Iran's Military Forces and Warfighting Capabilities

Iran's Military Forces and Warfighting Capabilities

The Threat in the Northern Gulf

**Anthony H. Cordesman
and Martin Kleiber**

Published in cooperation with the Center for Strategic and International Studies, Washington, D.C.

PRAEGER SECURITY INTERNATIONAL
Westport, Connecticut · London

Library of Congress Cataloging-in-Publication Data

Cordesman, Anthony H.
    Iran's military forces and warfighting capabilities : the threat in the Northern Gulf /
    Anthony H. Cordesman and Martin Kleiber.
        p. cm.
    Includes bibliographical references and index.
    ISBN 978–0–313–34612–5 (alk. paper)
1. Iran—Military policy. 2. National security—Iran. 3. Iran—Armed Forces. I. Kleiber, Martin. II.
Title.
UA853.I7C634 2007a
355′.033255—dc22   2007029599

British Library Cataloguing in Publication Data is available.

Library of Congress Catalog Card Number: 2007029599
ISBN-13: 978–0–313–34612–5

First published in 2007

Praeger Security International, 88 Post Road West, Westport, CT 06881
An imprint of Greenwood Publishing Group, Inc.
www.praeger.com

Printed in the United States of America

The paper used in this book complies with the
Permanent Paper Standard issued by the National
Information Standards Organization (Z39.48–1984).

10 9 8 7 6 5 4 3 2 1

Contents

Figures

Introduction

There is always a debate among national security experts as to the extent a country should be judged by its intentions or by its capabilities. The fact is, however, that both intentions and capabilities are always uncertain, even in the short term. They become progressively more uncertain with time. Domestic politics change perceptions and strategy, reality intervenes with plans, and external factors reshape both intentions and capabilities over time. States may or may not behave as they say, as they plan, or as rational actors. In practice, crises sometimes lead to radical changes in intentions that can escalate or mutate as a given crisis develops.

INTENTIONS VERSUS CAPABILITIES IN A DIVIDED STATE

Iran is no different in this respect from any other state. As Figures 1.1, 1.2, and 1.3 show, Iran is not a dominant regional military power by any standard, but it does have significant military assets and capabilities to wage defensive and asymmetric wars. Iran also has a well-established military and strategic literature that show a consistent Iranian interest in modern strategy, tactics, and technology.

There is no doubt from the writings of some of its institutions that Iran has its "realists" who look beyond nationalism and religious ideology and are capable of objectively assessing the costs, benefits, and risks in a given course of action. Iran's weapons development programs reflect a similar understanding of both modern conventional warfighting and the "revolution in military affairs," as well as the range of advances being made in the tactics and technology for asymmetric warfare.

Iran is, however, politically more volatile than many of its neighbors, and its decision-making processes are more driven by ideology and religion. Its security structure is still controlled by the Supreme Leader, not its president, and is still divided between its regular forces, the Revolutionary Guards, and its intelligence services. Its economy is weak and chronically mismanaged, and population pressure

Total Main Battle Tanks in Inventory

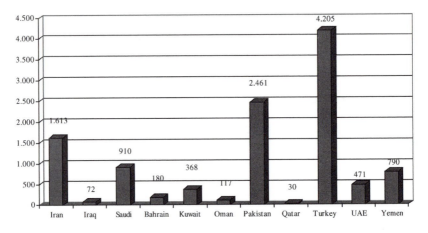

Total Fixed Wing Combat Aircraft

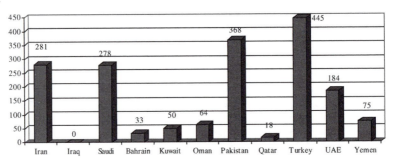

Source: International Institute for Strategic Studies (IISS), *Military Balance, 2007.*

Figure 1.1 Iran's Forces Relative to Those of Other Major Neighboring Military Powers in 2007

continues to be a problem in spite of a diminished birthrate. The uncertain relations between President Mahmoud Ahmadinejad and Supreme Leader Ali Khamenei, as well as between the more radical and moderate forces within the Iranian government and society, add to the difficulties in determining Iran's current intentions, much less its future ones.[1]

The Uncertain Voices of Iran's Leaders

Iran has an extraordinarily complex political structure, with the façade of democracy covering a state that is still under theocratic rule and which permits only candidates that meet the approval of its ruling religious elite to run for office. Its executive branch consists of a Supreme Leader appointed for life by the Assembly of Experts. This Assembly of Experts is elected by popular vote for an eight-year term; the last

Figure 1.2 Gulf Military Forces in 2007—Part One

	Iran	Iraq*	Bahrain	Kuwait	Oman	Qatar	Saudi Arabia†	UAE	Yemen
Total Manpower									
Total Active	545,000	136,400	11,200	15,500	41,700	12,400	199,500	50,500	66,700
Regular	420,000	136,400	11,200	15,500	41,700	12,400	124,500	50,500	66,700
National Guard & Other	125,000	0	0	0	6,400	0	75,000	0	0
Reserve	350,000	0	0	23,700	0	0		0	40,000
Paramilitary	40,000	25,400+	10,160	6,600	4,400	0	15,500+	0	70,000
Army and Guard									
Manpower	540,000‡	134,400	8,500	11,000	31,400	8,500	150,000	50,500	60,000
Regular Army Manpower	350,000	134,000	8,500	11,000	25,000	8,500	75,000	50,500	60,000
Reserve	350,000	0	0	0	0	0		0	40,000
Total Main Battle Tanks§	1,613	?	180	368	117	30	1,055	469	790
Active Main Battle Tanks	1,300	?	120	293	100	25	710	330	650
Active AIFV/Recce, Lt. Tanks	725+	?	71	up to 450	182	108	1,270+	579(40)	330
Total APCs	640	?	235	321	191	226	3,190	860	710
Active APCs	540	?	205	281	185	162	2,630	570	240
ATGM Launchers	75	0	15	118+	50	148	2,000+	305	71

	25	181	170	28	24	113	13	0	310+
Self-Propelled Artillery									
Towed Artillery	310	93	238(48)	12	108	0	26	?	2,010
MRLs	294	72(48)	60	4	?	27	9	?	876+
Mortars	502	155	400	45	101	78	21	?	5,000
SSM Launchers	28	6	10+	0	0	0	0	0	42+
Light SAM Launchers	800	40+	1,000+	66	54+	48	78	0	Some
AA Guns	530	62	0	0	26	Some	27	?	1,700
Air Force Manpower	5,000	4,000	18,000	2,100	4,100	2,500	1,500	900	52,000
Air-Defense Manpower	2,000	0	16,000	0	0	0	0	0	15,000
Total Combat Capable Aircraft	75(40)	184	291	18	48	50	33	0	281
Bombers	0	0	0	0	0	0	0	0	0
Fighter Ground Attack	41	155	171	18	12	39	12	0	186+
Fighter/Interceptor	30	–	106	0	0	0/14	21	0	74
Recce/FGA Recce	0	7	15	0	12	0	0	0	6+
AEW C4I/BM		0	5	0	0	0	0	0	1
MR/MPA†	0	0	0	0	0	0	0	0	5
OCU/COIN/CCT	0	11	14	0	16	19	0	0	0
Other Combat Trainers	6	0	50	0	0	0	0	0	35

Transport Aircraft**	82+	3	4	4	16	6	45	23	18
Tanker Aircraft	4	0	0	0	0	0	11	0	0
Total Helicopters	311	12	47	45	41	25	127	107+	20
Armed Helicopters**	104	0	40	32	0	19	32	55	8
Other Helicopters**	524	12	7	8	41	6	156	52	12
Major SAM Launchers	2,500+	0	15	36	40	9	5,284	Some	57
Light SAM Launchers	Some	0	78	48	54+	66	0	40+	120
AA Guns	Some	0	–	Some	26	–	1,140	–	–

AIFV = Armored Infantry Fighting Vehicle; Recce = Reconnaissance; APC = Armored Personnel Carrier; ATGM = Anti-Tank Guided Missile; MRL = Multiple Rocket Launcher; SSM = Surface-to-Surface Missile; SAM = Surface-to-Air Missile; AA = Anti-Aircraft; FGA = Fighter Ground Attack; AEW = Airborne Early Warning; MR/MPA = Maritime Reconnaissance/Maritime Patrol; OCU = Operational Conversion Unit; COIN = Counter Insurgency; CCT = Command and Control Technology.

Note: Equipment in storage is shown in the higher figure in parentheses or in a range. Air Force totals include all helicopters, including army-operated weapons, and all heavy surface-to-air missile launchers.

* The figures for Iraq are as of March 2007 and are taken from reporting by the U.S. Department of Defense.

† Saudi totals for reserve include National Guard Tribal Levies. The total for land forces includes active National Guard equipment. These additions total 450 AIFVs, 730 (1,540) APCs, and 70 towed artillery weapons. As for the National Guard, some estimates put the manpower at 95,000–100,000.

‡ Iranian total includes roughly 120,000 Revolutionary Guard actives in land forces and 20,000 in naval forces.

§ Total tanks include tanks in storage or conversion.

** Includes navy, army, National Guard, and royal flights, but not paramilitary.

Sources: Adapted from interviews, International Institute for Strategic Studies (IISS), *Military Balance, 2007; Jane's Sentinel, Periscope;* and Jaffee Center for Strategic Studies, *The Military Balance in the Middle East* (JCSS, Tel Aviv).

Figure 1.3 Gulf Military Forces in 2007—Part Two

	Iran	Iraq*	Bahrain	Kuwait	Oman	Qatar	Saudi Arabia†	UAE	Yemen
Total Naval Manpower	38,000‡	1,100	1,200	2,000	4,200	1,800	15,500	2,500	1,700
Regular Navy	18,000	1,100	1,200	2,000	4,200	1,800	12,500	2,500	1,700
Naval Guards	20,000	0	0	500	0	0	0	0	0
Marines	5,000	–	–	–	–	–	3,000	–	–
Major Surface Combattants									
Missile	5	0	3	0	2	0	11	4	0
Other	0	0	0	0	0	0	0	0	0
Patrol Craft									
Missile	10	0	4	10	4	7	9	8	8
(Revolutionary Guards)	10	–	–	–	–	–	–	–	–
Other	44	0	4	0	7	–	57	6	5
Revolutionary Guards (Boats)	40+	–	–	–	–	–	–	–	–
Submarines	3	0	0	0	0	0	0	0	0
Mine Vessels	5	0	0	0	0	0	7	0	6

Amphibious Ships	12	0	0	0	1	0	0	0	1
Landing Craft	9	–	4	2	4	0	8	5	6
Support Ships	25	2	4	4	4	–	7	2	2
Naval Air	2,600	–	–	–	–	–	–	–	–
Naval Aircraft									
Fixed Wing Combat	5	0	0	0	0	0	0	0	0
MR/MPA	10	0	0	0	(7)	0	0	0	0
Armed Helicopters	19	0	0	0	0	0	21	14	0
SAR Helicopters	–	0	0	13	0	0	4	4	0
Mine Warfare Helicopters	3	0	0	0	0	0	0	0	0
Other Helicopters	19	–	1	–	–	–	19	–	–

MR/MPA = Maritime Reconnaissance/Maritime Patrol; SAR = Search and Rescue.

Note: Equipment in storage is shown in the higher figure in parentheses or in a range. Air Force totals include all helicopters, including army-operated weapons, and all heavy surface-to-air missile launchers.

* The figures for Iraq are as of March 2007 and are taken from reporting by the U.S. Department of Defense.

† Saudi totals for reserve include National Guard Tribal Levies. The total for land forces includes active National Guard equipment. These additions total 450 AIFVs, 730 (1,540) APCs, and 70 towed artillery weapons. As for the National Guard, some estimates put the manpower at 95,000–100,000.

‡ Iranian total includes roughly 120,000 Revolutionary Guard actives in land forces and 20,000 in naval forces.

Sources: Adapted from interviews, International Institute for Strategic Studies (IISS), Military Balance, 2007; Jane's Sentinel, Periscope; and Jaffee Center for Strategic Studies, The Military Balance in the Middle East (JCSS, Tel Aviv).

election was held on December 15, 2006, at the same time as municipal elections. In practice, however, the only candidates that can run for the Assembly of Experts are those screened and approved by the Supreme Leader.[2]

Iran's president is elected by popular vote for a four-year term (eligible for a second term and a third nonconsecutive term). Once again, only candidates approved by the Supreme Leader and the ruling elite can run. The last election was held on June 17, 2005. It led to a runoff between two candidates on June 24, 2005. Mahmoud Ahmadinejad was elected president with 62 percent of the vote over former President Ali Akbar Hashemi-Rafsanjani, who won 36 percent. The next election is due in 2009, and a growing number of crackdowns on moderate political figures indicate that the choice of candidates may be even more restrictive in the future.

Unlike virtually all other governments that claim to be the result of a democratic process, the Supreme Leader, not the president, has control over the armed forces, the security services, the intelligence branch, and the courts. In addition, the government is controlled by three oversight bodies:

- The Assembly of Experts is an elected body of 86 religious scholars subject to the same tight screening process that limits the number of candidates for all elected offices in Iran. As is noted above, this body has constitutional responsibility for determining the succession of the Supreme Leader—based on his qualifications in the field of jurisprudence and commitment to the principles of the Islamic Revolution of 1979, reviewing his performance, and deposing him if deemed necessary;

- The Expediency Council, or Council for the Discernment of Expediency, is a policy advisory and implementation board consisting of more than 40 permanent members. It is supposed to represent all major government factions, including the heads of the three branches of government and the clerical members of the Council of Guardians. Its permanent members are appointed by the Supreme Leader for five-year terms. It also has temporary members that include Cabinet members and Majles committee chairmen, who are supposed to be selected when issues under their jurisdiction come before the Expediency Council. The Expediency Council exerts supervisory authority over the executive, judicial, and legislative branches and resolves legislative issues on which the Majles and the Council of Guardians disagree. Since 1989, the Supreme Leader has used it to obtain advice on matters of national policy, and it was given authority to act as a supervisory body over the government in 2003.

- The Council of Guardians of the Constitution, Council of Guardians, or Guardians Council is a 12-member board made up of six clerics chosen by the Supreme Leader and six jurists selected by the Majles from a list of candidates recommended by the judiciary (which in turn is controlled by the Supreme Leader) for six-year terms. It is supposed to determine whether proposed legislation is both constitutional and faithful to Islamic law, vets candidates for suitability, and supervises national elections.

The legislative branch consists of a unicameral Islamic Consultative Assembly or Majles-e-Shura-ye-Eslami or Majles. It has 290 seats and members are elected by popular vote to serve four-year terms. Once again, however, only those approved by the Supreme Leader and the ruling elite can run. The last elections were held on

February 20, 2004, with a runoff held May 7, 2004. The next elections are to be held in February 2008. According to the Central Intelligence Agency's (CIA's) analysis, conservatives and Islamists won 190 seats, reformers won 50, independents won 43, religious minorities won 5, and 2 seats cannot be categorized. Iran does not have political parties in the conventional sense of the term. As the CIA notes,

> formal political parties are a relatively new phenomenon in Iran and most conservatives still prefer to work through political pressure groups rather than parties, and often political parties or groups are formed prior to elections and disbanded soon thereafter; a loose pro-reform coalition called the 2nd Khordad Front, which includes political parties as well as less formal pressure groups and organizations, achieved considerable success at elections to the sixth Majles in early 2000; groups in the coalition include: Islamic Iran Participation Front (IIPF), Executives of Construction Party (Kargozaran), Solidarity Party, Islamic Labor Party, Mardom Salari, Mojahedin of the Islamic Revolution Organization (MIRO), and Militant Clerics Society (Ruhaniyun); the coalition participated in the seventh Majles elections in early 2004; following his defeat in the 2005 presidential elections, former MCS Secretary General Mehdi KARUBI formed the National Trust Party; a new apparently conservative group, the Builders of Islamic Iran, took a leading position in the new Majles after winning a majority of the seats in February 2004.[3]

There is no independent rule of law or protection of human rights. The Supreme Leader and his proxies effectively control the legal system. There is a Supreme Court and a four-member High Council of the Judiciary that have a single head and overlapping responsibilities. They are charged with supervising the enforcement of all laws and establishing judicial and legal policies. In practice, security-related issues are either extrajudicial or handled in specialized lower courts like the special clerical court, the revolutionary court, and the special administrative court. These courts normally are firmly under the control of the office of the Supreme Leader and the security services.

The end result is a security structure where the legislature and the legal system play only a limited role and where most key decisions are made by the equivalent of a national security council controlled by the Supreme Leader, bodies like the Iranian Revolutionary Guards, elements within the security services, and other coordinating and decision-making bodies whose structures, compositions, and power bases are not made public and remain unclear.

Given this complex mix of titular and real power, it is not surprising that Iran's various leaders make both moderate and hard-line statements, although the frequency of hard-line statements has increased steadily since the election of President Ahmadinejad on August 3, 2005. Its politicians, officials, and senior officers sometimes claim to be moderate and acting in defense of the nation. They also, however, sometimes make sweeping threats. Iranian rhetoric interacts with that of neighboring states, the United States, and Israel. They rarely speak in ways that encourage a balanced and objective indication of what Iranian leaders really think.[4]

This does not mean that various Iranian leaders should not be taken seriously, however, including Iranian leaders' most extreme statements. History is filled with examples of nations whose leaders have acted out their most extreme views; calling the United States and Israel "Satans," denying the Holocaust, calling for the end of Israel, and posturing over the use of long-range missiles are not statements that can be ignored. At the same time, other Iranian statements are very realistic, reflect a far more balanced understanding of the military situation, and offer the possibility of negotiation and reaching more stable forms of compromise.

The sheer range of Iranian views becomes clear from even a brief chronology of the mix of statements Iranian officials, officers, and strategic analysts made regarding the issue of Iran's nuclear program and security during 2005–2007. It should be noted, however, that the hard-line statements have increasingly predominated since 2006, and internal crackdowns on more moderate officials, political figures, and scholars increased steadily in 2007.

- **June 21, 2007:** Top Iranian nuclear negotiator Ali Larijani said in an interview: "They can pass another resolution, and we would make another, longer stride. Therefore they cannot solve the Iranian nuclear program."[5]

- **June 3, 2007:** President Ahmadinejad said at a speech near Teheran: "Even if all the world powers are slitting their own throats, the Iranian people are invincible and will remain invincible."[6]

- **May 24, 2007:** President Ahmadinejad said in a speech in Isfahan: "Our recommendation to you is this—stop your mischievous deeds as the Iranian nation has the nuclear technology for industrial purposes and will not retreat even a single step."[7]

- **April 23, 2007:** President Ahmadinejad said in a Spanish television interview that Iran prefers to remain within the nuclear nonproliferation treaty and resist U.N. sanctions peacefully. And "if the European Union wants to play an appropriate role in international relations, it should act independently....In the political sense, too, those who look at the world logically can understand that the use of nuclear weapons is already a thing of the past."[8]

- **April 17, 2007:** "We are employing the maximum effort to realise our projects in Natanz. Today in Natanz there is a continuous movement to install the centrifuges," the head of Iran's atomic energy agency Gholam Reza Aghazadeh said. He added that Iran "would continue with the installation until it has 50,000 centrifuges" and would complete that task within two to four years.[9]

- **April 16, 2007:** President Ahmadinejad said at a public speech broadcast on TV: "The Iranian people will resist until the end on acquiring their rights and will not shift an inch," referring to the standoff over the country's nuclear program.[10]

- **April 6, 2007:** Ahmed Jannati, Head of the Iranian Guardians Council, said, "Today, people around the world are experiencing an Islamic awakening and have become anti-American and Anti-Israeli. The time of American and Israel's power is over and they are rapidly going down the path of annihilation. It might take some time but it will happen while America and Israel are unaware them selves...God willing and contrary to what Iran's enemies like America, Britain, and Israel want, the Iranian nation will soon obtain its nuclear fuel cycle and become independent in producing nuclear fuel. Iran is going towards this goal fast."

- **April 5, 2007:** Iran's chief nuclear spokesman Ali Larijani said in a telephone conversation with the European Union's (EU's) top diplomat, Javier Solana, "The Islamic Republic of Iran is ready to negotiate only on non-diversion (of its nuclear programme for military purposes) and not on its nuclear rights...Iran will not accept any preconditions or suspension for a time. Nor can suspending enrichment be a precondition or the result of negotiations."[11]

- **April 3, 2007:** Major General Hassan Firoozabadi, Chief of Staff of the Iranian Armed Forces, said, " International Zionism and the Palestine usurping Israel with the support of the reactionary neoconservatives of the US are a new plan...Americans and the West will lose with this plan. But the Islamic countries are in danger."[12]

- **April 2007:** Hamid Reza Taraghi, Head of the International Affairs Office of the Islamic Coalition Party (a group close to the Iranian leadership, said, "Because US military configurations in the Persian Gulf are very similar to those before the Iraq Invasion, and because the neoconservatives in the American Administration are prone to this sort of stupidity and craziness, we have been fully prepared in terms of hardware and military arsenals but also software and information for electronic warfare."[13]

- **March 21, 2007:** The Supreme Leader, Ayatollah Ali Khamenei, was quoted as saying in a televised speech, "Until today, what we have done is in accordance with international regulations...But if they take illegal actions, we too can take illegal actions and will do so."[14]

- **March 16, 2007:** Major General Ataollah Salehi, commander in chief of the regular army, warns the United States and other Western states not to make a "stupid move" over Iran's nuclear program and said any such nation will be "surprised" by Iran's military response.[15]

- **March 14, 2007:** In an apparent reaction to plans for further United Nations Security Council (UNSC) sanctions, President Ahmadinejad was quoted as saying during a speech in Tehran, "Enemies oppose development and progress of the Iranian nation, because the Iranians are standard bearers of justice and advocates of freedom and will not yield to threats or bullying...Enemies are concerned that Iran may turn into a model for other nations of the world to follow...Issuing such torn pieces of paper... will not have an impact on the Iranian nation's will." He also reiterated that Iran will not give up uranium enrichment.[16]

- **February 26, 2007:** According to the Islamic Republic News Agency (IRNA), chief nuclear negotiator Ali Larijani said that if the United States made a formal request for talks, Iran will respond positively but would not accept conditions.[17]

- **February 25, 2007:** President Ahmadinejad was quoted as saying, "The train of the Iranian nation is without brakes and a rear gear...We dismantled the rear gear and brakes of the train and threw them away some time ago."[18]

- **February 24, 2007:** General Yahya Rahim Safavi, the chief of the Islamic Revolutionary Guards Corps (IRGC), was quoted as saying, "Iran's enemies, through hiring some mercenaries and with their wishful thinking, want to create instability but...the armed forces will strongly suppress anti-revolutionaries and rebels who are dependent to foreigners."[19]

- **February 21, 2007:** According to the Islamic Republic News Agency, President Ahmadinejad said in a speech, "Iran will not retreat one iota in its path to nuclear victory."[20] General Yahya Safavi, the chief of the IRGC, said the IRGC is posturing itself for asymmetric warfare, and the United States cannot make changes in Middle East security unless Iran cooperates.[21]

- **February 17, 2007:** Iran's Supreme Leader Ayatollah Ali Khamenei stated on Iranian state television that Iran's nuclear program is the country's "future and destiny" and a way of ensuring the Islamic Republic's progress because Iran's oil and gas reserves "would not last forever." The Supreme Leader also criticized those who claim Iran should not be pursuing a nuclear program given the high international costs this would entail.

- **February 14, 2007:** The foreign policy advisor to the Supreme Leader, Ali Akbar Velayati, said in an interview with the French *Libération*, "There are no limits within the negotiations [about Iran's nuclear program]."[22]

- **February 8, 2007:** Supreme Leader Ayatollah Ali Khamenei warned the United States that Iran will retaliate against American interests worldwide if his country is attacked.[23]

- **February 1, 2007:** President Ahmadinejad was quoted as saying, "We [Iran] are rapidly becoming a superpower...Our strength does not come from military weapons or an economic capability...Our power comes from our capability to influence the hearts and souls of people, and this scares them."[24]

- **January 31, 2007:** Ali Said, Khamenei's personnel representative to the IRGC, stated, "If America abandons its self-centeredness, and village headman position, Iran...could fulfill its mission in the region and help resolve regional issues."[25]

- **January 24, 2007:** Iranian Foreign Minister Manouchehr Mottaki told reporters at a press conference with Bahraini Foreign Minister Shaykh Khalid bin-Ahmad al-Khalifah, "We are ready for any possible action taken by America."[26]

- **January 15, 2007:** An Iranian government spokesman said that Iran is planning to install 3,000 centrifuges despite the provisions in United Nations Security Council Resolution (UNSCR) 1737.[27]

- **January 8, 2007:** Supreme Leader Ayatollah Ali Khamenei said that Iran would not halt the development of its nuclear program, despite UNSCR 1737. He was quoted as saying in a public speech, "The Iranian people will definitely not give up their right and the authorities have no right to give up this great achievement."[28]

- **December 26, 2006:** Iran's parliament passed a bill calling on the government to revise its cooperation with the International Atomic Energy Agency (IAEA) in response to UNSCR 1737. Out of 207 parliamentarians, 167 voted for the bill, which urged the government to restrict its cooperation with the IAEA and "accelerate Iran's nuclear activities."[29]

- **December 24, 2006:** President Ahmadinejad, in a reaction to the passing of UNSCR 1737, called the resolution "illegal" and "superficial."[30]

- **December 5, 2006:** President Ahmadinejad warned Europe against endorsing proposed measures by the UN against its nuclear program. He said Iran will respond by downgrading relations with the EU.[31]

- **November 12, 2006:** General Yahya Rahim-Safavi, Commander General of the IRGC, spoke about Iran's missile power on Iranian TV. He was quoted as saying that Iran is prepared to transfer ballistic missile technology to "neighboring and friendly countries."

Further, he said that the United States and "the Zionist regime" are the two threats from outside of Iran's region. In case of a contingency, the general expects them to attack Iran with long-range missiles and fighter planes. Therefore, Iran employs a strategy of "utilizing long-range and surface-to-surface missiles," although the intentions of the Iranian government are peaceful.[32] He also said, "The Americans have major weaknesses. In fact, the Americans have demonstrated their weaknesses and points of strength in wars in Afghanistan and Iraq. We have precisely planned our strategy in line with their weaknesses and strengths.[33]

- **November 11, 2006:** Iran's top nuclear negotiator, Ali Larijani, at meetings in Moscow called the Republican defeat in the U.S. Congressional elections a "landmark victory for the Iranian nation." Larijani said Iran remains ready for dialogue and warned against adopting the European group's sanctions resolution and, concerning Iran's position in case of a UN resolution, "We will review our relations with the IAEA [the International Atomic Energy Agency] if the U.N. adopts the Euro-troika resolution without taking into account the amendments made by Russia."[34]

  In addition, President Ahmadinejad said "the enemy cannot do a damn thing" to stop Tehran's nuclear program and "[b]y God's grace, our powerful nation will continue its path."[35]

- **October 10, 2006:** Supreme Leader Ayatollah Ali Khamenei, according to state television reports, proclaimed that Iran will step up its nuclear program and stand firm in the face of international pressure to suspend uranium enrichment. He was quoted as saying, "Our policy is clear progress proposing transparent logic and insisting on the nation's rights without backing down."[36]

- **October 2, 2006:** Mohammad Saeedi, Deputy Chief of Iran's Atomic Energy Agency, made the following remarks on French radio: "To be able to arrive at a solution, we have just had an idea. We propose that France create a consortium for the production of enriched uranium... That way France, through the companies Eudodif and Areva, could control in a tangible way our enrichment activities."[37]

- **September 22, 2006:** According to First Vice President Parviz Davoudi, Supreme Leader Ayatollah Ali Khamenei prohibits the use of any nuclear weapons. Davoudi was quoted as saying, "Any aggressor should purge the idea of invading Iran from its mind because our armed forces are serious and powerful enough to counterattack."[38]

- **September 20, 2006:** Supreme Leader Ayatollah Ali Khamenei said before members of the Iranian armed forces that his country must be ready to confront all foreign aggressors and that a strong military is important to deter what he called his country's "enemies."[39]

- **September 17, 2006:** During a visit in Venezuela, President Ahmadinejad called his host, President Hugo Chavez, his "brother" and "the champion of the struggle against imperialism." Ahmadinejad continued, "We have thoughts, objectives and interests in common... We must be able to make these ideas reality with the aim of achieving justice and peace."[40]

- **September 5, 2006:** Former Iranian President Mohammad Khatami said that U.S. forces should stay in Iraq until that country's government can assume greater responsibility itself. Khatami was quoted as saying "We can't leave this newly formed government at the mercy of terrorists and insurgents."[41]

- **August 27, 2006:** President Ahmadinejad made the following remarks concerning Iran's nuclear program during a televised speech: "The great decision of the Iranian nation for progress and acquiring technology is a definite decision. There is no way back from this path." He was also quoted as saying that the United States should give up nuclear weapons because it cannot be trusted with them. Chief nuclear negotiator Ali Larijani said in an Iranian radio interview, "Production of nuclear fuel is our strategic aim...Any measure to deprive Iran of its right will not change our mind about our aim." Muhammad Reza Baqeri added in an interview with the IRNA, "It [halting uranium enrichment] is our red line. We will never do it."[42]

- **August 23, 2006:** Supreme Leader Ayatollah Ali Khamenei promised to continue pursing Iran's nuclear program, despite the threat of UN sanctions. He was quoted as saying, "The Islamic Republic of Iran has made its decision and, in the issue of nuclear energy, will continue its path powerfully...and it will receive the sweet fruits of its efforts."[43]

- **June 26, 2006:** Supreme Leader Ayatollah Ali Khamenei said that there is no use negotiating between the United States and Iran because Iran will not surrender "our undeniable right of using nuclear technology." He continued, "We are willing to negotiate over controls, inspections and international guarantees."[44]

- **June 25, 2006:** Javad Vaeidi, Deputy Chief Nuclear Negotiator, said in Vienna, "Today, the power of Iran in the region has put us in the position to help with the security and the stability of the region. If we go after nuclear weapons, this would lead other countries in the region also to go after nuclear weapons...That would be neither in the interest of Iran, nor in the interest of the countries of the region."[45]

- **May 6, 2006:** General Yahya Rahim-Safavi, Commander General of the IRGC, said, "we no longer consider any of our neighbors on their own as a major threat against our country. We know that the military threats against us are from beyond the region and the Guards Corps has changed its strategy."[46]

- **March 5, 2005:** Brigadier General Mohammed Ali Jafari, previous head of the IRGC, said, "According to the IRGC asymmetric doctrine, and in order to realize its defense capacity in scope and depth, the IRGC ground force has been organizing and equipped its units, on the basis of a battalion-based plan, for the past two years. The main characteristic of this strengthening measure has been to pay particular attention to the volume of the battalion's firepower—with special stress on its anti armor and anti-helicopter capacity—as well as self reliance and great mobility of the combat battalions."[47]

- **January 25, 2005:** Motjtaba Zlnur, a high-ranking official in the IRGC, stated, "This is another weak point of the enemy, because we have certain methods for fighting in the sea so that war will spread into the sea of Oman and the Indian Ocean...We will not let the enemy inside our borders."[48]

- **April 20, 2004:** Brigadier General Amir Bakhtiari, a professor at the IRGC Command and Staff University, wrote, "although in terms of combat capability the American Army and its allies have advanced military equipment and arms, this does not mean we cannot fight against them...(It is) important and essential to change and replace military training and planning and to use unknown operational tactics and methods such as irregular and guerrilla warfare and rapid response and deterrent operations."[49]

At the same time, Iran has unique divisions within its military services between conventional and unconventional forces. It has elements throughout its state security system that are deeply ideological, nationalist, and committed to forms of Shi'ite Islamist extremism. The divisions between its presidency and Supreme Leader raise serious questions as to who is actually in charge in any given instance, and how objective decision-making will be, particularly at a time when the president is a radical populist who seems to have strong eschatological religious beliefs and may be far more willing to take risks than the mainstream in Iranian strategic and military thinking.

Iran's Military Exercises

Iran's military exercises provide a similar mix of propaganda and pragmatism. It is impossible to accurately describe Iran's exercises without access to classified material. On many occasions, Iran has deliberately mischaracterized the actual nature of the exercises, grossly exaggerated their size, and practiced "defensive" tactics and maneuvers whose true character was clearly offensive.

Once again, however, a chronology of recent Iranian military exercises provides insights into the range of Iranian views. It reveals both some of Iran's possible intentions and the difficulties in translating Iran's public statements about its intentions into anything more than a guess. At the same time, it shows Iran's increasing concern about the risk of a U.S. attack or invasion and its focus on asymmetric warfare both in defending its territory and as a means of conducting indirect or proxy attacks on the United States and on its own neighbors.

- **Planned for September 2007:** On July 19, the Iranian Minister of Defense announced that Iran is planning to hold military maneuvers in September 2007 that will include air force exercises in which the Azarakhsh aircraft will be tested. Little is known about the Azarkhsh fighter—it is believed to be based on the U.S.–made F-5F fighter and it may contain some modifications with comparatively modern avionics.[50]

- **March 22, 2007:** The Iranian navy started large-scale exercises in the Persian Gulf. Iran test-fired a "new" land-to-sea missile that it claims has a range of 180 miles. Rear Admiral Ali Fadavi of the Naval Branch of the IRGC said, "We have successfully fired a cruise missile....hitting targets in the Sea of Oman and northern Indian Ocean...This missile can hit all kinds of big warships in all of the Persian Gulf, Sea of Oman, and northen Indian Ocean."[51]

- **February 24, 2007:** The Ashura and Al-Zahra battalions of the Basij forces based in Khash began a nine-day military exercise named Persian Gulf 3. According to Iranian sources, these exercises are military and cultural drills. One senior Basij officer was reported to have said that the major objectives include delaying, rescue, anti-riot, and anti-heliborne operations as well as urban defense missions.[52]

- **February 21, 2007:** Six Ashura battalions—1,500 Basij forces—began a series of cultural, military, rescue, and sports exercises in Iranshahr and Bampur named Sarallah Boulevard Martyrs. According to the Iranian media, machine gun fire was heard near the training sites. Later, the Iranian media reported that the 1,500 Basij forces included an unspecified number of local nomads.[53]

- **February 19, 2007:** The IRGC began three-day exercises, named Eqtedar, in 16 of Iran's provinces. At the same time, Basij forces—reportedly 11 battalions—around the country started preparation drills. These included detailed exercises in guerrilla tactics and asymmetric warfare designed to defeat what effectively was a U.S. invasion. According to state media, 20 IRGC brigades took part in the Eqtedar exercises and missile tests were to be conducted. Iranian military sources later specified this information to 20 mechanized and infantry divisions of the IRGC. According to one senior IRGC commander, the Eqtedar exercises were the biggest in the running Iranian year (since March 21, 2006). Apparently, Fajir-3 and Fajir-5 as well as Zelzal missiles were fired.

  The second phase of this maneuver focused on defending against air raids, air strikes, and airborne attacks—apparently carried out by 3,000 "teams" (out of a claimed 9,000 operational teams) with "620 antiaircraft artilleries." The third phase of the exercises consisted of massive defensive operations. Finally, the commanding general stated that "declaring the readiness of all Iranian people to defend their holy territory" was the message of the exercises.

  After the exercises, the commander of the IRGC ground forces summarized them as follows: "During this three-day military maneuver, in addition to testing a new generation of missiles, armored and anti-armor weapons and a variety of artillery ammunition, our forces will also practice firing 750 types of weapons, including various missiles and artilleries."[54] He further explained that the exercises consisted of three stages, the first encompassed defensive artillery fire drills—apparently involving the 64th artillery and Al-Hadid missile groups of the IRGC—and occupying passageways, straits, and critical locations.

  The general also noted that for the first time in its military exercises the anti-air operations were carried out through a "visual surveillance network installed all around the country." According to other Iranian sources, the IRGC successfully launched guided missiles from FT-27 (likely T-72) tanks in the Ramsheh district of Esfahan in the first phase of the exercises, apparently the first time such tests took place.

- **February 7, 2007:** Air force and naval forces of the IRGC launched a two-day exercise (named "Saeqeh" for the air forces and "Raad" for the navy), primarily to test the country's missile defense capability. It was reported that Iran also successfully test-fired its recently acquired Tor-M1 SAM system as well as its Raad anti-ship missile. At the beginning of the exercises, the Iranian news agency IRNA reported that the exercises took place in the central and southern Gulf and the Sea of Oman. One stated objective of the exercises was to enhance defensive capabilities.

- **January 22, 2007:** The IRGC test-fired its Zalzal and Fajir-5 missiles during maneuvers in the Garmsar region, southeast of Tehran. Basij forces held exercises in parts of Kerman, Sistan-Baluchestan and Hormozgan provinces. The exercises were initially planned for three days, but on the last day it was decided to extend them one more day.[55]

- **November 2–13, 2006:** Iran launched its Great Prophet II exercises on November 3. The exercises were started with successful firings of the Shahab-2 and Shahab-3 missiles in Qom province. The Great Prophet II exercises are generally seen as a phase of greater intensity in the continuous, nationwide Blow of Zolfaqar exercises that began in August in the wake of the Israel-Lebanon War. They involved a range of asymmetric and guerrilla warfare efforts that adopted tactics used in Iraq, in the Hezbollah-Israel War, and other areas for defeating a conventional invasion modeled on U.S. concepts of operations.

According to one source, Iran simultaneously launched about 20 missiles on November 2, 2006, a combination of Shahab-3, Shahab-2, Zolfaqar-73, Fateh-110, Scud-B, and Zelzal-2 missiles.[56] The same source reports that the missile offensive was controlled and launched through an Iranian version of the North Korean command and control system for nuclear missile strikes.

The source reports that missile-carrying transporter-erector-launcher vehicles roamed Iran for at least a couple of weeks, without any communications signature. They converged on time to the test area (which simulates several forward bases) and launched simultaneously. There were no failures, no problems, no delays, and no electronic signature that could have provided a forewarning to the enemy.

The same source reports that a senior IRGC commander in the ballistic missiles forces stated that from a technical point of view, the coordinated ballistic missile launch also had the characteristics of a disarming first strike in the context of a region-wide strategic offensive. The officer stressed that the simulated missile offensive saturated a wide array of enemy objectives in a wide zone stretching between 300 and 2,000 kilometers from Iran.

The second stage of the exercises began with ground force maneuvers during the night of November 5–6. According to IRGC Brigadier General Ali Fazli, the objective of the offensive is to reach "up to 1,450 kilometers into enemy territory, first by air strikes and ultimately by ground forces. In the first night, the IRGC leading elements infiltrated nearly 300 kilometers, using light vehicles while passing through a friendly area. Then the IRGC deployed elite forces—according to Iranian sources about "1,800 self-sufficient teams, Saberin Special Forces, air units and executive teams also gave full logistical support to the [local] troops in surrounding and demolishing the enemy's forces in the region"[57] simulating operations into the deep rear of the enemy in co-ordination with "local troops."[58]

Iranian media claim that coast-to-sea, sea-to-sea, and nighttime operations were part of the exercise. Reportedly, all branches of the IRGC were involved, and the exercises took place in 14 provinces. During the first stage of the exercises, about 20,000 Basij and IRGC forces were used; they included the Tehran Sarallah operational headquarters, four teams from the mechanized division Mohammad Rasulallah, Special Forces of Division 10 Seyyedolshohada, and 45 battalions of Ashura from the Greater Tehran and Tehran Province Basij. Apparently, the objective for these forces was to defend against a potential attack on Tehran.

During the night of November 6–7, the objective for the Iranian forces was to include attacks by teams of Saberin Special Forces and IRGC Marines on oil rigs and coastal oil facilities in the Persian Gulf.[59]

According to Western media reports, the second stage of this exercise included an operation to cope with chemical warfare, a heliborne operation, an anti-heliborne operation, paramotor and paraglider flights, night combat, and countering enemy infiltration.[60] These exercises also took place in large portions of the Gulf. During the exercises, the IRGC test-fired Shahab-2 and Shahab-3 missiles as well as its Noor, Kowsar, Zolfaqar, Fateh-110, Zelzal, and Nasr anti-sea missiles. In addition, the IRGC tested new automatic cannons and rocket launchers, a new sniper rifle, and rocket launchers according to the semi-official ISNA news agency.

Apparently, the Blow of Zolfaqar and Great Prophet II exercises were not executed within the frame of a specific military mission. According to some reports, they were primarily aimed at showing Iranian leadership and other nations the capabilities and will of the Iranian military.

- **August 19, 2006:** Iran's state television and Western media reported the test-firing of ten submarine-launched, sea-to-surface Saegheh missiles on August 20, one day after large-scale military exercises named Zarbat-e-Zolfaqar started across the country.[61] Apparently as a reaction to the Israel-Lebanon War, Iran launched a series of exercises under the blanket name Zarbat-e-Zolfaqar that were to continue for months with differing degrees of intensity. The exercises were held in 16 provinces and in the Persian Gulf and the Sea of Oman.

    Iranian forces fired the Thaqeb, Iran's first missile that is fired from underwater and flies above the surface to hit its target. Amphibious assault and sea denial operations were also executed by the Iranian forces. It is not clear which naval warfare missiles were used; they may be the same that were introduced in the April exercises, which some experts believe to be modified Russian vintage weapons. The Zarbat-e-Zolifqar maneuver was followed by two-day-long air force exercises.

    Basij forces started exercises in the Sumarin region of Ardabil. According to Iranian sources, three Al-Zahra battalions and 11 Ashura battalions—about 4,000 men and women—took part.[62]

- **May 2006:** The IRGC conducted flight tests for the Shahab-3 missile. Allegedly, between July 1998 and this exercise, Iran test-fired ten Shahab-3 missiles, half of which were unsuccessful flights.[63]

- **March 31, 2006:** Iranian forces began seven-day exercises with approximately 17,000 soldiers from the northern extremity of the Persian Gulf to the Strait of Hormuz, from the Strait of Hormuz to Chahbahar, and a stretch of 40 kilometers off the Iranian coast. Iranian Rear Admiral Mohammad Ebrahim Dehghan said the strait of Hormuz was to be one of the focal points of the exercise.

    The first phase lasted until April 6. According to reports, the IRGC and the regular armed forces employed submarines, surface combatants, missiles, jet fighters and gunships, short- and middle-range missiles, and practiced using surface-to-surface missiles to destroy an enemy's oil, military, and security installations. The IRGC test-fired a radar-guided version of the Chinese C-701 anti-ship missile. Iran called one test an "ultra-horizon" missile, which is fired from helicopters and jet fighters, which could be a description for the C-701, and the Fajr-3 missile, which can reportedly evade radar and use multiple warheads to hit several targets simultaneously. Iran also test-fired the Noor anti-ship missile, a version of the Chinese C-802, which, according to Iranian sources, was successfully fired from a helicopter (apparently an Mi-17). Iranian sources further report the successful launch of the Kosar, or SL-10, missile.

    Iranian sources claim the IRGC was using unmanned reconnaissance airplanes and helicopters capable of launching long-range missiles. The defense ministry also says it has test-launched an improved intermediate-range ballistic missile, likely a Shahab-3 version.

    Iranian sources claim that the naval forces fired a new, indigenously developed anti-sea missile with a radar-evading warhead. Information provided through official Iranian channels claims that the missile was faster than any other previously known and was using a "stealth" warhead. In addition, Iran claims to have employed a "flying boat," most likely some sort of hovercraft or catamaran-based vessel; one source claimed that the vessel was a vintage Russian Ekranoplan vehicle.[64] Western sources speculate that the missile either closely resembled the Russian Shkval or may even be a modified version of older Russian technology. Iranian sources also mentioned a radar-decoy package that apparently comes along with the missile.

The second phase of the Noble Prophet exercises commenced on April 6, when a torpedo was fired at a target in the Strait of Hormuz. According to Iranian sources, over 17,000 soldiers and over 500 naval vessels (other Iranian sources mentioned 1,500 vessels) took part in this phase of the exercises.

- **December 8, 2005:** What is thought to be the largest Iranian naval exercises to date (Lovers of Velayat) started with submarine forces that performed offensive and defensive operations against other submarines and surface vessels, as well as the deployment of minesweepers in the Sea of Oman. According to Iranian military sources, fighter bombers were involved in anti-submarine warfare, too. Additionally, it is reported that surface-to-sea missiles and anti-aircraft guns were fired in advanced stages of the exercises.[65]

- **October 3, 2005:** The Meqdad military exercises began in an area covering about 110 square kilometers. According to Iranian souces, 12 Ashura battalions, 16 resistance areas, and 400 civic resistance bases participated in the exercise. The objective of these exercises reportedly was to enhance operational readiness in desert, asymmetrical, and relief and rescue operations as well as preparation for disaster relief.[66]

- **May 11, 2005:** The Unity-84 naval exercises began in a 12,000-square-mile area in the Sea of Oman. According to Iranian sources, surface vessels, submarines, missile cruisers, hovercraft, shore-to-sea missiles, and combat aircraft of the navy took part in the exercise. The same Iranian source describes the operations of the Kilo-class submarines as follows: "quick rotation, landing at the bottom of the sea, chasing the vessels of the hypothetical enemy and moving forces to pre-determined positions." Apparently, Ghadir submarines participated in the exercises also.[67]

- **November 2004:** Iran held the Peyrovan-e Velayat exercises in late November. Reportedly, army aviation bombers practiced against enemy attacks (sic). Army aviation Cobra helicopters attacked infrastructure and troop movements in dozens of sorties. Jet fighters and reconnaissance aircraft also were involved.[68] Chinook and AB-212 helicopters transported rapid-reaction units to several locations. The helicopter operations were conducted with simultaneous infantry and artillery support.[69]

- **September 2004:** The "new" IRGC held exercises named Ashura 5. Apparently these exercises were conducted in order to assess the reorganization in tactics for warfare against so-called light targets and evolving threats. These reportedly included asymmetric warfare operations based on observations of U.S. campaigns in Afghanistan and Iraq. According to Iranian sources, armored and light units as well as missile forces took part in the exercises. Apparently, the Basij forces used the exercises to test Iran's special air forces.[70]

- **July 2004:** Iran held large-scale military exercises named Tondar-5 in Dasht-e Abbas and Fakkeh. Reportedly, heliborne troop movements and infantry attacks with attack helicopter support were used to train offensive and counter-Special Forces operations.[71]

Short of mind reading, it is difficult to be certain of the true nature of what many exercises were really designed to test or signal. It is clear, however, that some exercises were clearly designed to fight a U.S. naval task force in the Gulf and Gulf of Oman and to deter a U.S. invasion or sea-based air attack. Others reveal a systematic effort to prepare the Iranian regular forces, the IRGC (Islamic Revolutionary Guard Corps), Basij for a land invasion and attack on Iran's cities by the United States, as well as operations in the oil-rich province of Khuzestan in the southwest and the Baluchi areas in the southeast.

Many aspects of the exercises reflect new tactics and the use of new weapons that must be regarded as potentially threatening. As is discussed in the chapters that follow, such Iranian activities show Iran's interest in expanding its capabilities in warfighting that can extend far beyond Iran's borders and defense of Iran's territory.

It should also be noted that this chronology is based on publicly announced activities. It is clear than many of the Iranian exercises include additional activities. For example, various reports claim Iran has tested several measures to increase its long-range aerial strike capability. According to a report in *Jane's,* Iran undertook aerial strike and refueling exercises. They began with deployments out of the Tactical Air Base 7 in Shiraz, southwest Iran, took place at night, and involved planes flying at very low altitudes. The exercises simulated "operational scenarios that would entail night-time refueling of an Iranian attack aircraft, at low altitude over the Mediterranean, outward bound en route to the target."[72]

Iran conducts air-defense exercises involving fighter and surface-to-air missile tactics clearly modeled on the lessons of both Iraqi efforts to defeat U.S. and British air operations during the Gulf War in 1991, the period of containment through 2003, and the U.S.–British invasion in 2003. These involve a range of deception and electronic warfare tactics, various forms of information warfare and countermeasures, and efforts to deny the United States the ability to gather signals intelligence, communications intelligence, and imagery. For obvious reasons, U.S. government experts will not comment on the details of such Iranian activities.

Iran's "Traveling Circus(es)" of Security Voices

At another level, Iran has developed a mix of think tanks, strategic spokespersons, and "dialogue" that involves an awkward mixture of professional apologists and extremists. Iran has sometimes sent such individuals as a virtual "traveling circus" to other countries or meetings in Iran. Such spokespersons, who somewhat distance themselves from the regime, then claim Iranian actions are misunderstood, grand bargains are at hand that can resolve all differences, and Iran's problems are the result of Western misunderstanding and a failure to listen, be "fair," and accept a true dialogue.

Many of the individuals involved may well be sincere, but they almost all sharply understate the level of new military developments in Iran, the nature of Iran's nuclear and missile activities, and Iran's ties to extremist and militant movements in other countries. Many have been political scientists or voices with little known connection to Iran's national security apparatus, but an increasing number are de facto intelligence agents and/or regime voices masquerading as independent thinkers.

The recent crackdown on moderates and any open form of opposition since the beginning of 2007 has made it steadily more difficult for truly independent figures to travel and more dangerous for them to speak, and a number have been threatened or arrested. Coupled with a skilled diplomacy based on obfuscation and denial, and official statements designed more to counter outside pressure than reflect Iran's true intentions, the end result is a "moderate" smokescreen that does far more to hide Iran's intentions than reveal them.

The Iranian extremist side of this equation is much freer to speak, although its rhetoric is often clearly intended to serve domestic or foreign propaganda purposes. Iran's president, some of its more radical clerics, and leaders and ex-leaders in the IRGC produce a steady stream of hard-line rhetoric and threats. This is reinforced by occasional statements by more mainstream leaders and by military exercises and overseas operations that are often described in extreme terms or tied to hard-line scenarios and non-Iranian extremist groups. All nations have their less rational voices, nationalist rhetoric, and posturing for domestic consumption. Iran, however, sometimes carries it to extremes beyond the usual limits of "extremism."

EXTERNAL SOURCES OF INSTABILITY

Iran's strategic posture makes it a critical player in events in the Gulf region, Central Asia, and in the flow of world energy exports regardless of its own goals and intentions. It has long been the focus of U.S., Russian, and European attention and now increasingly is a key focus for Chinese, Indian, and Japanese concerns over energy security. At the same time, Iran cannot control its strategic environment. It is no more able to predict the future nature and behavior of key neighbors like Iraq and Pakistan than any other nation. Key activities like its pursuit of nuclear weapons can provoke preventive or preemptive strikes based on accurate or false perceptions of Iranian progress.

Iran's strategic geography compounds its problems. Iran's territory extends from the Caspian Sea to the Gulf. It is the second largest country in the Gulf, and one of the largest in the Middle East, with an estimated area of 1.648 million square kilometers. Its land boundaries are virtually a catalog of unstable states and sectarian and ethnic tensions: Afghanistan, 936 kilometers; Armenia, 35 kilometers; Azerbaijan-proper, 432 kilometers; Azerbaijan-Naxcivan exclave, 179 kilometers; Iraq, 1,458 kilometers; Pakistan, 909 kilometers; Turkey, 499 kilometers; and Turkmenistan, 992 kilometers.

Iran has a 2,440-kilometer coastline on the Persian Gulf and the Gulf of Oman that places it within minutes of flying time of the southern Gulf's energy, power, and desalination facilities. Iran also borders the Caspian Sea (740 kilometers), a sea where major debates still exist about maritime rights and boundaries.[73]

Iran has experienced many serious strategic challenges over the past three decades, which still shape much of its strategic planning and debates. After the Islamic

Revolution of 1979, Iran was left without one of its formerly closest allies, the United States, which has considered Iran an adversarial power since the hostage crisis in 1979. In addition to the domestic turmoil created by the Revolution, Iranian oil production and income dropped sharply. Iran went from earning some 17 percent of all OPEC (Organization of the Petroleum Exporting Countries) revenues in the late 1970s to an average of around 10 percent from 1980 to the present.[74] It had to fight a bloody war against Iraq that lasted eight years and came at a great cost to Iran in terms of human life, strategic prestige, military capability, and economic development.

Following the Iran-Iraq War, the Iranian government failed to manage the nation's finances effectively and implement even basic reforms to develop its economy. Moreover, Iran suffered from low oil prices during much of the 1990s. This caused Iran's military readiness to decline and its economy to stagnate. While the Gulf War of 1990–1991 and the sanctions on Iraq that followed greatly weakened a once victorious Iraq, it also triggered a major expansion in the U.S. presence in the Gulf. Iran faced a different threat from the Taliban, which drove millions of Afghanis into Iran as refugees and was violently anti-Shi'ite. While the American military campaigns in Afghanistan and Iraq in 2001 and 2003 largely eliminated such threats, they also led to a massive American military presence on two of Iran's borders.

The "nuclearization" of India and Pakistan did not create a direct threat to Iran, but did change the nature of the balance of power in the region. More significantly, the rise of neo-Salafi Islamic fundamentalism created a direct religious and political challenge to Iran and all Shi'ites. While movements like Al Qa'ida are divided over how openly they attack Shi'ites, some key leaders like Abu Musab al-Zarqawi have called for a Sunni jihad against Shi'ites, and others have called Shi'ites polytheists and apostates. Iran increasingly faced a struggle for the future of Islam and one that affected all Shi'ites, including those in Iraq, Lebanon, and Syria—where Iran had direct strategic interests.

The failure of the Israeli-Palestinian peace process and Israeli-Syrian negotiations made it impossible for Iranian "moderates" to back away from hostility to Israel. It also allowed hard-liners to make the Israeli-Palestinian war of attrition that began in 2000 a rallying call for support of Hezbollah in Lebanon and anti-peace Palestinian groups like Hamas and the Palestinian Islamic Jihad (PIJ). Since that time, Iran has steadily increased its aid to such groups, provided them with arms or attempted to do so, and provided significant funding. It worked with Syria to turn Hezbollah in Lebanon into a major military force and to equip it with large numbers of rockets and missiles. This played a major role in triggering and shaping the course of the Israeli-Hezbollah War in 2006.

Even during Mohammad Khatami's presidency, Iran's more extreme statements and actions helped paralyze efforts to restore relations with the United States and led President George W. Bush to label Iran part of the "axis of evil" and the United States to call Iran the leading terrorist nation. Since the election of Ahmadinejad as president in 2005, Iranian anti-Iraeli and anti–U.S. rhetoric has become much stronger and more consistent, and President Ahmadinejad has questioned the existence of the Holocaust and called for the end of Israel. It has, however, sometimes been unclear as to just how sincere Iran's motives have been in launching such verbal attacks on Israel. In some cases, this rhetoric has also been used to defuse Arab hostility toward Iran or rationalize actions that were designed to increase Iran's military power and strategic influence in the Gulf region.

Strategic Uncertainty and the Gulf

The geography and strategic character of the "Persian" or "Arabian" Gulf creates major strategic uncertainties for Iran, its neighbors, and the world. It is a 600-mile-long body of water that separates Iran from the Arabian Peninsula, and it is one of the most strategic waterways in the world due to its importance in world oil transportation. Incidents in the Gulf can escalate quickly in ways that neither Iran nor its potential opponents intend. Iran's actions in Lebanon and in dealing with Hamas and the PIJ can provoke other unintended crises, and Iran is caught up in a broader, Sunni-dominated struggle for the future of Islam where some key Sunni Islamist extremist movements deny the legitimacy of Shi'ite beliefs. Military history is rarely determined by intentions and policy in peacetime, and crisis management often becomes an oxymoron as events spiral out of control, misperceptions dominate actions, and escalation becomes both asymmetric and an end in itself.

The Gulf countries (Bahrain, Iran, Iraq, Kuwait, Qatar, Saudi Arabia, and the United Arab Emirates) produce nearly 30 percent of the world's oil, while holding 57 percent (715 billion barrels) of the world's crude oil reserves. Iran alone is estimated to hold 11.1 percent of the world oil reserves (132.0 billion barrels of oil), and 15.3 percent of the world's natural gas reserves [970.8 trillion cubic feet (Tcf)].[75] Besides oil, the Persian Gulf region also has huge reserves of natural gas (2,462 Tcf), accounting for 45 percent of total proven world gas reserves.

Iran's coastline is particularly important because tanker and shipping routes pass so close to Iran's landmass, the islands it controls in the Gulf, and its major naval bases. At its narrowest point (the Strait of Hormuz), the Gulf narrows to only 34 miles wide, with Iran to the north and Oman to the south. The key passages through the Strait consist of 2-mile-wide channels for inbound and outbound tanker traffic, as well as a 2-mile-wide buffer zone.

The oil that flows through the Strait of Hormuz accounts for roughly 40 percent of all world traded oil, and the 17 million barrels per day (MMBD) or more of oil that normally are shipped through the Strait of Hormuz go eastward to Asia (especially Japan, China, and India) and westward (via the Suez Canal or the Sumed pipeline). Any closure of the Strait of Hormuz would require use of longer alternate routes. Such routes are now limited to the approximately 5-MMBD-capacity East-West pipeline across Saudi Arabia to the port of Yanbu, and the Abqaiq-Yanbu natural gas liquids line across Saudi Arabia to the Red Sea, although the Gulf Cooperation Council (GCC) seems to have agreed to construct a new strategic pipeline through Oman to a port on the Gulf of Oman.[76]

Iran has long been involved in significant territorial disputes with its neighbors over control of the islands in the Gulf and offshore oil and gas resources. It faced the Iran-Iraq War from 1980 to 1988, a "tanker war" with the United States over tanker movements through the Gulf from 1987 to 1988, and the risks posed by Iraq's invasion of Kuwait in 1990–1991.

Ever since the time of the Shah, there has been a dispute between Iran and the United Arab Emirates (UAE) over ownership of three strategically important islands near key tanker routes to the Strait of Hormuz—Abu Musa, Greater Tunb Island, and Lesser Tunb Island. The three islands were first seized by the Shah after British withdrawal from the Gulf in the early 1970s and were then occupied by Iranian troops in 1992. In 1995, the Iranian Foreign Ministry claimed that the islands were "an inseparable part of Iran."

Iran has since rejected a 1996 proposal by the GCC for the dispute to be resolved by the International Court of Justice (ICJ), an option supported by the UAE. The GCC issued a statement reiterating its support for the UAE's sovereignty over Abu Musa and the Tunbs on December 31, 2001, declared Iran's claims on the islands as "null and void," and backed "all measures...by the UAE to regain sovereignty on its three islands peacefully." It has repeatedly attempted to persuade Iran to agree to refer the issue to the ICJ. Iran again refused the UAE's offer of arbitration by the International Court of Justice in September 2006, and the risk of a future clash or conflict remains. In addition, Iran and Qatar have both claimed ownership of the North Field (where most of Qatar's gas reserves are), and the issue has never been fully resolved.

The strategic importance of the Gulf will also increase significantly with time. According to the reference case estimate in the Energy Information Administration's *International Energy Outlook 2006,* Gulf oil production is expected to reach about 28.3 MMBD by 2010, 31.1 MMBD by 2020, and 36.8 MMBD by 2020; compared to about 18.7 MMBD in 1990, 21.7 MMBD in 2000, and 23.7 MMBD in 2003. This would increase Gulf oil production capacity to 33 percent of the world total by 2020 (107.6 MMBD and 36 percent by 2030 (123.3 MMBD), up from 28 percent in 2000.[77]

As Figure 1.4 shows, the Gulf's importance as a percent of total world exports will most likely also increase, and the total volume of Gulf exports will increase from 22.5 to 34.3 MMBD. While much of this increase will go to Asia, it will also make a sharp increase in indirect U.S. and European dependence on the Gulf. Asia is so dependent on Gulf oil that a large amount of the energy Asia uses in producing goods for export to the United States and Europe comes from Gulf oil exports. The exact rise that will actually occur in Gulf exports is highly unpredictable, but parametric modeling of other price and economic growth cases shows that significant rises seem highly likely over the next two decades.

The Problem of the United States and Israel

The second problem is that the potential for serious misunderstanding is greatly complicated by the fact that the United States is not only by far the most dominant military power in the Gulf region, but still has no formal dialogue with Iran and has

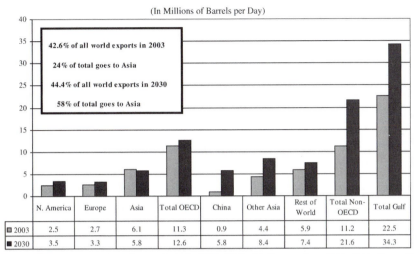

(In Millions of Barrels per Day)

42.6% of all world exports in 2003

24% of total goes to Asia

44.4% of all world exports in 2030

58% of total goes to Asia

	N. America	Europe	Asia	Total OECD	China	Other Asia	Rest of World	Total Non-OECD	Total Gulf
2003	2.5	2.7	6.1	11.3	0.9	4.4	5.9	11.2	22.5
2030	3.5	3.3	5.8	12.6	5.8	8.4	7.4	21.6	34.3

Source: DOE/EIA, International Energy Outlook, 2006, DOE, Washington, June 2006, Table 7, p. 34. http://www.eia.doe.gov/oiaf/ieo/index.html. OECD = Organization for Economic Co-operation and Development.

Figure 1.4   The Growing Volume of Gulf Oil Exports, 2003–2030

never decisively moved away from labeling Iran as part of an axis of evil. Ideological beliefs and misperceptions dominate U.S. attitudes toward Iran as well as Iranian attitudes toward the United States.

The U.S. administration sometimes seems as divided in its approach to Iran between pragmatism and ideology as Iran's leadership. The U.S. Congress can be as reckless in its rhetoric and debates as any in the Iranian Majlis. U.S. think tanks have their own traveling circuses of American apologists for Iran that ignore the military realities in the Gulf. At the same time, the United States has even louder groups calling for preemptive attacks, hard-line treatment of Iran, more sanctions, and for prevention of any official dialogue with Iran.

Israel adds its own dimension to the Iranian and U.S. dialogue of the deaf, a problem sometimes made worse by U.S. supporters of Israel that are far more reckless in what they say than Israeli officials and officers. Israeli concerns are at least partially justified by Iranian actions in Lebanon and the potential emergence of Iranian nuclear forces as an existential threat to Israel, but the combination of Iranian, U.S., and Israeli actions and perceptions creates pressures and risks that encourage escalation, overreaction, and strategic "accidents."

FOCUSING ON CAPABILITIES RATHER THAN ON INTENTIONS

These pressures and uncertainties do not mean that every effort should not be made to understand Iran's true military and strategic intentions or to establish a true dialogue among Iran, its neighbors, the United States, and Israel. From a military viewpoint, however, they do mean that Iran is a state whose military forces must be assessed largely in terms of their capabilities, and not guesses about the intentions of its present leader. Its political structure is too unstable to predict, and its real-world choice of defensive or offensive options is more likely to be determined by its perceptions of its opportunities and risks in actual future contingencies than its current policies and strategy.

Seen from this perspective, Iran is not a "weakling." At the same time, it is not capable of succeeding in any major act of offensive military operations or of becoming any form of regional "hegemon." It meets effective resistance from its neighbors and the United States. At the same time, Iran does present five major kinds of current and potential threats:

- *The first is as a conventional military power.* Iran has limited capabilities today, but could become a much more threatening power if it modernized key elements of its forces and its neighbors did not react.

- *The second is as an asymmetric threat that can seek to intimidate or attack using unconventional forces.* Iran has established a large mix of unconventional forces that can challenge its neighbors in a wide variety of asymmetric wars, including a low-level war of attrition.

- *The third is to some extent an extension of the second. Iran's asymmetric and unconventional capabilities give it the ability to use proxies and partners in the form of both state and nonstate actors.* Iran's support of Shi'ite militias in Iraq, ties to elements in the Iraqi government, partnership with Syria, and ties to Hezbollah in Lebanon are all practical examples of such activities.

- *The fourth is a potential nuclear power armed with long-range missiles. Iran is a declared chemical weapons power.* Its biological weapons efforts are unknown, but it seems unlikely that it remained passive in reaction to Iraq's efforts. It has openly made the acquisition of long-range missiles a major objective, and its nuclear research and production programs almost certainly are intended to produce nuclear weapons.

- *Finally, Iran presents a potential religious and ideological threat in a region and Islamic world polarized along sectarian lines.* For all of the talk about a clash between civilizations, the potential clash within Islam seems far more dangerous. The risk that Sunni and Shi'ite extremists can provoke a broader split between sects and nations could push Iran into a more aggressive religious and ideological struggle.

These are potential threats, not predictions of Iranian actions. They all can be contained with the right choice of policies and military actions. Barring major shifts in its regime, Iran not only is deterrable, but is a nation that will probably respond to the proper security incentives over time. The real question may well be whether Iran's neighbors and the United States provide the right mix of deterrence and incentives, not Iran's current and potential strength.

Iran's Changing Role in Regional Security

Iran is the region's most populous country with 68.7 million people and a population growth rate of 1.1 percent for 2006.[1] It is the one Gulf country that is not Arab, but has a unique Persian character. This is true even though U.S. sources estimate that the Persian-speaking part of the population makes up 58 percent of the total versus 26 percent for Turkic and Turkic dialects, 9 percent for Kurdish, 2 percent for Luri, 1 percent for Balochi, 1 percent for Arabic, 1 percent for Turkish, and 2 percent for other. In terms of ethnicity, U.S. estimates classify the population as 51 percent Persian, 24 percent Azeri, 8 percent Gilaki and Mazandarani, 7 percent Kurd, 3 percent Arab, 2 percent Lur, 2 percent Baloch, 2 percent Turkmen, and 1 percent other.[2]

Iran has its own Shi'ite Islamist fundamentalism at a time when Sunni neo-Salafi fundamentalism is seeking control of the Gulf and the Arab world. It does, however, have significant religious minorities. The population is 89 percent Shi'a Muslim, 9 percent Sunni Muslim, and 2 percent Zoroastrian, Jewish, Christian, and Baha'i. Iran's opposition to Israel and the United States, on the one hand, and its ties to Iraq, Syria, and Lebanon, on the other hand, both defuse Sunni and Arab hostility and increase its influence inside and outside the Gulf.[3]

Iran has always been a key player in regional security, and the role it plays has long been a destabilizing one. The Revolution that deposed the Shah in 1979 brought radical clerical leaders like Ayatollah Ruhollah Khomeini to power. It was followed by the seizure of American diplomats as hostages and Iranian efforts to export its "Islamic Revolution" to other Gulf States like Bahrain and to the Islamic world. Since that time, the United States and several European nations have consistently accused Iran of supporting terrorism. This usually took the shape of supporting proxy groups such as Hezbollah, Hamas, and Islamic Jihad. In addition, neighboring states such as Saudi Arabia and Bahrain have accused Iran of supporting local Shi'ite groups that carried out attacks against Saudi and Bahraini targets, including the 1996 Al-Khobar bombing and several attacks during the 1970s.

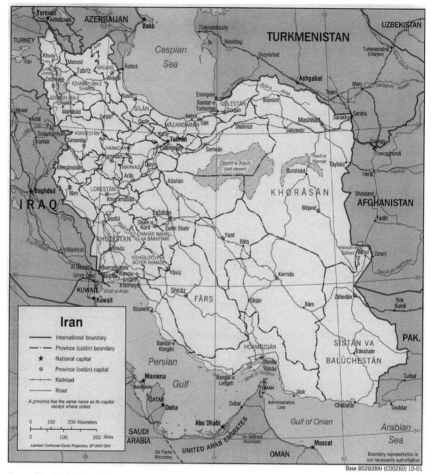

Source: CIA, "Iran," 2002, available at http://www.lib.utexas.edu/maps/middle_east_and_asia/iran_pol01.jpg

Figure 2.1   Iran

Iran has said it has abandoned its goal of spreading Iranian influence and an "Islamic" revolution in the southern Gulf States, but Iran's strategic intentions are now being questioned by many strategic and defense planners in the Gulf. The election of Mahmoud Ahmadinejad as Iran's president on August 3, 2005, made a radical populist Iran's leading civil leader. His hard-line views and his rhetoric about the return of the hidden imam have made Iran increasingly suspect to its neighbors, as well as to the rest of the world. Iran's meddling in Iraq's internal affairs and aid to Shi'ite militias like Hezbollah have raised growing concerns among Iran's Sunni neighbors. Leaders in Saudi Arabia, Egypt, and Jordan have accused Iran of wanting to create a "Shi'ite crescent" that includes Iran, Iraq, Lebanon, and Syria.

Iran's power and influence have been increased by several external developments. Two of Iran's main enemies, the Taliban regime and Saddam Hussein, have been toppled by the United States since the terrorist attacks on the United States on September 11, 2001. Iran no longer faces a threat from either neighbor and may acquire an ally in Iraq, where a Shi'ite majority has come to power. Hezbollah's success in fighting Israel in the summer of 2006 has been credited in part to Iranian investment, advisory efforts, and arms transfers. This has enhanced the credibility of Iran's ability to use nonstate actors and asymmetric warfare. The same has been true of Iran's support of Shi'ite militias in Iraq and support of Palestinian rejectionist movements like Hamas and the Palestinian Islamic Jihad.

At the same time the same invasions that toppled these two regimes have led to a major U.S. military presence in both states and a much larger U.S. air and naval presence in the Gulf. This has increased U.S.–Iranian tension and Iran's pressure on its neighbors. Iran has long used the U.S. presence in the region as a reason to condemn countries such as Kuwait and Saudi Arabia for their close alliance with the United States. In 2006, there were more than 130,000 U.S. troops in the countries on two of Iran's borders. In addition, the U.S. traditional presence in the Gulf, especially in Bahrain, Kuwait, and Qatar, has not changed.

The most destabilizing issue affecting Iran's role in regional security is the potential proliferation of nuclear weapons. Iran's nuclear program has been under growing scrutiny by the International Atomic Energy Agency, the EU-3 (France, Germany, and the United Kingdom), the United States, and most of Iran's neighboring states. So has the fact that it is developing a family of long-range missiles like the Shahab-3. There is increasing concern that Iran is seeking long-range nuclear strike capabilities that would be a destabilizing force in the region.

The inauguration of Mahmoud Ahmadinejad to the presidency compounded these concerns. His statements about the Holocaust and his rhetoric about the end of times have made Iran's nuclear program an existential threat to Israel. Most of Iran's neighbors in the southern Gulf also cannot ignore the fact that they, too, are "one city" target states in the sense that even one or two nuclear strikes on their capital city would destroy enough of their government, population, and economy so they could never recover from such strikes in anything like their present form.

The other side of the story is that Iran has been more conservative in modernizing its conventional military forces. Iran has never rebuilt the level of conventional forces it had before its defeat in its war with Iraq in 1988. Iran's conventional military readiness, effectiveness, and capabilities have declined since the end of the Iran-Iraq War, and Iran has not been able to find a meaningful way to restore its conventional edge in the region. As is discussed in detail, Iran has been able to order only $2.3 billion worth of new arms agreements during 1997–2004, although most recent trends give evidence for an increase in foreign weapon procurement. Saudi Arabia ordered $10.5 billion, Kuwait $3.1 billion, and the United Arab Emirates ordered $12.0 billion. Even a small nation like Oman spent $2.5 billion. This inability to modernize its conventional forces is seen by many experts as one of the reasons for Iran's "nuclear ambitions" and its focus on building its asymmetric capabilities.

Military Spending, Arms Imports, and Military Manning

Iran has faced major problems in modernizing and financing its military forces ever since the Revolution in 1979. The United States and other Western powers ceased to sell Iran weapon systems, spare parts, munitions, and technical expertise for its existing weapons programs shortly after the Revolution. Iran built up major supplies of Chinese, Russian, and other Eastern bloc weapons during the Iran-Iraq War, but its defeat in that war in 1988 resulted in the loss of some 40–50 percent of its land forces.

IRANIAN MILITARY SPENDING AND ARMS IMPORTS

Iran has faced serious financial problems in funding its force modernization, compounded by the systematic mismanagement of its economy. Iran's economy is overdependent on oil export revenues, with such revenues representing around 80–90 percent of total export earnings and 40–50 percent of the government budget; according to one source, revenues from oil monopoly rents comprised 63 percent of Iranian state revenues in 2004.[1]

Reporting by the U.S. Energy Information Agency (EIA) notes that strong oil prices have boosted Iran's oil export revenues and helped Iran's economic situation over the last few years. Iran's oil export revenues have increased steadily, from $32 billion in 2004, to $45.6 billion in 2005, with estimates for 2006 at $46.9 billion. Estimates for the Iranian year from March 2006 to March 2007 are about $54 billion. As a result, Iran's real gross domestic product increased by around 6.1 percent in 2005.[2]

Iran's state-run, oil-rentier economy has run into structural problems that, if they continue, will adversely affect the development of the armed forces. The official figure for inflation is around 16 percent per year, and unofficial estimates place the figure at 40–50 percent. Iranian budget deficits remain a chronic problem, in part due to large-scale state subsidies on foodstuffs and gasoline. The Iranian parliament (Majlis) decided in January 2005 to freeze domestic prices for gasoline and other fuels at 2003 levels.[3]

In March 2006, parliament reduced the government's gasoline subsidy allocation for fiscal year 2006/2007 to $2.5 billion, compared with a request of $4 billion and costs of over $4 billion for imports in the previous year. On March 7, 2007, the Majlis voted to freeze annual subsidies for gasoline at $2.5 billion, which will lead to a price hike by about 25 percent, projected to take effect in May 2007.[4] In 2006, the National Iranian Oil Company said it had used nearly its entire $2.5-billion budget for gasoline imports, but legislators have stated their opposition to providing the additional $3.5 billion necessary to pay for imports through the end of the fiscal year, in March 2007.

The EIA reports that the lack of job opportunities for the country's young and rapidly growing population is another major problem. Official unemployment in Iran was reported to be around 11 percent in 2006, but was significantly higher among young people. Iran has attempted to diversify its economy by investing some of its oil revenues in other areas, including petrochemicals.

Iran has also sought to attract billions of dollars worth of foreign investment by creating a more favorable investment climate, by reducing restrictions and duties on imports, and by creating free-trade zones. However, there has only been very limited progress, and Iran has fallen far short of its goals. Badly structured incentive programs, overambitious project requirements, poorly structured incentives, a hostile reaction to Iran's new president, and the ongoing debate over Iran's nuclear programs have all been significant factors.[5]

As Figure 3.1 shows, Iran has used its rising oil revenues to finance higher military spending. According to the International Institute for Strategic Studies (IISS), Iran's military budget has been steadily increasing over the past few years, rising from $2.3 billion in 2000, to $3.36 billion in 2003, and to $6.2 billion in 2006—this represents a 170-percent increase in Iran's military budget since 2000.[6] Figure 3.1 does, however, show that the other Gulf States have also increased their military spending as well, and Iranian spending lags far behind Saudi Arabia and even farther behind the total spending of the southern Gulf States.

The increase in military spending also has led to an increase in Iran's arms imports. Figure 3.2 shows the trend in new Iranian arms deliveries by supplier from 1993 to 2005. There has been a steady contraction in new arms deliveries from $2.6 billion during 1993–1996, to $1.9 billion during 1997–2000, and to $0.5 billion during 2001–2004, yet this number can be expected to increase because of an underlying recent increase in settled agreements.

Russia and China, Iran's two major suppliers, have experienced sharp declines in their exports to Iran. For example, Russian arms exports to Iran declined from $1.3 billion during 1993–1996 to $0.1 billion during 2001–2004, while China's arms deliveries to Iran declined from $0.9 billion during 1993–1996 to $0.1 billion during 2001–2004.

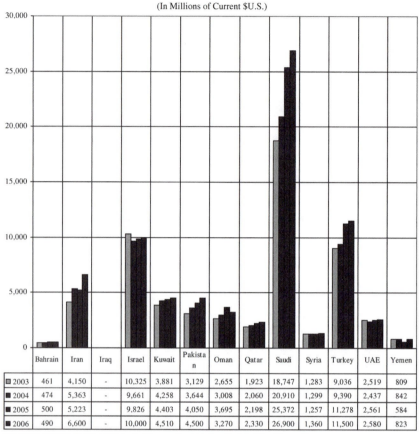

(In Millions of Current $U.S.)

	Bahrain	Iran	Iraq	Israel	Kuwait	Pakistan	Oman	Qatar	Saudi	Syria	Turkey	UAE	Yemen
2003	461	4,150	-	10,325	3,881	3,129	2,655	1,923	18,747	1,283	9,036	2,519	809
2004	474	5,363	-	9,661	4,258	3,644	3,008	2,060	20,910	1,299	9,390	2,437	842
2005	500	5,223	-	9,826	4,403	4,050	3,695	2,198	25,372	1,257	11,278	2,561	584
2006	490	6,600	-	10,000	4,510	4,500	3,270	2,330	26,900	1,360	11,500	2,580	823

Note: Israeli, Pakistani, Turkish, and Yemeni military spending totals do not include U.S. military assistance.
Source: IISS, *Military Balance 2007.*

Figure 3.1   Comparative Gulf Military Spending

In 2005, however, Russia concluded arms and technology transfer agreements with Iran that increased Iranian imports considerably. Russia agreed to deliver 29 comparatively modern TOR-M1 surface-to-air missiles (SAMs), as well as provide technological upgrades on Su-24 and MiG-29 aircraft and T-72 main battle tanks.[7] The TOR-1 SAMs reportedly were received in early 2007.[8]

Iran's new arms agreements have illustrated a more mixed trend. As shown in Figure 3.2, the combined value of new agreements over arms purchases increased from $1.2 billion between 1993 and 1996, to $1.5 billion between 1997 and 2000, fell to $0.8 billion between 2001 and 2004, before the total of new agreements almost tripled to $2.2 billion during 2002–2005. Russia's share in the total value of arms imports rose from $0.2 billion between 1993 and 1996 to $0.4 billion between 1997 and 2000, and then remained the same at $0.4 billion between 2002 and

Deliveries   (In Current Million $U.S.)

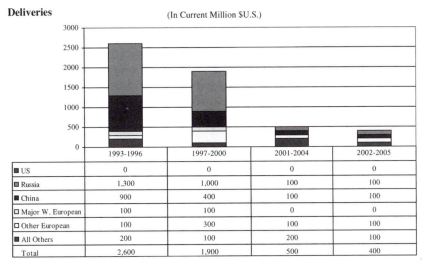

	1993-1996	1997-2000	2001-2004	2002-2005
■ US	0	0	0	0
▣ Russia	1,300	1,000	100	100
■ China	900	400	100	100
▢ Major W. European	100	100	0	0
▢ Other European	100	300	100	100
■ All Others	200	100	200	100
Total	2,600	1,900	500	400

New Agreements

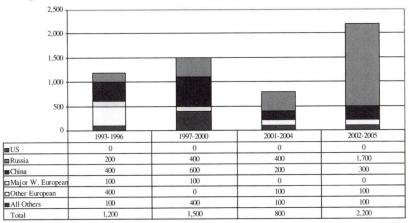

	1993-1996	1997-2000	2001-2004	2002-2005
■ US	0	0	0	0
▣ Russia	200	400	400	1,700
■ China	400	600	200	300
▢ Major W. European	100	100	0	0
▢ Other European	400	0	100	100
■ All Others	100	400	100	100
Total	1,200	1,500	800	2,200

Source: Richard F. Grimmett, Conventional Arms Transfers To Developing Nations, 1998-2005, CRS, October 23, 2006; Richard F. Grimmett, Conventional Arms Transfers To Developing Nations, 1997-2004, CRS, August 29, 2005; Richard F. Grimmett, Conventional Arms Transfers To Developing Nations, 1993-2000, CRS, August 16, 2001.

Figure 3.2   Iran's Arms Imports by Supplier, 1993–2005

2004, but more than quadrupled between 2002 and 2005, which represented an almost 80-percent share of all new delivery agreements.

China's new arms agreements with Iran increased from $0.4 billion during 1993–1996 to $0.60 billion during 1997–2000, and then dropped to $0.20 billion during 2001–2004. China has long been known to be a significant provider of missile technology to Iran. Western European countries had no new arms agreements during 2001–2004, and the amount coming from "All Others" decreased from $400 million during 1997–2000 to $100 million during 2001–2004.

As is discussed later, these expenditures have led to some carefully focused purchases that have increased Iran's military capabilities in several important areas. They have not, however, been large enough to offset the steady aging of most of Iran's military inventory, its inability to obtain parts and upgrades for much of its Western-supplied equipment, and anything close to parity with the level of weapons and technology in U.S., British, and many other Gulf forces. Iran has tried to compensate by creating its own military industries, but such efforts have as yet had only a limited impact. As Figures 3.3 and 3.4 show, Iran's arms imports and delivery agreements have not reached the levels of several other of the Gulf Cooperation Council states.

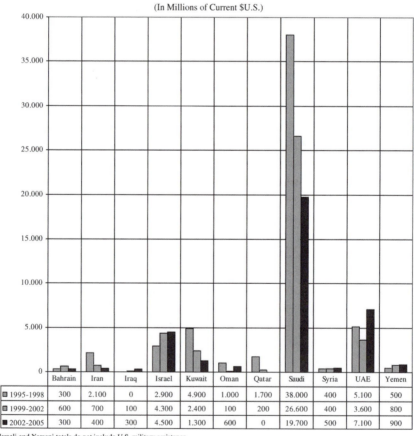

(In Millions of Current $U.S.)

	Bahrain	Iran	Iraq	Israel	Kuwait	Oman	Qatar	Saudi	Syria	UAE	Yemen
◨ 1995-1998	300	2.100	0	2.900	4.900	1.000	1.700	38.000	400	5.100	500
◨ 1999-2002	600	700	100	4.300	2.400	100	200	26.600	400	3.600	800
◼ 2002-2005	300	400	300	4.500	1.300	600	0	19.700	500	7.100	900

Israeli and Yemeni totals do not include U.S. military assistance.

Source: Richard F. Grimmett, Congressional Research Service, various reports.

Figure 3.3   Comparative Gulf New Arms Deliveries

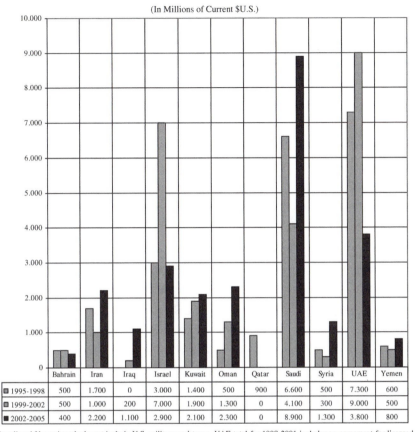

(In Millions of Current $U.S.)

	Bahrain	Iran	Iraq	Israel	Kuwait	Oman	Qatar	Saudi	Syria	UAE	Yemen
1995-1998	500	1.700	0	3.000	1.400	500	900	6.600	500	7.300	600
1999-2002	500	1.000	200	7.000	1.900	1.300	0	4.100	300	9.000	500
2002-2005	400	2.200	1.100	2.900	2.100	2.300	0	8.900	1.300	3.800	800

Israeli and Yemeni totals do not include U.S. military assistance. UAE total for 1998-2001 includes an agreement for licensed production 80 F-16 aircraft worth $6.432 billion.

Source: Richard F. Grimmett, Congressional Research Service, various reports.

Figure 3.4   Comparative Gulf New Arms Import Agreements

IRANIAN MILITARY MANPOWER

Iran maintained active armed forces totaling some 545,000 men in 2007, although some 220,000 of this total were 18-month conscripts who receive limited training and had only marginal military effectiveness. Iran also had an army reserve of some 350,000 men, although the men in these reserves received negligible training, and Iran lacked the equipment, supplies, and leadership cadres to make effective use of such reserves without months of reorganization and training.

Iran's military manpower problems are shaped by a number of factors. Iran divided its armed forces into regular and revolutionary components following the Revolution in 1979, creating a split between the regular forces that existed under the Shah and the Revolutionary Guards installed during the rule of the Ayatollah

Ruhollah Khomeini. This split has been reinforced by highly compartmented or "stovepiped" military forces, which have made only limited progress in joint warfare.

Military training is often subject to political problems and ideological interference, and many large-scale exercises are sometimes more to "posture" in front of the United States and Iran's neighbors than improve combat readiness. The combat-trained military personnel Iran developed during the Iran-Iraq War have virtually all left the service. Iran is now a largely conscript force with limited military training and little combat experience. The deep divisions between "moderates" and "hard-liners" in Iran's government have inevitably politicized the armed forces, which remain under the command of the supreme religious leader, the Ayatollah Ali Khamenei.

Iran must also deal with the language, ethnic, and sectarian divisions described earlier. While these have not produced acute tensions in the past, the divisions among Persian, Azeri, Arab, and Kurd do present problems. Language is an issue,

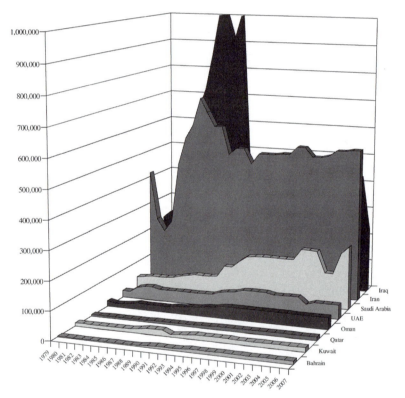

Note: Saudi totals include full-time active National Guard, Omani totals include Royal Guard, Iranian totals include Revolutionary Guards, and Iraqi totals include Republican Guards and Special Republican Guards.

Source: International Institute for Strategic Studies (IISS), *Military Balance*, various editions; *Jane's, Sentinel Security Assessment;* and *Military Technology.*

Figure 3.5   Comparative Trends in Gulf Total Active Military Manpower, 1979–2007

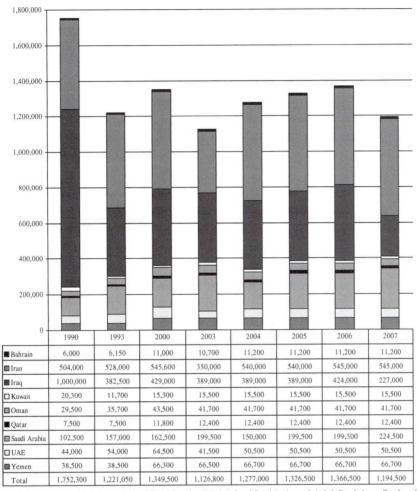

	1990	1993	2000	2003	2004	2005	2006	2007
■ Bahrain	6,000	6,150	11,000	10,700	11,200	11,200	11,200	11,200
▣ Iran	504,000	528,000	545,600	350,000	540,000	540,000	545,000	545,000
■ Iraq	1,000,000	382,500	429,000	389,000	389,000	389,000	424,000	227,000
☐ Kuwait	20,300	11,700	15,300	15,500	15,500	15,500	15,500	15,500
▣ Oman	29,500	35,700	43,500	41,700	41,700	41,700	41,700	41,700
■ Qatar	7,500	7,500	11,800	12,400	12,400	12,400	12,400	12,400
▣ Saudi Arabia	102,500	157,000	162,500	199,500	150,000	199,500	199,500	224,500
☐ UAE	44,000	54,000	64,500	41,500	50,500	50,500	50,500	50,500
▣ Yemen	38,500	38,500	66,300	66,500	66,700	66,700	66,700	66,700
Total	1,752,300	1,221,050	1,349,500	1,126,800	1,277,000	1,326,500	1,366,500	1,194,500

Note: Saudi totals include full-time active National Guard. Omani totals include Royal Guard. Iranian totals include Revolutionary Guards, and Iraqi totals include Republican Guards and Special Republican Guards.

Source: Estimated by authors based on data from the International Institute for Strategic Studies (IISS), *Military Balance*, various editions; Jane's, *Sentinel Security Assessment;* and *Military Technology.*

Figure 3.6 Total Active Military Manpower in All Gulf Forces, 1990–2007

particularly in the conscript intake, and the impact of sectarian differences is growing. Experts disagree significantly over the details of Iran's linguistic, ethnic, and religious structure, but the Central Intelligence Agency (CIA) makes the following estimate:

- Persian speaking population is 58% of the total versus 26% for Turkic and Turkic dialects, 9% for Kurdish, 2% for Luri, 1% for Balochi, 1% for Arabic, 1% for Turkish, and 2% for others. These data describe shares of the population that speak a particular language or dialect as their first language.

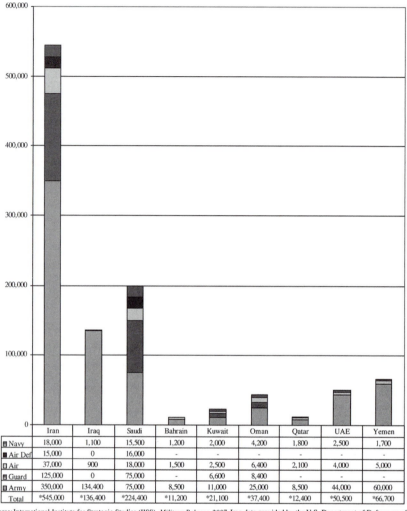

	Iran	Iraq	Saudi	Bahrain	Kuwait	Oman	Qatar	UAE	Yemen
Navy	18,000	1,100	15,500	1,200	2,000	4,200	1,800	2,500	1,700
Air Def	15,000	0	16,000	-	-	-	-	-	-
Air	37,000	900	18,000	1,500	2,500	6,400	2,100	4,000	5,000
Guard	125,000	0	75,000	-	6,600	8,400	-	-	-
Army	350,000	134,400	75,000	8,500	11,000	25,000	8,500	44,000	60,000
Total	*545,000	*136,400	*224,400	*11,200	*21,100	*37,400	*12,400	*50,500	*66,700

Source: International Institute for Strategic Studies (IISS), *Military Balance, 2007.* Iraq data provided by the U.S. Department of Defense as of March 5, 2007.

Figure 3.7 Total Gulf Military Manpower by Country by Service in 2007

- Ethnic Population is divided by 51% Persian, 24% Azeri, 8% Gilaki and Mazandarani, 7% Kurd, 3% Arab, 2% Lur, 2% Baloch, 2% Turkmen, and 1% other.

- In terms of religious affiliation, the population consists of 89% Shi'a Muslim, 9% Sunni Muslim, and 2% Zoroastrian, Jewish, Christian, and Baha'i.[9]

At the same time, Iran is the most populous Gulf State and can draw on large reserves of military age manpower. The comparative trends in military manpower are shown in Figures 3.5, 3.6, and 3.7. The CIA estimates that Iran has some 4.8

million men fit for military service in the ages 18–49 and that some 862,000 males reach the military age of 18 each year.

To put these numbers in perspective, Iraq has some 15.7 million men fit for military service in the ages 18–49, and some 289,000 males reach the military age of 18 each year. Saudi Arabia has some 6.6 million men fit for military service in the ages 18–49, and some 247,000 males reach the military age of 18 each year. A smaller Gulf State like Oman, with a comparatively large native population, has some 581,000 men fit for military service in the ages 18–49, and some 26,400 males reach the military age of 18 each year. Bahrain, Kuwait, Qatar, and the United Arab Emirates all have comparatively small pools of native manpower.[10]

4

The Iranian Army

As Figure 4.1 shows, the Iranian Army (Artesh) is large compared to those of other countries in the Gulf region. It has some 350,000 men (220,000 conscripts) organized into four corps, with four armored divisions, six infantry divisions, six artillery groups, two commando divisions, an airborne division, aviation groups, and other smaller independent formations. These latter units include independent armored, infantry, and commando brigades. Iran's strength in terms of comparative active land force manpower [Army and Islamic Revolutionary Guard Corps (IRGC)] is shown in Figure 4.1.

In practice, each Iranian division has a somewhat different organization. For example, only one Iranian division (the 92nd) is well enough equipped to be considered a true armored division, and two of the armored divisions are notably larger than the others. Two of the infantry divisions (28th and 84th) are more heavily mechanized than the others.[1] The lighter and smaller formations in the regular army include the 23rd Special Forces Division, which was formed in 1993–1994, and the 55th paratroop division. According to one source, the 23rd Special Forces Division has 5,000 full-time regulars and is one of the most professional units in the Iranian Army.

The regular army also has a number of independent brigades and groups. These include some small armored units, one infantry brigade, one airborne and two to three Special Forces brigades, coastal defense units, a growing number of air-defense groups, five artillery brigades/regiments, four to six army aviation units, and a growing number of logistic and supply formations. The land forces have six major garrisons and 13 major casernes. There is a military academy at Tehran and a signal-training center in Shiraz.[2] The airborne and Special Forces train at a facility in Shiraz, too.[3]

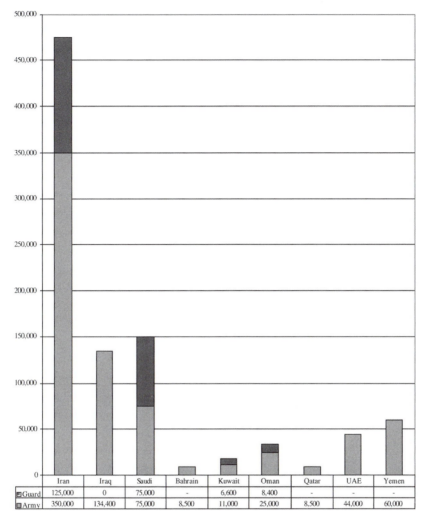

	Iran	Iraq	Saudi	Bahrain	Kuwait	Oman	Qatar	UAE	Yemen
■ Guard	125,000	0	75,000	-	6,600	8,400	-	-	-
■ Army	350,000	134,400	75,000	8,500	11,000	25,000	8,500	44,000	60,000

Note: Saudi totals include full-time active National Guard, Omani totals include Royal Guard, Iranian totals include Revolutionary Guards, and Iraqi totals include Republican Guards and Special Republican Guards.
Source: Estimated by authors based on data from the International Institute for Strategic Studies (IISS), *Military Balance*, various editions; Jane's, *Sentinel Security Assessment;* and *Military Technology.*

Figure 4.1   Total Active Army Manpower in All Gulf Forces 2007

IRANIAN TANK STRENGTH

Iran's comparative strength in total armored fighting vehicles and main battle tanks is shown in Figures 4.2, 4.3, and 4.4. It should be noted that Iran's Army has a higher proportion of combat-worn and obsolescent equipment than any of its major Gulf neighbors except Iraq, and the United States can decisively intervene with massively superior land and air forces against any offensive Iranian conventional military operation at any time.

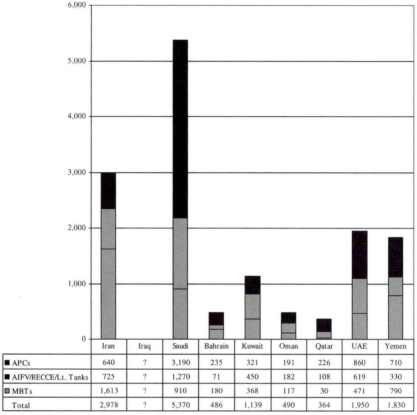

	Iran	Iraq	Saudi	Bahrain	Kuwait	Oman	Qatar	UAE	Yemen
■ APCs	640	?	3,190	235	321	191	226	860	710
■ AIFV/RECCE/Lt. Tanks	725	?	1,270	71	450	182	108	619	330
▨ MBTs	1,613	?	910	180	368	117	30	471	790
Total	2,978	?	5,370	486	1,139	490	364	1,950	1,830

Source: International Institute for Strategic Studies (IISS), *Military Balance, 2007.*

Figure 4.2   Total Gulf Operational Armored Fighting Vehicles, 2007

Iran has steadily rebuilt its armored strength since the Iran-Iraq War, although its forces are still significantly smaller than under the Shah. It has some 1,613 main battle tanks (MBTs) in 2007, and the number has risen steadily in recent years. Iran had a total of 1,145 in 2000, 1,565 in 2003, and 1,613 in 2006. The International Institute for Strategic Studies (IISS) estimates that Iran's inventory of main battle tanks now includes some 168 M-47/M-48s and 150 M-60A1s, 100 Chieftain Mark 3/5s, 540 T-54/T-55s/Type-59s, 75 T-62s, 480 T-72/T-72Ss, and 100 Zulfiqars. Its T-72 strength has increased from its level in the 1990s to it current strength of 480. (Other estimates indicate that Iran may have as many as 300 Type 59s and/or 150–250 Type-69IIs.)

Only 480–580 of Iran's main battle tanks can be described as "modern" by common standards—the T-72s and the Zulfiqars. Iran has some 865 other armored fighting vehicles, 550–640 armored personnel carriers (APCs), 2,010 towed artillery weapons, 310 self-propelled artillery weapons, more than 870 multiple rocket

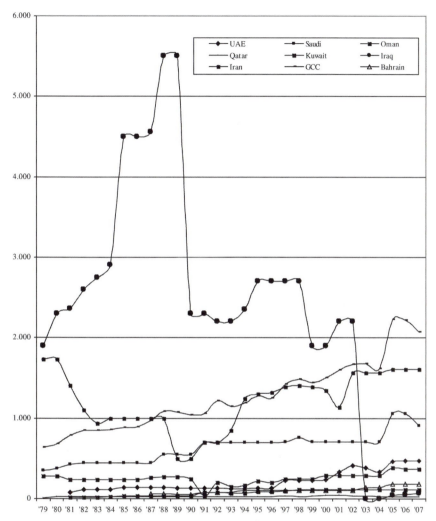

Note: Iranian totals include Revolutionary Guards, and Iraqi totals include Republican Guards and Special Republican Guards.
Source: Estimated using data from the International Institute for Strategic Studies (IISS), *Military Balance*, and various editions.

Figure 4.3   Total Operational Main Battle Tanks in All Gulf Forces, 1979–2007

launchers, about 1,700 air-defense guns and large numbers of light anti-aircraft (AA) missiles, large numbers of anti-tank weapons and guided missiles, and some 50 attack helicopters. This is a large inventory of major weapons, although many are worn and obsolete.

Given that Iran's armored forces reportedly are structured with 55 tanks in one battalion, and three battalions in one armored brigade, this leaves Iran with about three armored brigades equipped with modern tanks. These units would be mostly

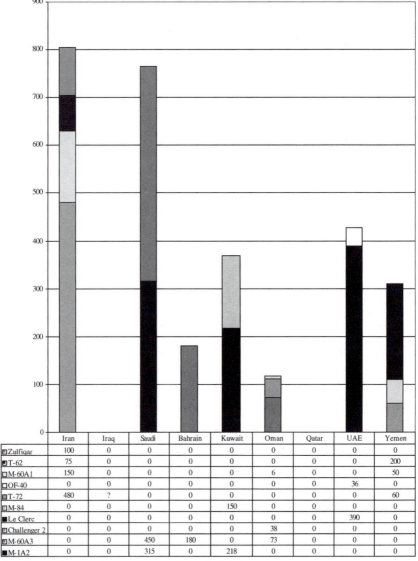

	Iran	Iraq	Saudi	Bahrain	Kuwait	Oman	Qatar	UAE	Yemen
Zulfiqar	100	0	0	0	0	0	0	0	0
T-62	75	0	0	0	0	0	0	0	200
M-60A1	150	0	0	0	0	6	0	0	50
OF-40	0	0	0	0	0	0	0	36	0
T-72	480	?	0	0	0	0	0	0	60
M-84	0	0	0	0	150	0	0	0	0
Le Clerc	0	0	0	0	0	0	0	390	0
Challenger 2	0	0	0	0	0	38	0	0	0
M-60A3	0	0	450	180	0	73	0	0	0
M-1A2	0	0	315	0	218	0	0	0	0

Source: International Institute for Strategic Studies (IISS), *Military Balance*, 2007.

Figure 4.4   Medium- to High-Quality Main Battle Tanks by Type, 2007

made up of T-72s because Iran tends to keep tanks of a specific kind in one unit. Any long campaign may quickly deplete Iran's capabilities to repair and replace its vehicles. Though Iran builds some of the T-72s in license, it appears doubtful that it has the resources to quickly service three brigades of T-72s with spare parts.

However, it has to be acknowledged that Iran now faces a near power vacuum in Iraq, which is slowly being equipped to fight counterinsurgency battles, but has lost virtually all of the major weapons and equipment it had in 2003 and is being equipped just with limited amounts of armor. Iran also possesses a relatively large mix of modern infantry fighting vehicles—the BMP-2 and variants. This allows it to field a significant number of reasonably modern tanks and infantry vehicles in some units. The Iranian Army appears to be able to deploy about three brigades with fairly modern equipment for integrated warfare. This is not a guarantee that it actually does so in its order of battle, and it does not say anything about the level of training among the troops.

As for tank mission readiness and quality, only part of Iran's total tank inventory is operational. It is uncertain how many of Iran's Chieftains and M-47/M-48s are operational, since the total number of Chieftains includes the remainder of 187 improved FV4030/1 versions of the Mark 5 Chieftain that were delivered to the country before the fall of the Shah. Smaller problems seem to exist throughout the rest of the force, and some experts estimate that Iran's sustainable operational tank strength may be fewer than 1,000 tanks. Furthermore, Iran's Chieftains and M-60s are at least several decades old, and most of them have been in service for more than 30 years. The M60s, the T-72s, and the Zulfiqars are Iran's only tanks with anything approaching modern fire-control systems, sights, and armor-piercing ammunition.

Iran's Most Modern Tanks

Iran's T-72Ss are export versions of the Soviet T-72B. Some have been built under license in Iran and are armed with a 125-mm 2A46M smoothbore gun. They have a relatively modern IA40-1 fire-control system and computer, a laser range finder, and a night and day image intensifying sighting system, which most likely is of inferior quality. The T-72S is powered by an 840-horsepower V-84MS diesel engine, has upgraded suspension and mine protection capabilities, and a combat weight of 44.5 tons. Russian sources indicate that Iran has ordered 1,000 T-72Ss from Russia.

According to one report, the T-72S can also fire a Svir 9M119 (AT-11) laser beam-riding guided anti-tank guided missile (ATGM) to a range of 4,000 meters.[4] Global Security reports that Iran has developed a tank upgrade package called the Type-72Z in order to extend the operational life of the T-54/T-55 MBTs, and its Chinese-made Type-59 equivalents, which originally were armed with a 100-mm gun. If these reports are accurate, they have been fitted with a copy of the 105-mm M68 rifled tank gun in service with Iran on the M60A1 MBT. The Armament Industries Division of the Defense Industries Organization has the capability to bore tank and artillery barrels, such as the 122-mm Russian D-30.[5]

The Type 72Z (Type-59) is also reported to have a Slovenian Fontana EFCS-3 computerized fire-control system to improve its first round kill capability both while the Type T72Z MBT is static or moving. Some may have been fitted with a roof-mounted laser-warning device, possibly coupled to a commander's display and smoke-grenade launchers on each side of the turret.

Global Security provides the following additional data of the Type T-72Z:

[T]he upgraded Type 72Z is powered by the V-46-6 V-12 diesel engine developing 780hp as part of a new a new powerpack, which also includes the SPAT 1200 transmission for use in automatic or semi-automatic modes. The V-46 V-12 diesel engine is also installed in early production T-72 series MBTs, such as the T-72 and T-72A, and Iran could obtain these from various sources besides Russia.

. . . Last year, the Shahid Kolah Dooz Industrial Complex revealed it had developed a new ERA package that can be rapidly fixed to the T-54/ T-55, T-72 and other MBTs to improve battlefield survivability against chemical energy (CE) and kinetic energy (KE) attack. This Iranian ERA package is similar to that being made and marketed by Russia and has been installed on Russian MBTs, such as the T-80BV, for some years. The Iranian ERA armor system comprises one composite layer. This protects against KE and CE projectiles and an extra energetic material that provides protection against KE attack. Iranian sources said this system can be dropped from a height of 5m; will not be activated from small arms fire up to 30mm in caliber or grenades; and is resistant to napalm type weapons.[6]

As mentioned earlier, Iran has developed its own main battle tank called the Zul-fiqar (Zolfaqar), which it claims is made largely out of Iranian-made components. It entered the prototype stage in 1997 and is reported to have a 125-mm smoothbore gun and welded steel turret of Iranian design. One source notes that Iran opened its own production line for T-72 tanks in 1997, too.[7] According to one report, the Zulfiqar is powered by a V-46-6-12 V-12 diesel engine with 780 horsepower and uses a SPAT 1200 automatic transmission. This engine is used in the Soviet T-72, but the tank transmission design seems to be closer to that of the U.S. M-60. Further, some reports claim that the development of the Zulfiqar resembles the Brazilian Osorio tank, a discontinued but fairly modern tank, which incorporated many Western-made parts.[8] The Zulfiqar seems to have a relatively modern fire-control system, and Iran may have improved its T-72s with a similar upgrade.

The Zulfiqar's combat weight is reported to be 36 tons, and its maximum speed supposedly reaches 65 kilometers per hour at a power-to-weight ratio of 21.7 horse-power per ton. The tank is equipped with a 7.62-mm coaxial and a 12.7-mm roof-mounted machine gun. It uses the modern Slovenia Fontana EFCS-3 computerized fire-control system to provide a fully stabilized fire-on-the-move capability. It may have a roof-mounted laser-warning device, and it could use the same reactive armor system discussed earlier. Roughly 100 Zulifqars are thought to be in service.

Holdings of Older Tanks

Iran has extended the service life of some of its T-54s, T-55s, and T-59s by improving their armor and fire-control systems and by arming them with an Iranian-made M-68 rifled 105-mm gun similar to the one used in the M-60A1. Reportedly, the Armament Industries Division of the Iranian Defense Industries Organization produces this gun. The Revolutionary Guards is reported to have a special variant of the T-54 called the Safir-74. Iran also claims to have developed explosive reactive armor add-ons for its tanks, although the effectiveness of such armor remains unclear. In broad terms, it is far easier to claim to have made meaningful updates of tanks this old, with all of their basic design, internal crew space, and power train problems, than actually implement them in combat-effective form.

Some of Iran's 168 M-47/M-48s include an upgraded version of the M-47M. The American firm of Bowen-McLaughlin-York, which also built a vehicle manufacturing plant in Iran, upgraded these tanks between 1970 and 1972. The M-47Ms have many of the components of the M-60A1, including the diesel engine, automatic transmission, suspension, gun-control system, and fire components. The upgrade is said to have resulted in an extended operating range of the M-47 from 130 to 600 kilometers, and increased storage space to hold 79 rounds by eliminating the bow-mounted machine gun thereby reducing the crew to four. An estimated 150 conversions were delivered to Iran, but this took place well over 30 years ago; the number still in service is unclear, and even the upgrades are now worn and obsolete.

The fact remains that Iran has both serious qualitative and quantitative problems. In spite of its tank imports and production since the Iran-Iraq War, Iran's total operational main battle tank holdings are sufficient to fully equip only five to seven of its divisions by Western standards. Iran can sustain only about half the number of its main battle tanks for any period of extended maneuver warfare. At present, however, Iran's tanks are dispersed in relatively small lots among all of its regular army and some of its IRGC combat units—all of the IRGC units generally have only small tank force cadres, and it is unclear to what extent these forces will be armored in the future. The 92nd Armored Division is the only Iranian division that has enough tanks to realistically be considered an armored division, even by regional comparisons.

OTHER IRANIAN ARMOR

Iran's comparative strength in other armored fighting vehicles is shown in Figures 4.5 through 4.8. Iran possessed about 1,000–1,360 armored infantry fighting vehicles (AIFVs) and APCs in its operational inventory in 2007, although counts are contradictory and it is difficult to estimate what parts of Iran's holdings are fully operational and/or sustainable for any length of time in combat. The IISS, for example, estimates an inventory of 690 light tanks and armored infantry fighting vehicles and 640 APCs. Virtually all estimates indicate, however, that Iran has only about half of the equipment it would need to fully mechanize its forces at its disposal.[9]

Iran appears to have retained 70–80 British-supplied Scorpions out of the 250 it received before the fall of the Shah. These light tanks are tracked weapon systems equipped with 76-mm guns. However, the Scorpion is more than 20 years old, and as few as 30 may be fully operational. Iran has developed a new light tank called the Towsan or Tosan-1 ("Wild Horse" or "Fury") with a 90-mm gun. It is reported to have entered the prototype stage in 1997, and some may already be in service.

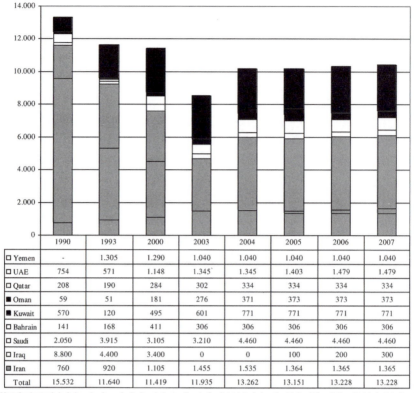

	1990	1993	2000	2003	2004	2005	2006	2007
☐ Yemen	-	1.305	1.290	1.040	1.040	1.040	1.040	1.040
☐ UAE	754	571	1.148	1.345`	1.345	1.403	1.479	1.479
☐ Qatar	208	190	284	302	334	334	334	334
■ Oman	59	51	181	276	371	373	373	373
■ Kuwait	570	120	495	601	771	771	771	771
☐ Bahrain	141	168	411	306	306	306	306	306
☐ Saudi	2.050	3.915	3.105	3.210	4.460	4.460	4.460	4.460
☐ Iraq	8.800	4.400	3.400	0	0	100	200	300
▦ Iran	760	920	1.105	1.455	1.535	1.364	1.365	1.365
Total	15.532	11.640	11.419	11.935	13.262	13.151	13.228	13.228

Note: Iranian totals include active forces in the Revolutionary Guards. Saudi totals include active National Guard. Omani totals include Royal Household Guard.
Source: International Institute for Strategic Studies (IISS), *Military Balance, 2007.*

Figure 4.5   Total Operational Other Armored Vehicles [Light Tanks, Light Armored Vehicles (LAVs), AIFVs, APCs, and Reconnaissance (Recce)] in Gulf Forces, 1990–2007

As far as other armored fighting vehicles are concerned, Iran had some 210 BMP-1s and 400 BMP-2 equivalents in service. The BMPs are Soviet-designed systems, but have serious ergonomic and weapons-suite problems. The BMPs are amphibious, but are hard to fight from and hard to quickly exit under combat conditions. The BMP-1 was designed in the early 1960s and first appeared in public in 1967. It has a 73-mm, 2A20 gun that fires a rocket-assisted, fin-stabilized HEAT projectile with an effective range of 800–1,300 meters against armored targets. It fires the same ammunition as the RPG-7 infantry rocket-propelled grenade launcher. A launching rail for the AT-3 SAGGER anti-tank guided missile is located above the gun with an effective range of up to 3,000 meters.[10]

The newer BMP-2s were developed in the 1980s. A new two-man turret has a 30-mm automatic gun that can be used against land targets, aircraft, and helicopters.

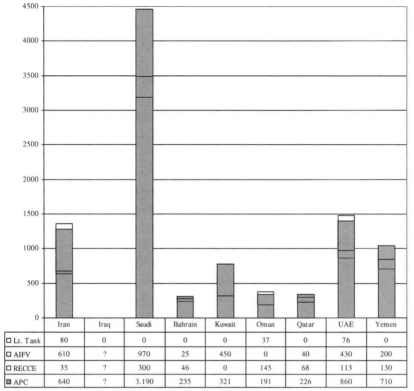

	Iran	Iraq	Saudi	Bahrain	Kuwait	Oman	Qatar	UAE	Yemen
☐ Lt. Tank	80	0	0	0	0	37	0	76	0
☐ AIFV	610	?	970	25	450	0	40	430	200
☐ RECCE	35	?	300	46	0	145	68	113	130
■ APC	640	?	3.190	235	321	191	226	860	710

Note: Iranian totals include active forces in the Revolutionary Guards. Saudi totals include active National Guard. Omani totals include Royal Household Guard.
Source: International Institute for Strategic Studies (IISS), *Military Balance, 2007.*

Figure 4.6   Gulf Other Armored Fighting Vehicles by Category, 2007

An ATGM launcher is mounted on top of the turret that can use AT-4 SPIGOT or AT-5 SPANDREL anti-armor missiles. Because the BMP-2 has a larger turret, it has two roof hatches in the rear fighting compartment, rather than the four on the BMP-1. Each side of the troop compartment has three firing ports with associated roof-mounted periscopes.

The BMP-2 is fully amphibious and the upper part of the track has a sheet metal cover deeper than that of the BMP-1 that is filled with a buoyancy aid. A French SNPE explosive reactive armor (ERA) kit and others are available for use on the BMP-2. The Iranian versions have armor that can protect only against small arms and light automatic weapons. The Iranian versions lack thermal vision systems and modern fire-control systems, and their main weapons are difficult to operate in combat even from static positions.[11]

Further, Iran has at least 35 EE-9 Cascavel armored reconnaissance vehicles, and one estimate indicates an inventory of 100. The Cascavel is a 6 × 6 armored car that was developed in the 1970s by Engesa of Brazil. Some versions have good 90-mm

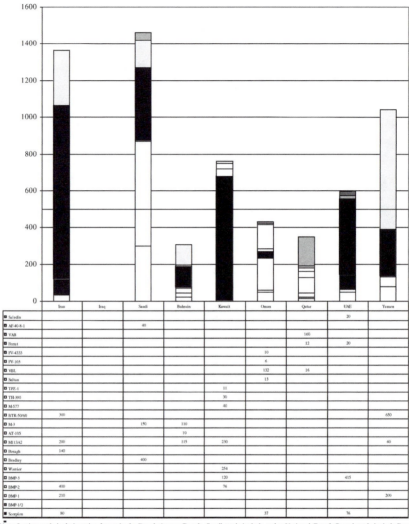

	Iran	Iraq	Saudi	Bahrain	Kuwait	Oman	Qatar	UAE	Yemen
Saladin								20	
AF-40-8-1			40						
VAB							160		
Ferret							12	20	
FV-4333						10			
FV-103						6			
VBL						132	16		
Sultan						13			
TPZ-1					11				
TH-390						30			
M-577					40				
BTR-50/60	300								650
M-3		150		110					
AT-105				10					
M113A2	200			115		230			60
Boragh	140								
Bradley			400						
Warrior					254				
BMP-3					120			415	
BMP-2	400				76				
BMP-1	210								200
BMP-1/2									
Scorpion	80						37	76	

Note: Iranian totals include active forces in the Revolutionary Guards. Saudi totals include active National Guard. Omani totals include Royal Household Guard.

Source: International Institute for Strategic Studies (IISS), *Military Balance, 2007.*

Figure 4.7   Armored Infantry Fighting Vehicles, Reconnaissance Vehicles, LAVs, and Light Tanks by Type, 2007

gun turrets, an acceptable design for Third World combat, but it lacks modern armor, modern sensors, and fire control. Earlier versions have had some transmission and engine problems.[12]

Iran's Army had some 200 tracked M-113s and other Western APCs, and a mix of BTR-40s, BTR-50s, and BTR-60s, numbering 300 in total. These are obsolescent systems that are combat worn and have limited endurance and sustainability under

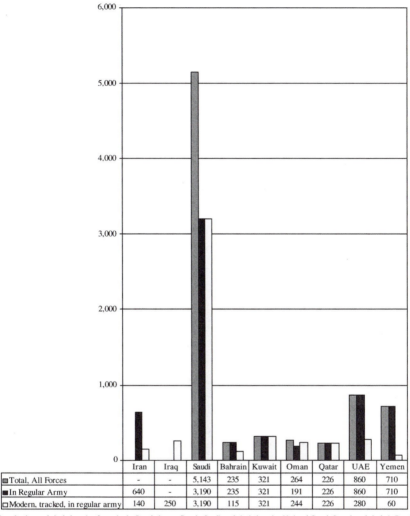

	Iran	Iraq	Saudi	Bahrain	Kuwait	Oman	Qatar	UAE	Yemen
▣ Total, All Forces	-	-	5,143	235	321	264	226	860	710
▪ In Regular Army	640	-	3,190	235	321	191	226	860	710
▢ Modern, tracked, in regular army	140	250	3,190	115	321	244	226	280	60

Note: Iranian totals include active forces in the Revolutionary Guards. Saudi totals include active National Guard. Omani totals include Royal Household Guard.
Source: International Institute for Strategic Studies (IISS), *Military Balance, 2007.*

Figure 4.8   Armored Personnel Carriers in Gulf Armies, 2007

combat conditions. They are vulnerable to all modern guided and unguided weapons and have limited firepower.

The M-113 is a lightly armored, tracked battle taxi, rather than a full fighting vehicle. The BTR-40 is an armored vehicle on a truck chassis and is so old as to be obsolete. The BTR-50 is a wheeled armored vehicle dating back to the 1950s, with light armor and capable of carrying 20 soldiers, plus 2 crewmembers. The Russian BTR-60 is an eight-wheeled APC developed in the late 1950s, but is still very lightly armored and its tires are highly vulnerable to gunfire and fragmentation damage. The version in most common service has a one-man turret, a 14.5-mm KPV-T MG, a coaxial 7.62-mm MG and day/night sights. The close fighting version of the vehicles is difficult to exit quickly and safely under combat conditions.[13]

Iran is producing an armored fighting vehicle called the Boragh (Boraq) and a lighter APC called the Cobra or BMT-2, of which some 140 are in service. The Boragh seems to be a copy of a Chinese version of the BMP-1, and Iran may have gotten access to Soviet technology when it negotiated producing the BMP-1 in license. These negotiations eventually failed, but may have given Iran much of the practical production technology it needed.

The Boragh is fully tracked and amphibious and has a combat weight of 13 tons. It can carry 8–12 people, plus 2 crew members. Reports differ as to its armament—perhaps reflecting different variants. Initial reports indicate that it has a turret armed with a 73-mm smoothbore gun and an ATGM launcher. It may, however, lack the commander's position that exists in the BMP-1, and it may be armed with a 12.7-mm machine gun. Iran has developed an armor package designed to fit over the hull of the Boragh to provide protection against 30-mm armor-piercing ammunition.[14] Variants with 120-mm mortars, one-man turrets with Iranian-made Toophan ATGMs, and AT-4 ATGMs, and others with 73-mm BMP-2 turret guns also seem to be deployed.

One source reports in 2005 that Iran manufactured an infantry fighting vehicle under the name Towsan that features the complete turret of the Russian BMP-2, including a 30-mm cannon and roof-mounted anti-tank missile launchers.[15] Since the name Towsan is used for a light tank model (see above), it is possible that the Towsan is a platform based on the BMP-2 that comes in variations and is labeled light tank or infantry fighting vehicle accordingly. It should be noted, however, that Iran also uses the name Towsan for its version of the Russian AT-5A (9M113 Konkurs) anti-tank guided missile that it began producing in the early 2000s, and the armored vehicle is also called a Tosan-1 and reported to be a light tank.

The Cobra or BMT-2 is a low-profile, wheeled troop carrier that can hold seven personnel. Some of its versions may have twin ZU-23-2 23-mm AA guns. Others have 30-mm guns.

Iran had an unknown number of British Chieftain bridge-laying tanks and a wide range of specialized armored vehicles as well as some heavy equipment transporters. Iran is steadily improving its ability to support armored operations in the field and to provide recovery and field repair capability. However, its exercises reveal that these capabilities still remain limited relative to those of U.S. forces as they lack recovery and field-repair capability in combination with poor interoperability. Most likely, these problems will seriously limit the cohesion, speed, and sustainability of Iranian armored operations.

Iran's armored warfare doctrine seems to be borrowed from U.S., British, and Russian sources without achieving any coherent concept of operations. Even so, Iran's armored doctrine is improving more quickly than its organization and exercise performance. Iran's armored forces are very poorly structured, and the country's equipment pool is dissipated between far too many regular and IRGC units. As mentioned before, Iran has only one armored division—the 92nd Armored Division—with enough tanks and other armor to be considered a true armored unit.

IRANIAN ANTI-ARMOR WEAPONS

Iran has large holdings of anti-tank guided weapons and has been manufacturing copies of Soviet systems, while buying missiles from China, Russia, and the Ukraine. It has approximately 50–75 Tube-launched Optically tracked Wire-guided missiles (TOW) and 20–30 Dragon anti-tank guided missile launchers that were originally supplied by the United States, although the operational status of such systems is uncertain.

It has Soviet and Asian versions of the AT-2, the AT-3, and the AT-5. Iran seems to have at least 100–200 AT-4 (9K111) launchers, but it is impossible to make an accurate estimate because Iran is producing its own copies of the AT-3, and other Russian designed anti-tank guided weapons. Iran also has some 750 RPG-7V, RPG-11, RPG-29, and 3.5-inch rocket launchers, roughly 150 M-18 57-mm, 200 M-20 75-mm, and B-10 82-mm, and 200 M-40 106-mm and B-11 107-mm recoilless guns.

Iran produces various anti-tank weapons. These include an improved version of the man-portable RPG-7 anti-tank rocket with an 80-mm tandem HEAT warhead instead of the standard 30-mm design, the NAFEZ anti-tank rocket, and a copy of the Soviet SPG-9 73-mm recoilless anti-tank gun. It has acquired the RPG-29 "Vampire," which it supplied to Hezbollah forces before the Israeli-Hezbollah War in 2006. This is a modern rocket-propelled grenade launcher with improved sighting and ergonomics, and a much more lethal warhead.

Iran makes a copy of the Russian AT-3 9M14M (SAGGER or Ra'ad) anti-tank guided missile. This is a crew-operable system with a guidance system that can be linked to a launcher holding up to four missiles. It has a maximum range of 3,000 meters, a minimum range of 500 meters, and a flight speed of 120 meters per second. Iran is also seeking more advanced technology from Russia. The United States maintains that a Russian company sold Iran Krasnopol artillery shells while the company denies any connection with Iran.[16] Prospective sanctions are likely to deter arms manufacturers from filling the many needs of the Iranian military.

The Iranian copy of the AT-3 is made by the Shahid Shah Abadi Industrial Group in Tehran, and it seems to be an early version that lacks semiautomatic guidance. Hence, the operator must sight the target, rather than use a joystick, to guide the missile to the target by using the light from the missile. The Iranian version of the AT-3 also seems to have a maximum armored penetration capability of 500 mm, which is not enough to penetrate the forward armor of the latest Western and Russian main battle tanks. Russia has, however, refitted most of its systems to the semiautomatic line of sight guidance and warheads capable of penetrating 800 mm. Iran may have or be acquiring such capability, and it would significantly improve the lethality of its anti-armor forces.

Iran also makes an improved copy of the TOW missile, which it has reverse engineered from the missiles it received from the United States. This missile is said to exist in both a Toophan and a Toophan 2 version. The Toophan is said to use the same wire-guided, optically tracked guidance system as the TOW, have a 3.6-kilogram high-explosive anti-tank warhead that can penetrate up to 550 mm of steel armor, a maximum range of 3,850 meters, and a top speed of 310 meters per seconds.[17] The Toophan 2 is said to have a more lethal missile and warhead component.

Other new projects reportedly include the Tondar-1, Towsan-1, and Super Dragon anti-tank missiles, some of which are supposed to be advanced laser-guided missiles. Some sources claim that the Tondar is a modified version of the Chinese C-801 missile, which is an anti-ship missile. Another source, based on Iranian announcements in September 1999, states that development for the Tondar was announced as a new anti-tank missile in September 1999.[18]

Iran reportedly developed and began production of the Towsan-1 in 2000. It allegedly is based on the Russian AT-5A. The AT-5A can be fired from vehicles and later models of the AT-4 SPIGOT launcher. It uses a gas generator to expel the missile from the launch tube that allows the missile to be launched directly at the target, rather than in an upward arc.[19] The missile is a relatively modern wire-guided system that tracks the position of an incandescent infrared bulb on the missile relative to the target and transmits appropriate commands to the missile using the wire that trails behind the missile. It is jam resistant, and a skilled operator can override the automatic guidance. It is a relatively effective and accurate system.

The Super Dragon missile is said to be based on U.S. Dragon anti-tank missiles that were delivered to Iran before 1979.[20] It seems questionable that Iran would initiate a development program for a comparatively low-value weapon some 30 years after its introduction that the U.S. Army found to be largely ineffective. The confusion surrounding some of the reporting on these weapons is evidenced, however, by the fact that another source states that the Towsan and the Super Dragon are essentially the same weapon.[21]

IRANIAN ARTILLERY STRENGTH

Iran's comparative artillery strength is shown in Figures 4.9, 4.10, and 4.11. Iran has some 3,200 operational medium and heavy artillery weapons and multiple rocket launchers, and some 5,000 mortars. Its towed artillery consists largely of Soviet and some Chinese designs. Its holdings of self-propelled artillery include 60 2S1122-mm howitzers, and some Iranian copies. There were some 180 aging M-109 155-mm weapon systems of which Iran has produced its own systems as part of the "Thunder" series. Iran further has some 70 aging 170-mm, 165-mm, and 203-mm weapon systems. It also has large numbers of multiple rocket launchers, including some 700 107-mm weapons, 150–200 122-mm weapons, 20-odd 240-mm weapons, and some 333-mm weapons. It manufactures its own multiple rocket launchers, including the long-range Fajr series.

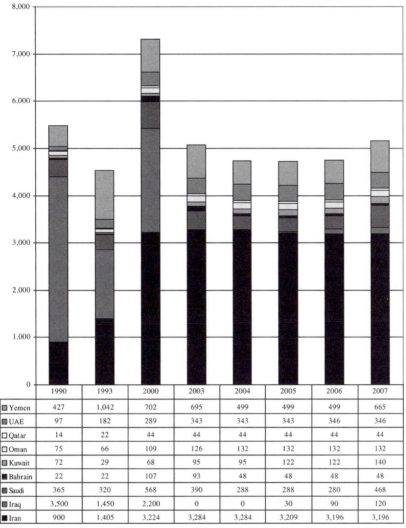

	1990	1993	2000	2003	2004	2005	2006	2007
Yemen	427	1,042	702	695	499	499	499	665
UAE	97	182	289	343	343	343	346	346
Qatar	14	22	44	44	44	44	44	44
Oman	75	66	109	126	132	132	132	132
Kuwait	72	29	68	95	95	122	122	140
Bahrain	22	22	107	93	48	48	48	48
Saudi	365	320	568	390	288	288	280	468
Iraq	3,500	1,450	2,200	0	0	30	90	120
Iran	900	1,405	3,224	3,284	3,284	3,209	3,196	3,196

Note: Iranian totals include active forces in the Revolutionary Guards. Saudi totals include active National Guard. Omani totals include Royal Household Guard.
Source: International Institute for Strategic Studies (IISS), *Military Balance*, various editions.

Figure 4.9   Total Operational Self-Propelled and Towed Tube Artillery and Multiple Rocket Launchers in Gulf Forces, 1990–2007

This total is very high compared to the artillery strength of most regional powers, and it reflects Iran's continuing effort to build up artillery strength that began during the Iran-Iraq War. Iran had to use artillery as a substitute for armor and airpower during much of the Iran-Iraq War and generally used relatively static fire. However, Iran's reliance on towed artillery and slow-moving multiple rocket launchers limits

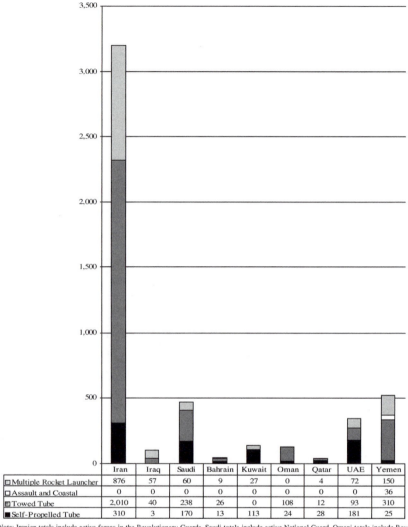

	Iran	Iraq	Saudi	Bahrain	Kuwait	Oman	Qatar	UAE	Yemen
☐ Multiple Rocket Launcher	876	57	60	9	27	0	4	72	150
☐ Assault and Coastal	0	0	0	0	0	0	0	0	36
☐ Towed Tube	2,010	40	238	26	0	108	12	93	310
■ Self-Propelled Tube	310	3	170	13	113	24	28	181	25

Note: Iranian totals include active forces in the Revolutionary Guards. Saudi totals include active National Guard. Omani totals include Royal Household Guard. Many Iraqi weapons are holdings, and not in active service.
Source: International Institute for Strategic Studies (IISS), *Military Balance, 2007.*

Figure 4.10   Total Operational Gulf Artillery Weapons, 2007

Iran's combined arms maneuver capabilities, and Iran has failed to develop effective night and beyond-visual-range targeting capability.

Holdings of Tube Artillery

Some 2,100 of Iran's weapons are towed tube artillery weapons, versus 310 self-propelled tube weapons, and 700–900 were vehicle-mounted or towed multiple

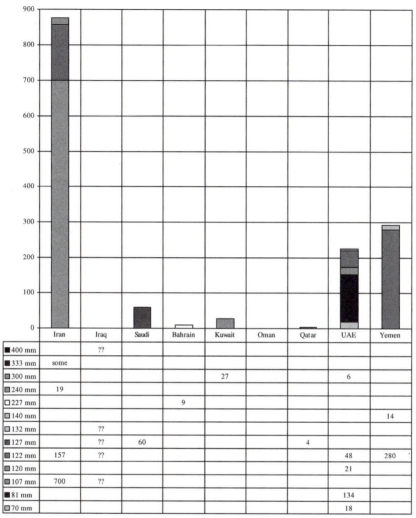

	Iran	Iraq	Saudi	Bahrain	Kuwait	Oman	Qatar	UAE	Yemen
■ 400 mm		??							
■ 333 mm	some								
▢ 300 mm					27			6	
▨ 240 mm	19								
▢ 227 mm			9						
▨ 140 mm									14
▨ 132 mm		??							
■ 127 mm		??	60				4		
▨ 122 mm	157	??						48	280
▨ 120 mm								21	
▨ 107 mm	700	??							
■ 81 mm								134	
▢ 70 mm								18	

Note: Iranian totals include active forces in the Revolutionary Guards. Saudi totals include active National Guard. Omani totals include Royal Household Guard. Iraq has a total of approximately 200 Multiple-Rocket Launchers.
Source: International Institute for Strategic Studies (IISS), *Military Balance*, 2007.

Figure 4.11   Gulf Inventory of Multiple Rocket Launchers by Caliber, 2007

rocket launchers. Iran's holdings of self-propelled weapons still appear to include a substantial number of U.S.–supplied systems, including 25–30 M-110 203-mm howitzers, 20–30 M-107 175-mm guns, and 130–150 M-109 155-mm howitzers. These weapons are worn, have not been modernized in over 15 years, and for the most part lack modern fire-control systems and artillery radars. Many also lack sustainability, and a considerable number may not be operational. As with virtually all U.S.–made equipment, it can be assumed that its operational status decreases rapidly in combat operations due to the limited availability of spare parts. Iran does, however, claim to have modernized its M109s with newer fire-control computers and enhanced ammunition.

Iran understands that it has less than a quarter of the self-propelled artillery it needs to properly support its present force structure and that maneuverable artillery is critical to success in dealing with Iraqi and other maneuver forces. However, 310 self-propelled weapon systems are enough to equip the three brigades that could be equipped with advanced tanks and infantry fighting vehicles (see above). Iran is attempting to compensate for the resulting lack of modern artillery and artillery mobility by replacing its U.S.–made self-propelled weapons with other self-propelled systems.

Iran has purchased 60–80 Soviet 2S1 122-mm self-propelled howitzers, and it has developed an indigenous version called Raad (Thunder 1/Thunder 2). Thunder 1 is a 122-mm weapon similar to Russian designs. This vehicle seems to be a modification of a Russian 122-mm gun, with a firing range of 15,200 meters and a road speed of 65 kilometers per hour. It may use the Iranian-made Boragh chassis, a modification of the Chinese Type WZ 501 armored infantry fighting vehicle.[22]

Thunder 2 is a "rapid fire" 155-mm self-propelled weapon that is claimed to be able to fire five rounds per minute and move at a speed of 70 kilometers (43 miles) per hour on the battlefield (a claim that is almost certainly grossly exaggerated given real-world problems in tank targeting and fire control while tanks are in motion). The gun's range is reported as 30 kilometers (19 miles), and it is reported to have a laser range finder and a semiautomatic loading system. Both Thunder 1 and Thunder 2 are now in deployment.[23]

Iran has some 5,000 mortars. These include 107-mm and 120-mm heavy mortars and 800–900 81-mm and 82-mm mortars. The Iranian Army has at least several hundred of its heavy mortars mounted on armored vehicles.

The 700–900 multiple rocket launchers in Iran's inventory are evidence of its tactical emphasis on massed, static firepower. All of Iran's MRLS (Multiple Rocket Launcher System) fire unguided rockets, some of them with inertial guidance, with effective ranges from about 10 to 200 kilometers and, in contrast to ballistic missiles, exclusively use solid propellants.

It is difficult to estimate Iran's inventory; according to one source, its holdings include roughly 10 M-1985 (M-1989 is tube artillery) 240-mm multiple rocket launchers, 500–700 Chinese Type-63 and Iranian Haseb and Fajr-1 107-mm multiple rocket launchers, and 100+ Soviet BM-21 and Soviet BM-11 122-mm launchers, as well as some Fajr-5 333-mm weapon systems. Another source mentions about 700 Chinese Type-63 in addition to Haseb and Fajr-1 107-mm systems; 50 Hadid, 100 BM-21, and 7 BM-11 122-mm systems; 9 M-1985 and 10 Fajr 240-mm systems; an unspecified number of Fajr-5 333-mm systems; and some Iran-130 (Nazeat variant) and Nazeat 355-mm systems.[24] The Haseb uses a 12 tube launcher, the Hadid a 12/30/ or 40 tube launcher, usually mounted on a vintage Mercedes-Benz truck.

In 2006, it was reported that the Fajr-5 system was being overhauled with a new Mercedes-Benz truck platform. Apparently, the new chassis has improved capabilities in terms of mobility, yet the crucial improvement lies in the improved fire-control system. With the new truck, one command vehicle can assume fire control for one entire MLRS troop. The same source describes the order of battle for the Iranian rocket artillery:

> Two troops make up a battery and, with typically two batteries per battalion, this pro-vides for some 16 launchers at battalion level. At battery level there is a command post vehicle based on a 4 x 4 truck chassis with a meteorological unit and battalion command vehicle at battalion level. At troop level there is also a repair facility, two transportation and loading vehicles and two loading vehicles. Fire missions are normally carried out through the chain of command, with each launcher equipped with its own mission com-puter that receives information via a datalink. In addition to controlling the system from inside the launch platform, the new system features a remote fire capability from a dis-tance of 1,000 m and also a fire capability from the command post vehicle that could be up to 20 km away.[25]

Multiple Rocket Launchers

Iran has produced its own multiple rocket launchers. These include some 50 122-mm, 40-round Hadid rocket launcher systems. In addition, Iran produces variants of Chinese and Russian 122-mm rockets called the Hadid/Arash (modified versions of the BM-21) and the Noor. Iran has transferred large numbers of its shorter-range rockets to Hezbollah in Lebanon.[26] It supplied most of the extended range versions of the Katyushas that Hezbollah used in the fighting against Israel in 2006.

The Noor is also the name for an Iranian rocket, SSM or ASCM, based on the Chinese YJ-82.[27] The DM-3b is said to be an active radar sensor that is used in the final stages of flight to acquire and home in on ship targets. A joint program between Iran's Aerospace Industries Organization and the China Aerospace Science and Industry Corporation developed the Noor.[28] The Falaq-1 and Falaq-2 series are examples of vehicle-mounted unguided rocket systems in the Iranian arsenal. The Falaq-1 fires a 240-mm rocket with 50 kilograms of explosives and can reach a target up to ten kilometers away. The Falaq-2 is slightly larger, its warhead is about twice as heavy, and it flies almost a full kilometer farther.[29]

Iran's land forces operate a number of Iranian-made long-range unguided missiles, including the Shahin 1 and 2, Oghab, and Nazeat. They also include some ten large 240-mm artillery rockets with a range of up to 40–43 kilometers called the Fajr-3. Some of these systems played a major role in triggering Israel's war against Hezbollah in Lebanon in 2006, and the key longer-range systems seem to include the following:[30]

- The Hadid (sometimes variants are called Arash or Noor) is a truck-mounted 122-mm system, usually configured as a 16- or 30-round launcher, with a maximum range of approximately 20 kilometers. Apparently, this system is based on the Soviet BM-21 MLRS. The Hadid is in service with both the Iranian Army as well as the IRGC.[31]

- The Shahin 1 (sometimes called the Fajr-4) is a trailer-launched 333-mm caliber unguided, high-explosive artillery rocket. Two rockets are normally mounted on each trailer, and they have a solid propelled-rocket motor, a maximum range of 75 kilometers, and a 175-kilogram conventional or chemical warhead. The Shahin evidently can be equipped with three types of warheads: a 180-kilogram high-explosive warhead, a warhead using high-explosive submunitions, and a warhead that uses chemical weapons. There is a truck-mounted version, called the Fajr-5, with a rack of four rockets. A larger Shanin 2, with a range of 20 kilometers, is also deployed.

- The Fajr-3 is a truck-mounted system with a 12-round launcher for 240-mm rockets. It has a maximum range of 43 kilometers and a 45-kilogram payload in its warhead. Apparently, it was produced under license on the basis of the North Korean M-1985, which in turn was based on Russian designs.[32]

- The Fajr-5 is a truck-mounted 33-mm caliber unguided artillery rocket with a solid propelled-rocket motor, a maximum range of 75 kilometers (another source reports 90 kilometers),[33] and a 175-kilogram conventional or chemical warhead. This rocket reportedly is based on the Chinese WS-1 302-mm system. The launching system carries four rockets, and they can evidently be equipped with three types of warheads: a kilogram high-explosive warhead, a warhead using high-explosive submunitions, and a warhead that uses chemical weapons. One source reports that Hezbollah in Iran received an Iranian 302-mm missile, referred to as "Iranian Khaibar 1." This appears to be either a version of the Fajr-5 or, due to the fact that its caliber is 302 mm, it could be a direct application of the Chinese WS-1 system. The same source reports that the range of the Khaibar 1 is 100 miles, thereby putting in doubt the claim that it closely resembles the Fajr-5.[34]

- The Oghab is a 230-mm caliber unguided, high-explosive artillery rocket, is usually launched from a three-tube launcher that is spin stabilized in flight, has a maximum range of 34 kilometers (some sources state 45 kilometers),[35] and has a 70-kilogram high explosives fragmentation warhead—although chemical warheads may be available. While it may have a chemical warhead, it has an operational circular error probable (CEP) that has proven to be in excess of 500 meters at maximum range. This missile was one of the first developed in Iran's artillery long-range missile program after the Revolution of 1979. The Oghab became operational in the 1980s. Further, Iran has no ability to target accurately the Oghab or any other long-range missile against mobile or point targets at long ranges, other than a limited ability to use remotely piloted vehicles (RPVs). According to U.S. sources, Iran developed a modified version of the Oghab that could be carried and fired from F-4 and F-14 fighter aircraft.[36]

- The Nazeat is a Transporter-Erector-Launcher launched system with conventional and possibly chemical and biological warheads. The full details of this system remain unclear, but it seems to be based on Chinese technology, particularly the CSS-8—early versions may have been the Mushak 120, 160, and 200 systems—and it uses a solid fuel rocket, with a simple inertial guidance system. Nazeat units are equipped with communications vans, meteorological vans, and a global positioning system (GPS) for surveying the launch site. Some reports indicate there are two variants of the Nazeat solid-fueled rocket system—a 355.6-mm caliber rocket with a 105-kilogram range and a 150-kilogram (one source reports 1,300-kilogram payload)[37] warhead usually called Nazeat-6, and the Nazeat-10, a 450-mm caliber rocket with a reported range of

130–150 kilometers and a 250-kilogram warhead. The Nazeat-6 apparently is fired from the same launcher as the Oghab. Both systems have maximum closing velocities of Mach 4–5, but both also appear to suffer from poor reliability and accuracy. Other reports indicate all Nazeats have a 335.6-mm caliber, and there are four versions of progressively larger size, with ranges from 80 to 120 kilometers. It is claimed to have a CEP within 5 percent of its range. Some reports state Nazeat-4 and Nazeat-5 missiles are in stock with the IRGC; the latter is reported to carry a payload of 175 kilograms and have an effective range of 70 kilometers.[38]

- The Zelzal 1 is a 610-mm long-range rocket, which can carry a 600-kilogram payload up to 125 kilometers.

- The Zelzal 2 is a 610-mm long-range rocket, with a warhead with a 600-kilogram payload and a maximum range of up to 210 kilometers. A single rocket is mounted on a launcher on a truck. It is unguided, but is spin stabilized and is claimed to have a CEP within 5 percent of its range. According to Israeli intelligence, IRGC units in Lebanon received the Zelzal 2 in 2002.[39] Apparently, this missile has also been named Mushak 200.[40]

- The Fateh 110, and an apparently improved version named A-110, is a developmental system believed to be similar to the Chinese CSS-7, CSS-8 (the Iranian version is also called Tondar-69), and perhaps M-11 systems, which is a surface-to-surface system derived from the Russian SA-2 surface-to-air missile. It is a 610-mm rocket with a 600-kilogram payload. Apparently it has a maximum range of 200 kilometers and may have entered production by now. Reportedly, Iranian sources repeatedly claimed that the Fateh 110 has a very high degree of precision, prompting some observers to assume that the rocket employs a comparatively sophisticated optical guidance package.[41] Some reports state the Fateh 110 is either based on the Mushak 160 or a parallel development program.

One source states that in mid-2001, Iran decided to discontinue the Zelzal program due to budget constraints. Such reports are unverifiable to date; most observers count Zelzal in the Iranian inventory as of 2007.[42] Some reports claim that the Fateh 110 is the successor to the Zelzal program or, at least, is based on the latter. Similar performance data on the two systems may corroborate such assumptions. As is the case with virtually all long-range artillery rockets, the numbers of holdings cannot be confirmed independently. Even if the Zelzal production was given up six years ago, it is likely that stockpiles still exist and are in service.

Modern Targeting and Fire-Control Systems and Artillery Tactics

Iran has made limited progress in deploying artillery fire-control and battle management systems, counterbattery radar capability, and long-range target acquisition capability, but its capability is improving steadily and it makes increasing use of RPVs to support its self-propelled weapons. Iran has actively sought more modern fire-control and targeting systems since the mid-1980s, and the equipment it supplied to Hezbollah forces in Lebanon—while not the state of the art in Iran—showed

Iran has made growing progress in developing effective planning, fire-control, targeting, and damage assessment systems.

Any estimate of artillery capability must take into account the quality of the process that begins with target reconnaissance and ends with actual fire control of modern weapons and damage assessment. Hence, numbers and firepower of artillery systems cannot count as real capabilities if they are not supported by precise and quick battlefield information systems.

In late 2006, it was reported that Iran had developed and had begun production of two new surveillance radar systems, named 110-S and 110-D. The Q-band 110-S reportedly weighs 25 kilograms, is equipped with a GPS receiver, and is man portable but can also be mounted on a vehicle. The radar apparently can detect a heavy vehicle at a distance of 6.5 kilometers away, a light vehicle at 5 kilometers, and a single person at 2.8 kilometers away with a claimed target accuracy of 10 meters in range.[43]

The man-portable or vehicle-mounted 110-D radar operates in the X-band. Detection ranges for this system have been reported at 18 kilometers for an individual person, 30 kilometers for a light, and 40 kilometers for a heavy vehicle.

Some experts believe that these two radar systems are based on foreign designs, perhaps with a few Iranian-made improvements. It is impossible to judge to what extent Iran can indigenously develop and build a modern radar system, but the production of the 110-S and 110-D radars shows that Iran is undertaking efforts to acquire the knowledge and means to reach this capability. It also was reported that Iran is selling the two radar systems on the export market, which is an indication that Iran has mastered the development and assembly of relatively modern battlefield radar systems.

IRANIAN ARMY AIR-DEFENSE SYSTEMS

Iranian land forces have a total of some 1,700 anti-aircraft guns, including 14.5-mm ZPU-2/-4s, 23-mm ZSU-23-4s and ZU-23s, 35-mm M-1939s, 37-mm Type 55s, and 57-mm ZSU-57-2s. Iran also had 100–180 Bofors L/70 40-mm guns and moderate numbers of Skyguard 35-mm twin anti-aircraft guns (many of which may not be operational). Its largest holdings consisted of unguided ZU-23-2s (which it can manufacture) and M-1939s.

It is unclear how many of these systems are really operational as air-defense weapons, and most would have to be used to provide very short-range "curtain fire" defense of small point targets. They would not be effective against a modern aircraft using an air-to-ground missile or laser-guided weapon. The only notable exception is the ZSU-23-4 radar-guided anti-aircraft gun. Iran has 50–100 fully operational ZSU-23-4s. The weapon is short ranged and is vulnerable to electronic countermeasures, but is far more lethal than Iran's unguided guns.

Iran had large numbers of SA-7 (Strela 2M) and SA-14 (Strela) man-portable surface-to-air missiles, some more modern SA-16s and HN-5/HQ-5s, as well as Misaq man-portable surface-to-air missiles. It may also have up to 500 SA-18s, which are advanced man-portable surface-to-air missiles.[44] It had some U.S.–made Stinger man-portable surface-to-air missiles it bought from Afghan rebels, but these may no longer be operational or may have been used for reverse-engineering purposes.

Iran also has some (up to 50) Swedish RBS-70 low-level surface-to-air missiles. Iran seems to be producing some version of the SA-7, perhaps with Chinese assistance. It is not clear whether Iran can do this in any large number. Iran's land-based air-defense forces are also acquiring growing numbers of Chinese FM-80s, a Chinese variant of the French-designed Crotale. Some reports indicate that it has some SA-8s, but these may be token transfers obtained for reverse-engineering purposes.

In January 2007, Iran acquired 29 Tor-M1 SAMs that it had ordered two years before from Russia. Shortly thereafter, it was reported that Iran test-fired the system during military exercises. The TOR-M1 is an anti-aircraft system against low-flying targets. It usually is mounted on a tracked vehicle, each of which carries eight missiles (SA-15 Gauntlet). The TOR-M1 must be considered an advanced system in its system class, and it certainly is among Iran's most advanced air-defense assets. The TOR-M1 has advanced abilities to resist jamming, and it can detect targets as far as 25 kilometers away.

Apparently, Iran has been negotiating since 2001 with Russia over a possible purchase of the S-300 SAM (with SA-10c missiles), which is one of the most advanced mobile air-defense systems. Iran allegedly also expressed interest in purchasing the even more advanced S-400 SAM.[45] Another source states that Iran already possesses the S-300, yet most other observers have not confirmed such assertions.[46] The S-300 would give Iran a powerful anti-air asset that can effectively target aircraft and missiles flying at low and high altitudes, as well as operate in a heavily jammed environment. At the delivery of the Tor-M1 system, Russia apparently announced the possibility for further cooperation in air-defense systems.

It has been reported that Russian companies have installed the 36D6 (Tin Shield) radar system in Iran around Bushehr as well as in Syria. This comparatively advanced, very mobile radar system can target low- to high-altitude targets and provide fire-control surveillance and can be used as part of the S-300 PMU SAM system, although it has not been confirmed that Iran uses this system.

Jane's reported in July 2007 that Iran acquired "at least 10 96K6 Pantsyr-S1E self-propelled short-range gun and missile air-defence systems" from Russia. In this deal, Iran apparently will receive the systems, which originally were earmarked for Syria, in late 2008 and retain the option to buy dozens more.[47]

Little else is known about the quantities of Iran's anti-air assets. The Tor-M1 certainly is a formidable system, but probably is not sufficient for defending against a prolonged campaign of missile and bomb attacks. Iran's anti-aircraft guns are certainly no match against missile attacks from high altitudes. Much of Iran's combat strength will also depend on a centralized radar system, which it currently lacks. A few patches of advanced radar systems, whose performance under Iranian command is not proven, do not suffice to defend against sustained stealth aircraft and missile attacks. Iran does not operate a modern Airborne Warning and Control System (AWACS). Plans to acquire American AWACS aircraft were thwarted by the Revolution of 1979. Further, there is no indication of Iranian capabilities for advanced electronic countermeasures. In a worst-case scenario for Iran, its forces may find themselves strapped of their most effective system before they will even face an enemy aircraft.

IRANIAN ARMY AVIATION

Iran pioneered its use of army aviation and attack helicopters during the time of the Shah, but built up its holdings of helicopters far more quickly than it expanded its training and maintenance capability. As a result, it had an ineffective and unsustainable force at the time the Shah fell. Its inability since that time to obtain adequate spare parts to help in modernizing the aircraft has long made Iranian operational helicopter holdings uncertain.

The Iranian Army seems to retain 50 AH-1J Sea Cobra attack helicopters, 20 CH-47Cs, 50 Bell-214A/Cs, 68 AB-205As, 10 AB-206s, and 25 Mi-8/Mi-17 transport and utility helicopters. There are also reports that Iran signed orders for 4 Mi-17s in 1999 and 30 Mi-8s in 2001. Army aviation bases are located in Bakhtaran, Ghale Morghi, Isfahan, Kerman, Mashad, Tehran, and Masjed Soleiman.[48]

These Western-supplied transport and support helicopters have low operational readiness, and they have little sustained sortie capability. They are, however, regularly used in Iranian military exercises. In January 2007, reports surfaced that Iran had bought U.S. military surplus parts. In one case, customs officials confirmed that parts for the Chinook helicopter entered Iran.[49] However, it is not known whether these parts were obtained by the Iranian armed forces and whether or not they proved to be useful.

IRANIAN ARMY UNMANNED AERIAL VEHICLES

Iran is believed to operate a number of unmanned aerial vehicles (UAVs). The IISS *Military Balance* for 2007 states that the Iranian Army operates an unspecified number of Mohajer-II/-III/-IV UAVs. Other sources name earlier UAVs in service with the Iranian Army, but their status remains unknown. The Qods Aviation Industries reportedly began designing, developing, and manufacturing UAVs in the mid-1980s, and today it produces the Mohajer UAVs. The first products, however, Tallash I, Tallash II, Saeqeh I, and Saeqeh II, were drones that hardly had any capabilities other than serving as aerial targets, although the Saeqeh II reportedly can be GPS guided.

The more advanced Mohajer-II/-III/-IV UAVs can be used for reconnaissance, jamming, and communications missions. The Mohajer-II is a fully capable unmanned reconnaissance aircraft that can be used for surveillance, electronic countermeasures, and communications relay. Weaknesses of this UAV are its limited operational radius of 50 kilometers and the fact that it is launched by compressed nitrogen from a truck-mounted rail. It has an operational radius of 50 kilometers, a maximum speed of 180 kilometers per hour, and a ceiling of 11,000 feet. The Mohajer-III (Dorna) has an operational radius of about 100 kilometers. The Mohajer-IV (Hodhod) reportedly carries advanced jamming systems, is equipped with infrared cameras with real-time data transmission, and has an operational radius of 150 kilometers and/or seven hours.

Further, Iran developed a set of UAVs named the Ababil series. According to one source, the Ababil-5/-T/-B/-S variants exist. The Ababil-5 is a medium-range reconnaissance and surveillance UAV; the Ababil-T is a short-/medium-range attack UAV; the Ababil-B and Ababil-S variants are believed to be newer variants primarily designed for information systems research (ISR) missions. The Ababil UAVs are launched from a truck-mounted launcher.

During the Israeli-Hezbollah War of summer 2006, it was reported that Israeli forces shot down a Mirsad-1 UAV believed to be supplied by Iran.[50] This UAV is almost certainly the Iranian Mohajer-1 or a variant thereof. Further, Hezbollah is believed to have received eight Ababil UAVs.

On February 10, 2007, a senior IRGC officer stated that a stealth UAV (drone) with a range of 700 kilometers was entering mass production in Iran.[51] According to the officer, the UAV is supposed to be used in ISR missions. It is not clear to which line of UAVs the comments refer. It may very well be that the claim is simply a false statement given to confuse recipients.

Iran is also seeking to create a significant RPV force that borrows in many ways from Israeli technical developments and doctrine. It has produced some such RPVs, such as the Mohajer series—and several exercise reports refer to their use. It has sold some of these systems to Hezbollah, but insufficient data are available to assess this aspect of Iranian capabilities.

IRANIAN ARMY'S COMMAND, CONTROL, COMMUNICATIONS, COMPUTERS, AND INTELLIGENCE

Iranian Army communications have improved, as have Iranian battle management and communications exercises. They are now capable of better coordination between branches, the density of communications equipment has improved, and the functional lines of communication and command now place more emphasis on maneuver, quick reaction, and combined arms. Iran has also improved its electronic intelligence communications intelligence, jamming, and countermeasure capability and has been aided by Syria since the two countries signed a new defense cooperation agreement on November 14, 2005, and ratified it in January 2006.[52] However, Iranian battle management and communications capabilities seem to remain relatively limited.

Iran's holdings still consist largely of aging VHF (very high frequency) radio with some HF (high frequency) and UHF (ultra high frequency) capability. This equipment cannot handle high traffic densities, and secure communications are poor. Iran still relies heavily on analog data handling and manually switched telephone systems. It is, however, acquiring a steadily growing number of Chinese and Western encryption systems and some digital voice, fax, and telex encryption capabilities.

FORCE TRENDS AND SUMMARY CAPABILITIES

Iran's Army has improved its organization, doctrine, training, and equipment for land force operations. Its order of battle is still mixed, and some units are far more capable than others. It still, however, is capable of defending against any army in the region and is trained and organized for defense in depth. The facts that most of Iran's cities are a considerable distance from its borders, much of its terrain is defendable, and it has no neighboring powers capable of meaningful amphibious operations give it additional defensive advantages.

The Iranian Army is not organized for offensive maneuver warfare and would have serious problems in sustaining offensive operations against a well-organized defender. It certainly, however, is capable of deploying into Iraq, if the United States or United Kingdom should leave. The Iraqi Army is no longer capable of armored warfare or fighting major conventional battles. Iran might also be able to move against Kuwait and the Saudi Gulf coast if neither power had U.S. support. It does not, however, have strong air support and would face major problems if the Saudi Air Force was fully committed. Much would depend on whether Saudi forces deployed to defend the Gulf land approaches before Iran acted.

The Iranian Army and Revolutionary Guards have steadily improved their capabilities to fight a defensive battle against a U.S. invasion of Iran, or any other invading conventional force. There has also been a similar improvement in the organization and arming of Iranian naval and air forces for this mission. While Iranian propaganda and training literature have often sharply exaggerated the resulting improvements in Iranian capabilities, and of Iran's new missiles and "secret weapons," there is no doubt that Iran is now far better organized to fight a defensive war of attrition than in the past and use a range of asymmetric means to challenge U.S. military efforts—including the use of proxies and unconventional forces in Iraq, Afghanistan, and Lebanon. As has been discussed earlier, its exercises have also become progressively more tailored to this mission, and some are well structured and show close attention to the lessons of fighting against conventional forces in Iraq and Lebanon.

The Iranian Army and Air Force are not, however, well trained, equipped, or organized to fight the United States in a conventional airland battle. Iran still is a slow-moving force with limited armored maneuver capability and artillery forces better suited for defense in depth, the static use of mass fire than the efficient use of rapidly switched and well-targeted fire, and dispersed asymmetric warfare.

Sustainability is limited, as is field recovery and repair capability. Overall manpower quality is mediocre because of a lack of adequate realistic training and a heavy reliance on conscripts.

This does not mean, however, that the Iranian Army could not fight a less conventional battle in depth if U.S. forces should invade. It has closely studied U.S. strengths and weaknesses in recent wars and does increasingly train in guerrilla and asymmetric tactics, although the level of real-world coordination it has achieved with the IRGC is uncertain. It could draw upon the IRGC forces and a mobilized Basij and seek to force the United States into a war of attrition in which the Iranian Army avoided direct conventional battles as much as possible, focused on ambush tactics and the use of terrain and deception, and fought as small, dispersed elements— "swarming" to create a significant presence only when this had a serious chance of imposing significant casualties.

Both the Iranian Army and the IRGC also are actively seeking to improve their ability to use anti-tank weapons in dispersed ambush tactics, as a substitute for direct armored battles, and to try to improve anti-attack helicopter tactics as well as deal with heliborne troop movements. The success of such tactics in the face of U.S. intelligence, surveillance, and reconnaissance capabilities is uncertain.

The Iranian Army has no present air-defense capabilities that can counter the all-weather targeting and standoff precision-strike capabilities of U.S. air forces of the kind the United States used in its invasion of Iraq. Its purchase of the TOR M-1 short-range air-defense system could, however, give it some improved air-defense capability if this unit was deployed with the Iranian Army and used with considerable skill.

One report sees the regular army (Artesh) as assuming more modern capabilities, doctrine, and command systems, leaving other tasks to the IRGC and the Basij. According to the report, the Iranian Artesh thus is likely to increase the size of its army aviation service with an increasing number of attack and transport helicopters in service.[53]

Iran is reported to have created a rapid deployment force around the beginning of 2005. This unit reportedly equals the size of a combat brigade, and its primary focus is to respond "to any military situation inside or outside Iran."[54] Among its assets are C-130 aircraft for transport, armored vehicles, anti-tank missiles, and artillery. No further information about this unit exists, but it appears questionable if the stated objectives can be met, and it remains even more questionable how Iran is planning to deploy artillery systems for a brigade-sized unit outside the country "within hours."

The overall mix of Iranian Army combat arms, support forces, and logistic and sustainment elements (as shown in Figure 4.12) has some capability for power projection and armored maneuver warfare, but does not train seriously for long-range maneuver and does little serious training for amphibious warfare or deployment by sea in the face of hostile defense. Its logistics, maintenance, and sustainment systems are largely defensive and designed to support Iranian forces in defending Iran out of

Figure 4.12   Iranian Army's Force Structure Trends, 1990–2007

	1990	2000	2005	2006	2007
Manpower	305,000	350,000	350,000	350,000	350,000
Active	305,000	350,000	350,000	350,000	350,000
Conscripts	250,000	220,000	220,000	220,000	220,000
Combat Units					
Army Headquarters	3	4	4	4	4
Armored Division	0	4	4	4	4
Mechanized Division	4	0	0	0	0
Infantry Division	6	6	6	6	6
Airborne Brigade	1	1	1	1	1
Special Operations Brigade	1	1	1	1	1
Commando Division	0	1	2	2	2
Armored Brigade	Some	0	0	0	Some
Mechanized Brigade	Some	1	1	0	0
Artillery Battalion	0	4–5	4–5	4–5	6
Mechanized Battalion	28	0	0	0	0
(Army) Aviation Group	0	Some	Some	Some	Some
Main Battle Tanks	500	1,345	1,613	1,613+	1,613+
T-54/Type-59	Some	400	540	540	540
T-62	Some	75	75	75+	75+
T-72	Some	480	480	480	480
Chieftain Mk 3/5	Some	140	100	100	100
M-47/-48	Some	150	168	168	168
M-60A1	Some	100	150	150	150
Zulfiqar	0	0	100	100	100
Light Tanks	30	80	80+	80+	80+
Scorpion	30	80	80	80	80
Towsan	0	0	Some	Some	Some
Reconnaissance	130	35	35	35	35
EE-9 Cascavel	130	35	35	35	35
Armored Infantry Fighting Vehicles	100+	440	610	610	610
BMP-1	100+	300	210	210	210

BMP-2	0	140	400	400	400
Armored Personnel Carrier	500	550	640	640	640
BTR-50/-60	Some	300	300	300	300
M-113	Some	250	200	200	200
Boragh	0	0	140	140	140
TOWED	Some	2,170	2,010	2,010	2,010
105 mm: M-101A1	339+	130	130	130	130
105 mm: Oto Melara	36	0	0	0	0
122 mm: D-30	0	600	540	540	540
122 mm: PRC type-54	0	100	100	100	100
130 mm: M-46/Type-59	125	1,100	985	985	985
152 mm: D-20	0	30	30	30	30
155 mm: WAC-21	0	20	15	15	15
155 mm: M-71	50	0	0	0	0
155 mm: M-114	0	70	70	70	70
155 mm: FH-77B	18	0	0	0	0
155 mm: GHN-45	130	100	120	120	120
203 mm: M-115	30	20	20	20	20
Self-Propelled	140	290	310+	310+	310+
122 mm: 2S1	0	60	60	60	60
122 mm: Thunder 1	0	0	Some	Some	Some
155 mm: M-109	100	60	180	180	180
155 mm: Thunder 2	0	0	Some	Some	Some
170 mm: M-1978	0	10	10	10	10
175 mm: M-107	30	30	30	30	30
203 mm: M-110	10	30	30	30	30
Multiple Rocket Launchers	Some	764+	876+	876+	876+
107 mm: PRC Type-63	Some	600	700	700	700
107 mm: Haseb	0	0	Some	Some	Some
107 mm: Fajr 1	0	0	Some	Some	Some
122 mm: Hadid/Arash/Noor	0	50	50	50	50
122 mm: BM-21	65	100	100	100	100
122 mm: BM-11	Some	5	7	7	7
240 mm: M-1985	0	9	9	9	9

240 mm: Fajr 3	0	0	10	10	10
333 mm: Fajr 5	0	0	Some	Some	Some
Mortars	3,000+	6,500	5,000	5,000	5,000
60 mm:	0	Some	Some	Some	Some
81 mm:	Some	Some	Some	Some	Some
82 mm:	0	Some	Some	Some	Some
107 mm: M-30	Some	Some	Some	Some	Some
120 mm: M-65	3,000	Some	Some	Some	Some
Surface-to-Surface Missiles	Some	Some	Some	42+	42+
Scud-B/-C Launchers, est. 300 MSLS	Some	10	12–18	12–18	12–18
Shahab-3	Some	Some	Some	Some	Some
CSS-8	0	25	30	30	30
Oghab	Some	Some	Some	Some	Some
Shaheen 1/-2	Some	Some	Some	Some	Some
Nazeat	Some	Some	Some	Some	Some
Surface-to-Air Missiles	some	some	some	some	some
SA-7	Some	Some	Some	0	0
SA-14	Some	Some	Some	0	0
SA-16	Some	Some	Some	0	0
HQ-7	Some	Some	Some	Some	Some
Anti-Tank Guided Weapons	Some	Some	75	75	75
ENTAC	Some	0	0	0	0
SS-11/-12	Some	0	0	0	0
Dragon	Some	0	0	0	0
AT-3 SAGGER	0	0	Some	Some	Some
AT-4 Spigot	0	Some	Some	Some	Some
AT-5 Spandrel	0	0	Some	Some	Some
Saeqhe 1/-2	0	0	Some	Some	Some
Toophan	0	0	Some	Some	Some
Rocket Launchers	0	Some	Some	Some	Some
73 mm: RPG-7	0	Some	Some	Some	Some
Recoilless Launchers	Some	Some	Some	Some	Some
57 mm	Some	0	0	0	0

75 mm: M-20	Some	Some	Some	Some	Some
82 mm: B-10	0	Some	Some	Some	Some
106 mm: M-40	Some	Some	200	200	200
107 mm: B-11	0	Some	Some	Some	Some
Air-Defense Guns	1,500	1,700	1,700	1,700	1,700
14.5 mm: ZPU-2/-4	Some	Some	Some	Some	Some
14.5 mm: ZSU-23-4	Some	Some	Some	Some	Some
23 mm: ZSU-57-2SP	0	Some	Some	Some	Some
35 mm: M-1939	0	Some	Some	Some	Some
37 mm: S-60	0	0	0	Some	Some
37 mm: Type-55	Some	Some	Some	0	0
57 mm: ZPU-2	0	Some	0	Some	Some
57 mm: ZU-23	0	0	Some	Some	Some
57 mm: S-60	0	0	Some	0	0
Surface-to-Air Missiles	230	Some	Some	Some	Some
I-Hawk	30	0	0	0	0
RBS-70	200	0	0	0	0
SA-7/-14/-16	Some SA-7	Some SA-7	Some	Some	Some
HQ-7	0	0	Some	Some	Some
QW-1	0	0	Some	Some	Some
Unmanned Aerial Vehicle (UAV)	0	0	Some	Some	Some
Mohajer-II/-III/-IV	0	0	Some	Some	Some
Aircraft	49+	77	36	17	17
Cessna 185	40+	50	10	10	10
F-27	2	19	2	2	2
Falcon 20	2	8	20	1	1
Turbo Commander 690	5	0	4	4	4
Helicopters	410	556	223	223	223
AH-1J Attack	100	100	50	50	50
CH-47C Heavy Transport	10	40	20	20	20
Bell 214A/C	250	165	50	50	50
Bell 204	0	30	0	0	0
AB-205A	35	40	68	68	68

AB-206	15	90	10	10	10
AB-12	0	12	0	0	0
Mi-8/-17	0	0	25	25	25
Hughes 300C	0	5	0	0	0
RH-53D	0	9	0	0	0
SH-53D	0	10	0	0	0
SA-319	0	10	0	0	0
UH-1H	0	45	0	0	0

Source: IISS, *Military Balance,* various editions, including 1989–1990, 1999–2000, 2004–2005, 2005–2006, 2006, and 2007.

local bases. It does not practice difficult amphibious operations, particularly "across the beach" operations. Iran could, however, deploy into Kuwait and cross the border into Iraq. It can also move at least brigade-sized mechanized units across the Gulf by amphibious ship and ferry if it does not meet significant naval and air opposition to any such movement. It lacks the air strength and naval air- and missile-defense capabilities to be able to defend such an operation.

The Islamic Revolutionary Guards Corps (Pasdaran)

The Islamic Revolutionary Guards Corps (IRGC) is a product of the Iranian Revolution of 1979. Ayatollah Ruhollah Khomeini established the force to protect the Islamic order of the new Iranian government. The IRGC has since evolved to be a major political, military, and economic force in Iran. It is believed to have close ties to the Supreme Leader, but has its own factions—some of which have loyalties to President Mahmoud Ahmadinejad, who is a veteran of the IRGC. It is far more political and ideological than the regular armed forces. A number of senior officers in the IRGC have relatives or close ties to Iran's leading clerics.

The IRGC (Pasdaran) has contributed some 125,000 men to Iran's forces in recent years and has substantial capabilities for asymmetric warfare and covert operations. This includes the Al Quds Force and other elements that operate covertly or openly overseas, working with Hezbollah of Lebanon, Shi'ite militias in Iraq, and Shi'ites in Afghanistan. It was members of the IRGC that seized 15 British sailors and Marines, who seem to still have been in Iraqi waters, in March 2007.[1]

The IRGC operates most of Iran's surface-to-surface missiles and is believed to have custody over potentially deployed nuclear weapons, most or all other chemical, biological, radiological, and nuclear (CBRN) weapons, and to operate Iran's nuclear-armed missile forces if they are deployed.

The links between the IRGC and Iran's nuclear program are so close that its leaders were singled out under the UN Security Council Resolutions passed on December 23, 2006, and March 24, 2007, and had their assets frozen. The commander, Major General Yahya Rahim Safavi, deputy commander, Brigadier General Morteza Rezaie, and the heads of the IRGC ground forces, the naval branch, the Al Quds (Qods) Force, and the Basij (Mobilization of the Oppressed Force) were all involved.[2]

UN Security Council Resolution 1747, passed on March 24, 2007, included a wide range of Iranian officials involved in nuclear or ballistic missile activities, including the following members of the IRGC command structure:

- Ministry of Defense and Other Officials
  - Fereidoun Abbasi-Davani [Senior Ministry of Defence and Armed Forces Logistics (MODAFL) scientist with links to the Institute of Applied Physics, working closely with Mohsen Fakhrizadeh-Mahabadi, designated below];
  - Mohsen Fakhrizadeh-Mahabadi [Senior MODAFL scientist and former head of the Physics Research Centre (PHRC). The International Atomic Energy Agency has asked to interview him about the activities of the PHRC over the period he was the head, but Iran has refused];
  - Seyed Jaber Safdari (Manager of the Natanz Enrichment Facilities);
  - Amir Rahimi [Head of Esfahan Nuclear Fuel Research and Production Center, which is part of the Atomic Energy Agency of Iran's (AEOI's) Nuclear Fuel Production and Procurement Company, which is involved in enrichment-related activities];
  - Mohsen Hojati [Head of Fajr Industrial Group, which is designated under Resolution 1737 (2006) for its role in the ballistic missile programme];
  - Mehrdada Akhlaghi Ketabachi [Head of Shahid Bagheri Industrial Group (SBIG), which is designated under Resolution 1737 (2006) for its role in the ballistic missile programme];
  - Naser Maleki [Head of SHIG, which is designated under Resolution 1737 (2006) for its role in Iran's ballistic missile programme. Naser Maleki is also a MODAFL official overseeing work on the Shahab-3 ballistic missile programme. The Shahab-3 is Iran's long-range ballistic missile currently in service]; and
  - Ahmad Derakhshandeh [Chairman and Managing Director of Bank Sepah, which provides support for the AIO and subordinates, including Shahid Hemmat Industrial Group (SHIG) and SBIG, both of which were designated under Resolution 1737 (2006)];
- Iranian Revolutionary Guard Corps key persons
  - Brigadier General Morteza Rezaie (Deputy Commander of IRGC);
  - Vice Admiral Ali Akbar Ahmadian (Chief of IRGC Joint Staff);
  - Brigadier General Mohammad Reza Zahedi (Commander of IRGC Ground Forces);
  - Rear Admiral Morteza Safari (Commander of IRGC Navy);
  - Brigadier General Mohammad Hejazi (Commander of the Bassij resistance force);
  - Brigadier General Qasem Soleimani (Commander of the Qods force); and
  - General Zolqadr (IRGC officer, Deputy Interior Minister for Security Affairs).[3]

IRGC LAND FORCES

The IRGC has small elements equipped with armor and has the equivalent of conventional army units, and some units are trained for covert missions and asymmetric warfare, but most of its forces are lightly equipped infantry trained and equipped for internal security missions. These forces are reported to have between 120,000 and 130,000 men, but such totals are uncertain. They also include conscripts recruited from the same pool as regular army conscripts, and training and retention levels are low. The IRGC land forces do, however, control the Basij (Mobilization of the Oppressed) and other paramilitary forces if they are mobilized for war.

Some sources, like the International Institute for Strategic Studies (IISS), report a force structure with 20 "divisions," but most IRGC units seem to be battalion-sized elements. According to a *Jane's* report, estimates of the IRGC's organization differ sharply. Some sources claim that there are two armored, five mechanized, ten infantry, one Special Forces division, and about 15–20 independent brigades. The report concludes that many alleged divisions are equivalent to large brigades and the personnel numbers of the IRGC could support only three to five divisions.[4] The total manpower pool of the IRGC could support only about five to six light infantry divisions. There is also supposed to be one airborne brigade.

The IRGC often claims to conduct very large exercises, sometimes with 100,000 men or more. The exact size of such exercises is unclear, but they are often a small fraction of IRGC claims. With the exception of a limited number of more elite elements, training is limited and largely suitable for internal security purposes. Most forces would require substantial refresher training to act in any mission other than static infantry defense and using asymmetric warfare tactics like hit-and-run operations or swarming elements of forces when an invader appears vulnerable.

The IRGC is, however, the center of much of Iran's effort to develop asymmetric warfare tactics to counter a U.S. invasion. Work by Michael Connell of the Center for Naval Analysis notes that the IRGC has been systematically equipping, organizing, and retraining its forces to fight decentralized partisan and guerrilla warfare. It has strengthened the anti-tank and anti-helicopter weaponry of IRGC battalions and stressed independent battalion-sized operations that can fight with considerable independence even if Iran loses much of the coherence in its command, control, communications, and intelligence capabilities.[5] Its exercises have included simulated attacks on U.S. AH-64 attack helicopters with Iran's more modern man-portable surface-to-air missiles, using mines and using improvised explosive device (IED)-like systems to attack advancing armored forces.

The IRGC, like the army and the Basij, have attempted to develop and practice deception, concealment, and camouflage methods to reduce the effectiveness of U.S. and other modern imagery coverage, including dispersing into small teams and avoiding the use of uniformed personnel and military vehicles. While the credibility and effectiveness of such tactics are uncertain, the IRGC claims to be adopting tactics to avoid enemy radars and satellites. Both the IRGC and the army have also attempted to deal with U.S. signals and communications intelligence collection capabilities by making extensive use of buried fiber optics and secure communications and developing more secure ways to use the Internet and commercial landlines. Iran claims to be creating relatively advanced secure communications systems, but its success is uncertain.[6]

Connell notes that the IRGC is developing such tactics in ways that could form a layered or "mosaic" defense with the army and air forces, where the IRGC kept up constant pressure on any advancing U.S. forces. He indicates that the IRGC has developed special stay-behind units or "cells" that would include some 1,800 to 3,000 teams of three to four soldiers whose main mission would be to attack U.S. lines of supply and communication, strike at elements in rear areas, and conduct ambushes of combat troops. This could include sending units forward into countries like Iraq and Afghanistan to attack U.S. forces there, or encourage local forces to do so, and sending teams to raid or infiltrate the southern Gulf States friendly to the United States.[7]

At the same time, Connell notes that if the Iranian Army was defeated and an attacker like the United States moved into Iran's territory, the IRGC, the Iranian Army, and the Basij are now organized and trained to fight a much more dispersed war of attrition in which force elements would disperse and scatter, carrying out a constant series of attacks on U.S. forces wherever they deployed as well as against U.S. lines of communication and supply. Such elements would have great independence of action rather than relying on centralized command. The IRGC and the Iranian Army have clearly paid close attention to both the limited successes that Saddam's Fedayeen had against the U.S. advance on Baghdad, and the far more successful efforts of Iraqi insurgents and militias in attacking U.S. and other Coalition forces following the fall of Baghdad.

One technique such forces organize and practice is using cities and built-up areas as defensive areas that provide concealment and opportunities for ambushes and for the use of swarming tactics, which forces an attacker to disperse large numbers of forces to try to clear and secure given neighborhoods. Connell indicates that some 2,500 Basij members staged such an exercise in the Western suburbs of Tehran in February 2007. Once again, Iran can draw on the lessons of the fighting in Iraq. It also, however, employed such tactics with great success against Iraqi forces during the Iran-Iraq War, and it has closely studied the lessons of urban and built-up area fighting in Somalia and Lebanon.

The IRGC remains the center of Iran's hard-line security forces, but has become steadily more bureaucratic and less effective as a conventional fighting force since the end of the Iran-Iraq War in 1988. Corruption and careerism are growing problems, and the IRGC's role in the defense industry has led to financial abuses. At this point in time, it is the elite elements of the IRGC that give it real meaning beyond serving the regime's need to control its population.

One source identifies a trend that will eventually render the regular army more technologically advanced and more modern in general. According to this report, the IRGC, in contrast, is to focus on "less traditional defense duties," such as enforcing border security, commanding the country's ballistic missile and potential weapons of mass destruction forces, and preparing for a closing of the Strait of Hormuz with military means.[8]

THE IRGC AIR FORCE

The air force of the IRGC is believed to operate Iran's three Shahab-3 intermediate-range ballistic missiles units (whose true operational status remains uncertain) and may have had custody of its chemical weapons and any biological weapons. While the actual operational status of the Shahab-3 remains uncertain, Iran's Supreme Leader, Ayatollah Ali Khamenei, announced in 2003 that Shahab-3 missiles had been delivered to the IRGC. In addition, six Shahab-3s were displayed in Tehran during a military parade in September 2003.[9]

It is not clear what combat formations exist within the IRGC, but the IRGC may operate Iran's ten EMB-312 Tucanos.[10] It also seems to operate many of Iran's 45 PC-7 training aircraft, as well as some Pakistani-made trainers at a training school near Mushshak, but this school may be run by the regular air force. It has also claimed to manufacture gliders for use in unconventional warfare. These are unsuitable delivery platforms, but could at least carry a small number of weapons.[11]

THE IRGC NAVAL FORCES

The IRGC has a naval branch that is described in more detail in Chapter 7. It has some 20,000 men, including marine units of some 5,000 men. Such a force could deliver conventional weapons, bombs, mines, and CBRN weapons into ports and oil and desalination facilities. It is operational in the Gulf and the Gulf of Oman and could operate elsewhere if given suitable sealift or facilities.

The naval branch has bases in the Gulf, many near key shipping channels and some near the Strait of Hormuz. These include facilities at Al-Farsiyah, Halul (an oil platform), Sirri, Abu Musa, Bandar Abbas, Khorramshahr, and Larak. It also controls Iran's coastal defense forces, including naval guns and an HY-2 Seersucker land-based anti-ship missile unit deployed in five to seven sites along the Gulf coast.

Its forces can carry out extensive raids against Gulf shipping, carry out regular amphibious exercises with the land branch of the IRGC against objectives like the islands in the Gulf, and could conduct raids against Saudi Arabia or other countries on the southern Gulf coast. They give Iran a major capability for asymmetric warfare. The Guards also seem to work closely with Iranian intelligence and appear to be represented unofficially in some embassies, Iranian businesses and purchasing offices, and other foreign fronts.

The IRGC naval forces have at least 40 light patrol boats, 10 Houdong guided missile patrol boats armed with C-802 anti-ship missiles, and a battery of HY-2 Seersucker land-based anti-ship missiles. Some of these systems could be modified to carry a small CBRN weapon, but hardly are optimal delivery platforms because of their limited-range payload and sensor/guidance platforms unsuited for the mission.

PROXY AND COVERT CBRN OPERATIONS

The IRGC has a complex structure that includes both political and military units. It has separate organizational elements for its land, naval, and air units, which include both military and paramilitary units. The Basij and the tribal units of the Pasdaran are subordinated to its land unit command, although the commander of the Basij often seems to report directly to the Commander-in-Chief and Minister of the Pasdaran and through him to the Leader of the Islamic Revolution.

The IRGC has close ties to the foreign operations branch of the Iranian Ministry of Intelligence and Security (MOIS), particularly through the IRGC's Qods force. The Ministry of Intelligence and Security was established in 1983 and has an extensive network of offices in Iranian embassies. It is often difficult to separate the activities of the IRGC, the Vezarat-e Ettela'at va Amniat-e Keshvar, and the Foreign Ministry, and many seem to be integrated operations managed by a ministerial committee called the "Special Operations Council" that includes the Leader of the Islamic Revolution, President, Minister of Intelligence and Security, and other members of the Supreme Council for National Defense.[12]

Other elements of the IRGC can support proxy or covert use of CBRN weapons. They run some training camps inside Iran for outside "volunteers." Some IRGC still seem to be deployed in Lebanon and actively involved in training and arming Hezbollah, other anti-Israeli groups, and other elements.[13] The IRGC has been responsible for major arms shipments to Hezbollah, including large numbers of AT-3 anti-tank guided missiles, long-range rockets, and some Iranian-made Mohajer unmanned aerial vehicles.[14]

Iran exported thousands of 122-mm rockets and Fajr-4 and Fajr-5 long-range rockets to Hezbollah in Lebanon, including the *Arash* with a range of 21–29 kilometers. These reports give the Fajr-5 a range of 75 kilometers with a payload of 200 kilograms. Iran seems to have sent such arms to Hezbollah and some various Palestinian movements, including some shiploads of arms to the Palestinian Authority.[15]

It has provided arms, training, and military technology to Shi'ite militias in Iraq and may have provided such support to Sunni Islamist extremists as well, which led to attacks on U.S. and Coalition forces. These transfers have included relatively advanced shaped charge and triggering components, which have sharply increased the lethality of militia and insurgent attacks using IEDs on U.S. and Coalition armor. There were also growing indicators that similar training, weapons, and other aid were being provided to Shi'ite forces and Taliban elements in Afghanistan in 2007.

THE AL QUDS (QODS) FORCE

The IRGC has a large intelligence operation and unconventional warfare component. Roughly 5,000 of the men in the IRGC are assigned to the unconventional warfare mission. The IRGC has the equivalent of one Special Forces division, plus additional smaller formations, and these forces are given special priority in terms of training and equipment. In addition, the IRGC has a special Al Quds Force that plays a major role in giving Iran the ability to conduct unconventional warfare overseas using various foreign movements as proxies.[16]

In January, Iran's Supreme National Security Council (SNSC) decided to place all Iranian operations in Iraq under the command of the Al Quds Force. At the same time, the SNSC decided to increase the personnel strength of the Al Quds to 15,000.[17] Current force strength data for the Qods are not available.

The Al Quds Force is under the command of Brigadier General Qassem Soleimani and has supported nonstate actors in many foreign countries. These include Hezbollah in Lebanon, Hamas and the Palestinian Islamic Jihad in the Gaza Strip and the West Bank, the Shi'ite militias in Iraq, and Shi'ites in Afghanistan. Links to Sunni extremist groups like Al Qa'ida have been reported, but never convincingly confirmed.

Many U.S. experts believe that the Al Quds Forces has provided significant transfers of weapons to Shi'ite (and perhaps some Sunni) elements in Iraq. These may include the shaped charge components used in some IEDs in Iraq and the more advanced components used in explosively formed projectiles, including the weapon assembly, copper slugs, radio links used to activate such devices, and the infrared triggering mechanisms. These devices are very similar to those used in Lebanon, and some seem to operate on the same radio frequencies. Shaped charge weapons first began to appear in Iraq in August 2003, but became a serious threat in 2005.[18]

On January 11, 2007, the director of the Defense Intelligence Agency stated in a testimony before the U.S. Senate Select Committee on Intelligence that Iran's Islamic Revolutionary Guard Corps-Qods Force has the lead for its transnational terrorist activities, in conjunction with Lebanese Hezbollah and Iran's MOIS.[19] Other sources believe that the primary mission of the Al Quds Force has been to support Shi'ite movements and militias, and such aid and weapons transfers seem to have increased significantly in the spring of 2007.

The Al Quds is also believed to play a continuing role in training, arming, and funding Hezbollah in Lebanon and to have begun to support Shi'ite militia and Taliban activities in Afghanistan. Experts disagree on the scale of such activity, how much it has provided support to Sunni Islamist extremist groups rather than Shi'ite groups, and over the level of cooperation in rebuilding Hezbollah forces in Lebanon since the cease-fire in the Israel-Hezbollah War of 2006. The debates focus on the scale of such activity and the extent to which it has been formally controlled and authorized by the Supreme Leader and the president, however, and not over whether some level of activity has been authorized.

The exact relationship between the Al Quds Force, Hamas, and the Palestinian Islamic Jihad is even more speculative. Some Iranian arms shipments have clearly been directed at aiding anti-peace and anti-Israeli elements in the Gaza Strip. There is some evidence of aid in training, weapons, and funding to hostile Palestinian elements in both the Gaza Strip and the West Bank. Open sources do not, however, provide a clear picture of the scale of such activity.

Some reports indicate that the budget for the Al Quds Force is a classified budget directly controlled by Supreme Leader Khamenei and is not reflected in the Iranian general budget. The active elements of the Al Quds service operate primarily outside Iran's borders, although it has bases inside and outside of Iran. The Al Quds troops are divided into specific groups or "corps" for each country or area in which they operate. There are Directorates for Iraq; Lebanon, Palestine, and Jordan; Afghanistan, Pakistan, and India; Turkey and the Arabian Peninsula; Asian countries of the former Soviet Union; Western nations (Europe and North America); and North Africa (Egypt, Tunisia, Algeria, Sudan, and Morocco).

The Al Quds Force has offices or "sections" in many Iranian embassies, which are closed to most embassy staff. It is not clear whether these are integrated with Iranian intelligence operations or if the ambassador in each embassy has control of, or detailed knowledge of, operations by the Al Quds staff. However, there are indications that most operations are coordinated between the IRGC and offices within the Iranian Foreign Ministry and MOIS. There are separate operational organizations in Lebanon, Turkey, Pakistan, and several North African countries. There are also indications that such elements may have participated in the bombings of the Israeli Embassy in Argentina in 1992 and the Jewish Community Center in Buenos Aires in 1994—although Iran has strongly denied any involvement in either.[20]

The Al Quds Force seems to control many of Iran's training camps for unconventional warfare, extremists, and terrorists in Iran and countries like the Sudan and Lebanon. In Sudan, the Al Quds Force is believed to run a training camp of unspecified nature. It has at least four major training facilities in Iran. The Al Quds Force has a main training center at Imam Ali University that is based in the Sa'dabad Palace in Northern Tehran. Troops are trained to carry out military and terrorist operations and are indoctrinated in ideology. There are other training camps in the Qom, Tabriz, and Mashhad governorates and in Lebanon and the Sudan. These include the Al Nasr camp for training Iraqi Shi'ites and Iraqi and Turkish Kurds in northwest Iran and a camp near Mashhad for training Afghan and Tajik revolutionaries. The Al Quds Force seems to help operate the Manzariyah training center near Qom, which recruits foreign students in the religious seminary and which seems to have trained some Bahraini extremists. Some foreigners are reported to have received training in demolition and sabotage at an IRGC facility near Isfahan, in airport infiltration at a facility near Mashad and Shiraz, and in underwater warfare at an IRGC facility at Bandar Abbas.[21]

On January 11, 2007, the U.S. military in Iraq detained five men accused of providing funds and equipment to Iraqi insurgents. According to U.S. military sources, these men had connections to the Al Quds Force.[22] On January 20, 2007, gunmen dressed as U.S. soldiers entered the Provincial Joint Coordination Center in Karbala and killed and wounded several U.S. servicemen. According to some sources, including U.S. military intelligence, the gunmen were members of the Al Quds Force. The sophisticated planning and execution of this attack made it unlikely that any Iraqi group was involved in it.[23]

General David H. Petraeus, the commander of U.S. forces in Iraq, stressed the growing role of the Al Quds Force and the IRGC in testimony to Congress in April 2007. He noted that the United States had found Al Quds operatives in Iraq and seized computers with hard drives that included a 22-page document that had details on the planning, approval process, and conduct of an attack that killed five U.S. soldiers in Karbala. Petraeus noted,

> They were provided substantial funding, training on Iranian soil, advanced explosive munitions and technologies as well as run-of-the-mill arms and ammunition...in some cases advice and in some cases even a degree of direction...Our sense is that these records were kept so that they could be handed in to whoever it is that is financing them ...And again, there's no question...that Iranian financing is taking place through the Al-Quds force of the Iranian Republican Guards Corps.[24]

Israeli defense experts state that they believe the IRGC and the Al Quds Force not only played a major role in training and equipping Hezbollah, but may have assisted it during the Israeli-Hezbollah War in 2006. Israeli intelligence officers claim to have found command and control centers, and a missile and rocket fire-control center, in Lebanon that was of Iranian design. They feel the Al Quds Force played a major role in the Hezbollah anti-ship missile attack on an Israeli Navy Sa'ar-class missile patrol boat and that Iranians and Syrians supported Hezbollah with intelligence from facilities in Syria during the fighting.

THE BASIJ

Like the IRGC, the Basij force grew out of the Revolution of 1979 by direct intervention of Ayatollah Khomeini. On January 1, 1981, the Basij was put under command of the IRGC. The Basij is a popular reserve force of about 90,000 men, with an active and reserve strength of up to 300,000 and a mobilization capacity of nearly 1,000,000 men. It has up to 740 regionally commanded battalions, which consist of about 300–350 personnel each. It is controlled by the IRGC and consists largely of youths, men who have completed military service, and the elderly.

Apparently, the Basij began to place emphasis on riot control and internal security missions in the mid-1990s. Therefore, it has created a formal military-style command system and set up special battalions for internal security missions (Ashura).[25]

Its mission has, however, increasingly been broadened to providing reserves and small combat elements for the IRGC in defending against a U.S. invasion. It would serve as a mobilization base for the IRGC, as well as provide cadres and small units for independent action against invading forces. It would also serve as a "stay behind" force and attack isolated U.S. units and rear areas. According to Connell, the IRGC has formed a wartime mobilization plan for the IRGC called the "Mo'in Plan," where Basij battalions would be integrated into the IRGC in wartime as part of the IRGC regional defense structure.[26]

It is far from clear how effective the Basij would really be in such missions. Similar forces have been created in a number of countries, including Iraq. In many cases, they have not materialized as a meaningful resistance force. Iran does, however, have extensive experience in creating and using such forces dating back to the Iran-Iraq War, and the fighting in Iraq since 2003 has shown that small cadres of activists using IEDs, car bombs, and suicide bombs can have a major political and military impact.

ROLE IN IRAN'S INDUSTRIES

The IRGC plays a major role in Iran's military industries. Its lead role in Iran's efforts to acquire surface-to-surface missiles and weapons of mass destruction gives it growing experience with advanced military technology. As a result, the IRGC is believed to be the branch of Iran's forces that plays the largest role in Iran's military industries.[27] It also operates all of Iran's Scuds, controls most of its chemical and biological weapons, and provides the military leadership for missile production and the production of all weapons of mass destruction.

The IRGC is a powerful economic force, controlling key elements of Iraq's defense industry. It seems to operate part of Iran's covert trading network, a system established after the fall of the Shah to buy arms and military parts through various cover and false flag organizations. It is not clear, however, how much of this network is controlled by the IRGC versus the Ministry of Defense. For example, the same UN resolution dealing with Iran's nuclear proliferation listed a wide range of entities where the role of the IRGC is often unclear:

- Ammunition and Metallurgy Industries Group (AMIG) (Ammunition Industries Group) (AMIG controls 7th of Tir, which is designated under resolution 1737 (2006) for its role in Iran's centrifuge programme. AMIG is in turn owned and controlled by the Defence Industries Organisation (DIO), which is designated under resolution 1737 (2006))

- Esfahan Nuclear Fuel Research and Production Centre (NFRPC) and Esfahan Nuclear Technology Centre (ENTC) (Parts of the Atomic Energy Organisation of Iran's (AEOI) Nuclear Fuel Production and Procurement Company, which is involved in enrichment-related activities. AEOI is designated under resolution 1737 (2006))

- Kavoshyar Company (Subsidiary company of AEOI, which has sought glass fibres, vacuum chamber furnaces and laboratory equipment for Iran's nuclear programme)

- Parchin Chemical Industries (Branch of DIO, which produces ammunition, explosives, as well as solid propellants for rockets and missiles)

- Karaj Nuclear Research Centre (Part of AEOI's research division)

- Novin Energy Company (aka Pars Novin) (Operates within AEOI and has transferred funds on behalf of AEOI to entities associated with Iran's nuclear programme)

- Cruise Missile Industry Group (aka Naval Defence Missile Industry Group)

- (Production and development of cruise missiles. Responsible for naval missiles including cruise missiles)

- Bank Sepah and Bank Sepah International (Bank Sepah provides support for the Aerospace Industries Organisation (AIO) and subordinates, including Shahid Hemmat Industrial Group (SHIG) and Shahid Bagheri Industrial Group (SBIG), both of which were designated under resolution 1737 (2006)

- Sanam Industrial Group (subordinate to AIO, which has purchased equipment on AIO's behalf for the missile programme)
- Ya Mahdi Industries Group (subordinate to AIO, which is involved in international purchases of missile equipment) Iranian Revolutionary Guard Corps entities[28]

It is clear that the IRGC has become a leading contracting organization, bidding for other contracts including at least some oil and gas projects. Like most Iranian entities associated with government projects, it is reported to get many contracts out of favoritism and/or without competitive bidding. It is believed to now be as corrupt as civil entities and religious foundations like the Bunyods.

OTHER PARAMILITARY FORCES

Iran also has 45,000–60,000 men in the Ministry of Interior serving as police and border guards, with light utility vehicles, light patrol aircraft (Cessna 185/310s and AB-205s and AB-206s), 90 coastal patrol craft, and 40 harbor patrol craft. The rest of Iran's paramilitary and internal security forces seem to have relatively little capability in any form of warfighting mission.

6

The Iranian Air Force

The Iranian Air Force (IAF) still is numerically strong, but most of its equipment is aging, worn, and has limited mission capability. It has some 52,000 men: 37,000 in the air force in 2007, and 15,000 in the Air Defense force, which operates Iran's land-based air defenses. There are over 300 combat aircraft in the inventory [the International Institute for Strategic Studies (IISS) estimates 281 combat aircraft]. Operational command is divided into three commands and their subsequent units—Eastern, Western, and Southern.

Many of Iran's aircraft are either not operational or cannot be sustained in extended air combat operations. This applies to 50–60 percent of Iran's U.S.– and French-supplied aircraft and some 20–30 percent of its Russian- and Chinese-supplied aircraft. It has nine fighter-ground attack squadrons with 162–186 aircraft; seven fighter squadrons with 70–74 aircraft; a reconnaissance unit with 4–8 aircraft; and a number of transport aircraft, helicopters, and special purpose aircraft. The air force operates most of Iran's land-based air defenses, including some 150 I-Hawks, 45 HQ-21s, 10 SA-5s, 30 Rapiers, 15 Tigercats, and additional forces equipped with light surface-to-air missiles.

The Iranian Air Force is headquartered in Tehran with its training, administration, and logistics branches, as well as a major central Air Defense Operations Center. The headquarters has a political directorate and a small naval coordination staff. It has three major regional headquarters: Northern Zone (Badl Sar), Central Zone (Hamaden), and Southern Zone (Bushehr).

Each regional zone seems to control a major air-defense sector with subordinate air bases and facilities. The key air-defense subzones and related bases in the Northern Zone are located at Badl Sar, Mashhad, and Shahabad Kord. The subzones and bases in the Central Zone are at Hamadan and Dezful, and the subzones and bases in the Southern Zone are at Bushehr, Bandar Abbas, and Jask. Iran has large combat air bases at Mehrabad, Tabriz, Hamadan, Dezful, Bushehr, Shiraz, Isfahan, and Bandar Abbas. It has smaller bases at least at 11 other locations. Shiraz provides interceptor training and is the main base for transport aircraft.

IRANIAN AIR STRENGTH

Iran's comparative air strength is shown in Figures 6.1 through 6.6. Once again, Iran now can take advantage of a near power vacuum in Iraq. At the same time, these

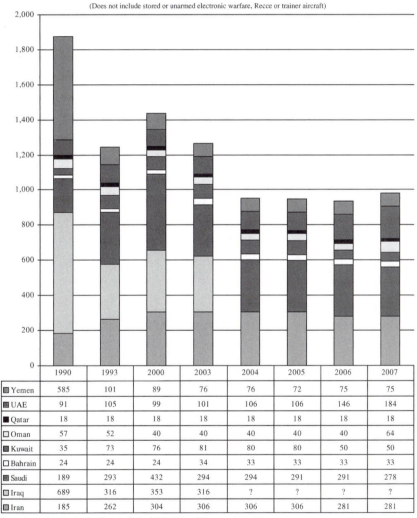

(Does not include stored or unarmed electronic warfare, Recce or trainer aircraft)

	1990	1993	2000	2003	2004	2005	2006	2007
▣ Yemen	585	101	89	76	76	72	75	75
▣ UAE	91	105	99	101	106	106	146	184
■ Qatar	18	18	18	18	18	18	18	18
☐ Oman	57	52	40	40	40	40	40	64
▣ Kuwait	35	73	76	81	80	80	50	50
☐ Bahrain	24	24	24	34	33	33	33	33
▣ Saudi	189	293	432	294	294	291	291	278
☐ Iraq	689	316	353	316	?	?	?	?
▣ Iran	185	262	304	306	306	306	281	281

Source: International Institute for Strategic Studies (IISS), *Military Balance*, various editions.

Figure 6.1   Total Operational Combat Aircraft in All Gulf Forces, 1990–2007

Fixed-Wing Combat Aircraft

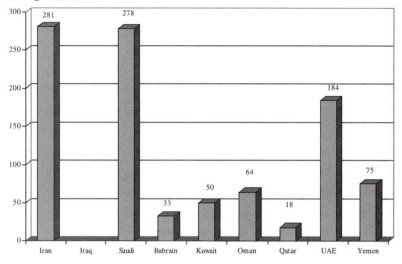

Armed and Attack Helicopters

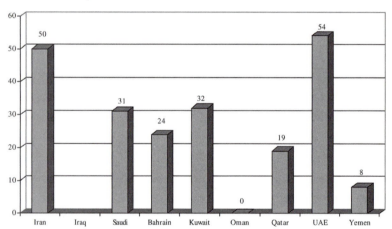

Note: Only armed or combat-capable fixed wing combat aircraft are counted, not other trainers or aircraft. Note: Yemen has an additional 5 MiG-29S/UB on order. Iraq totals are for March 2003, before the Iraq War

Source: International Institute for Strategic Studies (IISS), *Military Balance, 2007.*

Figure 6.2   Total Gulf Holdings of Combat Aircraft, 2007

figures show that Iran's air strength is considerably more limited relative to its southern Gulf neighbors than its land force strength, and this is particularly true if force quantity is taken into account along with force quality. Furthermore, such calculations again ignore the fact that the United States can decisively intervene with massively superior force at any time.

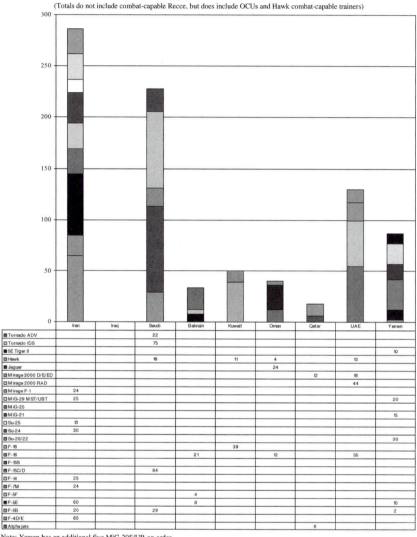

(Totals do not include combat-capable Recce, but does include OCUs and Hawk combat-capable trainers)

	Iran	Iraq	Saudi	Bahrain	Kuwait	Oman	Qatar	UAE	Yemen
■ Tornado ADV			22						
▨ Tornado IDS			75						
■ 5E Tiger II									10
▨ Hawk			18		11	4		13	
■ Jaguar						24			
▨ Mirage 2000 D/E/ED							12	18	
▨ Mirage 2000 RAD								44	
■ Mirage F-1	24								
▢ MiG-29 MST/UBT	25								20
▨ MiG-25									
■ MiG-21									15
▢ Su-25	13								
■ Su-24	30								
▨ Su-20/22									30
▢ F-18					39				
■ F-16				21		12		55	
■ F-15S									
■ F-15C/D			84						
▢ F-14	25								
■ F-7M	24								
▢ F-5F				4					
■ F-5E	60			8					10
▨ F-5B	20		29						2
▢ F-4D/E	65								
■ Alpha jets							6		

Note: Yemen has an additional five MiG-29S/UB on order.
Source: International Institute for Strategic Studies (IISS), *Military Balance, 2007*.

Figure 6.3   Gulf High- and Medium-Quality Fixed-Wing Fighter, Fighter Attack, Attack, Strike, and Multirole Combat Aircraft by Type, 2007

Force Quantity

As is the case with most aspects of Iranian military forces, estimates of Iran's exact air strength differ by source. The IISS estimates the air force has 14 main combat squadrons. These include nine fighter ground-attack squadrons, four with at least 65 U.S.–supplied F-4D/Es, four with at least 60 F-5E/F, and one with

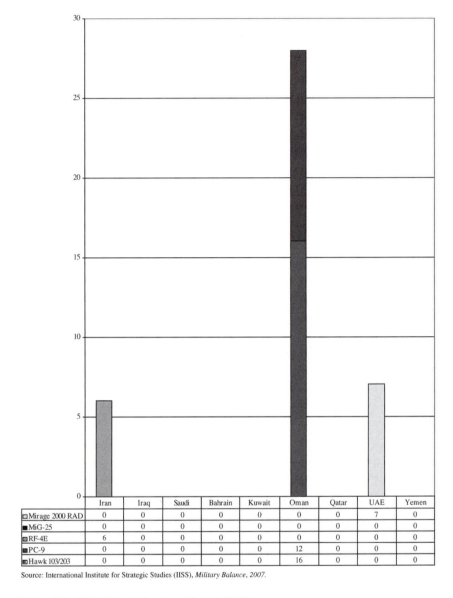

Source: International Institute for Strategic Studies (IISS), *Military Balance, 2007.*

Figure 6.4   Gulf Reconnaissance Aircraft, 2007

30 Soviet-supplied Su-24MK, 13 Su-25K, and 24 French F-1E Mirage aircraft. Iran possesses some MiG-29, Su-25K, and 24MK, and Mirage F-1E Iraqi aircraft it seized during the Gulf War. Another source reports that Iran has five fighter squadrons, two with 25 U.S.–supplied F-14s each, two with 25–30 Russian/Iraqi-supplied

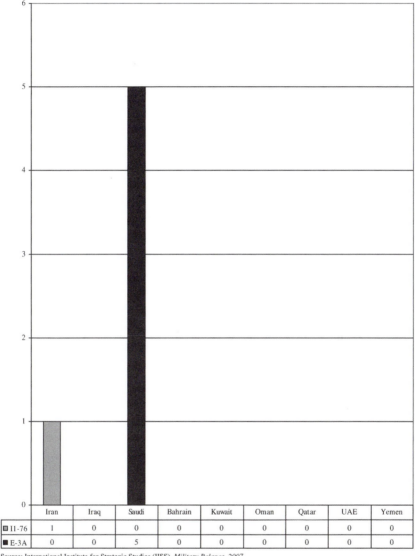

	Iran	Iraq	Saudi	Bahrain	Kuwait	Oman	Qatar	UAE	Yemen
Il-76	1	0	0	0	0	0	0	0	0
E-3A	0	0	5	0	0	0	0	0	0

Source: International Institute for Strategic Studies (IISS), *Military Balance*, 2007.

Figure 6.5 Sensor, Airborne Warning and Control System, Command, Control, Communications, Computers, and Intelligence (C⁴I), Early Warning, and Electronic Intelligence (ELINT) Aircraft, 2007

MiG-29A/-UBs, and one with 24 Chinese supplied F-7Ms.[1] How many of these are operational is not known.

Iran has upgraded some of its F-5s, although the details are controversial. Iranian sources claim that Iran upgraded the F-5E/F as part of the "Offogh-project," which

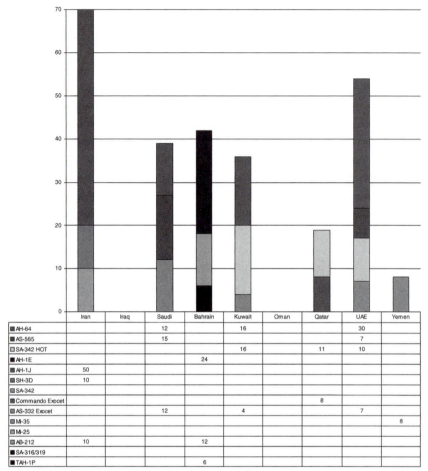

	Iran	Iraq	Saudi	Bahrain	Kuwait	Oman	Qatar	UAE	Yemen
■ AH-64			12		16			30	
■ AS-565			15					7	
▨ SA-342 HOT					16		11	10	
■ AH-1E				24					
■ AH-1J	50								
▨ SH-3D	10								
▨ SA-342									
■ Commando Exocet							8		
▨ AS-332 Exocet			12		4			7	
▨ M-35									8
▨ M-25									
▨ AB-212	10				12				
■ SA-316/319									
■ TAH-1P				6					

Source: International Institute for Strategic Studies (IISS), *Military Balance, 2007.*

Figure 6.6   Gulf Attack, Antiship and ASW Helicopters, 2007

improved the range of the F-5E APQ-159 radar and allows the aircraft to carry advanced missiles like the PL7, AIM-9P Sidewinders, and R-60 Aphids.[2] Similarly, Iranian sources claim that Iran has upgraded the APQ-120 Radar on its F-4Es by almost doubling its range, by adding automatic targeting and moving target indication capabilities, and has modified them to carry and fire the Kh-58 anti-radiation missile with its associated targeting pod as well as R-73 and PL-7 short-range air-to-air missiles.[3]

According to one source, Iran has improved its Su-24s within-flight refueling capability, an Upaz-A buddy refueling system to extend the range of other aircraft, installed active radar jammers and electronic countermeasures, and upgraded some aspects of the weapons launch and target software.[4] These reports cannot be fully confirmed.

Some reports indicate that Iran ordered an unknown number of TU-22M-3 "Backfire C" long-range strategic bombers from either Russia or the Ukraine.[5] While discussions to buy such aircraft seem to have taken place, no purchases or deliveries have ever been confirmed. Similarly, there have been rumors that Iran might have Su-30 fighter aircraft; however, such reports have not been confirmed either by official Iranian or Western sources. Another source reports that China may supply 90 FC-1 and 60 J-10/F-10 aircraft to Iran.[6] China's ability to export such aircraft in the near term is uncertain, however, given the needs of its own forces. It is also questionable if China would provoke the United States by making such a sale.

Force Quality

Iranian sources claim that the IAF's F-14s have been modified to increase their AWG-9's radar range and capability and that Iran has integrated the R-73 air-to-air missile (AAM) and various air-to-ground weapons with the aircraft. Claims that Iran is manufacturing upgraded AIM-54A Phoenix long-range air-to-air missiles do not seem to be correct.[7] Iran has acquired spare parts for F-14 aircraft from U.S. overstock through intermediaries.[8] As a consequence, the U.S. Defense Logistics Agency tightened its supervision of surplus goods sales. One source states that Iran claims to be able to produce up to 70 percent of all F-14 parts indigenously. However, Iran continues to make constant efforts to acquire F-14 and other U.S. aircraft parts on the world market. It is questionable whether or not Iran can keep more than 30 F-14 aircraft serviceable.[9]

The export versions of the MiG-29A have limited radar and avionics capabilities relative to the Russian model, but Iranian sources claim that Iran has modified avionics, integrated Western AAMs into the weapons options, equipped the aircraft with indigenously developed 99-lmp gallon (450-liter) external fuel tanks under project "Khorsid," and given some in-flight refueling capability.[10] These reports cannot be fully confirmed.

The F-7M is the export version of the Chinese J-7 and is derived from the MiG-21. These are aging designs with limited avionics for air-to-air and air-to-ground combat. Their use in combat is not confirmed, but one source reports that Iranian movies showed the aircraft conducting 810-kilometer-deep raids into Iraq against Iraqi Air Force airfields on April 4, 1981. Another movie claims Iran downed some 70 Iraqi aircraft in air combat in 1981, and another claims the aircraft were used in air-to-ground attacks toward the end of the war.[11] Such claims are propaganda. Iranian air raids on Iraq had little effectiveness, and large-scale air-to-air combat never took place.

The Iranian Air Force has a small reconnaissance squadron with six RF-4E Phantom aircraft. It has one RC-130, and other intelligence/reconnaissance aircraft, together with large numbers of transports and helicopters. The C-130 reportedly serves as a long-range maritime reconnaissance aircraft.[12]

Mission Capability

Most Iranian squadrons can perform both air-defense and attack missions, regardless of their principal mission—although this does not apply to Iran's F-14 (air-defense) and Su-24 (strike/attack) units. Iran's F-14s were, however, designed as dual-capable aircraft, and it has not been able to use its Phoenix air-to-air missiles since the early 1980s. Iran has claimed that it is modernizing its F-14s by equipping them with Improved Hawk (I-Hawk) missiles adapted to the air-to-air role, but it is far from clear that this is the case or that such adaptations can have more than limited effectiveness. In practice, this means that Iran might well use the F-14s in nuclear strike missions. They are capable of long-range, high payload missions and would require minimal adaptation to carry and release a nuclear weapon.[13]

It should be noted that in addition to conventional warfighting capabilities, Iran has a large number of attack and air-defense aircraft that could carry a small- to medium-sized nuclear weapon long distances, particularly since such strikes are likely to be low-altitude one-way missions. (These were the mission profiles in both NATO and Warsaw Pact theater nuclear strike plans.) Several might conceivably be modified as drones or the equivalent of "cruise missiles" using autopilots, on-board computers, and an add-on global positioning system.

Airlift and Support Capability

Iran has moderate airlift capabilities for a regional power. The Iranian Air Force's air transport assets included 3 B-707 and 1 B-747 tanker transports and 5 transport squadrons with 4 B-747Fs, 1 B-727, 17 C-130E/Hs, 3 Commander 680s, 10 F-27s, 1 Falcon 20A, 1 Il-76, 40 Iran-140s, 9 Y-12s, 2 Y-7s, 10 PC6Bs, and 2 Jetstars. Iran planned to acquire up to 14 Xian Y-7 transporters by 2006.[14]

The IAF's helicopter strength includes 2 AB-206As, 27–30 Bell 214Cs, 2 CH-47s, and 30 Mi-17 and Iranian-made Shabaviz 206-1 and 2-75 transport helicopters.

IRGC Air Units

The Islamic Revolutionary Guards Corps (IRGC) also has some air elements. It is not clear what combat formations exist within the IRGC, but the IRGC may operate Iran's 10 EMB-312.[15] It seems to operate many of Iran's 45 PC-7 trainers, as well as some Pakistani-made trainers at a training school near Mushhak, but this school may be run by the regular air force. It has also claimed to manufacture gliders for use in unconventional warfare.

The IRGC has not recently expanded its air combat capabilities.[16] According to one report, Iran is undertaking efforts to build up a long-range air strike capability. To this end it is equipping its Su-24 fighter aircraft with new probe pods so they can be refueled in-flight by Iran's U.S.–supplied Boeing 707 and 747 air tankers.[17] Apparently, the IRGC is in charge of overseeing the long-range strike program and has conducted refueling training over Syria.

Air Weaponry

Iran still deploys F-14s with Phoenix air-to-air missiles, but it is unclear whether such missiles are operational, and the same is true of reports that Iran has adapted the Hawk surface-to-air missile for air-to-air combat use on the F-14. Iran does, however, operate a range of other AAMs, which are becoming increasingly more capable.

Iran manufactures at least one fairly modern air-launched missile named Fajr-e Darya. This is an air-launched anti-ship/anti-ground missile, which is based on the Chinese C-701, a TV-guided missile with an effective range of 15 kilometers. Its Iranian land-launched equivalent is called Kossar. This Kossar or Kossar 3 appears to be a radar-guided missile with a range of 25 kilometers and a 29-kilogram warhead. Iran also operates the AGM-379/-20 (Zoobin) air-to-surface missile, apparently its first precision-guided missile. This weapon has an effective range of about 25–30 kilometers and uses the same warhead as the GBU-67/9 (Qadr), which is a similar, TV-guided missile with a 20-kilometer range.

In the past, Iran reportedly fitted Chinese-made YJ-1 missiles to F-4 Phantom aircraft and conducted trial launches in 1997. It is also believed that Iran may be manufacturing YJ-1 missiles under the project name Karus. Since Iran is not known to operate F-4 aircraft anymore, no reliable information exists about the continuance of the Karus program or any variants thereof.[18] Iran also demonstrated a new missile that it called the Qassed or "Messenger" that its F-4Es could carry in pairs and which Iran said was a 2,000-pound, rocket-assisted, precision-guided standoff weapon that could be used to attack both land and naval targets.

IRANIAN AIRCRAFT DEVELOPMENT

Iran is producing light turboprop aircraft and a light utility helicopter. It is making enough progress so that it will probably be able to produce a jet trainer and heavier helicopters, but it is unclear how effective it can be in producing modern combat aircraft.[19] Iran has some ambitious claims about aircraft production that it had not as yet backed up with confirmed production and deployments.

Russian firms and the Iranian government tried to reach an agreement over license production of the MiG-29, but repeated attempts have failed. Likely due to the difficulty the regime has had in procuring new aircraft, Iran has been developing three new attack aircraft. The indigenous design and specifics of one of the fighters in development, the Shafagh, were unveiled at the Iran Airshow in 2002.

The Shafagh seems to be a single engine fighter-trainer with some features similar to the Yak-130, but Iran Defense Net reports that it is a single-engined, tandem two-seat aircraft that resembles the Yak-130 from its nose to just aft of the wings' trailing edges, "but has a twin-tail design similar to the defunct Polish 'Skorpion' ground attack aircraft. The wing area is larger and the angle of sweep appears more pronounced than the Yak jet trainer, presenting the possibility of the aircraft being capable of sustained supersonic speeds of perhaps just over Mach 1 . . . It is equipped with digital avionics and MFD, marking a major step forward in the technology employed by Iran's aviation industries...A light interceptor/ground attack version with an uprated engine is on the cards to fill the gap created by the retirement of the IRIAF's F-5E/F Tiger IIs."[20] Some sources indicate Iran hopes to have a prototype by 2008, though it is unclear what the production numbers will be and what the real-world timetable for deployment may be.[21]

Little is known about the other two fighters in development, the Saegheh and the Azarakhsh. They have been reportedly derived from the F-5F, and some sources report the Azarakhsh is a scaled-up version of that fighter that is 10–15 percent larger. The Azarakhsh is said to use an upgraded version of N-019 Topaz (N-019ME) radar. Iran's acting commander of the air force said that Azarakhsh had reached mass-production stage on May 17, 2000, but it is unclear that any had entered active Iranian Air Force inventory. Other sources state that the Saeghe may have replaced the Azarkash development program. Reportedly, the Saeghe made its maiden flight in the summer of 2005, and pictures have been reported depicting a Saeghe fighter flying in an exercise in August and September 2006.[22]

Other claims have been made, however, that the Azarakhsh may be an advanced fighter type being built by Malek Ashtar and is the same as the M-ATF air superiority fighter. There are some reports that Iran is experimenting with composites in the Azarakhsh and is seeking to give it a locally modified beyond-visual-range radar for air-to-air combat.[23]

The Saeghe is being developed by MATSA (Iran's Air Force Technology and Electronics Center) at Mehrabad. It seems to be a modified F-5 fighter that has been rebuilt in a twin-fin configuration. Iran has already shown it can overhaul and modify some of its inventory of F-5As and F-5Bs.[24]

According to some reports, Iran has developed another indigenous fighter design called the Owj (Zenith). The Federation of American Scientists reports that Iran's Defense Industries Organization has announced plans for the production of the propeller-driven Parastu (Swallow) and jet-powered Dorna (Lark) training aircraft, and there are also claims of the testing of the first Iranian-designed helicopter.[25] Iran also has some indigenous capability to produce combat aircraft and drones.

One source notes that Iran may have manufactured some advanced avionics systems that were developed by Russia for the MiG-I-2000 fighter. Apparently, Russia no longer pursues the development of this aircraft, but may have cooperated with Iran in the early stages of development and/or transferred expertise.[26]

Iranian sources in early 2007 reported that the Iranian Defense Minister inaugurated an overhaul facility for the Mi-171 helicopter. The Mi-171 is a vintage Russian-designed transport/utility helicopter. At the event, he was quoted as saying, "At present, we are planning, preparing designs and carrying out studies on the helicopter."[27]

IRANIAN AIR FORCE READINESS AND EFFECTIVENESS

In spite of Iran's efforts, readiness and force quality remain major issues. The Iranian Air Force still has many qualitative weaknesses, and it is far from clear that its current rate of modernization can offset the aging of its Western-supplied aircraft and the qualitative improvements in U.S. and southern Gulf forces. The air force also faces serious problems in terms of sustainability, command and control, and training. In addition, Iran has a pilot quality problem.

Many of its U.S.-trained pilots were purged at some point during the Revolution. Its other U.S.-trained pilots and ground-crew technicians have aged to the point where most have probably long retired from service. Iran lacks advanced test range, combat simulation capabilities, and aggressor squadron training, and Iranian pilots have not had advanced air-to-air combat and air attack training for more than 15 years. One source does, however, report that Iranian pilots receive about 180 flight hours annually.[28] This number could indicate a comparatively high amount of training; yet it is not clear what the quality of the flight training is, and the number has not been confirmed by other sources.

Iran has only token numbers of advanced strike aircraft, and these consist of export versions of the SU-24 and dual-capable MiG-29s that do not compete with modern U.S. aircraft or the most modern aircraft in southern Gulf forces. Exercises like the Holy Prophet and Force of Zolfaghar exercises that Iran held in 2006 show that it is slowly improving its capability for joint land-air and air-sea operations. Iranian exercises and statements provide strong indications that Iran would like to develop an advanced air-defense system, the ability to operate effectively in long-range maritime patrol and attack missions, effective joint warfare capabilities, and strike/attack forces with the ability to penetrate deep into Iraq, the southern Gulf States, and other neighboring powers.

Iran's exercises, military literature, and procurement efforts also make it clear that its air planners understand the value of airborne early warning and C^4I systems, the value of airborne intelligence and electronic warfare platforms, the value of remotely piloted vehicles, and the value of airborne refueling.

As is the case with its army, the Iranian Air Force and land-based air-defense forces have benefited by Iran's cooperation with Syria and Syrian transfers of Russian methods, tactics, and technology in areas like signals intelligence (SIGINT), electronic intelligence, communications intelligence (COMINT), and command and control.[29] Iran has even sought to create its own satellite program.[30] Israel and other sources claim that Iran has several joint SIGINT bases in Syria and that Iran and Syria established a joint intelligence center with Hezbollah during the Israel-Hezbollah War in the summer of 2006.

Further, the air force's efforts at sheltering and dispersal indicate that it understands the vulnerability of modern air facilities and the standoff attack capabilities of advanced air forces like those of the United States.

The Iranian Air Force must also deal with the fact that its primary challenge now consists of the U.S., British, and Saudi air forces. They are high-technology air forces that operate the airborne warning and control system, have some of the most advanced electronic warfare and targeting systems in the world, and have full refueling capability. They use sophisticated, computer-aided aggressor training and have all of the range and training facilities for beyond-visual-range combat and standoff attacks with air-to-surface munitions.

Iran has no advanced airborne control system capabilities, although it does have maritime patrol aircraft with some capability for such missions and may be able to use the radars on its F-14s to support other aircraft from the rear. According to the IISS, Iran does still have five operational P-3MP Orions and may have made its captured Iraqi IL-76 Candid AEW aircraft operational. These assets would give it some basic airborne warning and command and control capabilities, but these are obsolescent to obsolete systems. They are also likely to be highly vulnerable to electronic warfare and countermeasures, and long-range air-to-air missile attack, even with Iranian modifications and updates. There are some reports Iran may be seeking a version of the Russian AN-140 AEW aircraft, but these could not be deployed much before 2015.[31]

Its overall C^{4}I system is an inadequate mix of different sensors, communications, and data processing systems. It has limited electronic warfare capabilities by U.S. standards, although it may be seeking to acquire two Beriev A-50 Mainstay Airborne Early Warning (AEW) aircraft and has converted some aircraft to provide a limited ELINT/SIGINT capability.

Iran's air-defense aircraft consist of a maximum operational strength of two squadrons of 25 export versions of the MiG-29A and two squadrons of 25-30 F-14As. The export version of the MiG-29A has significant avionics limitations and vulnerability to countermeasures, and it is not clear if Iran has any operational Phoenix air-to-air missiles for its F-14As or has successfully modified its I-Hawk missiles for air-to-air combat. The AWG-9 radar on the F-14 has significant long-distance sensor capability in a permissive environment, but is a U.S.–made system in a nearly 30-year-old configuration that is now vulnerable to countermeasures.

Iran might risk using its fighters and AEW aircraft against an Israeli strike. It seems doubtful that Israel could support a long-range attack unit with the air defense and electronic assets necessary to provide anything like the air defense and air-defense suppression assets that would support a U.S. strike. A U.S. strike could almost certainly destroy any Iranian effort to use fighters, however, and destroy enough Iranian surface-to-air missile defenses to create a secure corridor for penetrating into Iran and against key Iranian installations. The United States could then maintain such a corridor indefinitely with restrikes.

While Iran practices realistic individual intercept training, it fails to practice effective unit or force-wide tactics and has shown only limited capability to fly large numbers of sorties with its U.S.–supplied aircraft on even a surge basis. It has limited refueling capabilities—although it has four B-707 tanker/transporters and may have converted other transports. The Iranian Air Force lacks advanced training facilities and has only limited capability to conduct realistic training for beyond-visual-range combat and standoff attacks with air-to-surface munitions. Ground-crew training and proficiency generally seem mediocre—although the layout of Iranian air bases, aircraft storage and parking, the deployment of equipment for maintenance cycles, and the other physical signs of air unit activity are generally better organized than those of most Middle Eastern air forces.

IRANIAN LAND-BASED AIR DEFENSE

If one looks at Iran's overall air defense capability, Figure 6.7 shows that Iran has force "quantity"—at least in terms of total holdings versus operational weapons. Its air defenses, however, have limited "quality." In addition to its fighter defenses, Iran seems to have assigned about 12,000–15,000 men in its air force to land-based air-defense functions, including at least 8,000 regulars and 4,000 IRGC personnel. It is not possible to distinguish clearly between the major air-defense weapons holdings of the regular air force and of the IRGC, but the air force appears to operate most major surface-to-air missile (SAM) systems.

Total holdings seem to include 30 Improved Hawk fire units (12 battalions/150+ launchers), 45–55 SA-2 and HQ-2J/23 (CSA-1) launchers (Chinese-made equivalents of the SA-2), and possibly 25 SA-6 launchers. The air force also had three Soviet-made long-range SA-5 units with a total of 10–15 launchers—enough for six sites. Iran has developed and deployed its own domestically manufactured SAM dubbed the Shahab Thaqeb. The SAM requires a four-wheeled trailer for deployment and closely resembles the R440 SAM.[32]

Iran's holdings of lighter air defense weapons include five Rapier squadrons with 30 Rapier fire units, 5–10 Chinese FM-80 launchers, 10–15 Tigercat fire units, and a few RBS-70s. Iran also holds large numbers of man-portable SA-7s, HN-5s, and SA-14s, plus about 2,000 anti-aircraft guns—including some Vulcans and 50–60 radar-guided and self-propelled ZSU-23-4 weapons.[33] Some of these weapons have been exported to Hezbollah in Lebanon and Shi'ite fighters in Iraq. One source claims that Tehran supplied Hezbollah with SA-7s, SA-14s, SA-16s, and Mithaq-1s (based on Chinese QW-1) man-portable SAMs.[34]

It is not clear which of these lighter air-defense weapons were operated by the army, the IRGC, or the air force. The IRGC clearly had larger numbers of man-portable surface-to-air launchers, including some Stingers that it had obtained from Afghanistan. It almost certainly had a number of other light air-defense guns as well.

There are no authoritative data on how Iran now deploys its land-based air defenses, but Iran seems to have deployed its new SA-5s to cover its major ports, oil facilities, and Tehran. It seems to have concentrated its Improved Hawks and Soviet- and Chinese-made SA-2s around Tehran, Isfahan, Shiraz, Bandar Abbas, Kharg Island, Bushehr, Bandar Khomeini, Ahwaz, Dezful, Kermanshah, Hamadan, and Tabriz.

Although Iran has made some progress in improving and updating its weapons, sensors, and electronic warfare capability and has learned much from Iraq's efforts to defeat U.S. enforcement of the "no-fly zones" during 1992–2003, its current defenses are outdated and poorly integrated. All of its major systems are based on technology that is now more than 35 years old, and all are vulnerable to use of active and passive countermeasures. Iran is trying to reduce this vulnerability by improving

Figure 6.7   Gulf Land-Based Air-Defense Systems, 2007

Country	Major SAM	Light SAM	AA Guns
Bahrain	8 I-Hawk	60 RBS-70 18 Stinger 7 Crotale	15 Oerlikon 35 mm 12 L/70 40 mm
Iran	2,400 I-HAWK MIM-23B 10 SA-5 45 HQ-2J (SA-2) SA-2 15 TigercatFIM-92A Stinger 29 Tor-M1	SA-7/14/16, HQ-7 HN-5 30 Rapier FM-80 (Ch Crotale) Oerlikon SA-7 Grail	1,700 Guns ZU-23, ZSU-23-4, ZSU-57-2, KS-19 ZPU-2/4, M-1939
Iraq	SA-2 SA-3 SA-6	Roland 1,500 SA-7 850 (SA-8 SA-9, SA-13, SA-14, SA-16)	6,000 Guns ZSU-23-4 23 mm, M-1939 37 mm, ZSU-57-2 SP, 57 mm 85 mm, 100 mm, 130 mm
Kuwait	24 I-Hawk Phase III MIM-23B 5/40 Patriot	12 Aspede 48 Starburst	35-mm Oerlikon
Oman	None	Mistral 2 SP 34 SA-7 Grail 34 Javelin 40 Rapier	10 GDF-005 35 mm (with Skyguard) 4 ZU-23-2 23 mm 12 L/60 40 mm
Qatar	None	10 Blowpipe 12 FIM-92A Stinger 9 Roland II 20 SA-7 24 Mistral	
Saudi	16/128 (2,048) I-Hawk 4-6/16-24 (640) PAC-2 17/68 (1,156) Shahine 2-4/160 PAC-2 launchers 17 ANA/FPS-117 radar	40+ Crotale 500 Stinger (ARMY) 500 Mistral (ADF) 500 Redeye (ARMY) 500 Redeye (ADF) 73-141 Shahine static 500 Stinger (ADF) 400 FIM-92A Avenger	50 AMX-30SA 30 mm 92 M-163 Vulcan 20 mm 70 L-70 40 mm (in store) 850 AMX-30SA

UAE	5/30 I-Hawk Bty.	20+ Blowpipe	42 M-3VDA 20 mm SP
		20 Mistral	20 GCF-BM2 30 mm
		12 Rapier	Javelin
		9 Crotale	
		13 RBS-70	
		Igla (SA-16)	
Yemen	Some SA-2, SA3, SA-6	Some SA-7, SA-9, SA13,	50 M-167 20 mm
	SA-7, SA-9, SA-13,	SA-14	20 M-163 Vulcan 20 mm
	SA-14	800 SA-7/9/13/14	50 ZSU-23-4 23 mm
			100 ZU-23-2 23 mm
			150 M-1939 23 mm
			120 S-60 37 mm
			40 KS-12 85 mm

Sources: International Institute for Strategic Studies (IISS), *Military Balance, 2007; Periscope;* JCSS, *Middle East Military Balance;* Jane's, *Sentinel Security Assessment;* and Jane's, *Defense Weekly.* Some data were adjusted or estimated by the authors.

its C^4I systems, jamming, tactics, and radars, but faces major limitations on what it can do without major new transfers of modern, advanced weapons and technology from a source like Russia.

Iran's air-defense forces are too widely spaced to provide more than limited air defense for key bases and facilities, and many lack the missile launcher strength to be fully effective. This is particularly true of Iran's SA-5 (S-200) sites, which provide long-range, medium-to-high altitude coverage of key coastal installations. These units seem to have been upgraded to the S-200VE "Vega-E" by BeloRussian special-ists.[35] However, too few launchers are scattered over too wide an area to prevent rel-atively rapid suppression.

Iran also lacks the low-altitude radar coverage, overall radar net, command and control assets, sensors, resistance to sophisticated jamming and electronic counter-measures, and systems integration capability necessary to create an effective air-defense net. Its land-based air defenses must operate largely in the point defense mode. Iran lacks the battle management systems and its data links are not fast and effective enough to allow it to take maximum advantage of the overlapping coverage of some of its missile systems—a problem further complicated by the problems in trying to net different systems supplied by Britain, China, Russia, and the United States. Iran's missiles and sensors are most effective at high to medium altitudes against aircraft with limited penetrating and jamming capability.

This situation may, however, change in the future, and improvements in Iran's land-based air defenses could be a factor in the timing of any U.S. or Israeli strikes. Iran purchased 20 Russian 9K331 TOR-M-1 (SA-15 Gauntlet) self-propelled surface-to-air missiles in December 2005.[36] This system was delivered and test-fired by Iran in January 2007. Global Security indicates that this is a modern short-range missile that has the capability to simultaneously attack two targets using a relatively high-powered and jam-resistant radar and has "electronic beam control and vertically launched missiles able to maintain high speed and maneuverability inside an entire engagement envelope; the high degree of automation of combat operation provided by the electronic equipment suite."[37] It is said to be capable of detecting targets at a distance of 25 kilometers and attacking them at a maximum distance of 12 kilometers. For what it is worth, Russian sources claim that the TOR is much more efficient than similar systems like France's Crotale and Britain's Rapier. According to Russian sources, the TORs will be deployed with priority first in Isfahan and then Bushehr, Tehran, and in the east of the country.[38]

The basic combat formation is a firing battery consisting of four transporter-launchers and radar (TLARs) and the Rangir battery command post. The TLAR carries eight ready missiles stored in two containers holding four missiles each. It is claimed to have an effective range of 1,500 to 12,000 meters against targets flying at altitudes between 10 and 6,000 meters. The maximum maneuvering load factor limit on the weapon is said to be 30 "Gs."[39] It should be noted that Russian manufacturer claims are no less exaggerated than those of European and U.S. manufacturers.

The system is designed to be effective against low-flying aircraft and the TOR is too range limited to have a major impact on U.S. stealth attack capability, although its real-world performance against cruise missiles still has to be determined. It might have more point defense lethality against regular Israeli and U.S. strike fighters like the F-15 and the F-16 using precision-guided bombs, but would be lethal only against such aircraft with standoff air-to-surface missiles if it could be deployed in the flight path in ways that were not detected before the attack profile was determined.

Iran also announced in February 2006 that it was mass producing a new man-portable, low-altitude, short-range air-defense missile called the Mithaq-2 (along with several other weapons and military exercise announcements that seemed timed to try to deter U.S. or Israeli military action).[40] The Mithaq-2 was said to be electronic warfare and infrared (IR)-flare resistant and seemed to be based on the Chinese QW-1 Vanguard.

If the Mithaq-2 is a copy of the Chinese QW-1, it is an IR-homing missile introduced in the mid-1990s. It may, however, be a variant of the QW-2 with an improved IR seeker. China claims it has an effective range of 500-5,000 meters at target altitudes of 30-4,000 meters. The maximum maneuvering load factor limit on the weapon is said to be 30 Gs. In spite of Iranian claims, it does not seem superior to the Russian SA-14s already in Iranian inventory and is too short ranged to have more than a minimal deterrent effect.[41]

Some reports indicate that Iran is seeking more modern Soviet SA-300 or S-400 missiles and to use Russian systems to modernize its entire air-defense system. One source does claim that in addition to the above-mentioned weapon systems, Iran has received the S-300 PMU and that it also operates the SA-6 system. If Iran could acquire, deploy, and bring such systems to a high degree of readiness, they would substantially improve Iranian capabilities. A report in *Jane's* claims that Iran is building surface-to-air missile defense zones around its nuclear facilities that will use a single battery of S-300PMU (SA-10) missiles to defend the Bushehr reactor and will deploy the S-300V (SA-12b) to provide wide area defense coverage of other targets that it will mix with the TOR-M1 to provide low-altitude point defense.

This is a logical Iranian approach to improving its defenses, and Iran has sought to purchase the S-300 in the past. It seems to have advanced electronic warfare capabilities, sensors, computer systems, and software. The SA-10 is reported to be able to intercept aircraft at a maximum slant range of 32,000 to 43,200 meters and a maximum effective defense perimeter of 150 kilometers (90 miles). The minimum effective interception altitude is claimed to be 10 meters. One variant of the missile is reported to have some ballistic missile defense capability and be able to engage ballistic missile targets at ranges of up to 40 kilometers (25 miles). Each battery is said to have a load of 32 missile rounds on its launchers, a battery deployment time as low as five minutes, and the ability to fire three missiles per second. A standard battery consists of an 83M6E2 command post, up to six 90Zh6E2 air-defense missile complexes, 48N6E2 air-defense missiles, and technical support facilities.[42]

If Iran were to get the S-300V (SA-12a and SA-12b), it would get a system with far more advanced sensors, electronic warfare capabilities, and significant point defense capabilities against ballistic missiles.[43] A Russian S-300V brigade has the following components: 9M82 SA-12b Giant missiles (two per launcher) and TELAR, 9M83 SA-12a Gladiator missiles (four per launcher), and TELAR, Giant and Gladiator launcher/loader vehicles, 9S15 Bill Board Surveillance Radar system, 9S19 High Screen Sector Radar system, 9S32 Grill Pan Guidance Radar system, and 9S457 Command Station. The SA-12a is a dual-role anti-missile and anti-aircraft missile with a maximum range between 75 and 90 kilometers. The SA-12b GIANT missile is configured as an ATBM (Anti-Tactical Ballistic Missile) role with a longer maximum range of between 100 and 200 kilometers. Each unit can detect up to 200 targets, track as many as 70 targets, and designate 24 of the targets to the brigade's four GRILL PAN radar systems for engagement.[44]

Iran would benefit even more if it could obtain the more advanced 300PMU3, which is more generally called the S-400, as well as the SA-20 or Triumf. There is no way to know how effective this system would be against stealth aircraft and the range of capabilities the United States can deploy, without access to classified information. Global Security describes the system as follows:

The *Triumf* S-400, also known as the S-300PMU3, is a new generation of air defense and theater anti-missile weapon developed by the Almaz Central Design Bureau as an evolution of the S-300PMU [SA-10] family. This new system is intended to detect and destroy airborne targets at a distance of up to 400 km (2- 2.5 times greater than the previous S-300PMU system). The main difference between the PMU-2 and the S-400 is greater engagement range of the latter, about 250 mi. against aircraft versus 125 mi., a larger number of targets it can track and improved electronic counter-countermeasures. The *Triumf* system includes radars capable of detecting low-signature targets. And the anti-missile capability of the system has been increased to the limits established by the ABM Treaty demarcation agreements—it can intercept targets with velocities of up to 4.8 km/sec, corresponding to a ballistic missile range of 3,500 km.

The system was developed through the cooperation of the Almaz Central Design Bureau, Fakel Machine Building Design Bureau, Novosibirsk Scientific Research Institute of Instruments, St. Petersburg Design Bureau of Special Machine Building and other enterprises.

The Fakel Machine Building Design Bureau has developed two new missiles for *Triumf.*

- The "big" missile [designation otherwise unknown] has a range of up to 400 km and will be able to engage "over-the-horizon [OTH]" targets using a new seeker head developed by Almaz Central Design Bureau. This seeker can operate in both a semiactive and active mode, with the seeker switched to a search mode on ground command and homing on targets independently. Targets for this missile include airborne early warning and control aircraft as well as jammers.

- The 9M96 medium-range missile, which comes in two versions (9M96E and 9M96E2), is designed to destroy aircraft and air-delivered weapons at ranges in excess of 120 km. The missile is small—considerably lighter than the ZUR 48N6Ye used in the S-300PMU1 systems and the *Favorit.* The missile is equipped with an active homing head and has an estimated single shot kill probability of 0.9 for manned aircraft and 0.8 for unmanned maneuvering aircraft. a gas-dynamic control system enables the 9M96 missile to maneuver at altitudes of up to 35 km at forces of over 20g, which permits engagement of non-strategic ballistic missiles with trajectory speed up to 4.8km/s. One 9M96 modification will become the basic long-range weapon of Air Force combat aircraft, and may become the standardized missile for air defense SAM systems, ship-launched air defense missile systems, and fighter aircraft. The 9M96E2 missiles is based on all-new components, use new high-energy solid fuel and an advanced guidance and control system that has made it possible to minimize their size. The 9M96E2 missile can intercept all types of aircraft, including tactical ballistic and medium-range theater missiles flying at altitudes from 5 meters to 30 kilometers. Their exceptionally high accuracy is ensured by the missile's main secret, the so-called transverse control engine, which rules out misses during the final approach trajectory. The transverse control engine is still without parallel in the world. Russia's top-of-the-line 9M96E2 guided air defense missile is being marketed by Russia's state-owned arms trader Rosvooruzhenye. A mockup of the missile was set up at an Athens arms exhibition in October 1998.

These new missiles can be accommodated on the existing SAM system launchers of the S-300PMU family. A container with four 9M96's can be installed in place of one container with the 5V55 or 48N6 missiles, and thus the standard launcher intended for four 48N6Ye missiles can accommodate up to 16 9M96Ye missiles. The *Triumf* air defense system can also use 48N6E missiles of the S-300PMU-1 system and 48N6E2 missiles of the S-300PMU-2 *Favorit* system, making it possible to smoothly change over to the production of the new generation system. It will include the previous control complex, though supporting not six but eight SAM systems, as well as multifunctional radar systems illumination and guidance, launchers, and associated autonomous detection and target indication systems.

The state tests of the S-400 system reportedly began in 1999, with the initial test on 12 February 1999 using the 48N6E missiles of the S-300PMU-1 system. As of May 1999 the testing of S-400 air defense system was reportedly nearing completion at Kapustin Yar, with the first systems of this kind to be delivered to the Moscow Air Force and Air Defense District in the fourth quarter of 1999. However, as of August 1999 government testing of the S-400 was slated to begin at the end of 1999, with the first system complex slated for delivery in late 2000. The sources of the apparent one-year delay in the program are unclear, though they may involve some combination of technical and financial problems with this program. Russian air defense troops conducted a test of the new anti-aircraft missile system S-400 on 07 April 2000. At that time, Air Force Commander Anatoly Kornukov said that serial production of the new system would begin in June 2000. Kornukov said air defense troops would get one S-400 launcher system by the end of 2000, but it would be armed with missiles of the available S-300 system.

On condition of normal funding, radars with an acquisition range of 500-600 km should become operational by 2002-2003. However, other sources report that while it was ordered by the Defence Ministry, the military has nothing to pay for it with, so it is unclear when the Russian military will get this new weapon.[45]

The S-400 would be far more expensive than the S-300, however, and its production and development status is uncertain. Making it effective would also require large numbers of systems and its integration into a fully modern C^4I, sensor, and radar network.

It is doubtful that Iran has taken delivery on any variant of the S-300 systems, or has yet been able to buy any variant of the S-300 or S-400 from Russia. In February 2006 the Russian Minister of Defense flatly denied any such sales had taken place.[46] Even if such systems are delivered, their real-world performance will be uncertain. In the past, Russia has also been careful to control some critical aspects of its weapons exports and sell degraded export versions.

FORCE TRENDS AND SUMMARY CAPABILITIES

Figure 6.8 shows that Iran has not modernized the bulk of its air and air-defense forces since the fall of the Shah in 1979 and has made only limited changes in many of its holdings since the end of the Iran-Iraq War in 1988. Iran's air- and land-based air-defense forces are only marginally better able to survive in air-to-air combat than Iraq's were before 2003.

Iran's command and control system has serious limitations in terms of secure communications, vulnerability to advanced electronic warfare, netting, and digital data transfer. Deliveries of the TOR-M1 are improving some aspects of its point defense capability, but have limited probable effectiveness against aircraft with stealth features and lack the range to deal with aircraft with modern long-range precision-guided weapons.

Figure 6.8   Iranian Air Force's Force Structure Trends, 1990–2007

	1990	2000	2005	2006	2007
Manpower	35,000	50,000	52,000	52,000	52,000
Active	35,000	50,000	52,000	52,000	52,000
Conscripts	0	0	0	0	0
Fighter	15	114	74	153	118
F-7M	0	24	24	24	24
F-14	15	60	25	25	25
MiG-29	0	30	25	0	25
F1-E Mirage	0	0	0	24	24
F-5B	0	0	0	20	20
F-5E	0	0	0	60	0
Fighter Ground Attack	104	140	186	102	168
F-4D/E	35	50	65	65*	65
F-5E/F	45	60	60	0	60
Ch J-6	24	0	0	0	0
Su-24	0	30	30	30	30
Su-25K	0	0	7	7	13
Mirage F1-E	0	0	24	0	0
Maritime Reconnaissance	2	5	3	5	5
P-3F	2	0	0	0	0
P-3MP	0	0	3	5	5
C-130H-MP	0	5	0	0	0
Reconnaissance	8	15	6	6+	6+
F-5	5	0	0	0	0
RF-4E	3	15	6	6+	6+
Transport	59	63	64+	65+	103+
Boeing 707	14	3	3	3	3
Boeing 747F	9	7	5	5	4
Boeing 727	0	1	1	1	1
C-130E/H	20	18	18	17	17
F-27	9	15	10	10	10
Commander 690	3	3	3	3	3
Falcon	3	4	1	1	1

PC-6B	0	10	10	10	10
Y-7	0	2	2	9	2
Y-12(II)	0	0	9	3	9
Jetstar	0	0	2	2	2
Il-76	0	0	Some	1+	1+
Iran-140 Fatanz	0	0	0	0	40
Utility	0	0	0	12	12
TB-21	0	0	0	8	8
TB-200	0	0	0	4	4
Helicopters	55 (none armed)	53 (none armed)	34 (none armed)	34+	34+
AB-206	2	2	2	2	2
Bell 214C	39	39	30	30	30
CH-47	10	5	2	2+	2+
S-61A	2	0	0	0	0
Shabaviz 2-75	0	0	0	Some	Some
Shabaviz2061	0	0	0	Some	Some
Training	84	132	151	119	119
F-33A/C/V	26	26	20	20	20
T-33	7	7	7	7	7
PC-7	46	40	40	40	40
EMB-312	5-6	15	15	15	15
MiG-29B	0	5	0	Some	0
FT-7	0	5	15	0	0
F-5B	0	20	20	0	0
TB-21	0	8	8	8	0
TB-200	0	4	4	4	0
MFI-17 Mushshaq	0	0	22	15	22
JJ-7	0	0	0	15	15
Surface-to-Air Missiles	105	190+	220+	2,500+	250
I-Hawk	0	100	150	2,400	150+
Rapier	30	30	30	30	30
Tigercat	25	15	15	15	15
SA-2/HQ-2J	50	45	15	45	45

SA-5	0	0	10	10	10
SA-7	0	Some	Some	Some	Some
FM-80 (Crotale)	0	Some	Some	Some	Some
Air-to-Air Missiles	Some	Some	Some	Some	Some
AIM-7 Sparrow	Some	Some	Some	Some	Some
AIM-9 Sidewinder	Some	Some	Some	Some	Some
AIM-54 Phoenix	Some	Some	Some	Some	Some
AA-8	0	Some	Some	Some	Some
AA-10	0	Some	Some	Some	Some
AA-11	0	Some	Some	Some	Some
PL-2A	0	0	Some	Some	Some
PL-7	0	Some	Some	Some	Some
Air-to-Surface Missiles	Some	Some	Some	Some	Some
AS-10	0	Some	Some	Some	Some
AS-11	0	Some	Some	Some	Some
AS-12	Some	0	0	0	0
AS-14	0	Some	Some	Some	Some
C-801K	0	0	Some	Some	Some
AGM-65A	0	Some	3,000	Some	Some
AGM-84 Harpoon	Some	0	0	0	0
Air-Defense Guns	0	0	Some	Some	Some
23 mm	0	0	Some	Some	Some
ZSU-23	0	0	Some	Some	Some
37 mm	0	0	Some	Some	Some
Oerlikon	0	0	Some	Some	Some

* IISS states total number of F-4 aircraft as 260+ yet does not include these in the total number of FGA (102).

Sources: IISS, *Military Balance,* various editions, including 1989–1990, 1999–2000, 2004–2005, 2005–2006, 2006, and 2007.

Iran does use both its air force and its air-defense forces in both exercises with an offensive character (usually conducted under the cover of a counteroffensive) and in defensive exercises that seem designed to deal with a U.S. invasion. The details of such exercises are unclear, but they seem to involve efforts to support the navy and the naval branch of the IRGC with air cover and air-launched strikes against U.S. vessels and forces and defense in depth of key military, defense industrial, and government facilities.

Iran practices dispersal and concealment of its air assets, both fixed and rotary wing. It also seems to have examined possible first-strike options and the use of fighters and surface-to-air missile defenses to create "traps" for U.S. and other attacking aircraft using the tactics similar to those used in Serbia and Iraq (which had little success). It has made extensive use of optical fibers and has developed its own approaches to secure communications, upgrade avionics, and linking ground-based radars to provide remote and "pop up" capabilities for its surface-to-air missile units.

It may have practiced emergency dispersal and concealment of its surface-to-air missile and other anti-aircraft forces and weapons. It does have contingency plans for dispersal of its lighter and man-portable surface-to-air missiles and air-defense weapons. The army, the IRGC, and the Basij practice anti-helicopter tactics and "ambushes."

It is far from clear, however, how effective the technology and tactics are in any of these aspects of Iranian force development. Given the gap in technology and professional experience, they may have limited effectiveness at best.

The Iranian Navy

The Iranian Navy had some 18,000 men in 2007. According to the International Institute for Strategic Studies (IISS), this total included two marine brigades of some 2,600 men and a 2,000-man naval aviation force. It has bases at Bandar Abbas, Bushehr, Kharg Island, Bandar Anzali, Chah Bahar, Bander-e Mahshahar, and Bander-e Khomeini, most of them opposing the Saudi coast.

The naval forces had 3 fleet submarines, 3 frigates, 2 corvettes, 11 missile patrol craft, 5 mine warfare ships, over 60 coastal and inshore patrol craft, some miniature submarines, and 13 amphibious ships. Its naval aviation branch is one of the few air elements in any Gulf navy, having 6 maritime patrol aircraft and 13 armed helicopters. When combined with the Islamic Revolutionary Guards Corps (IRGC) naval branch, this brought the total maritime strength of Iran to 38,000 men, with significant capabilities for both regular naval and asymmetric naval warfare.

Figures 7.1 through 7.4 show that Iran's total strength is limited when compared to that of its southern Gulf neighbors, and such calculations again ignore the fact that the United States can decisively intervene with massively superior force at any time. Iran has given the modernization of its lighter naval forces some priority, but its major surface ships are all old vessels with limited refits and aging weapons and fire-control systems.

Since the end of the Iran-Iraq War, Iran has attempted to compensate for the weaknesses of its surface fleet by obtaining new anti-ship missiles and missile patrol craft from China. Some reports also indicate that it has acquired midget submarines from North Korea, submarines from Russia, and modern mines.

Iran has expanded the capabilities of the naval branch of the IRGC, acquired additional mine warfare capability, and upgraded some of its older surface ships. Iran's exercises have included a growing number of joint and combined arms exercises with the land forces and the air force.

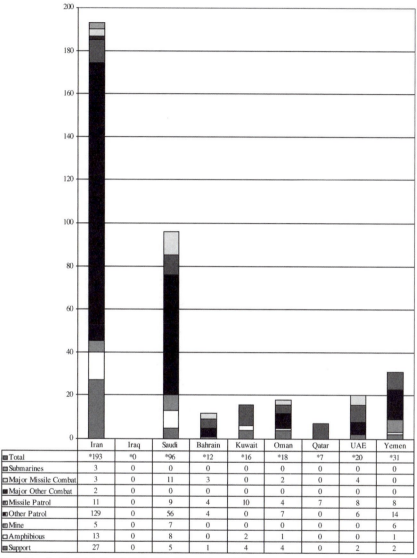

	Iran	Iraq	Saudi	Bahrain	Kuwait	Oman	Qatar	UAE	Yemen
■Total	*193	*0	*96	*12	*16	*18	*7	*20	*31
▨Submarines	3	0	0	0	0	0	0	0	0
▢Major Missile Combat	3	0	11	3	0	2	0	4	0
■Major Other Combat	2	0	0	0	0	0	0	0	0
▨Missile Patrol	11	0	9	4	10	4	7	8	8
▨Other Patrol	129	0	56	4	0	7	0	6	14
▨Mine	5	0	7	0	0	0	0	0	6
▢Amphibious	13	0	8	0	2	1	0	0	1
▨Support	27	0	5	1	4	4	0	2	2

Source: International Institute for Strategic Studies (IISS), *Military Balance, 2007.*

Figure 7.1   Gulf Naval Ships by Category, 2007

Iran has also improved its ports and strengthened its air defenses, while obtaining some logistic and technical support from nations like India and Pakistan. In August 2000, the Islamic republic announced that it had launched its first domestically produced light submarine, which is called the Al-Sabiha 15. Iran has stated it can be used for reconnaissance and laying mines.[1]

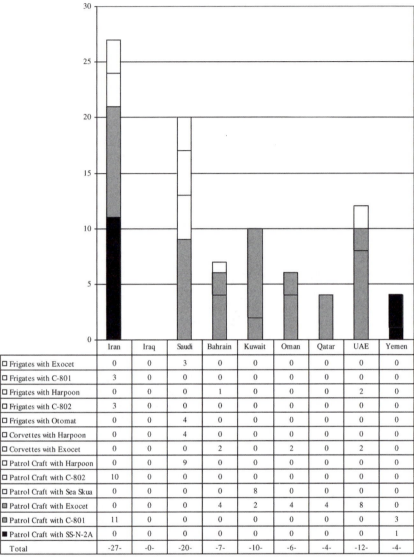

	Iran	Iraq	Saudi	Bahrain	Kuwait	Oman	Qatar	UAE	Yemen
☐ Frigates with Exocet	0	0	3	0	0	0	0	0	0
☐ Frigates with C-801	3	0	0	0	0	0	0	0	0
☐ Frigates with Harpoon	0	0	0	1	0	0	0	2	0
☐ Frigates with C-802	3	0	0	0	0	0	0	0	0
☐ Frigates with Otomat	0	0	4	0	0	0	0	0	0
☐ Corvettes with Harpoon	0	0	4	0	0	0	0	0	0
☐ Corvettes with Exocet	0	0	0	2	0	2	0	2	0
☐ Patrol Craft with Harpoon	0	0	9	0	0	0	0	0	0
☐ Patrol Craft with C-802	10	0	0	0	0	0	0	0	0
☐ Patrol Craft with Sea Skua	0	0	0	0	8	0	0	0	0
▨ Patrol Craft with Exocet	0	0	0	4	2	4	4	8	0
▨ Patrol Craft with C-801	11	0	0	0	0	0	0	0	3
■ Patrol Craft with SS-N-2A	0	0	0	0	0	0	0	0	1
Total	-27-	-0-	-20-	-7-	-10-	-6-	-4-	-12-	-4-

Source: International Institute for Strategic Studies (IISS), *Military Balance, 2007.*

Figure 7.2   Gulf Warships with Anti-Ship Missiles, 2007

One source claims that Iran may try to compensate for its problems in facing superior U.S., British, and Gulf forces by deploying "thousands" of boats in "swarming" or saturation attacks with at least some sort of armament.[2] While such boats would not be part of the Iranian Navy and most of them would be poorly equipped

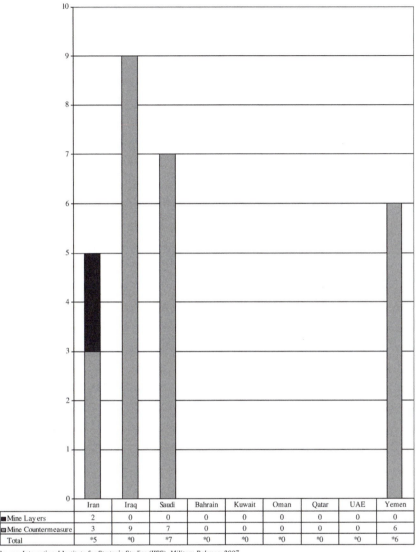

	Iran	Iraq	Saudi	Bahrain	Kuwait	Oman	Qatar	UAE	Yemen
■ Mine Layers	2	0	0	0	0	0	0	0	0
▨ Mine Countermeasure	3	9	7	0	0	0	0	0	6
Total	*5	*0	*7	*0	*0	*0	*0	*0	*6

Source: International Institute for Strategic Studies (IISS), *Military Balance, 2007.*

Figure 7.3   Gulf Mine Warfare Ships, 2007

to engage in combat operations, such assertions may offer insights into Iran's naval warfighting doctrine. Certainly, Iranian naval capabilities for asymmetric warfare need to be taken into account in considering both defense against unconventional operations in the Gulf and in planning operations that involve amphibious landings on Iran's Gulf coast.

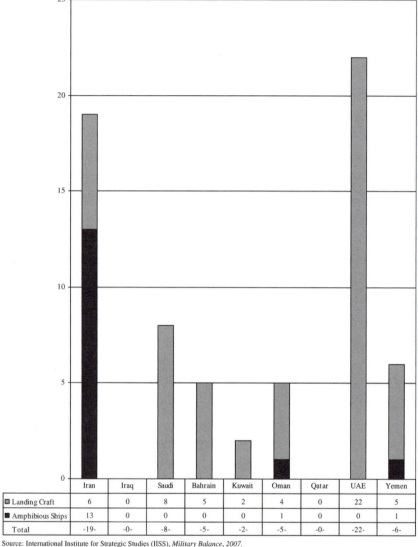

	Iran	Iraq	Saudi	Bahrain	Kuwait	Oman	Qatar	UAE	Yemen
▣ Landing Craft	6	0	8	5	2	4	0	22	5
■ Amphibious Ships	13	0	0	0	0	1	0	0	1
Total	-19-	-0-	-8-	-5-	-2-	-5-	-0-	-22-	-6-

Source: International Institute for Strategic Studies (IISS), *Military Balance, 2007.*

Figure 7.4   Gulf Amphibious Warfare Ships, 2007

MAJOR SURFACE SHIPS

Iran's major active surface ships are now all obsolete to obsolescent. Its main ships consist of two Bayandor- (PF103) class corvettes launched in 1963 and commissioned in 1964. These displace 1,135 tons fully loaded and have a crew of 140 each. They are armed with two 3-inch (76-mm) guns, two 40-mm anti-aircraft guns, and

20-mm guns. Their weapons control, search/track radars, and sonars have not been modernized since the mid-1960s, and their depth charge racks have been replaced by 20-mm guns. Some aspects of their electronic warfare capabilities, communications, and battle management system do seem to have been upgraded. The *Bayandor* and the *Naghdi* are probably the most active large surface ships in the Iranian Navy. However, neither is equipped with anti-ship and anti-air missiles, sophisticated weapons systems, sonars, or advanced electronic warfare equipment and sensors.[3]

Iran also has three somewhat more modern Alvand- (Vosper Mark 5) class frigates: the *Alvand,* the *Alborz,* and the *Sabalan.* These are 1,350-ton ships with a crew of 125 each. They were launched during 1967–1968 and commissioned during 1968–1969. Two have been upgraded to carry four Chinese C-802 anti-ship missiles each on twin launchers. The C-802 is a sea-skimming missile with a range of 120 kilometers, a 165-kilogram warhead, and a maximum speed of Mach 0.9. One ship retains the aging Sea Killer II launcher as its primary anti-ship weapon. This is an obsolete beam-riding radio command or optical tracking missile system with a 25-kilometer range and a small 70-kilogram warhead. It seems to have been fitted with BM-21 multiple rocket launchers for shore or offshore bombardment purposes.

The Alvand-class vessels also have one 76-mm (4.5-inch) gun with a maximum range of 25 kilometers. They have twin 35-mm guns, automatic loading anti-submarine mortars. All three ships are active, but the *Sabalan* took serious damage from the U.S. Navy during the Tanker War of 1987–1988, and the ships have not had a total refit since the early 1990s. The anti-submarine weapons (ASW) capabilities of these ships seem to be limited or nonfunctioning.

Reports state that in 2003 Iran announced that it would launch a 1,400 destroyer named *Mouj* and a 350-ton missile frigate named *Sina* the same year. So far Iran has not been known as having either vessel in service.[4]

IRAN'S SUBMARINE FORCES

Iran has attempted to offset some of the weaknesses of its major surface forces by obtaining three Type 877EKM Kilo-class submarines. The Kilo is a relatively modern and quiet submarine that first became operational in 1980. The Iranian Kilos are Type 877EKM export versions that are about 10 meters longer than the original Kilos and are equipped with advanced command and control systems. Each Type 877EKM has a teardrop hull coated with anechoic tiles to reduce noise. It displaces approximately 3,076 tons when submerged and 2,325 tons when surfaced. It is 72.6 meters long, 9.9 meters in beam, has a draught of 6.6 meters, and is powered by three 1,895 horsepower generator sets, one 5,900 shaft horse power electric motor, and one six-bladed propeller. It has a complement of 52 men and an endurance of 45 days. Its maximum submerged speed is 17 knots, and its maximum surface speed is 10 knots.

Each Kilo has six 530-mm torpedo tubes, including two wire-guided torpedo tubes. Only one torpedo can be wire guided at a time. The Kilo can carry a mix of 18 homing and wire-guided torpedoes or 24 mines. Russian torpedoes are available with ranges of 15–19 kilometers, speeds of 29–40 knots, and warheads with 100-, 205-, and 305-kilogram weights. Their guidance systems include active sonar homing, passive homing, wire guidance, and active homing. Some reports indicate that Iran bought over 1,000 modern Soviet mines along with the Kilos and that the mines were equipped with modern magnetic, acoustic, and pressure sensors. The Kilo has a remote anti-aircraft launcher with one preloaded missile in the sail, and Soviet versions have six SA-N-5 (Igla/SA-16) surface-to-air missiles stored inside. However, Russia supplied Iran only with the SA-14 (Strela). It can be modernized to carry Chinese YJ-1 or Russian Novator Alfa surface-to-surface missiles.[5]

The Kilo has a maximum surface speed of 10 knots, a maximum submerged speed of about 17 knots, a minimum submerged operating depth of about 30 meters, an operational diving depth of 240 meters, and a maximum diving depth of 300 meters. The submarine also has a surface cruise range of 3,000–6,000 nautical miles and a submerged cruise range of 400 nautical miles—depending on speed and combat conditions.[6]

In 2005, it was announced that Iran is developing a new class of submarines called Ghadir.[7] To this date no reliable information about that submarine's specifications has been available. According to Iranian media reports, Iran in May 2005 commenced production of a stealth submarine capable of firing missiles and torpedoes. An Iranian defense ministry spokesman referred to the new vessel as Ghadir.[8] In addition, Iran reportedly started producing mini-submarines in 2000. One of these vessels allegedly is called Al-Sabehat 15; it can accommodate two crew and three divers, and its mission supposedly is to plant mines and carry out reconnaissance missions.[9]

Iran's ability to use its submarines to deliver mines and fire long-range wake-homing torpedoes gives it a potential capability to strike in ways that make it difficult to detect or attack the submarine. Mines can be laid covertly in critical areas before a conflict, and the mines can be set to activate and deactivate at predetermined intervals in ways that make mining difficult to detect and sweep. Long-range homing torpedoes can be used against tanker-sized targets at ranges in excess of 10 kilometers and to attack slow-moving combat ships that are not on alert and/or that lack sonars and countermeasures.

At the same time, many Third World countries have found submarines to be difficult to operate. For example, Russia delivered the first two Kilos with two 120-cell batteries designed for rapid power surges rather than power over long periods. They proved to last only one to two years in warm waters versus five to seven years for similar batteries from India and the United Kingdom. Iran had to turn to India for help in developing batteries that are reliable in the warm waters of the Gulf. Iran has also had problems with the air conditioning in the ships, and their serviceability has been erratic. There are serious questions about crew capability and readiness, and all three submarines already need significant refits.

Iran faces significant operational problems in using its submarines in local waters. Many areas of the Gulf do not favor submarine operations. The Gulf is about 241,000 square kilometers in area and stretches 990 kilometers from the Shatt al-Arab to the Straits of Hormuz. It is about 340 kilometers wide at its maximum width and about 225 kilometers wide for most of its length. While heat patterns disturb surface sonars, they also disturb submarine sonars, and the advantage seems to be slightly in favor of sophisticated surface ships and maritime patrol aircraft.

The deeper parts of the Gulf are noisy enough to make ASW operations difficult, but large parts of the Gulf—including much of the southern Gulf on a line from Al Jubail across the tip of Qatar to about half way up the United Arab Emirates—are less than 20 meters deep. The water is deeper on the Iranian side, but the maximum depth of the Gulf—located about 30 kilometers south of Qeys Island—is still only 88 meters. This means that no point in the Gulf is deeper than the length of an SN-688 nuclear submarine. The keel to tower height of such a submarine alone is 16 meters. Even smaller coastal submarines have maneuver and bottom suction problems, cannot hide in thermoclines, or take advantage of diving for concealment or self-protection. This may explain why Iran is planning to relocate its submarines from Bandar Abbas, inside the Gulf, to Chah Bahar in the Gulf of Oman and is deepening the navy facility at Chah Bahar.[10]

The Strait of Hormuz at the entrance to the Gulf is about 180 kilometers long, but has a minimum width of 39 kilometers, and only the two deep-water channels are suitable for major surface ship or submarine operations. Further, a limited flow of fresh water and high evaporation makes the Gulf extremely salty. This creates complex underwater currents in the main channels at the Strait of Hormuz and complicates both submarine operations and submarine detection. There are some areas with considerable noise, but not of a type that masks submarine noise from sophisticated ASW detection systems of the kind operated by the United States and the United Kingdom. Further, the minimum operating depth of the Kilo is 45 meters, and the limited depth of the area around the Straits can make submarine operations difficult. Submarines are easier to operate in the Gulf of Oman, which is noisy enough to make ASW operations difficult, but such deployments would expose the Kilos to operations by U.S. and British nuclear attack submarines. It is unlikely that Iran's Kilos could survive for any length of time if hunted by a U.S. or British Navy air-surface-SSN (nuclear submarine) hunter-killer team.[11]

In any case, the effectiveness of Iran's submarines is likely to depend heavily on the degree of Western involvement in any ASW operation. If the Kilos do not face the U.S. or British ASW forces, they could operate in or near the Gulf with considerable impunity. If they did face U.S. and British forces, they might be able to attack a few tankers or conduct some mining efforts, but are unlikely to survive extended combat. This makes the Kilos a weapon that may be more effective in threatening Gulf shipping, or as a remote minelayer, than in naval combat. Certainly, Iran's purchase of the Kilos has already received close attention from the southern Gulf States and convinced them that they must take Iran more seriously.

Iran is also reported to have two types of miniature submarines for unconventional warfare operations. These seem to include at least three one-man submarines designed largely for covert underwater demolition and infiltration. Various sources state that in 1993, Iran acquired midget submarines from North Korea. Their quantity is not known; some sources estimate a total of eight submarines.[12] According to U.S. government estimates, another delivery of North Korean midget submarines took place in 2004. Admiral Lowell E. Jacoby reported this in a testimony in 2005 before the U.S. Senate Armed Services Committee:

> We judge Iran can briefly close the Strait of Hormuz, relying on a layered strategy using predominately naval, air, and some ground forces. Last year it purchased North Korean torpedo and missile-armed fast attack craft and midget submarines, making marginal improvements to this capability.[13]

Another observer states that the IRGC has midget submarines in its inventory. The vessels allegedly are used for sabotaging oil installations.[14] A *Jane's* report dated from February 2007 states that Iran possesses four mini-submarines and is building two more. The same report lists three submarines in service with the Iranian Navy and none in construction, thereby neither acknowledging the existence of a Ghadir submarine nor subsuming it under mini-submarines.[15]

ANTI-SHIP MISSILES AND SMALLER MISSILE CRAFT

Iran depends heavily on its ability to use smaller naval combat ships, especially ones carrying anti-ship missiles, to make up for its lack of airpower and modern major surface vessels. Iran's Western-supplied missiles are now all beyond their shelf life, and their operational status is uncertain. Iranian forces are now systems largely supplied by the People's Republic of China (PRC) and have replaced most Western-supplied missiles with Chinese ones.

The Iranian Navy's missile patrol boats include 9–11 operational 275-ton French-made Combattante II (Kaman-class) fast attack boats, out of an original total of 12. These boats are reported to be armed with two to four C-802 Sardine anti-ship missiles, one 76-mm gun, and to have maximum speeds of 37.5 knots.

The Kaman-class fast attack boats were originally armed with four U.S. Harpoon missiles, but their Harpoons may no longer be operational. At least five had been successfully converted with launchers that can carry two to four C-801/C-802s. Iran supplied the C-802s that Hezbollah successfully used against one of Israel's most modern Sa'ar Class-5 missile ships during the fighting in 2006.

The terminology for the C-801 and C-802 series of missiles in Iranian naval forces is confusing and sources contradict each other as to the variant used on given Iranian platforms. Some sources refer to all of these missiles as part of the CSS-N-4/YJ-1 series:[16]

- **The C-801/Raad.** Apparently, Iran has several hundred Raad in stock. One source notes that the missile "is clearly optimized for much longer ranges [than 150 kilometers], and Iran possesses sea-, and land-launched versions of this weapon and may develop an air-launched version based on the Chinese adaptation of the HY-2 for an air-launched version (YJ-6)."[17] Indeed, another source states that the Raad has a range of about 350 kilometers.[18]

- **The C-801A** anti-ship missile, also called the Yinji (Eagle Strike) missile, is a solid fueled missile. It can be launched from land and ships. It has a 512-kilogram warhead and cruises at an altitude of 20–30 meters and descends in its terminal phase to a height between 5 and 7 meters. The missile is believed to have a maximum speed of Mach 0.85. Some sources report a range of approximately 74 kilometers in the surface-to-surface mode, and it uses J-Band active radar guidance. Others report a range of 8–40 kilometers in the ship-mounted version. The Iranian-produced version of the C-801A is apparently called Tondar, although some sources refer to the C-802 as the Tondar.

- **The C-802/CSS-N-8/Saccade** is an upgraded CS-801. It uses a turbojet propulsion system with a rocket booster instead of the solid fueled booster in the CS-801. It has a maximum speed of Mach 0.9 and can be targeted by a radar—deployed on a smaller ship or aircraft operating over the radar horizon of the launching vessel.[19]

  Global Security reports that the weight of the subsonic (0.9 Mach) Yingji-802 is reduced from 815 kilograms to 715 kilograms, but its range is increased from 42 kilometers to 120 kilometers. The 165-kilogram (363-pound) warhead is just as powerful as that of C-801. The missile has a small radar reflectivity and flies only 5 to 7 meters above the sea surface in its terminal phase as it attacks the target. Its guidance equipment has moderate anti-jamming capability.[20]

  Global Security also reports that Iran imported the C-802 anti-ship cruise missile from 1992–1996, but that China suspended exports in 1996 after U.S. pressure. It says that Iran expected to purchase 150 C-802 missiles from China but received only half of them because of the arms suspension. It also reports that Iran possessed some 60 of the missiles deployed in coastal batteries on Qeshm Island in mid-1997.

  There are reports that North Korea and Iran jointly developed an advanced version of the C-802 cruise missile. The C-802s that Iran initially acquired were not advanced versions of the C-802 and were more vulnerable to countermeasures. As a result of these limits and the Chinese cutoff in sales, Iran is reported to have turned to North Korea. The Iranian version of this missile is called the Noor. Apparently, Iran is indigenously building all parts necessary for assembling the Noor.[21]

- **The C-801K/YJ-1** is a Chinese-supplied, air-launched anti-ship missile and variant of the CS-801. It, too, is a sea-skimming, high-subsonic cruise missile and has a range in excess of 40–50 kilometers (roughly 20 nautical miles). It has been test-fired by Iran's F-4Es, but Iran may be able to use other launch aircraft. This air delivery capability gives Iran what some analysts have called a "360 degree" attack capability, since aircraft can rapidly maneuver to far less predictable launch points than Iranian combat ships.[22]

- **The TL-6 or FL-9** radar-guided anti-ship missile is a fairly new system, which Iran acquired from China. The missile can carry a 30-kilogram warhead at a maximum speed of about Mach 0.8 to 0.9. Its effective range reportedly is up to 35 kilometers, and it is supposed to be launched mainly from fast attack craft. Iran apparently produces this missile based on Chinese technology under the name Nasr.

- **The TL-6B (C-704)** missile is not confirmed to be in service with the Iranian Navy, but reportedly Iran expressed interest in acquiring it. Alongside the Hongdu TL-10, Iran appears interested in the Chinese TL-6B anti-ship (C-704) missile. This weapon corresponds to the Nasr missile in terms of design and performance specifications, and it is not clear what improvements the TL-6B, which reportedly is radar guided, has over the TL-6.

- **The TL-10 (C-701) or FL-8** anti-ship missile comes in two versions, one TV guided (TL-10A), and one radar guided (TL-10B) with all-weather capability. The former is distinguished by a rounded glass nose, the latter by a smaller, solid nose for radar homing. Their technical specifications appear to be nearly identical; their warhead weighs 30 kilometers and reportedly flies up to 20 kilometers at Mach 0.85. This missile appears to be a smaller version of C-801. The TL-10 missiles apparently are also for use on fast attack craft. Iran reportedly produces this missile under license under the name Kosar. Many Iranian official sources claimed that the country produces the C-701 missiles indigenously; apparently it calls the electro-optical-guided version Kosar-1, the radar-guided version Kosar-3.[23] Apparently, the advantage of this missile lies in its smaller size, more flexible availability, and lower flight pattern.

In late August 2006, reports surfaced that claimed to show a successful test-firing of a new ASW missile, the Thaqeb. This missile can be fired from both underwater and above water and then flies to its target. The missile tests were shown on TV along with the presentation of a high-speed boat that allegedly flies over the water's surface. Some Western sources claim that these images show modified but largely outdated Russian equipment.

It has also been alleged that Iran is developing a new supersonic anti-ship missile. As of early 2007, Iran is reported to be in the design phase of the development for this missile. Further, Iranian efforts to build a new type of anti-ship missile may be linked to China's work on the C-803 missile, which in turn is based on the air-launched YJ-83. One caveat is always warranted when trying to establish links or cooperation between Iran and China: Iran may be cooperating with North Korean organizations, which develop weapon systems based on Chinese equipment.

In the early fall of 2006, Iran demonstrated new naval missile capabilities during its Force of Zolfaghar exercises. These included submarine-launched missiles that Iran called the Sagheb, but which seem to have been Chinese YJ-8s.[24] Another submarine-to-surface missile—the Thaqeb/Saturn—was test-fired in the Persian Gulf on August 27, 2006.

Iran now is believed to have at least 100 C-801s and C-802s. One source notes that Iran may have imported up to 100 C-801s and eight launchers in 1987–1988 and built its arsenal to 200 by 1994 as well as the ability to produce the C-801 indigenously (under the designation "Tondar").[25] Another sources notes that Iran may have deployed its C-701 missiles at launching bases under construction at Bandar Abbas, Bandar Lengeh, Bushehr, and Bandar Khomeini.[26]

Iran has sought to buy advanced anti-ship missiles from Russia, North Korea, and China, to buy anti-ship missile production facilities, and possibly even Chinese-made missile armed frigates. Some sources have claimed that Iran has bought eight Soviet-made SS-N-22 "Sunburn" or "Sunburst" anti-ship missile launch units from Ukraine and has deployed them near the Straits of Hormuz. However, U.S. experts have not seen firm evidence of such a purchase and doubt that Iran has any operational holdings of such systems. The "SS-N-22" is a title that actually applies to two different modern long-range supersonic sea skimming systems—the P-270 Moskit (also called the Kh-15 or 3M80) and the P80 or P-100 Zubi/Onika.

OTHER PATROL BOATS AND SURFACE CRAFT

Iran has a number of large patrol craft and fast attack craft (120+), and the IISS *Military Balance* for 2007 lists 140 patrol and coastal combatants. The operational ships of this type include three North Korean–supplied 82-ton Zafar-class (Chaho-class) fast attack craft with I-band search radars and armed with 23-mm guns and a BM-21 multiple rocket launcher, two Kavian-class (U.S. Cape-class) 148-ton patrol craft armed with 40-mm and 23-mm guns, and three Improved PGM-71 Parvin-class 98-ton patrol craft supplied in the late 1960s, armed with 40-mm and 20-mm guns.

There are some 87 inshore patrol boats displacing less than 100 tons each [including 11 China Cats (C 14), although only 9 of those are believed to be operational] and 37 small port patrol boats, plus large numbers of small boats operated by the IRGC. Most of these craft are operational and can be effective in patrol missions. They do, however, lack sophisticated weapon systems or air defenses, other than machine guns and SA-7s and SA-14s. However, many reports allege that China Cats carry C-701 anti-ship missiles, although missile craft are believed to be under the command of the IRGC. Apparently, further procurement of China Cats is likely, although details are unknown.[27]

Iran has five to six BH-7 and seven to eight SRN-6 hovercraft, believed to be operated by the IRGC. About half of these hovercraft may be operational. They are capable of speeds of up to 60–70 knots. They are lightly armed and vulnerable, but their high speed makes them useful for many reconnaissance and unconventional warfare missions. They can rapidly land troops on suitable beaches, but the beaching angle is critical and some beaches are not appropriate.

The IISS *Military Balance 2007* lists eight unmanned combat air vehicles (UCAVs), among them seven Wellingtons (another report lists six)[28] and one Iran-class vessel. The Wellingtons are large 1960s hovercrafts that were commissioned in the early 1970s. The Iran-class vessel is a smaller, albeit newer, development that is supposedly based on the SRN-6. It can accommodate 26 troops and two tons of equipment.[29]

IRANIAN MINE WARFARE CAPABILITIES

Mine warfare, amphibious warfare, anti-ship missiles, and unconventional warfare offer Iran ways of compensating for the weakness of its conventional air and naval forces. Iran's mine warfare vessels include two Type-292 and one Shahrock-class MSC-292/268 coastal minesweepers (used for training in the Caspian Sea). Two of these three ships, the *Shahrock* and the *Karkas,* are known to be operational. They are 378-ton sweepers that can be used to lay mines as well as sweep, but their radars and sonars date back to the late 1950s and are obsolete in sweeping and counter-measure activity against modern mines.

Iran has one to two operational Cape-class (Riazzi-class) 239-ton inshore mine-sweepers and seems to have converted two of its indigenously produced Ajar-class landing ship tanks (LSTs) for mine warfare purposes. Many of its small boats and craft can also lay mines. Both the Iranian Navy and the naval branch of the IRGC are expanding their capability for mine warfare. While Iran has only a limited number of specialized mine vessels, it can also use small craft, LSTs, Boghammers, helicopters, and submarines to lay mines. As a result, it is impossible to determine how many ships Iran would employ to plant or lay mines in a given contingency, and some of its mines might be air dropped or laid by commercial vessels, including dhows.

Iran has a range of Soviet-, Western-, and Iranian-made moored and drifting contact mines, and U.S. experts estimate that Iran has at least 2,000 mines. Another source claims that Iran's stockpiles amount to as many as 3,000 mines.[30] Iran has significant stocks of anti-ship mines and has bought Chinese-made and North Korean–made versions of the Soviet mines. It has claimed to be making its own nonmagnetic, acoustic, free-floating, and remote-controlled mines and has had Chinese assistance in developing the production facilities for such mines. It may have acquired significant stocks of nonmagnetic mines, influence mines, and mines with sophisticated timing devices from other countries.[31]

There also are reports that Iran has negotiated with China to buy the EM-52 or MN-52 rocket-propelled mine. The EM-52 is a mine that rests on the bottom of the sea until it senses a ship passing over it, and then it uses a rocket to hit the target. The maximum depth of the Straits of Hormuz is 80 meters (264 feet), although currents are strong enough to displace all but firmly moored mines.[32] Combined with modern submarine-laid mines and anti-ship missile systems like the CS-801/802 and the SS-N-22, the EM-52 would give Iran considerable capability to harass Gulf shipping and even the potential capability to close the Gulf until U.S. naval power and airpower could clear the mines and destroy the missile launchers and submarines.

Even obsolete moored mines have proven difficult to detect and sweep when intelligence does not detect the original laying and size of the minefield, and free-floating mines can be used to present a constant hazard to shipping. Bottom-influence mines can use acoustic, magnetic, or pressure sensors to detect ships passing overhead. They can use multiple types of sensor/actuators to make it hard to deceive the mines and force them to release, can be set to release only after a given number of ships pass, and some can be set to attack ships only of a given size or noise profile. Such mines are extremely difficult to detect and sweep, particularly when they are spaced at wide intervals in shipping lanes.

IRANIAN AMPHIBIOUS ASSETS

Iran has significant amphibious assets compared to other Gulf countries, and the regular navy and the naval branch of the IRGC operate independent marine forces. The navy is reported to have a 2,600-man, two brigade marine force. The role this force plays relative to the naval branch of the IRGC is unclear.

Its lift assets are large enough to move a battalion-sized force relatively rapidly; they include four Hengam-class (Larak-class) LST amphibious support ships (displacement of 2,940 tons loaded) that can carry up to six tanks, 600 tons of cargo, and 227 troops. They also include three Iran Hormuz-class (South Korean) landing ships, medium (2,014 tons loaded) that can carry up to nine tanks and berth 140 troops, and three Hormuz-21-class 180-ton LSTs (other sources report two) and three Fouque-class 176-ton landing ship logistics (LSLs). Several other Foque-class vessels reportedly are in service with the Iranian civilian navy.

These amphibious capabilities are not large enough to sustain large-scale operations across the Gulf, and Iran has no capacity to protect an amphibious operation against naval and air attack. Iran's amphibious ships give it the capability to deploy about 1,000 troops and, theoretically, about 30–40 tanks in an amphibious assault —but Iran has never demonstrated that it has an effective over-the-shore capability. It also lacks adequate firepower to support such a mission. Iran might use commercial ferries and roll-on–roll-off ships. Iran has also built up its capability to hide or shelter small ships in facilities on its islands and coastline along the Gulf and has the ability to provide them with defensive cover from anti-air and anti-ship missiles.

Iran has support ships, but these are generally insufficient to sustain "blue water" operations and support an amphibious task force. It has one Kharg-class 33,014-ton replenishment ship, two Bandar Abbas-class 4,673-ton fleet supply ships and oilers, one 14,410-ton repair ship, two 12,000-ton water tankers, seven 1,300-ton Delva-class support ships, five to six Hendijan-class support vessels, two floating dry docks, and 20 tugs, tenders, and utility craft to help support a large naval or amphibious operation.

Iran's training to date has focused on amphibious raiding, however, and not on operations using heavy weapons or larger operations. Iran lacks the air and surface power to move its amphibious forces across the Gulf in the face of significant air/ sea defenses or to support a landing in a defended area.

IRANIAN NAVAL AIR

The Iranian Navy's relative air strength is shown in Figure 7.5. It consists of around 2,600 men. Its key air systems include two to three operational P-3F Orion maritime patrol aircraft out of an original inventory of five. According to reports from the Gulf, none of the surviving P-3Fs have fully operational radars, and their crews often use binoculars, yet apparently one of the aircraft is designed to conduct early warning and fire-control missions.[33]

Iran is reported to also have three Da-20 Falcons fitted for electronic warfare and electronics intelligence missions. Their configuration and mission capability is unknown.

It has up to ten Sikorsky SH-3D ASW helicopters, three RH-53D mine-laying helicopters, and seven Agusta-Bell AB-212 helicopters. Another source lists six operational AB-212s and six RH-53MD Sea Stallion helicopters in service. Apparently, the unarmed Sea Stallions are used only for logistical missions; the AB-212s

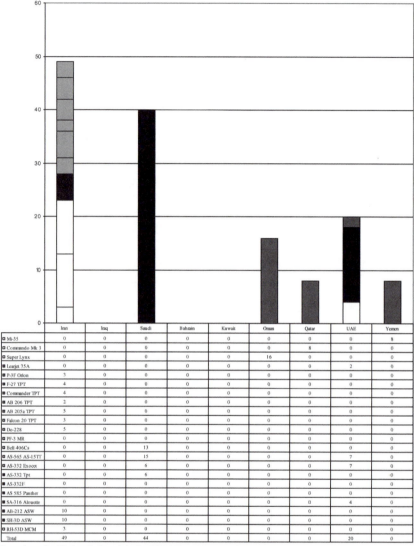

	Iran	Iraq	Saudi	Bahrain	Kuwait	Oman	Qatar	UAE	Yemen
Mi-35	0	0	0	0	0	0	0	0	8
Commando Mk 3	0	0	0	0	0	0	8	0	0
Super Lynx	0	0	0	0	0	16	0	0	0
Learjet 35A	0	0	0	0	0	0	0	2	0
P-3F Orion	3	0	0	0	0	0	0	0	0
F-27 TPT	4	0	0	0	0	0	0	0	0
Commander TPT	4	0	0	0	0	0	0	0	0
AB 206 TPT	2	0	0	0	0	0	0	0	0
AB 205a TPT	5	0	0	0	0	0	0	0	0
Falcon 20 TPT	3	0	0	0	0	0	0	0	0
Do-228	5	0	0	0	0	0	0	0	0
PF-3 MR	0	0	0	0	0	0	0	0	0
Bell 406Cs	0	0	13	0	0	0	0	0	0
AS-565 AS-15TT	0	0	15	0	0	0	0	7	0
AS-332 Exocet	0	0	6	0	0	0	0	7	0
AS-332 Tpt	0	0	6	0	0	0	0	0	0
AS-332F	0	0	0	0	0	0	0	0	0
AS 585 Panther	0	0	0	0	0	0	0	0	0
SA-316 Alouette	0	0	0	0	0	0	0	4	0
AB-212 ASW	10	0	0	0	0	0	0	0	0
SH-3D ASW	10	0	0	0	0	0	0	0	0
RH-53D MCM	3	0	0	0	0	0	0	0	0
Total	49	0	44	0	0	0	0	20	0

Source: International Institute for Strategic Studies (IISS), *Military Balance, 2007.*

Figure 7.5   Gulf Naval Aircraft and Helicopter Aircraft, 2007

are used for ASW, as well as for oil platform defense missions.[34] Iran uses air force AH-1J attack helicopters, equipped with French AS-12 missiles, in naval missions and has adapted Hercules C-130 and Fokker Friendship aircraft for mine-laying and patrol missions. The most significant recent development in Iran's capabilities to use airpower to attack naval targets has been the acquisition of the C-801K for its regular air force.

Like the air force, the Iranian Navy also seems to be making increased use of unmanned aerial vehicles (UAVs) and may be experimenting with UCAVs for special mission purposes.

The navy's transport and utility aircraft include 5 Do-228, 4 F-27 Friendship, and 4 Rockwell Turbo Commando 680 fixed-wing aircraft and 17 utility helicopters (5 AB-205A, 2 AB-206, and 10 AB-212).

It has to be kept in mind that naval aviation units play an important role in combination with surface-to-sea missiles, weapon systems that may play a crucial role in any contingency involving the Strait of Hormuz.

THE ROLE OF THE NAVAL BRANCH OF THE IRGC

Iran's unconventional warfare capabilities include the naval branch of the Islamic Revolutionary Guards Corps with some 18,000 men. This force has a major capability for asymmetric naval warfare. It also operates Iran's land-based anti-ship missiles and coastal defense artillery and includes a 5,000+ man marine force with at least one combat brigade.

It has been reported that the IRGC operates all of Iran's missile craft. Its missile patrol boats include ten 68-ton Chinese-built Thondor (Hudong)-class fast attack craft or missile patrol boats. These fast attack craft are equipped with I-band search and navigation radars, but do not have a major anti-air missile system. Iran ordered these ships for the naval branch of its Iranian Revolutionary Guards Corps in 1992, and all ten were delivered to Iran by March 1996. The vessels have a crew of 28. They carry four anti-ship missiles and are armed with the C-801 and C-802 missiles.

In addition to its land- and sea-based anti-ship missile forces, the naval guards can use large numbers of small patrol boats equipped with heavy machine guns, grenade launchers, anti-tank-guided weapons, man-portable surface-to-air missiles, and 106-mm recoilless rifles.

The IRGC also uses small launchers, and at least 30 Zodiak rubber dinghies, to practice rocket, small arms, and recoilless rifle attacks. Its other small craft were armed with a mix of machine guns, recoilless rifles, and man- and crew-portable anti-tank guided missiles. These vessels can reach top speeds over 35 knots and are difficult to detect by radar in anything but the calmest seas. Iran bases them at a number of offshore islands and oil platforms, and they can strike quickly and with limited warning. The naval branch of the IRGC also has naval artillery, divers, and mine-laying units. It had extensive stocks of scuba equipment and an underwater combat center at Bandar Abbas.[35] Iran is also improving the defenses and port capabilities of its islands in the Gulf, adding covered moorings, more advanced sensors, and better air defenses.

The IRC Naval Branch also deploys the Seersucker (C-201/HY-2/SY2).[36] This is a long-range, mobile anti-ship missile, which is designated the Sea Eagle-2 by the People's Republic of China and is sometimes referred to as the CSS-N-3. It is a large missile with a 0.76-meter diameter and a weight of 3,000 kilograms. It has an 80–90-kilometer range and a 450-kilogram warhead.

There are two variants of this missile. One uses radar active homing at ranges from the target of 8 kilometers (4.5 nautical miles). The other is set to use passive infrared homing and a radar altimeter to keep it at a constant height over the water. The Iranian version of the improved HY-2 is called Raad. The naval branch of the IRGC also uses this weapon.

According to Global Security, the system features long-range coverage and a large firing sector, enabling one missile battalion to cover a blockaded ocean area of 14,000 square kilometers. After the missile is fired, ground guidance and control are not necessary, and the firing position can remain concealed.

The truck-mounted radar associated with the HY-2 system provides surveillance and target-detection facilities and is also stated to perform target tracking. The design apparently originates from a Soviet naval search radar and probably operates in the C-band of the spectrum. The level flight altitude of the missile is low, and the system's anti-jam capabilities are moderately resistant to electronic countermeasures. The missile's large warhead can sink or severely damage a large combat ship. Iran has claimed that it has the capacity to manufacture HY-2s and other anti-ship cruise missiles indigenously. Global Security reports currently estimated that Iran has about 100 HY-2 missiles on eight to ten mobile launchers. Global Security reports that there are four variants of the missile and it is not clear which are currently deployed, but Iran does have the capability to upgrade the system.[37]

- HY-2A terminal guidance radar of the prototype missile was modified into a passive infrared target seeker that effectively raised the concealment and anti-jamming capabilities of the missile. The interception performance of this missile within guidance range can realize omnidirectional attacks on ship targets at sea.

- HY-2B, the conical scanning terminal guidance radar of the prototype missile, was modified to an advanced monopulse system radar that improved its resistance to sea waves interference and various forms of electronic jamming.

- HY-2C terminal guidance radar of the prototype missile was modified into a television-equipped target seeker that was able to effectively raise the concealment and anti-jamming capabilities of the missile as well as increase its hit probability.

- HY-2G uses a high-precision radio altimeter so that the level flight altitude of the missile can be lowered to 30-50 meters, raising penetration capabilities. The basic HY-2 uses active radar homing, while HY-2G adds a radio altimeter to permit a lower penetration altitude.

Iran can use IRGC forces to conduct the kind of low-intensity/guerrilla warfare that can be defeated only by direct engagement with land forces and can filter substantial reinforcements into a coastal area on foot or with light vehicles, making such reinforcement difficult to attack. Iran can use virtually any surviving small craft to lay mines and to place unmoored mines in shipping lanes. Its IRGC forces can use small craft to attack offshore facilities and raid coastal targets.

Finally, it is important to note the United States did not successfully destroy a single land-based Iraqi anti-ship missile launcher during the Gulf War, and the IRGC now has many dispersal launch sites and storage areas over a much longer coast. It also has a growing number of caves, shelters, and small hardened facilities. Such targets are sometimes difficult to detect until they are used, and they present added problems because they usually are too small and too numerous to attack with high-cost ordnance until it is clear they have valuable enough contents to merit such an attack.

NAVAL FORCE DEPLOYMENTS

The main forces of the Iranian Navy are concentrated in the Gulf and at Bandar Abbas just to the north of the Strait of Hormuz. Iran gives more importance to the security of its territorial sea in the Gulf area since in this direction it has highly complicated relations with various Arab nations, the United States, and Israel. Every year, the Iranian Navy conducts the so-called Nasr exercise with approximately 100 ships in the Gulf.[38] After the collapse of the Soviet Union, however, Iran's policy toward the Caspian Sea area has changed. According to the contracts between the Soviet Union and Iran, Tehran was not allowed to station its navy in the Caspian Sea. After the disintegration of the USSR, however, the fourth naval regional forces started representing the Iranian Navy in the Caspian.[39]

The Islamic republic has almost 3,000 personnel in the Caspian. The forces include up to 50 fighting ships and support vessels, the Marine Corps, coastal guard forces, and the sea aircraft. There are also training vessels in the fleet, including one Shahrokh MSC (Mine Sweeper Coastal) minesweeper, two Hamzeh ships, and others. Currently, Iran has the second largest fleet in the Caspian after Russia. The fleet, however, is outdated. This is why Tehran has been trying to strengthen its naval forces in the Caspian through various programs. It is reported that the government has numerous plans to modernize its fleet. According to these projects, the future fleet will include several divisions and separate battalions of ships and submarines.[40]

FORCE TRENDS AND SUMMARY CAPABILITIES

The detailed trends in Iran's naval forces are shown in Figure 7.6. Iran's efforts have steadily improved its capabilities to threaten Gulf shipping and offshore oil facilities, its capability to support unconventional warfare, and its ability to defend its offshore facilities, islands, and coastline. They have not, however, done much to help Iran to act as an effective blue water navy.

At the same time, the military capability of Iranian naval forces should not be measured in terms of the ability to win a battle for sea control against U.S. and British naval forces or any combination of southern Gulf States supported by U.S. and British forces. For the near future, Iran's forces are likely to lose any such battle in a matter of days. As a result, it is Iran's ability to conduct limited or unconventional

Figure 7.6 Iranian Navy's Force Structure Trends, 1990–2007

	1990	2000	2005	2006	2007
Manpower	14,500	20,600	18,000	18,000	18,000
Active	14,500	20,600	18,000	18,000	18,000
Conscripts	0	0	0	0	0
Submarines	0	5	3	3	3
SSK (RF Type 877/Kilo class)	0	3	3	3	3
SSI	0	2	0	0	0
Destroyers	3	0	0	0	0
Damavand (U.K. *Battle*)	1	0	0	0	0
Babr (U.S. *Sumner*)	2	0	0	0	0
Frigates	5	3	5	5	5
Alvand (U.K. *Vosper*)	3	3	3	3	3
Corvettes	2	0	2	2	2
Bayandor (U.S. PF-103)	2	0	2	2	2
Patrol and Coastal Combatants	34	64	56	250+	140
Patrol Missile Craft	10	20	10	10	11
Kaman (Fr Combattante II)	10	10	10	10	11
Houdong	0	10	0	0	0
Patrol Coastal/Inshore	24	42	35+	85	129
Kaivan	3	Some	0	0	2
Parvin	3	3	3	3	3
Chaho	3	Some	0	0	0
Zafar	0	3	3	3	?
Bogomol	0	1	0	0	?
China Cat	0	0	3	9	11
Mine Warfare	3	7	7	5	5
Sharokh (MSC)	2	1	1	1	1
Riazi (U.S. *Cape*)	0	1	2	2	2
Harischi (MSI)	1	1	0	0	0
Hejaz (Minelayer)	0	2	2	0	0
292 MSC	0	2	2	2	2

Amphibious	7	9	10	10	10
Hengam (LST)	4	4	4	4	4
Iran Hormuz (LST)	3	3	3	3	3
Hejaz (LST)	0	0	0	3	3
Foque (LSL)	0	2	3	3	3
Landing craft	4+	9+	200+	6	6
Support	8	25	25	27	27
AO	3	3	3	3	3
AT	1	1	1	1	1
AWT	?	0	2	2	2
Delvar (SPT)	?	7	5	7	7
Hendijan (SPT)	?	9	12	12	12
TRG	?	1	2	2	2
Maritime Reconnaissance	0	8	10	8	8
P-3F	0	3	5	5	?
Do-228	0	5	5	5	5
Anti-Submarine Weapons	9	9	20	10	10
SH-3D Sea King (Heli)	3	3	10	10	10
AB-212 (Heli)	6	6	10	0	0
Mine Countermeasures	2	2	3	3	3
RH-53D (Heli)	2	2	3	3	3
Transport	29	29	18	13	13
Commander	4	4	4	4	4
Falcon	1	1	3	3	3
F-27	4	4	4	4	4
AB-205 (Heli)	Some	Some	5	5	5
AB-206 (Heli)	Some	Some	2	2	2
AB-212 (Heli)	0	0	0	10	10
UCAV	0	0	0	0	8
Wellington	0	0	0	6	7
Iran	0	0	0	0	1

Sources: IISS, *Military Balance,* various editions, including 1989–1990, 1999–2000, 2004–2005, 2005–2006, 2006, and 2007.

warfare, or to threaten traffic through the Gulf, that gives Iran the potential ability to threaten or intimidate its neighbors.

Iran now practices a kind of layered defense where it would use its navy, air force, and IRGC forces to try to attack a U.S. fleet or force as far forward as possible in the Gulf, the Gulf of Oman, and the Indian Ocean. Some reports talk about a series of three "kill zones" along the areas from Bandar Abbas to the ports of Jask and Chabahar extending out into the Gulf of Oman and the Indian Ocean. One such report states that new submarine facilities are being built at Chabahar to allow rapid deployment directly into the Indian Ocean.[41] As has been noted earlier in Chapter 1, Motjtaba Zlnur, a high-ranking official in the IRGC, has stated that, "This is another weak point of the enemy because we have certain methods for fighting in the sea so that war will spread into the sea of Oman and the Indian Ocean...We will not let the enemy inside our borders."[42]

Iran has repeatedly made public announcements stating that it is focusing on long-range anti-ship missiles for submarine, surface, land, and air launch. It is unclear, however, how much of this focus represents a serious belief such systems would be effective and how much is a deterrent. Iran has claimed to have a variety of "smart," supersonic, and long-range missiles. In March 2007, it claimed to have tested a new anti-ship missile with a range of over 180 miles. It has also claimed to have "stealth" UAVs and UCAVs. Ali Shushtari, the Deputy Commander of the IRGC ground forces, said in March 2007, "We have built birds without passengers that can carry out suicide operations on the US Navy, at any depth necessary, to make them leave the region in disgrace."[43]

Iran must realize that it would lose most of the attacking elements, but may feel it would lose them in any case and that some of its anti-ship missiles could do serious damage. It may plan to keep its submarines and some mine-laying-capable vessels in reserve since these would be less vulnerable. The same would probably be true of any operational midget submarines, some of its anti-ship missile fast patrol boats, and many of its IRGC small craft and mobilized commercial and fishing vessels. It would make sense, however, for Iran to deploy floating mines in the Gulf and do its best to mine the shipping channels in the Strait of Hormuz as soon as possible to avoid losing the capability to do so because of a U.S. attack.

It would deploy its smaller vessels and the IRGC Naval Branch along the coast and the islands from areas near the Iraqi border to the Gulf of Oman, dispersing and concealing as many of its forces as possible. It would probably use some of its longer-range land-based anti-ship missiles as soon as they could acquire targets and try to disperse and conceal others and hold them in reserve. This would allow Iran to minimize the visibility of its naval forces, to strike at random intervals while trying to deny or harass both combat operations and commercial shipping, and to try to carry out a war of attrition at sea as well as on land.

Paramilitary, Internal Security, and Intelligence Forces

Iran has not faced a meaningful threat from terrorism. Its internal security forces are focused on countering political opposition. Figure 8.1 shows the force structure of Iran's paramilitary and internal security services. Since 1990, Iran has maintained the same force structure, and its key agencies have not changed since the early years of the Revolution.

The U.S. Department of State described the role of Iran's internal security apparatus as follows:

> Several agencies share responsibility for law enforcement and maintaining order, including the ministry of intelligence and security, the law enforcement forces under the interior ministry, and the IRGC [Islamic Revolutionary Guards Corps]. A paramilitary volunteer force known as the Basij and various informal groups known as the Ansar-e Hezbollah (Helpers of the Party of God) aligned with extreme conservative members of the leadership and acted as vigilantes. The size of the Basij is disputed, with officials citing anywhere from 11 to 20 million, and a recent Western study claiming there were 90 thousand active members and up to 300 thousand reservists. Civilian authorities did not maintain fully effective control of the security forces. The regular and paramilitary security forces both committed numerous, serious human rights abuses. According to HRW [Human Rights Watch] since 2000 the government's use of plainclothes security agents to intimidate political critics became more institutionalized. They were increasingly armed, violent, and well equipped, and they engaged in assault, theft, and illegal seizures and detentions.[1]

Iran maintains an extensive network of internal security and intelligence services. The main parts of the domestic security apparatus are made up of the Ministry of Intelligence and Security, the Basij Resistance Force, the intelligence unit of the

Figure 8.1   Iran's Paramilitary Forces' Force Structure, 1990–2007

	1990	2000	2005	2006	2007
Manpower	1,045,000	1,040,000	1,040,000	1,040,000	1,040,000
Active (Interior Ministry officers)	45,000	40,000	40,000	40,000	40,000
Reserve (includes rev. conscripts, Basij)	1,000,000	1,000,000	1,000,000	1,000,000	1,000,000
Patrol and Coastal Combatants	136	130	130	130	130
Misc. Boats and Craft	40	40	40	40	40
PCI	96	90	90	90	90
Aircraft	?	?	?	?	Some
Cessna 185/Cessna 310	?	?	?	?	Some
Helicopters	?	24	24	24	24
UTL Bell/205/206	?	24	24	24	24

Sources: IISS, *Military Balance,* various editions, including 1989–1990, 1999–2000, 2004–2005, 2005–2006, 2006, and 2007.

IRGC, and the law enforcement forces within the Ministry of Interior that largely are responsible for providing police and border control. The leadership of each of these organizations appears to be fragmented and dispersed among several, often competing, political factions. Public information on all Iranian security and intelligence forces is extremely limited and subject to political manipulation.

Key to most paramilitary and intelligence forces in Iran is the IRGC, as it holds control over several other organizations or parts thereof. All security organizations without exception report to the Supreme National Security Council (SNSC), as the highest body in the political chain of command. The phenomenon of the fragmented leadership of the security organizations is reflected in their relationship to the SNSC as different security organizations maintain special ties to certain elements of the SNSC. The Supreme Leader, Ali Khamenei, installed an advisory panel called Strategic Council on Foreign Policy in May 2006. This body is supposed to advise the Supreme Leader in a broad range of foreign policy matters. It can only be speculated what the implications of this body are, but its creation sends a caveat to observers that there may be some significant tension among the security components in Iran.

In addition, it has to be assumed that other state organizations, most notably the police services, exert varying control over internal security. As with virtually all other organizations, the IRGC is believed to have considerable leverage over these services.[2] The effectiveness of the internal security organizations is unclear and the political will to use them is hard to predict. After local unrest in the Iranian province of

Baluchistan in May 2006, police were unable to seize control of the situation against regional tribal forces.[3]

THE MINISTRY OF INTELLIGENCE AND SECURITY

The Ministry of Intelligence and Security (MOIS), or Vezarat-e Ettela' at va Aminat-e Keshvar (VEVAK), was installed following the Revolution to replace the now-disbanded National Organization for Intelligence and Security (SAVAK), which in turn was created under the leadership of U.S. and Israeli officers in 1957. SAVAK fell victim to political leadership struggles with the intelligence service of the IRGC during the Iran-Iraq War. A compromise solution resulted in the creation of MOIS in 1984.

In 2006, the MOIS employed about 15,000 civilian staff. Its major tasks included intelligence about the Middle East and Central Asia and domestic intelligence and monitoring of clerical and government officials,[4] as well as work on preventing conspiracies against the Islamic republic.[5] It can therefore be assumed that the Ministry maintains an elaborate domestic service network.

The MOIS staff is believed to maintain a professional service loyalty and therefore is not subject to easy mobilization by military, clergy, or other political forces. Some, however, believe that during former President Mohammad Khatami's rule the MOIS actively sought to rid the organization of hard-line officials.[6] Within Iran's political system there is constant argument about limiting parliamentary control over MOIS, indicating that the control over MOIS can be used as a powerful political instrument. Recently, there were efforts in Iran to extract the counterintelligence unit of MOIS and make it a separate entity. This proposal seems to be favored by Supreme Leader Ayatollah Ali Khamenei and some hard-line legislators.[7]

Until recently, the organization has remained under very limited public disclosure. In the 1990s, Ministry personnel were accused of killing political dissidents in Iran. Ensuing investigations have been covered up systematically. Apparently, MOIS has a comparatively large budget at its disposal and operates under the broader guidance of Ali Khamenei.[8] And it seems likely that the details about the Ministry's resources are partly undisclosed even to Iranian political officials.

THE IRGC INTELLIGENCE BRANCH

As part of the Islamic Revolution Guard Corps, the roughly 2,000 staff members of its intelligence force are a largely politicized force with a political mission. According to *Jane's*, their conformity and loyalty to the regime are unquestionable.[9]

The main task of the IRGC Intelligence Branch is to gather intelligence in the Muslim world. As far as domestic security is concerned, the organization targets the enemies of the Islamic Revolution and also participates in their prosecution and trials.[10] In addition, it works closely with the IRGC's Al Quds Force, which also operates covertly outside Iran.

THE BASIJ RESISTANCE FORCE

The Basij has already been mentioned briefly in the chapter on the IRGC (Chapter 5), but it performs broader functions than simply serving as a reserve for the IRGC. The IRGC oversaw the creation of a people's militia, a volunteer group it named the Basij Resistance Force (which means Mobilization of the Oppressed), in 1980. The Basij derives its legitimization from Article 151 of the Iranian Constitution, which calls upon the government to fulfill its duty according to the Quran to provide all citizens with the means to defend themselves. Numbering over 1,000,000 members,[11] the Basij is a paramilitary force, mostly manned by elderly men, youths, and volunteers who have completed their military service.

This force is organized in a regional and decentralized command structure. It has up to 740 regional "battalions," each organized into three to four subunits. Each battalion has 300–350 men. According to one source, about 20,000 Basij forces were organized in four brigades during an exercise in November 2006.[12] It maintains a relatively small active-duty staff of 90,000 and relies on mobilization in the case of any contingency.[13]

According to an IRGC general, a military exercise (Great Prophet II) conducted in the first two weeks of November 2006 employed 172 battalions of the Basij Resistance Force. According to the same source, the main mission of these troops was to guard "public alleyways and other urban areas."[14]

The Basij has a history of martyr-style suicide attacks dating back to the Iran-Iraq War, 1980–1988. Today, its main tasks are thought to assist locally against conventional military defense as well as quell civil uprisings. In addition, one of the Force's key roles has been to maintain internal security, including monitoring internal threats from Iranian citizens and acting as "a static militia force." The state of training and equipment readiness for the Basij is believed to be low. No major weapon systems have been reported for the inventory of the Basij.

The IRGC maintains tight control over the leadership of the Basij and imposes strict Islamic rules on it members. Recent comments by Iranian leaders indicate that the mission of the Basij is shifting away from traditional territorial defense to "defending against Iranian security threats." Furthermore, there are reports of an increased interest in improving the Basij under the leadership of President Mahmoud Ahmadinejad.[15] At the same time, the IRGC leadership questions the effectiveness of the Basij and might loosen its ties to the organization.[16]

In 1993, the Ashura Brigades were created from IRGC and Basij militia units as a response to anti-government riots. This unit is composed of roughly 17,000 men and women, and its primary purpose is to keep down civil unrest, although there has been some discontent expressed by senior leaders about using IRGC units for domestic contingencies.[17]

THE UNCERTAIN ROLE OF THE MINISTRY OF INTERIOR

The police forces, which comprise about 40,000 police under the Ministry of Interior (MoI), participate in internal security as well as border protection. The

Police-110 unit specializes in rapid-response activities in urban areas to disperse potentially dangerous public gatherings. The maritime police have 90 inshore patrol and 40 harbor boats. In 2003, some 400 women became the first female members of the police force since the 1978–1979 Revolution.[18]

The role of Iran's MoI is unclear, and open-source information regarding its structure and forces is limited. The same is true of other organizations in Iran's internal security apparatus. The Ansar-e Hezbollah is a paramilitary force that has gained questionable notoriety. It remains unclear to what extent it is attached to government bodies. Reportedly, the political Right in the government has repeatedly made use of it to fight and intimidate liberal forces in society. According to reports, the Ansar-e Hezbollah's military level of training appears to be very poor.[19]

Iran's Long-Range Missile Arsenal

The development of ballistic and cruise missiles as well as their incorporation into the order of battle for the Iranian forces remains an intractable issue, first, because of a lack of information on the missile program and, second, because the known information illustrates a trend that shows that Iran is on its way to master a broad range of missiles for military applications. U.S. Secretary of Defense Robert M. Gates said that he would like to see Iran freeze its missile technology development program.[1]

Iran continues to deploy surface-to-surface missiles and has its own systems in development. Generally, the Islamic Revolutionary Guards Corps (IRGC) is believed to control Iran's ballistic missiles. This, however, depends on the classification of missiles. The number assigned to the army versus the IRGC is unclear, but the IRGC seems to hold and operate most long-range missiles rather than the army. As Figure 9.1 shows, however, Iran has a variety of short-, medium-, and long-range missiles; while many are based on other missiles such as the SCUD and the short-range missiles that the Defense Intelligence Agency (DIA) labels CSS (acronym for the Chinese term for surface-to-surface missile), Iran has either developed them further or renamed them. One senior IRGC officer has laid out the strategic and tactical rationale behind Iran's weapons program:

> Our enemy's strategy is based on air and sea operations. That is, we believe that any future threat to us will come from the countries beyond our region. In our military analyses, we particularly consider the Americans and the Zionist regime as the two threats from beyond our region. Their strategy will be aerial operations, be it by long-range missiles or fighter planes. In the face of their air raids or missile attack, we have adopted the strategy of utilizing long-range or surface-to-surface missiles.[2]

The Iranian government stated as early as 1999 that it was developing a large missile body or launch vehicle for satellite launch purposes and repeatedly denied that it

Figure 9.1   Estimated Iranian Missile Profiles, 2007

Designation	Stages	Progenitor Missiles	Propellant	Range (Kilometers)	Payload (Kilograms)	IOC (Year)	Inventory
Fateh A-110	1	Zelzal	Solid	210	500	?	?
Tondar 69	1	CSS-8	Solid	150	150–200	?	Up to 200
Ghadr 110	?	?	?	2,500–3,000	?	?	?
M-9 variant	1	CSS-6	Solid	800	320	?	?
M-11 variant	1	CSS-7	Solid	400	?	?	?
Mushak-120	1	CSS-8, SA-2	Solid	130	500	2001	200
Mushak-160 (also Fateh 110)	1	CSS-8, SA-2	Solid	160	500	2002	?
Mushak-200 (also Zelzal 2)	1	SA-2	Solid	200	500	NA*	0
Saegheh	1?	?	Solid	75–225	?	?	?
Shahab-1	1	Soviet SSN-4, N. Korean SCUD-B	Liquid	300	987–1,000	1995	250–300
Shahab-2	1	Soviet SSN-4, N. Korean SCUD-C	Liquid	500	750–989	?	200–450
Shahab-3	1	N. Korean No Dong 1	Liquid	1,300	760–1,158	2002	25–100
Shahab-4	2	N. Korean Taep'o-dong-1	Liquid	3,000	1,040–1,500	NA	0
Ghadr 101	Multi	Pakistan Shaheen-1	Solid	2,500	NA	NA	0
Ghadr 110	Multi	Pakistan Shaheen-2	Solid	3,000	NA	NA	0
IRIS	1	China M-18	Solid	3,000	760–1,158	2005	NA
Kh-55	1	Soviet AS-15 Kent, Ukraine	Jet engine	2,900–3,000	200 kg nuclear	2001	12

Shahab-5	3	N. Korean Taep'o-dong-2	Liquid	5,500	390–1,000	NA	0
Shahab-6	3	N. Korean Taep'o-dong-2	Liquid	10,000	270–1,220	NA	0

* NA = not available.

Sources: Adapted from GlobalSecurity.org, available at http://www.globalsecurity.org/wmd/world/iran/
   missile.htm; the Federation of American Scientists, available at http://www.fas.org/nuke/guide/iran/
   missile; The Claremont Institute: Ballistic Missiles of the World, http://www.missilethreat.com/
   missiles/index.html.

was upgrading the Shahab series (especially the Shahab-3) for military purposes. Iran also continued to claim that the "Shahab-4" program is aimed at developing a booster rocket for launching satellites into space. In January 2004, Iran's Defense Minister claimed that Iran would launch a domestically built satellite within 18 months. This had still not taken place as of July 2007.[3]

In December 2005, the U.S. government announced its belief that Iran had built underground missile factories that were capable of producing Shahab-1s, Shahab-2s, and Shahab-3s, as well as testing new missile designs. It was also believed that Karimi Industries was housed at one of the secret bases, which is where work is taking place on perfecting Iran's nuclear warheads.[4] Most of Iran's missile development industry reportedly is located in Karaj near Tehran. Apparently, there are two large, underground tunnels between Bandar Abbas and Bushehr.[5]

One source notes that with improvements in its Shahab missile program, Iran has attained the capability to strike any place in the Middle East from hardened, fixed sites. Apparently, launch silos for the Shahab-3ER exist near Isfahan.[6]

U.S. officials insisted that information on the underground facilities did not come from Iranian opposition sources like the Mujahadeen-e-Khalq (MEK) and that it was reliable. They feel Iran has made significant strides in recent years using North Korean, Chinese, and Russian technology. If Iran begins work on the Shahab-5 and the Shahab-6 series, it may acquire delivery systems with the range to make it a global nuclear power, instead of merely a regional one. One observer has concluded that Iran is becoming self-sufficient in the production of ballistic missiles.[7] Another source claims that Iran is covering almost all the technological bases necessary to administer an advanced missile program;[8] reports of a possible space launch program support such assertions. Also, it is not unlikely that Iran is going to master cruise-missile technology in the near future. As one Israeli analyst concludes, "Iran's missile program is not a paper tiger."[9]

SHAHAB-1/SCUD-B

The Soviet-designed SCUD-B (17E) guided missile currently forms the core of Iran's ballistic missile forces. The missile was used heavily in the latter years of the Iran-Iraq War. In 2006, it was estimated that Iran had between 300 and 400

Shahab-1 and Shahab-2 variants of the SCUD-B and the "SCUD-C" in its inventory, although some earlier estimates for the SCUD-B ranged as low as 50.[10] These seem to be deployed in three to four battalions in a Shahab brigade.

Iran acquired its first Scuds in response to Iraq's invasion. It obtained a limited number from Libya and subsequently a larger number from North Korea. Some 20 such missiles and two MAZ-543P transporter-erector-launchers (TELs) were delivered in early 1985.[11]

It deployed these units with a special Khatam ol-Anbya force attached to the air element of the Pasdaran. Iran fired its first Scuds in March 1985. It fired as many as 14 Scuds in 1985, 8 in 1986, 18 in 1987, and 77 in 1988. Iran fired 77 Scud missiles during a 52-day period in 1988, during what came to be known as the "war of the cities." Sixty-one were fired at Baghdad, 9 at Mosul, 5 at Kirkuk, 1 at Tikrit, and 1 at Kuwait. Iran fired as many as five missiles on a single day, and once fired three missiles within 30 minutes. This still, however, worked out to an average of only about one missile a day, and Iran was down to only 10–20 Scuds when the war of the cities ended.

Iran's missile attacks were initially more effective than Iraq's attacks. This was largely a matter of geography. Many of Iraq's major cities were comparatively close to its border with Iran, but Tehran and most of Iran's major cities that had not already been targets in the war were outside the range of Iraqi Scud attacks. Iran's missiles, in contrast, could hit key Iraqi cities like Baghdad. This advantage ended when Iraq deployed extended-range Scuds.

The SCUD-B is a relatively old Soviet design that first became operational in 1967, designated as the R-17E or R-300E. Its thrust is 13,160 kgf (kilogram-force), its burn time is between 62 and 64 seconds, and it has an Isp of 62-Sl due to vanes steering drag loss of 4–5 seconds. The SCUD-B possesses one thrust chamber and is a one-stage rocket (it does not break into smaller pieces). Its fuel is TM-185, and its oxidizer is the AK-27I.[12]

The SCUD-B has a range of 290–300 kilometers with its normal conventional payload. The export version of the missile is about 11 meters long, 85–90 centimeters in diameter, and weighs 6,300 kilograms. It has a nominal circular error probable (CEP) of 1,000 meters. The Russian versions can be equipped with conventional high explosives, fuel air explosives, runway penetrating submunitions, and chemical and nuclear warheads. Its basic design comes from the old German V-2 rocket design of World War II. It has moveable fins and is guided only during powered flight.

The SCUD-B was introduced on the JS-3 tracked chassis in 1961 and appeared on the MAZ-543 wheeled chassis in 1965. The "SCUD-B" missile later appeared on the TEL based on the MAZ-543 (8 × 8) truck. The introduction of this new cross-country wheeled vehicle gave this missile system greater road mobility and reduces the number of support vehicles required.

The export version of the SCUD-B comes with a conventional high-explosive warhead weighing about 1,000 kilograms, of which 800 kilograms are the high-explosive payload and 200 are the warhead structure and fusing system. It has a single-stage storable liquid rocket engine and is usually deployed on the MAZ-543—an eight-wheel TEL. It has a strap-down inertial guidance, using three gyros to correct its ballistic trajectory, and it uses internal graphite jet vane steering. The warhead hits at a velocity above Mach 1.5.

The following timeline tracks the history of the Shahab-1 (SCUD-B) after it was first introduced in Iran in 1985:

- **1985:** Iran began acquiring SCUD-B (Shahab-1) missiles from Libya for use in the Iran-Iraq War.[13] About 20 SCUD-Bs were delivered along with two MAZ-543P TELs.[14]

- **1986:** Iran turned to Libya as a supplier of SCUD-Bs.[15] Syria is believed to have supplied Iran with a small number of SCUD-B missiles.[16]

- **1987:** A watershed year. Iran attempted to produce its own SCUD-B missiles, but failed. Over the next five years, it purchased 200–300 SCUD-B missiles plus 6–12 TELs from North Korea.[17]

- **1988:** Iran began producing its own SCUD-Bs, though not in large quantities.[18]

- **1991:** It is estimated that at approximately the time of the Gulf War, Iran stopped producing its own SCUD-Bs and began purchasing the more advanced SCUD-Cs (Shahab-2). This is said to be a system with an 800-kilogram warhead and a 500-kilometer range versus comparable profiles of 1,000 kilograms with 300 kilometers range for the SCUD-B or Shahab-1.[19]

- **1993:** Iran sent 21 missile specialists, led by Brigadier General Manteghi, to North Korea for training.[20]

- **October 1997:** Russia began training Iranian engineers on missile production for the Shahab-3.

- **1998:** Iran began testing its own Shahab-3s. Problems with finding or making an advanced guidance system hindered many of their tests, however. Meanwhile, Iran begins experimenting with the Shahab-4.

- **July 23, 1998:** Iran launched its first test flight of the Shahab-3. The missile flew for approximately 100 seconds, after which time it was detonated. It is not known if it malfunctioned, because the Iranians did not want to risk discovery.

- **July 15, 2000:** Iran had its first successful test of a Shahab-3.

- **Summer 2001:** Iran began production of the Shahab-3.

- **July 7, 2003:** Iran completes the final test of the Shahab-3. The missile is seen in Iranian military parades and displayed openly.

- **October 2003:** Iran claimed it was abandoning its Shahab-4 program, citing that the expected increase in range (2,200 to 3,000 kilometers) would cause too much global tension.

- **Late 2003:** Some sources indicated that Iran had begun only limited production of the Shahab-3.

- **August 11, 2004:** Iran decreases the size of the Shahab-3 warhead, making a move toward the feat of being able to mount a nuclear warhead to a Shahab-3. At this point, the modified Shahab-3 is often referred to as the Shahab-3M.

- **May 31, 2005:** Iran claimed that it successfully tested a new missile motor using solid-fuel technology with a range of 2,000 kilometers.

Experts estimate Iran bought 200–300 SCUD-Bs (Shahab-1s) and SCUD-Cs (Shahab-2), or the suitable components for Iranian reverse-engineered systems, from North Korea between 1987 and 1992 and may have continued to buy such missiles after that time.[21]

Israeli experts estimated that Iran had at least 250–300 SCUD-B missiles and at least 8–15 launchers on hand in 1997. Most current estimates indicate that Iran now has 6–12 Scud launchers and up to 200 SCUD-B (R-17E) missiles with a 230–310-kilometer range. Some estimates give higher figures. The International Institute for Strategic Studies (IISS) estimates in 2007 that Tehran had 18 launchers and 300 Scud missiles.[22] It is, however, uncertain how many of those are SCUD-Bs and how many are SCUD-Cs.

U.S. experts also believe that Iran can now manufacture virtually all of the SCUD-B, with the possible exception of the most sophisticated components of its guidance system and rocket motors. This makes it difficult to estimate how many missiles Iran has in its inventory and how many it can acquire over time, as well as to estimate the precise performance characteristics of Iran's missiles, since it can alter the weight of the warhead and adjust the burn time and improve the efficiency of the rocket motors.

SHAHAB-2/SCUD-C

Iran served as a transshipment point for North Korean missile deliveries during 1992 and 1993. Part of this transshipment took place using the same Iranian B-747s that brought missile parts to Iran. Others moved by sea. For example, a North Korean vessel called the *Des Hung Ho*, bringing missile parts for Syria, docked at Bandar Abbas in May 1992. Iran then flew these parts to Syria. An Iranian ship coming from North Korea and a second North Korean ship followed, carrying missiles and machine tools for both Syria and Iran. At least 20 of the North Korean missiles have gone to Syria from Iran, and production equipment seems to have been transferred to Iran and to Syrian plants near Hama and Aleppo.

The SCUD-C is an improved version of the SCUD-B. With superior range and payload, it is another tactical missile first acquired by Iran in 1990. It has an approximate range between 500 and 700 miles, a CEP of 50 meters, and it carries a 700–989-kilogram warhead. It has a diameter of 0.885 meters, a height of 11–12 meters, a launch weight of 6,370–6,500 kilograms, an unknown stage mass, an unknown dry mass, and an unknown propellant mass. In terms of propelling ability, its thrust is unknown, its burn time is unknown, and it has an effective Isp of 231. The SCUD-C possesses one thrust chamber and is a one-stage rocket (it does not break into smaller pieces). Its fuel is Tonka-250, and its oxidizer is the AK 20P.[23]

SCUD-C missile development was successfully completed and ready for production by 1987 (mainly by North Korea) and then distributed to Iran several years later. According to some reports, Iran has created shelters and tunnels in its coastal areas that it could use to store Scuds and other missiles in hardened sites to reduce their vulnerability to air attack.

The missile is more advanced than the SCUD-B, although many aspects of its performance are unclear. North Korea seems to have completed development of the missile in 1987, after obtaining technical support from China. While it is often called a "SCUD-C," it seems to differ substantially in detail from the original Soviet SCUD-B. It seems to be based more on the Chinese-made DF-61 than on a direct copy of the Soviet weapon.

Experts estimate that the North Korean missiles have a range of around 310 miles (500 kilometers), a conventional warhead with a high-explosive payload of 700 kilograms, and relatively good accuracy and reliability. While some experts feel the payload of its conventional warhead may be limited for the effective delivery of chemical agents, Iran might modify the warhead to increase payload at the expense of range and restrict the using of chemical munitions to the most lethal agents such as persistent nerve gas. It might also concentrate its development efforts on arming its SCUD-C forces with more lethal biological agents.

It is currently estimated that Iran has 50–150 SCUD-Cs in its inventory.[24] While early development of the SCUB-C tracks closely with that of the SCUD-B, the following timeline tracks the development of Iranian SCUD-C missiles since the Gulf War:

- **1991:** Iran apparently received its first shipment of about 100–170 North Korean SCUD-C missiles.
- **1994:** By this year, Iran had purchased 150–200 SCUD-Cs from North Korea.[25]
- **1997:** Iran began production of its own SCUD-C missiles. This is generally considered a technological leap for Iran, and it is believed that a large portion of its production capability and technology came from North Korea.[26]
- **2004–2006:** According to Iranian sources, Iran fired Shahab-2 missiles in most of its major military exercises.
- **Undated and unconfirmed:** According to one report, Iran set up a production line for Shahab-2 missiles in Syria.[27]

In spite of the revelations during the 1990s about North Korean missile technology transfers to Tehran, Iran formally denied the fact it had such systems long after the transfer of these missiles became a fact. Hassan Taherian, an Iranian foreign ministry official, stated in February 1995 "There is no missile cooperation between Iran and North Korea whatsoever. We deny this."[28]

A senior North Korean delegation did, however, travel to Tehran to close the deal on November 29, 1990, and met with Mohsen Rezaei, the former Commander of the IRGC. Iran either bought the missile then or placed its order shortly thereafter. North Korea then exported the missile through its Lyongaksan Import Corporation.

Iran imported some of these North Korean missile assemblies using its B-747s and seems to have used ships to import others.

Iran probably had more than 60 of the longer-range North Korean missiles by 1998, although other sources report 100, and one source reports 170. Iran may have five to ten SCUD-C launchers, each with several missiles. This total seems likely to include four North Korean TELs received in 1995.

Iran is seeking to deploy enough missiles and launchers to make its missile force highly dispersed and difficult to attack. Iran began to test its new North Korean missiles. There are reports it fired them from mobile launchers at a test site near Qom to a target area about 310 miles (500 kilometers) away south of Shahroud. There are also reports that units equipped with such missiles have been deployed as part of Iranian exercises like the Saeqer-3 (Thunderbolt 3) exercise in late October 1993.

Such missiles are likely to have enough range-payload to give Iran the ability to strike all targets on the southern coast of the Gulf and all of the populated areas in Iraq, although not the West. Iran could also reach targets in part of eastern Syria, the eastern third of Turkey, and cover targets in the border area of the former Soviet Union, western Afghanistan, and western Pakistan.

Accuracy and reliability do remain major uncertainties, as does the missile's operational CEP. Much would depend on the precise level of technology Iran deployed in the warhead. Neither Russia nor the People's Republic of China seems to have transferred the warhead technology for biological and chemical weapons to Iran or Iraq when they sold them the SCUD-B missile and CSS-8. However, North Korea may have sold Iran such technology as part of the SCUD-C sale. If it did so, such a technology transfer would save Iran years of development and testing in obtaining highly lethal biological and chemical warheads. In fact, Iran would probably be able to deploy far more effective biological and chemical warheads than Iraq had at the time of the Gulf War.

Iran can now assemble SCUD-C missiles using foreign-made components. It may soon be able to make entire missile system and warhead packages in Iran. Iran may be working with Syria in such development efforts, although Middle Eastern nations rarely cooperate in such sensitive areas.

SHAHAB-3

Iran appears to have entered into a technological partnership with North Korea after years of trading with the North Koreans for SCUD-Cs throughout the 1990s. The visit to North Korea in 1993 by General Manteghi and his 21 specialists seems a possible date when Iran shifted from procurement to development.

Iran did not have the strike capability to attack Israel with its limited-range Scuds. As a result, the Iranians seem to have begun using some of the designs for the North Korean No Dong medium-range ballistic missile in an attempt to manufacture their own version of the missile, the Shahab-3. Between 1997 and 1998, Iran began testing the Shahab-3. While Iran claimed Shahab-3's purpose was to carry payloads of submunitions, it is more likely that Iran would use the Shahab-3's superior range to carry a chemical, nuclear, or biological weapon.

Missile Development

Iran's new Shahab-3 series is a larger missile that seems to be based on the design of the North Korean No Dong 1/A and No Dong B missiles, which some analysts claim were developed with Iranian financial support. It also has strong similarities to the Ghauri missile. It is based on North Korean designs and technology, but is being developed and produced in Iran. This development effort is controlled and operated by the IRGC. Iranian officials, however, claimed that the production of the Shahab-3 missiles was entirely domestic. Former Iranian Defense Minister Ali Shamkhani argued in May 2005 that the production was comprised of locally made parts and that the production was continuing.[29]

As the following timeline shows, the Shahab-3 is a relatively young and constantly evolving system, but it has been tested several times:

- **October 1997:** Russia began training Iranian engineers on missile production for the Shahab-3.[30]

- **1998:** Iran began testing its own Shahab-3s. Problems with finding or making an advanced guidance system hindered many of Iran's tests, however. Meanwhile, Iran begins experimenting with the Shahab-4.[31]

- **July 23, 1998:** Iran launched its first test flight of the Shahab-3. The missile flew for approximately 100 seconds, after which time it was detonated. It is not known if it malfunctioned, because the Iranians did not want to risk discovery.[32]

- **July 15, 2000:** Iran had its first successful test of a Shahab-3, using a new North Korean engine.[33]

- **Summer 2001:** Iran claimed to have begun production of the Shahab-3.[34]

- **July 7, 2003:** Iran completed the final test of the Shahab-3. Allegations emerged that Chinese companies like Tai'an Foreign Trade General Corporation and China North Industries Corporation had been aiding the Iranians in overcoming the missile's final technical glitches.[35] The missile was seen in Iranian military parades and displayed openly. Iran announced at the same time an increase in the production rate of the Shahab-3 to several a month and introduction into service.[36]

- **September 22, 2003:** The Shahab-3 was displayed on mobile launchers at a military parade. Reportedly, the parade announcer said that the shown missile had a range of 1,000 miles.[37]

- **August 11, 2004:** Iran decreased the size of the Shahab-3 warhead with a significantly modified reentry vehicle and propulsion system, making a move toward being able to mount a nuclear warhead to a Shahab-3. At this point, the modified Shahab-3 is often referred to as the Shahab-3M.[38] The missile had a new, smaller, and "bottleneck" warhead. This kind of warhead has a slower reentry than a cone-shaped warhead and has advantages using warheads containing chemical and biological agents. Some estimated that it had a range of 2,000 kilometers for a 700-kilogram warhead, but this may be a confusion with another solid-fueled system. A second variant may exist with a larger fin, a meter less length, and less than a 1,500-kilometer range.[39]

- **September 19, 2004:** Another test took place, and the missile was paraded on September 21 covered in banners saying "we will crush America under our feet" and "wipe Israel off the map."[40]

- **May 31, 2005:** Iranian Defense Minister Ali Shamkhani claimed that Iran successfully tested a new missile motor using solid-fuel technology with a range of 1,500–2,000 kilometers, and a 700-kilogram warhead. Shamkhani was quoted as saying, "Using solid fuel would be more durable and increase the range of the missile."[41] It remains uncertain if this referred to the Shahab-3 or the modified Shahab-3, the IRIS missile.

- **September 2005:** Two new missiles were tested, again with a triconic or baby-bottle warhead some 3 meters long. Some experts speculate that it can disperse chemical and biological weapons or is better suited to a nuclear warhead. Others feel it is an air-burst warhead, capable of better dispersing chemical and/or biological weapons. Two Shahab-3 missiles with triconic warheads were displayed at a parade. These missiles were believed to be new variants of the Shahab-3.

- **February 16, 2006:** Iran is believed to have successfully completed four successful missile test launches this year, including one of a Shahab-3 and a Shahab-4 missile with ranges of 1,300 kilometers and 2,200 kilometers, respectively.

- **April 7, 2006:** The *London Telegraph* reports that Iran has succeeded in adapting the nose cone of the Shahab-3 missile to deliver a nuclear weapon. Allegedly, a modified Shahab-3 could carry the Pakistani version of a nuclear warhead, and it is rumored that Iran possesses this design.

- **November 23, 2006:** It was reported that Iran for the first time fired Shahab-3 missiles in an exercise in early November. Allegedly, a Shahab-3 version with a range of *1,900 kilometers* (with cluster bombs) was fired.

- **September 2006:** Iran was reported to have more than 30 Shahab-3s and 10 TELs, but this is not confirmed.[42]

- **November 2006:** Iran was reported to have successfully fired Shahab-2 and Shahab-3 missiles in military exercises. The Shahab-3 version, according to Iranian sources, carried cluster warheads, had a strike range of about 1,900 kilometers, and landed "a few meters away" from its intended target.[43]

As of early 2006, there had been some ten launches at a rate of only one to two per year. Roughly 30 percent had fully malfunctioned, and six launches had had some malfunction. Iran had also tested two major payload configurations.[44] One report states that the latest TELs used for launching a Shabab-3 need one hour to arrive at the launch site, set up the TEL, and fire the missile.[45] One observer was struck by the number of missiles the Iranian forces fired during the Great Prophet II exercises. Without providing numbers, his comments suggested that Iran fired a surprisingly large amount. While it is impossible to draw a precise inference on the number of missiles in stock, it can be assumed that Iran is capable of producing Shahab-3s in large quantities.[46]

Uncertain Performance[47]

Discussions of the Shahab-3's range-payload, accuracy, and reliability are uncertain and will remain speculative until the system is far more mature. A long-range ballistic missile requires at least 10–30 tests in its final configuration to establish its true payload and warhead type, actual range-payload, and accuracy. While highly detailed estimates of the Shahab-3's performance are available, they at best are rough engineering estimates and are sometimes speculative to the point of being sheer guesswork using rounded numbers.

Its real-world range will depend on both the final configuration of the missile and the weight of its warhead. Various sources now guess that the Shahab-3 has a range between 1,300 and 2,000 kilometers, but the longer-range estimate seems to be based on Iranian claims and assumptions about an improved version, not full-scale operational tests.[48]

U.S. experts believe that the original Shahab-3 missile had a nominal range of 1,100 to 1,300 kilometers, with a 1,200-kilogram payload. The basic system is said to have been 16.5 meters long, have a diameter of 1.58 meters, with a launch weight of 17,410 pounds. Iran has claimed that the Shahab-3 has a range of 2,000 kilometers. This may reflect different estimates of different versions of the missile.

Nasser Maleki, the head of Iran's aerospace industry, stated on October 7, 2004, "Very certainly we are going to improve our Shahab-3 and all of our other missiles." Tehran then claimed in September that the Shahab-3 could now reach targets up to 2,000 kilometers away, presumably allowing the missiles to be deployed a greater distance away from Israel's Air Force and Jericho-2 ballistic missiles.[49]

IRGC Political-Bureau Chief Yadollah Javani stated in September 2004 that the modified Shahab—sometimes called the Shahab-3A or Shahab-3M—could be used to attack Israel's Dimona nuclear reactor.[50] Iran performed another test on October 20, 2004, and Iran's Defense Minister, Ali Shamkani, claimed it was part of an operational exercise. On November 9, 2004, Iran's Defense Minister also claimed that Iran was now capable of mass producing the Shahab-3 and that Iran reserved the option of preemptive strikes in defense of its nuclear sites. Shamkani claimed shortly afterward that the Shahab-3 now had a range of more than 2,000 kilometers (1,250 miles).[51]

One leading German expert stresses the uncertainty of any current estimates and notes that range-payload trade-offs would be critical. He puts the range for the regular Shahab-3 at 820 kilometers with a 1.3-ton payload and 1,100 kilometers with a 0.7-ton payload. (An analysis by John Pike of GlobalSecurity.org also points out that missiles—like combat aircraft—can make trade-offs between range and payload. For example, the No Dong B has a range of 1,560 kilometers with a 760-kilogram warhead and 1,350 kilometers with a 1,158-kilogram warhead.[52]

He feels that an improved Shahab could use a combination of a lighter aluminum airframe, light weight guidance, reduced payload, increased propellant load, and increased burn time to increase range. He notes that little is really known about the improved Shahab-3, but estimates the maximum range of an improved Shahab-3 as still being 2,000 kilometers, that a 0.7–0.8-ton warhead would limit its range to 1,500 kilometers, and that a 0.8–1.0-ton warhead would reduce it to 1,200 kilometers. A 1.2-ton warhead would limit it to around 850 kilometers. He feels Iran may have drawn on Russian technology from the R-21 and the R-27. Photos of the system also show progressive changes in cable duct position, fins, and length in 2004 and 2005.[53]

The difference in range estimates may be a matter of Iranian propaganda, but a number of experts believe that Iranian claims refer to the modified Shahab-3D or the Shahab-3M and not the regular Shahab-3. There are reports that such modified versions use solid fuel and could have a range of up to 2,000 kilometers. They also indicate that the standard Shahab-3 remains in production, but the improved Shahab is now called the Shahab-3M.[54]

Much also depends on the missile warhead. In 2004, then U.S. Secretary of State Colin Powell accused Iran of modifying its Shahab-3 to carry a nuclear warhead based on documents the U.S. government had received from a walk-in source. While experts argued that this information was yet to be confirmed, others claimed that Iran obtained "a new nose cone" for its Shahab-3 missile.[55] In addition, other U.S. officials claimed that the source of the information provided "tens of thousands of pages of Farsi-language computer files" on Iranian attempts to modify their Shahab-3 missile to deliver a "black box," which U.S. officials believed to "almost certainly" refer to a nuclear warhead. These documents were said to include diagrams and test results, weight, detonation height, and shape, but did not include warhead designs.[56]

Media reporting indicates that the United States was able to examine drawings on a stolen laptop from Iran and found that Iran had developed 18 different ways to adapt the size, weight, and diameter of the new nose cone on its Shahab-3 missile. It was also reported, however, that Iran's effort to expand the nose cone would not work and that Iran did not have the technological capabilities to adapt nuclear weapons into its Shahab-3 missile. U.S. nuclear experts claimed that one reason for this failure was that the project "wasn't done by the A-team of Iran's program."[57]

Some experts believe that the new bottleneck warhead tested in 2004 was for the Shahab-3M and makes it more accurate and capable of air-burst detonations, which could be used to more effectively spread chemical weapons. Others believe a smaller warhead has increased its range. According to one source, the baby-bottle shaped missiles, which surfaced in 2004, represent an entirely new missile development if they carry a triconic warhead. Reportedly, the latter warhead does not fit on a Shabab-3 missile. Further, some analysts believe that this warhead would be the prime vehicle for a nuclear weapon.[58] The same source states that the SHIG (a unit known as Department 2500 or Shahid Karimi) started a project (project 111) between 2001 and 2003 to fit a nuclear warhead on a Shabab-3.[59]

As for other aspects of performance, it is again easy to be precise, but difficult to be correct. One source, for example, reports that the Shahab-3 has a CEP of 190 meters and carries a 750-989-1,158-kilogram warhead. The problem with all such reporting, however, lies in the definition of CEP: It is a theoretical engineering term that states that 50 percent of all the missiles launched will hit within a circle of the radius of the CEP. It also assumes that all missiles are perfectly targeted and function perfectly throughout their entire flight. It makes no attempt to predict where the 50 percent of the missiles that hit outside the circle will go, or missile reliability. Engineering estimates basing CEP on the theoretical accuracy of the guidance platform have also often proven to be absurdly wrong until they are based on the actual performance of large numbers of firings of mature deployed systems (the derived aim point method).[60]

The same source reports that the Shahab-3 has a height of 16 meters, a stage mass of 15,092 kilograms, a dry mass of 1,780–2,180 kilograms, and a propellant mass of 12,912 kilograms. In terms of propelling ability, its thrust is between 26,760–26,600 kgf, its burn time is 110 seconds, and it has an effective Isp of 226 and a drag loss of 45 seconds. According to this source, the Shahab-3 possesses one thrust chamber. Its fuel is TM-185, and its oxidizer is the AK 27I.[61]

High levels of accuracy seem possible for this missile, but this remains to be seen. If the system uses older guidance technology and warhead separation methods, its CEP could be anywhere from 1,000 to 4,000 meters (approximately 0.0015 to 0.001 CEP). If it uses newer technology, such as some of the most advanced Chinese technology, it could have a CEP as low as 190–800 meters. In any case, such CEP data are engineering estimates based on the ratios from a perfectly located target.

This means real-world missile accuracy and reliability cannot be measured using technical terms like CEP even if they apply to a fully mature and deployed missile. The definition of the term is based on the assumption that the missile can be perfectly targeted at launch and that it performs perfectly through its final guidance phase. True performance can be derived only from observing reliability under operational conditions and by correlating actual point of impact to a known aim point.[62]

A German expert notes, for example, that the operational CEP of the improved Shahab-3 is likely to be around 3 kilometers, but the maximum deviation could be 11 kilometers.[63] In short, unclassified estimates of the Shahab-3's accuracy and reliability available from public sources are matters of speculation, and no unclassified source has credibility in describing its performance in real-world, warfighting terms. In 2007, Yahja Safavi, the commander of the IRGC, announced on Iranian state television that Iran test-fired its latest version of the Shahab-3. According to the general, the missile used had a CEP of "several meters."[64] The CEP varies with the distance the missile flies, but most experts believe that a CEP of only several meters on a Scud-based missile is unrealistic.

This is not a casual problem, since actual weaponization of a warhead requires extraordinarily sophisticated systems to detonate a warhead at the desired height of burst and to reliably disseminate the munitions or agent. Even the most sophisticated conventional submunitions are little more than area weapons if the missile accuracy to target location has errors in excess of 250–500 meters, and a unitary conventional explosive warhead without terminal guidance is little more than a psychological or terror weapon almost regardless of its accuracy.

The effective delivery of chemical agents by either spreading the agent or the use of submunitions generally requires accuracies less than 1,000 meters to achieve lethality against even large point targets. Systems with biological weapons are inherently area weapons, but a 1,000-kilogram nominal warhead can carry so little agent that accuracies less than 1,000 meters again become undesirable. Nuclear weapons require far less accuracy, particularly if a "dirty" ground burst can be targeted within a reliable fallout area. There are, however, limits. For example, a regular fission weapon of some 20 kilotons requires accuracies under 2,500–3,000 meters for some kinds of targets like sheltered airfields or large energy facilities.

What is clear is that the Shahab could carry a well-designed nuclear weapon well over 1,000 kilometers, and Iran may have access to such designs. As noted earlier, the Shahab-3 missile was tested in its final stages in 2003 and in ways that indicate it has a range of 2,000 kilometers, which is enough to reach the Gulf and Israel. A. Q. Khan sold a Chinese nuclear warhead design to Libya with a mass of as little as 500 kilograms and a one-meter diameter. It is highly probable such designs were sold to Iran as well.

Mobility and Deployment

The Shahab-3 is mobile, but requires numerous launching support vehicles for propellant transport and loading and power besides its TELs.[65] The original version was slow in setting up, taking five hours to prepare for launch.[66] Some five different TELs have been seen, however, and some experts believe the current reaction time is roughly an hour.[67]

The Shahab-3's deployment status is highly uncertain. Some reports have claimed that the Shahab-3 was operational as early as 1999. Reports surfaced that development of the Shahab-3 was completed in June 2003 and that it underwent "final" tests on July 7, 2003. However, the Shahab-3 underwent a total of only nine tests from inception through late 2003, and only four of them could be considered successful in terms of basic system performance. The missile's design characteristics also continued to evolve during these tests. A CIA report to Congress, dated November 10, 2003, indicated upgrading of the Shahab-3 was still under way, and some sources indicated that Iran was now seeking a range of 1,600 kilometers.

Speculations about the possibility of replacing the liquid propulsion fuel with solid fuel for the Shahab-3 have been dismissed due to technical reasons. Apparently, reengineering the current design with solid fuel propulsion would lead to a completely modified missile. Rather, the development of a solid fuel propulsion system in a missile the size of the Shahab-3 would point to an entirely new line of missiles that are much more sophisticated than the Shahab-3. It has been reported that Iran operates Pakistani-designed Shaheen missiles, which use solid fuel propulsion. In addition, Iran is known to have received assistance in solid fuel propulsion technology by China. It is, however, unclear to what extent Iran has mastered or is using solid fuel missiles.[68]

There is an argument among experts as to whether the system has been tested often enough to be truly operational. The CIA reported in 2004 that Iran had "some" operational Shahab-3s with a range of 1,300 kilometers. Some experts feel the missile has since become fully operational and Iran already possesses 25–100 Shahab-3's in its inventory.[69] Iranian opposition sources have claimed that Iran has 300 such missiles. According to other sources, the IRGC operated six batteries in the spring of 2006 and was redeploying them within a 35-kilometer radius of their main command and control center every 24 hours because of the risk of a U.S. or Israeli attack. The main operating forces were deployed in the west in the Kermanshah and Hamadan provinces with reserve batteries farther east in the Fars and Isfahan provinces.[70]

A substantial number of experts, however, believe the Shahab-3 may be in deployment, but only in "showpiece" or "test-bed" units using conventional warheads and with performance Iran cannot accurately predict.

SHAHAB-3A/3M/3D/IRIS

In October 2004, the Mujahedin-e Khalq (MEK) claimed that Iran was developing an improved version of the Shahab-3 with a 2,400-kilometer range (1,500 miles). The MEK has an uncertain record of accuracy in making such claims, and such claims could not be confirmed. Mortezar Ramandi, an official in the Iranian delegation to the UN, denied that Iran was developing a missile with a range of more than 1,250 miles (2,000 kilometers).[71]

This new range for the Shahab-3 may have marked a significant move in Iranian technological capability, as some experts believe Iran switched the fuel source from liquid fuel to solid. The possible existence of a Shahab-3 with a solid fuel source created yet another variant of the Shahab-3 series, the Shahab-3D, or the IRIS missile.

Such a development of a solid fuel source might enable the Shahab-3D to enter into space and serve as a potential satellite launch vehicle. Perfecting solid fuel technology would also move Iran's missile systems a long way toward the successful creation of a limited range intercontinental ballistic missile (LRICBM), which is what the Shahab-5 and Shahab-6 are intended to accomplish.[72] On January 26, 2007, Iranian sources reportedly claimed that Iran has successfully converted one of its missiles into a satellite delivery vehicle.[73] This information remains unconfirmed.

If there is an IRIS launch vehicle, it apparently consists of the No Dong/Shahab-3 first stage with a bulbous front section ultimately designed to carry the IRIS second-stage solid motor, as well as a communications satellite or scientific payload.[74] The IRIS solid fuel missile itself may be the third-stage portion of the North Korean Taep'o-dong-1.[75]

The Shahab-3D alone is not capable of launching a large satellite probe into space, and it is possible that it is a test for the second- and third-stage portions of the upcoming IRBM Ghadr designs and the LRICBM Shahab-5 and Shahab-6.[76]

No test flights of the Shahab-3D have been recorded on video, but it is believed that they have taken place at a space launch facility.[77] The following timeline shows the reported tests of the Shahab-3D/IRIS:

- **July 22, 1998:** First test flight (exploded 100 seconds after takeoff).
- **July 15, 2000:** First successful test flight (range of 850 kilometers).
- **September 21, 2000:** Unsuccessful test flight (exploded shortly after takeoff). After the test, an Iranian source claimed that the missile was a two-stage/solid fuel propulsion system.
- **May 23, 2002:** Successful test flight.
- **July 2002:** Unsuccessful test flight (missile did not function properly).
- **June 2003:** Successful test flight. Iran declared this was the final test flight before deployment.
- **August 11, 2004:** Successful test flight of Shahab-3M. The missile now had a bottleneck warhead.
- **October 20, 2004:** Another successful test flight of Shahab-3M. Iran now claimed the modified missile had a range of 2,000 kilometers.[78]

SHAHAB-4

Iran may also be developing larger designs with greater range-payload using a variety of local, North Korean, Chinese, and Russian technical inputs. These missiles have been called the Shahab-4, the Shahab-5, and the Shahab-6. As of September 2006, none of these missiles were being produced, and the exact nature of such programs remained speculative.[79]

Some experts believe the "Shahab-4" has an approximate range between 2,200 and 2,800 kilometers. Various experts have claimed that the Shahab-4 is based on the North Korean No Dong 2, the three-stage Taep'o-dong-1 missile, the Russian SS-N-6 SERB, or even some aspects of the Russian SS-4 and SS-5,[80] but has a modern digital guidance package rather than the 2,000–3,000 meter CEP of early missiles like the Soviet SS-4, whose technology is believed to have been transferred to both North Korea and Iran.

Russian firms are believed to have sold Iran special steel for missile development, test equipment, shielding for guidance packages, and other technology. Iran's Shahid Hemmet Industrial Group is reported to have contracts with the Russian Central Aerohydrodynamic Institute, Rosvoorouzhenie, the Bauman Institute, and Polyus. It is also possible that Iran has obtained some technology from Pakistan.

One source has provided a precise estimate of some performance characteristics. This estimate of "Shahab-4 gives it an estimated height of 25 meters, a diameter of 1.3 meters, and a launch weight of 22,000 kilograms. In terms of propelling ability, its thrust is estimated to be around 26,000 kgf and its burn time is around 293 seconds. It is said to be a 2/3-stage rocket that possesses three thrust chambers, one for each stage. Its fuel for the first stage is heptyl, and its oxidizer is inhibited red fuming nitric acid."[81]

Iran has sent mixed signals about the missile development status. In October 2003, Iran claimed it was abandoning its Shahab-4 program, citing that the expected increase in range (2,200 to 3,000 kilometers) would cause too much global tension.[82] Some speculate that Iran may have scrapped its Shahab-4 program because it either was not innovative and large enough and/or to avoid controversy. The reason announced by some Iranians for creating a missile like the Shahab-4 was for satellite launches.

The IRIS/Shahab-3D, with its solid fuel source, however, has shown potential for space launches. The improved range and bottleneck warhead design offered by the Shahab-3M (which began testing in August 2004) may make the Shahab-4 simply not worth the effort or controversy.[83] According to unconfirmed reports by the National Council of Resistance of Iran (NCRI), a resistance group, Iran for the first time launched a Shahab-4 missile on August 17, 2004.[84]

According to German press reports, however, Iran is moving ahead in its development of the Shahab-4. In February 2006, the German news agency cited "Western intelligence services" as saying that Iran successfully tested the Shahab-4 missile with a range of 2,200 kilometers on January 17, 2006, and the test was announced on Iranian television several days later by the Commander of the IRGC.[85] These reports remain unverifiable.

Further, in May 2005, Ali Shamkhani, Iran's Minister of Defense announced the successful development of a "twin engine," which subsequently was interpreted as a two-stage missile with a solid propellant. Initial assumptions over an improved version of the Shahab-3 were refuted, as observers claimed that introducing a solid propellant, two-stage motor into a Shahab-3 made little sense.[86] Yet Iranian sources have not clarified their statements about the alleged new motor, therefore leaving open speculations whether the new engine was in use at all, perhaps in use with the Shahab-4 and Shahab-5 missiles, or whether it existed at all. The Pakistani Shaheen, on the other hand, is solid fueled. The IISS *Military Balance 2007* reports that Iran holds an unspecified number of Shaheen missiles. Perhaps Iran has modified the motor of that engine for its own program.

SHAHAB-5 AND SHAHAB-6

Israeli intelligence has reported that Iran is attempting to create a Shahab-5 and a Shahab-6, with a 3,000–5,000-kilometer range. These missiles would be based on the North Korean Taep'o-dong-2 and would be three-stage rockets. If completed, the Shahab-5 and the Shahab-6 would take Iran into the realm of intercontinental ballistic missiles (ICBMs) and enable Iran to target the U.S. eastern seaboard. The Shahab-5 and the Shahab-6 would possess a solid fuel third stage for space entry and liquid fuel for the first stage units.

It is alleged that Russian aerospace engineers are aiding the Iranians in their efforts. It is believed that the engineers will employ a version of Russia's storable liquid propellant RD-216 in the missile's first stage. The RD-216 is an Energomash engine originally used on the Skean/SS-5/R-14, IRBM, Saddler/SS-7/R-16, ICBM, and Sasin/R-26 ICBM missiles used in the Cold War. The effort to develop an ICBM with the Russian RD-216 engine in some sources has been named Project Koussar.[87] These reports remain uncertain, and Israeli media and official sources have repeatedly exaggerated the nature and speed of Iranian efforts.[88]

Neither the Shahab-5 nor the Shahab-6 has been tested or constructed. While no description of the Shahab-6 is yet available, extrapolations for the Shahab-5 have been made based on the North Korean Taep'o-dong-2. The Shahab-5 has an approximate range between 4,000 and 4,300 kilometers. The Shahab-5 has an unknown CEP, and its warhead capacity is between 700 and 1,000 kilograms. It has a height of 32 meters, a diameter of 2.2 meters, and a launch weight of 80,000–85,000 kilograms.

In terms of propelling ability, some experts estimate its thrust to be 31,260 kgf and its burn time to be 330 seconds. The Shahab-5 is a three-stage rocket that possesses six thrust chambers, four for stage one, and one for the two remaining stages. The Shahab-5 and the Shahab-6 would be considered long-range ICBMs.[89]

As of January 2006, Iran had not completed its plans for these missiles, and it had none in its inventory. In February 2006, German press reports, however, claimed that the Federal German Intelligence Service estimated that it was possible for Iran to acquire the Shahab-5 as early as 2007 with a range of 3,000–5,000 kilometers.[90] These estimates, however, are speculative and remain unconfirmed.

SATELLITE LAUNCH VEHICLE

As early as 1998 Iran announced its objective to establish a space program. One source reports that when Iran's Supreme Leader Ali Khamenei visited a defense fair the same year, images of a satellite launch vehicle (SLV) surfaced that apparently showed a SLV resembling the Shahab-3 with the letters IRIS painted on it.[91] Iran has never openly declared its space program assets, but on February 25, 2007, proclaimed that it had fired a test rocket into a suborbital altitude. This apparently was based on a vehicle identified as Shahab-4.[92] Out of the great multitude of speculations about the satellite launch, claims of the Shahab-4 with a two-stage, solid propellant motor seem to be the most prevalent. This may, however, simply be attributed to the fact that Iranian official sources distributed such information and other sources lacked any convincing evidence. Parts of the missile that was fired on February 25 apparently fell back to earth by parachute. This test caused considerable concern among Western observers. By the second week of March, the U.S. government had not issued an official statement about the event. However, the actual rocket launch so far has not revealed any significant technical breakthrough that was not previously known. It may or may not be the case that Iran signaled its intentions to speed up its ballistic missile program; there is simply not enough reliable data available that can give credible evidence to whether the launch is a step toward the acquisition of an ICBM or not.

According to one source, Iran is working on the following satellite projects:

- Zoreh: Allegedly, Iran was the contractor for this communication satellite, but did not engineer any of the parts for it. The satellite was supposed to be launched by a Russian vehicle.
- Safrir 313: This is a 20-kilogram heavy, Iranian-made satellite that was supposed to be launched in early 2005; as of July 2007 this has not taken place.
- Mesbah: Reportedly, this is a 70-kilogram satellite produced by an Italian-Iranian joint venture. It was supposed to be launched by a Russian vehicle.
- Sina 1: This is a Russian communication and observation satellite. Apparently, the Iranian role consisted of a tracking and data retrieval station and possibly to expand cooperation with a successor satellite named Sina 2.[93] Reportedly, the Sina 1 was Iran's first satellite that it launched into space. The launch occurred in October 2005.[94]

One analyst speculates about the difficulties in discerning Iranian space vehicle launch capabilities as follows:

> Though an indigenously built Iranian satellite launch vehicle could exist, the launch of a North Korean-manufactured Taepodong-2 with an Iranian flag painted on it is far more likely (although any Iranian-built missile would likely be nearly identical to the Taepodong-2 and in grainy imagery of such a launch it could be impossible to tell one from the other). Either way, any Iranian satellite launch vehicle will look strikingly similar to the Taepodong family, and there would almost certainly be North Korean scientists on the ground at the launch site.[95]

CSS-8 OR TONDAR 69

Jane's reports that Iran may have some 200 Chinese CSS-8, or M-7/Project 8610 short-range missiles. These are Chinese modifications of the SA-2 surface-to-air missile for use as a surface-to-surface system. It has a 190-kilogram warhead and a 150-kilometer range. Up to 90 may have been delivered to Iran in 1992, and another 110 may have been delivered later. The system is reported to have poor accuracy.[96]

BM-25/SS-N-6

Reportedly, Iran concluded an agreement with North Korea to buy 18 IRBMs (initially called BM-25) that in return are reverse-engineered Russian SS-N-6 SLBMs. Apparently, Iran tested a BM-25 in January 2006; the missile is reported to have flown more than 3,000 kilometers. Several sources claim that the BM-25 has a range of up to 4,000 kilometers.[97]

Iran is believed to have received 18 missiles; an Israeli source reportedly confirmed the delivery, but claimed that the missile's range was 2,500 kilometers.[98] One source claims that the initial SS-N-6 used a complicated propulsion as well as guidance system, and it appears questionable that North Korea and/or Iran are capable of making the necessary adjustments to create a land-launched version and achieving a range of over 2,000 miles.[99] No test of this missile in either North Korea or Iran have so far been confirmed.

GHADR 101 AND GHADR 110

The uncertainties surrounding Iran's solid fuel program and the existence or non-existence of the Shahab-3 are compounded by reports of a separate missile development program. The Iranian exile group NCRI claimed in December 2004 that the Ghadr 101 and the Ghadr 110 were new missile types that used solid fuel and were, in fact, IRBMs. Their existence has never been confirmed, and conflicting reports make an exact description difficult. One analyst claims that the Russian Kh-55 cruise missile (see below) is being reengineered by Iran under the name Ghadr.[100]

At the time, U.S. experts indicated that the Ghadr is actually the same as the Shahab-3A/Shahab M/Shahab-4, which seemed to track with some Israeli experts who felt that Iran was extending the range/payload of the Shahab-3 and that reports of both the Gadr and the Shahab-4 were actually describing the Shahab-3A/3M.[101] Another source claims that Ghadr missiles can be compared to SCUD-E missiles.[102] The SCUD-E designation has been used to describe Taep'o-dong-1 and No Dong 2 missiles.

In May 2005, Iran tested a solid fuel motor for what some experts call the Shahab-3D, possibly increasing the range to 2,500 kilometers, making space entry possible, and setting the stage for the Shahab-5 and the Shahab-6 to be three-stage rockets resembling ICBMs.[103] This test showed that Iran had developed some aspects of a successful long-range, sold fuel missile design, but did not show how Iran intended to use such capabilities.

The NCRI again claimed in March 2006 that Iran was moving forward with the Ghadr solid fuel IRBM. It also claimed that Iran had scrapped the Shahab-4 because of test failures and performance limitations. It reported that Iran had substantial North Korean technical support for the Ghadr, that it was 70 percent complete, and had a range of 3,000 kilometers. One Israeli expert felt that the NCRI was confusing a solid-state, second-stage rocket for the liquid-fueled Shahab-4 with a separate missile.[104]

Work by Dr. Robert Schmucker indicates that Iran is working on solid-fueled systems, building on its experience with solid fuel artillery rockets like its Fateh 110A1 and with Chinese support in developing solid fuel propulsion and guidance. The Fateh, however, is a relatively primitive system with strap-down gyro guidance that is not suited for a long-range ballistic missiles, although it is reported to be highly accurate.[105]

As is the case with longer-range variants of the Shahab, it is probably wise to assume that Iran is seeking to develop options for both solid- and liquid-fueled IRBMs and will seek high-range payloads to ensure it can deliver effective CBRN payloads even if it cannot produce efficient nuclear weapons. It is equally wise to wait for systems to reach maturity before reacting to vague possibilities rather than real-world Iranian capabilities.

RADUGA KH-55 GRANAT/KH-55/AS-15 KENT

The Raduga Kh-55 Granat is a Ukrainian-/Soviet-made armed nuclear cruise missile first tested in 1978 and completed in 1984.[106] The Russian missile carries a 200-kiloton nuclear warhead, and it has a range of 2,500–3,000 kilometers. It has a theoretical CEP of about 150 meters and a speed of Mach 0.48–0.77.

Its guidance system is reported to combine inertial-Doppler navigation and position correction based on in-flight comparison of terrain in the assigned regions with images stored in the memory of an on-board computer. It was designed to deliver a high-yield nuclear weapon against fixed-area targets and has little value delivering conventional warheads. While it was originally designed to be carried by a large bomber, and its weight makes it a marginal payload for either Iran's Su-24s or F-14As, it has land and ship launch capability. It can also be adapted to use a much larger nuclear or other CBRN warhead by cutting its range, and it may be a system that Iran can reverse engineer for production.[107]

Russian President Boris Yeltsin made further manufacture of the missile illegal in 1992.[108] Still, the Ukraine had 1,612 of these missiles in stock at the end of 1991, and it agreed to give 575 of them to Russia and scrap the rest.[109] The plans to give the missiles to Russia in the late 1990s proved troublesome, however, and an organization was able to forge the documents regarding 20 missiles and listed them as being sold to Russia, while in fact 12 seem to have been distributed to Iran and 6 to China (the other two are unaccounted for).[110] It was estimated that the missiles were smuggled to Iran in 2001.[111]

Ukrainian officials confirmed the illegal sale on March 18, 2005, but the Chinese and Iranian governments were silent regarding the matter. While some U.S. officials downplayed the transaction, the U.S. Department of State expressed concern that the missiles could give each state a technological boost.[112] The missiles did not contain warheads at the time of their sale, and they had passed their service life in 1995 and were in need of maintenance.[113] It is, however, feared that Iran could learn from the cruise missiles technology to improve its own missile program and the missiles could be fitted to match Iran's Su-24 strike aircraft.[114] According to one source, Parchin Missile Industries and China South Industries Group are to reverse engineer the missile, but as of July 2007 are likely still at an early stage of the process.[115]

The availability of the Kh-55 is impeded by the fact that this missile in its original design can be launched only from long-range Tupolev bombers, which Iran does not possess. It is therefore not unlikely that the Kh-55 primarily serves for research purposes and/or reverse engineering of its small fan jet engine, especially since the turbo fan engine for the Kh-55 was manufactured in Ukraine. The Kh-55 therefore may serve as an important stepping-stone in the development of cruise missile capabilities.[116]

With the Kh-55 cruise missile, Iran already possesses the capability to strike targets in Western Europe, an option that is widely believed to alter strategic and political considerations between the United States and its allies. Iran's capability in this regard, however, remains a theoretical one. It is highly doubtful that Iran possesses the means to employ a Kh-55 according to its widely stated technical capabilities. Even though the Kh-55 may have a maximum range of 3,000 kilometers, there are numerous technical obstacles that Iran would have to overcome before launching a cruise missile. As mentioned, it is not known if Iran possesses the launching capabilities. As the country lacks the original launching platform (a Tu-95/Bear H bomber), it would need to adapt its aircraft or naval vessels to be operational to fire a Kh-55. There is currently no indication that Iran possesses aircraft or ships with such capability, yet one analyst claims that Iran might develop the capability to launch a cruise missile based on the Kh-55 from its Su-24 and F-14A aircraft.[117] The Kilo-class submarines in Iran's possession are not fitted to launch Kh-55 missiles, only short-range SS-N-27 cruise missiles.

Second, long-range cruise missiles require long-range navigation systems. Iran does not have access to the GPS (Global Positioning System), TERCOM (Terrain Contour Matching), or GLONASS (Global Navigation Satellite System) systems. In 2000, the Iranian defense minister announced that Iran was beginning to produce its own laser gyros, which are at the core of any modern navigation system. Without satellite-guided navigation, the CEP of a missile that flies 3,000 kilometers is over 1,000 meters.

According to reports, Iran may be involved in three advanced missile programs: the improvement of the Shabab-series missiles, the BM-25/SS-N-6, and the Kh-55. There is no reliable information available whether Iran is pursuing three distinct programs or not. It seems unlikely that this is the case since intelligence has failed to report a single test of the BM-25/SS-N-6 or the Kh-55. It may be that these two programs are used to study the missile technology and/or are suspended due to a lack of funds. A Russian general remarked in November 2006, during Iran's military exercises, that Iran does not possess the capability to produce intercontinental ballistic missiles.[118]

M-9 AND M-11 MISSILES

For over a decade there has been speculation whether or not Iran acquired Chinese M-9 and M-11 missiles, which are based on the Russian Scud designs. It seems evident that Iran expressed interest in these missiles, but apparently China did not deliver any missiles because of U.S. pressure. One source notes that China may have delivered one or two stereotypes in the early 1990s.[119] Some experts continuously speculate whether deliveries have taken place illegally, despite China's pledge to not sell the missiles, although most reports do not confirm that any of the missiles are in stock with Iranian forces.

FURTHER DEVELOPMENTS

In late January 2007, it was reported that Iran has converted a ballistic missile into a satellite launch vehicle. Reports assume that the missile is either a version of the Shahab-3 or the Ghadr 110, based on the reported weight of 30 tons.[120] According to the latest DIA estimates, Iran may develop a 3,000-mile ICBM by the year 2015. The advances in missile technologies have substantiated evidence that there is close cooperation between North Korean and Iranian space missile programs, but no reliable information about this is available.[121]

Iran's Weapons of Mass Destruction Program: Chemical and Biological Weapons

There is no simple or reliable way to characterize Iran's ability to acquire weapons of mass destruction and the means to deliver them. Iran is clearly attempting to acquire long-range ballistic missiles and cruise missiles, but it has never indicated that such weapons would have chemical, biological, radiological, and nuclear (CBRN) warheads. Iran has never properly declared its holdings of chemical weapons, and the status of its biological weapons programs is unknown.

There have been strong indications of an active Iranian interest in acquiring nuclear weapons since the time of the Shah and that Ayatollah Ruhollah Khomeini revived such efforts after Iraq invaded Iran and began to use chemical weapons. There is, however, no reliable history of such efforts or a "smoking gun" that conclusively proves their existence.

The Iranian leadership has consistently argued that its nuclear research efforts are designed for peaceful purposes, although various Iranian leaders have made ambiguous statements about acquiring weapons of mass destruction and Iranian actions strongly suggest that Iran is trying to acquire nuclear weapons. Whether such Iranian deniability is plausible or not is highly questionable, but Iran has been able to find some alternative explanation for even its most suspect activities, and there is no present way to disprove its claims with open-source material.

CHEMICAL WEAPONS

The various claims and counterassertions about Iran's current chemical weapons capabilities are as hard to substantiate as they are to rebut. Open sources are limited and conflicting, and Iranian claims go unchecked. Outside governments have provided some useful summary assessments of Iranian chemical weapons program, but few details.

Official Estimates of Iranian Capability

The Central Intelligence Agency (CIA) has reported that Chinese entities were still trying to supply Iran with chemical warfare (CW)-related chemicals between 1997 and 1998. The U.S. sanctions imposed in May 1997 on seven Chinese entities for knowingly and materially contributing to Iran's CW program remain in effect. In addition, the CIA estimated in January 1999 that Iran obtained material related to chemical warfare from various sources during the first half of 1998. It already has manufactured and stockpiled chemical weapons, including blister, blood, and choking agents and the bombs and artillery shells for delivering them. However, Tehran is seeking foreign equipment and expertise to create a more advanced and self-sufficient CW infrastructure.

The last unclassified U.S. formal assessment of this aspect of Iranian proliferation was released in 2001, and it provided only a broad summary:

> Iran has acceded to the Chemical Weapons Convention (CWC) and in a May 1998 session of the CWC Conference of the States Parties, Tehran, for the first time, acknowledged the existence of a past chemical weapons program. Iran admitted developing a chemical warfare program during the latter stages of the Iran-Iraq war as a "deterrent" against Iraq's use of chemical agents against Iran. Moreover, Tehran claimed that after the 1988 cease-fire, it "terminated" its program. However, Iran has yet to acknowledge that it, too, used chemical weapons during the Iran-Iraq War.
>
> Nevertheless, Iran has continued its efforts to seek production technology, expertise and precursor chemicals from entities in Russia and China that could be used to create a more advanced and self-sufficient chemical warfare infrastructure. As Iran's program moves closer to self-sufficiency, the potential will increase for Iran to export dual-use chemicals and related equipment and technologies to other countries of proliferation concern.
>
> In the past, Tehran has manufactured and stockpiled blister, blood and choking chemical agents, and weaponized some of these agents into artillery shells, mortars, rockets, and aerial bombs. It also is believed to be conducting research on nerve agents. Iran could employ these agents during a future conflict in the region. Lastly, Iran's training, especially for its naval and ground forces, indicates that it is planning to operate in a contaminated environment.[1]

In mid-May 2003, the Bush administration released a statement to the Organization for Prohibition of Chemical Weapons in which the United States accused Iran of continuing to pursue production technology, training, and expertise from abroad. The statement asserted that Iran was continuing to stockpile blister, blood, choking, and some nerve agents. This was followed by an unclassified report that the CIA released in November 2003, which stated that "Iran is a party to the Chemical Weapons Convention (CWC). Nevertheless, during the reporting period it continued to seek production technology, training, and expertise from Chinese entities that could further Tehran's efforts to achieve an indigenous capability to produce nerve agents. Iran likely has already stockpiled blister, blood, choking, and probably nerve agents—and the bombs and artillery shells to deliver them—which it previously had manufactured."[2]

John R. Bolton, then Under Secretary for Arms Control and International Security at the U.S. Department of State, reported on Iran's chemical program in testimony to the House International Relations Committee Subcommittee on the Middle East and Central Asia in 2005. He reported, however, only in summary terms:[3]

> We believe Iran has a covert program to develop and stockpile chemical weapons. The U.S. Intelligence Community reported in its recent unclassified Report to Congress on the Acquisition of Technology Relating to Weapons of Mass Destruction and Advanced Conventional Munitions, also known as the "721 Report," that Iran continues to seek production technology, training, and expertise that could further its efforts to achieve an indigenous capability to produce nerve agents. A forthcoming edition of the 721 report is expected to state that, "Iran may have already stockpiled blister, blood, choking, and nerve agents—and the bombs and artillery shells to deliver them—which it previously had manufactured."
>
> Iran is a party to the Chemical Weapons Convention (CWC). The CWC's central obligation is simple: no stockpiling, no development, no production, and no use of chemical weapons. The overwhelming majority of States Parties abide by this obligation. Iran is not, and we have made this abundantly clear to the Organization for the Prohibition of Chemical Weapons (OPCW). Although Iran has declared a portion of its CW program to the OPCW, it is time for Iran to declare the remainder and make arrangements for its dismantlement and for the destruction of its chemical weapons.

European assessments seem to agree with those of the U.S. Department of Defense (DOD) and the CIA, but there have been only limited public reports. The German Federal Customs Administration published a report in November 2004 that stated, "Iran has an emerging chemical industry. Its CW program obtains support, according to accounts received, from China and India. It probably possesses chemical agents such as sulphur mustards, Tabun, and hydrogen cyanide, possibly also Sarin and VC. Iran is attempting to acquire chemical installations and parts thereof, as well as technology and chemical precursors."[4]

Arms Control Estimates of Iranian Capability

Arms control efforts have not provided meaningful transparency, and ratifying the CWC has not guaranteed the end of Tehran's CW programs; it has only meant that if Iran is violating the treaty, it is an "illegal" activity.

Unfortunately, there have been no meaningful inspections or independent analysis of Iran's chemical weapons program. Iran did submit a statement in Farsi to the CWC secretariat in 1998, but this statement consisted only of questions as to the nature of the required compliance. It has not provided the CWC with detailed data on its chemical weapons program. Iran also stridently asserted its right to withdraw from the Convention at any time.

NGO Estimates of Iranian Capability

Some nongovernmental organization (NGO) reporting does provide more detail. A study by the Monterey Institute indicates there are a number of sites in Iran that may be related to Iran's chemical warfare effort:[5]

- **Abu Musa Island:** Iran holds a large number of chemical weapons, principally 155-millimeter artillery shells, in addition to some weaponized biological agents.

- **Bandar Khomeini:** This is allegedly the location of a chemical weapons facility, run by the Razi Chemical Corporation, established during the Iran-Iraq War to manufacture chemical weapons.

- **Damghan:** This is the location of either a chemical weapons plant or warhead assembly facility. It is primarily involved in 155-millimeter artillery shells and Scud warheads.

- **Isfahan:** This is a suspected location of a chemical weapons facility, possibly operated by the Polyacryl Iran Corporation.

- **Karaj:** Located about 14 kilometers from Tehran, this is the site of an alleged storage and manufacturing facility for chemical weapons. Reports suggest that this facility was built with Chinese assistance.

- **Marvdasht:** The Chemical Fertilizers Company is suspected to have been a manufacturing facility for mustard agents during the Iran-Iraq War.

- **Parchin:** This is the location of at least one munitions factory and is suspected of being a major chemical weapons production facility. Reports of uncertain reliability indicate that the plant was in operation no later than March 1988. In April 1997, a German newspaper reported that, according to the German Federal Intelligence Service, the factories at Parchin were producing primary products for chemical warfare agents.

- **Qazvin:** A large pesticide plant at this location is widely believed to produce nerve gas.

- **Mashar:** Iranian opposition groups have made allegations, of uncertain reliability, that a warhead filling facility is operated at this location.

The Nuclear Threat Initiative summarized what is and is not known about the status of Iran's chemical weapons as follows in January 2006:[6]

Despite its acquisition of precursors from abroad, Iran is allegedly working to develop an indigenous CW production capability. The CIA believes that "Teheran is rapidly approaching self-sufficiency and could become a supplier of CW-related materials to other nations." As of 1996, the Department of Defense claimed that Iran had stockpiled almost 2000 tons of toxic chemical agents and was continuously working on expanding its CW program. Iran has several advanced research institutions employing various chemicals for a variety of reasons, including pesticide production, pharmaceutical research, and other medical studies. Iran has also conducted several military exercises to date that have included defensive chemical and biological weapons maneuvers.

Iran continues to deny any allegations that it is actively pursuing an offensive CW program. In 1996, it held the first regional seminar on the national implementation of the CWC in Tehran so that government authorities could familiarize themselves with their duties and obligations under the treaty. It also held a mock "trial inspection" at the Shahid Razkani chemical factory to allow inspectors to see how such a procedure was conducted. Iran submitted a declaration on its chemical facilities and its past CW stockpile, it has destroyed chemical weapons production equipment in the presence of OPCW inspectors, and it has undergone a number of OPCW inspections of its chemical industrial facilities. Iran continues to play an active role at the Organization for the Prohibition of Chemical Weapons (OPCW), is recognized as a member in good standing, and currently serves on its executive council. Although U.S. and Israeli intelligence agencies continue to insist Iran maintains a stockpile of chemical weapons, no challenge inspections of Iranian facilities have been requested, and none of the allegations made regarding the stockpiling of CW can be verified in the unclassified domain. However, Iran continues to retain a strong incentive for developing a defensive CW program.

BIOLOGICAL WEAPONS

Any analysis of Iran's biological weapons effort must be even more speculative. In 1997, the U.S. DOD asserted that the Iranian biological warfare (BW) program "is in the research and development [R&D] stage, [but] the Iranians have considerable expertise with pharmaceuticals, as well as the commercial and military infrastructure needed to produce basic biological warfare agents."[7]

The Department of State updated its findings in 2001 as follows:[8]

Iran has a growing biotechnology industry, significant pharmaceutical experience and the overall infrastructure to support its biological warfare program. Tehran has expanded its efforts to seek considerable dual-use biotechnical materials and expertise from entities in Russia and elsewhere, ostensibly for civilian reasons. Outside assistance is important for Iran, and it is also difficult to prevent because of the dual-use nature of the materials and equipment being sought by Iran and the many legitimate end uses for these items.

Iran's biological warfare program began during the Iran-Iraq war. Iran is believed to be pursuing offensive biological warfare capabilities and its effort may have evolved beyond agent research and development to the capability to produce small quantities of agent. Iran has ratified the BWC [Biological Weapons Convention].

Since that time, the United States has not significantly updated its unclassified estimates, except to state that such Iranian R&D efforts continue. The problem is whether such statements are a suspicion, a strong probability, or a fact. Iran does have extensive laboratory and research capability and steadily improving industrial facilities with dual-use production capabilities. Whether it has an active weapons development program or not, however, is a controversial matter.

The reality is that many nations now have the biotechnology, the industrial base, and the technical expertise to acquire biological weapons. Not only does most civil technology have "dual use" in building weapons, but the global dissemination of biological equipment has made control by supplier nations extremely difficult. Even when such controls do still apply to original sellers, they have little or no impact on the sellers of used equipment, and a wide range of sensitive equipment is now available for sale to any buyer on the Internet.

This makes it almost impossible to disprove a nation's interest in biological weapons. Moreover, there is little meaningful distinction between a "defensive" and an "offensive" capability. Nations can claim to be conducting defensive research, acquiring key gear for defensive purposes, and practicing defensive training and maneuvers.

So far, Iran has not demonstrated any such defensive activities, but there is an active debate over whether it has a biological weapons program.

Possible Early Indicators That Iran Might Have a BW Program

There is a long history of indicators that Iran might have some form of BW program. Reports first surfaced in 1982—during the Iran-Iraq War—that Iran had imported suitable type cultures from Europe and was working on the production of mycotoxins—a relatively simple family of biological agents that require only limited laboratory facilities for small-scale production. Many experts believe that the Iranian biological weapons effort was placed under the control of the Islamic Revolutionary Guards Corps (IRGC), which is known to have tried to purchase suitable production equipment for such weapons.

U.S. intelligence sources reported in August 1989 that Iran was trying to buy two new strains of fungus from Canada and the Netherlands that can be used to produce mycotoxins. German sources indicated that Iran had successfully purchased such cultures several years earlier. Some universities and research centers may be linked to the biological weapons program. The Imam Reza Medical Center at Mashhad University of Medical Sciences and the Iranian Research Organization for Science and Technology were identified as the end users for this purchasing effort, but it is likely that the true end user was an Iranian government agency specializing in biological warfare.

Since the Iran-Iraq War, various reports have surfaced that Iran may have conducted research on more lethal active agents like anthrax, hoof-and-mouth disease, and biotoxins. Iranian groups have repeatedly approached various European firms for equipment and technology that could be used to work with these diseases and toxins.

Unclassified sources of uncertain reliability have identified a facility at Damghan as working on both biological and chemical weapons research and production and believe that Iran may be producing biological weapons at a pesticide facility near Tehran.

Reports also surfaced in the spring of 1993 that Iran had succeeded in obtaining advanced biological weapons technology in Switzerland and containment equipment and technology from Germany. According to these reports, this led to serious damage to computer facilities in a Swiss biological research facility by unidentified agents. Similar reports indicated that agents had destroyed German biocontainment equipment destined for Iran. More credible reports by U.S. experts indicate that Iran might have begun to stockpile anthrax and botulinum in a facility near Tabriz, can now mass manufacture such agents, and has them in an aerosol form. None of these reports, however, can be verified.

The Uncertain Nature of Iran's BW Program Since the Mid-1990s

The CIA reported in 1996, "We believe that Iran holds some stocks of biological agents and weapons. Tehran probably has investigated both toxins and live organisms as biological warfare agents. Iran has the technical infrastructure to support a significant biological weapons program with little foreign assistance." It also reported that Iran has "sought dual-use biotech equipment from Europe and Asia, ostensibly for civilian use," and that Iran might be ready to deploy biological weapons. Beyond this point, little unclassified information exists regarding the details of Iran's effort to "weaponize" and produce biological weapons.

Continuing Alarms and Excursions

Iran announced in June 1997 that it would not produce or employ chemical weapons including biological toxins. However, the CIA reported in June 1997 that Iran had obtained new dual-use technology from China and India during 1996.

Furthermore, the CIA reported in January 1999 that Iran continued to pursue dual-use biotechnical equipment from Russia and other countries, ostensibly for civilian uses. Its BW program began during the Iran-Iraq War, and Iran may have some limited capability for BW deployment. Outside assistance is both important and difficult to prevent, given the dual-use nature of the materials and equipment being sought and the many legitimate end uses for these items.

In 2001, an allegation from the former director of research and development at the Cuban Center for Genetic Engineering and Biotechnology surfaced that claimed Cuba had assisted the Iranian bioweapons program from 1995 to 1998. The authenticity of the director's claims has not been established.[9]

A report produced by an Iranian insurgent group, the Mujahedin-e Khalq (MEK) Organization, asserted in 2003 that Iran had started producing weaponized anthrax and was actively working with at least five other pathogens, including small pox. The MEK was the same organization that produced early evidence of Iran's noncompliance with the terms of the Nuclear Non-Proliferation Treaty (NPT). Iran issued a vehement denial of these charges in a May 16, 2003, press release. The accuracy of either set of statements remains uncertain.

The Possible Role of Outside Suppliers

Russia has been a key source of biotechnology for Iran. Russia's world-leading expertise in biological weapons also makes it an attractive target for Iranians seeking technical information and training on BW agent production processes. This has led to speculation that Iran may have the production technology to make dry storable and aerosol weapons. This would allow it to develop suitable missile warheads, bombs, and covert devices.

In testimony to the Senate Committee on Foreign Relations, John A. Lauder, the Director of the Nonproliferation Center at the CIA, asserted the following in 2000:[10]

Iran is seeking expertise and technology from Russia that could advance Tehran's biological warfare effort. Russia has several government-to-government agreements with Iran in a variety of scientific and technical fields.

—Because of the dual-use nature of much of this technology, Tehran can exploit these agreements to procure equipment and expertise that could be diverted to its BW effort.

—Iran's BW program could make rapid and significant advances if it has unfettered access to BW expertise resident in Russia.

The CIA reported in November 2003, "Even though Iran is part of the BWC, Tehran probably maintained an offensive BW program. Iran continued to seek dual-use biotechnical materials, equipment, and expertise. While such materials had legitimate uses, Iran's biological warfare program also could have benefited from them. It is likely that Iran has capabilities to produce small quantities of BW agents, but has a limited ability to weaponize them."[11] John R. Bolton, then Under Secretary for Arms Control and International Security at the U.S. Department of State, testified the following to the House International Relations Committee in 2004:[12]

The U.S. Intelligence Community stated in its recent 721 Report that, "Tehran probably maintains an offensive BW program. Iran continued to seek dual-use biotechnical materials, equipment, and expertise. While such materials had legitimate uses, Iran's biological warfare (BW) program also could have benefited from them. It is likely that Iran has capabilities to produce small quantities of BW agents, but has a limited ability to weaponize them."

Because BW programs are easily concealed, I cannot say that the United States can prove beyond a shadow of a doubt that Iran has an offensive BW program. The intelligence I have seen suggests that this is the case, and, as a policy matter therefore, I believe we have to act on that assumption. The risks to international peace and security from such programs are too great to wait for irrefutable proof of illicit activity: responsible members of the international community should act to head off such threats and demand transparency and accountability from suspected violators while these threats are still emerging. It would be folly indeed to wait for the threat fully to mature before trying to stop it.

Iran is a party to the Biological Weapons Convention (BWC) and the 1925 Protocol for the Prohibition of the Use in War of Asphyxiating, Poisonous or Other Gases, and of Bacteriological Methods of Warfare. Like the CWC, the central obligation of the BWC is simple: no possession, no development no production and, together with the 1925 Protocol, no use of biological weapons. The overwhelming majority of States Parties abide by these obligations. We believe Iran is not abiding by its BWC obligations, however, and we have made this abundantly clear to the parties of this treaty. It is time for Iran to declare its biological weapons program and make arrangements for its dismantlement.

POSSIBLE CBW WARFIGHTING CAPABILITY

These factors make it almost impossible to know how Iran may use any capabilities it does possess. It does not overtly train its forces for offensive chemical warfare, and its current and future warfighting capabilities are unknown.

Iran has stated its objection to the use of CBW in war on religious grounds—based on Khomeini's statements in the 1980s—and legal obligation under international conventions. Most experts do, however, believe that Iran at least used confiscated Iraqi chemical shells against Iraqi forces. It had definitely instituted its own program to produce chemical weapons and may have used its weapons. The International Institute for Strategic Studies pointed out in its 2005 study of Iran's weapons that "[d]espite a similar record with respect to nuclear weapons and the NPT, Iran conducted undeclared nuclear activities in violation of the treaty for over 20 years. Whether Iran has carried out similar activities in violation of its CWC and BWC obligations cannot be determined definitively from the available public information."[13]

It does seem likely that Iran at least retains some capability to make chemical weapons, and it may have inactive or mothballed facilities. There have been no public reports of active production, but this is possible. Iraq produced small lots of mustard gas weapons at the laboratory level before its major production facilities came online and showed that it could produce at the batch level with relatively small and easy-to-conceal facilities. Iran's purchases also indicate that it could have a significant stock of precursors; and some less lethal weapons can be made out of refinery and petrochemical by-products.

Any assessment of Iranian capabilities must also take account of the fact that Iraq began to use chemical weapons against Iran in the early 1980s and that Iran has had at least a quarter of a century in which to react to a real-world threat, six years of which were spent dealing with a nation seeking to acquire chemical, biological, and nuclear weapons to destroy it. Iranian military literature also has extensively reprinted Western and other literature on CBRN weapons, and Iran actively collects such literature on a global basis.

It seems clear that Iran has the technology base to produce mustard gas and non-persistent nerve agents—including reasonable stable agents and binary weapons—and may have the technology to produce persistent nerve agents as well. It probably has technical knowledge of "third-generation" and "dusty" agents. It has had the opportunity to reverse engineer captured Iraqi weapons and may have received aid in weapons design from Russian, Chinese, and North Korean sources. It certainly has monitored UN reporting on the Iraqi chemical and biological programs and may have acquired considerable detail on these programs, their strengths and weaknesses, and Iraq's sources abroad.

Iran almost certainly has the ability to make effective chemical artillery shells and bombs and unitary rocket and missile warheads. It can probably design effective cluster bombs and warheads. It may have sprayers for use by aircraft, helicopters, and unmanned aerial vehicles (UAVs). Iran's ability to develop lethal missile warheads is far more problematic. The timing and dissemination problems are far more difficult and may be beyond Iran's current technical skills.

The past history of Iranian efforts at complex program management and systems integration, however, has shown that Iran has serious problems in translating its technical expertise into practice. The knowledge of how to do things rarely leads to similar capability to actually do them, particularly when programs remain concealed and are largely "mothballed" or have low levels of activity.

Testing chemical weapons presents serious problems when the test goes beyond static tests or relatively crude measurements of how well given weapons disseminate the agent. It is particularly difficult in the case of missile warheads. It is possible to determine lethality in rough terms from residues, but this requires repeated testing using actual weapons in a variety of real-world conditions. There are no reports of such testing, but it is more than possible that they could be successfully concealed. Unlike most biological weapons, the operational lethality of chemical weapons can be safely tested against live animals. Again, there are no reports of such testing, but it is more than possible that they could be successfully concealed.

The history of actual chemical warfare, however, indicates that the results of such tests can be extremely unrealistic and that operational lethality has rarely approached anything like engineering and test predictions. The "scale-up" of individual weapons results into predictions of real-world results from using large numbers of weapons has produced particularly misleading results. Moreover, as is the case with biological weapons, temperature, weather, sunlight, wind, surface conditions, and a number of external factors can have a major impact on lethality.

These factors, coupled with the difficulty in measuring incapacity or deaths in less than hours to days, also means Iran and other users would have to carry out any chemical campaign with little ability to predict its actual lethality or carry out effective battle damage assessment. Such considerations might not be important, however, when the goal was terror, panic, area denial, forcing an enemy to don protection gear and decontaminate, or accept casualties in addition to other casualties from military operations.

At the same time, all of these factors combine to indicate that even if Iran does have plans and doctrine for using chemical weapons and has made serious efforts to estimate their lethality and effectiveness, such plans are unlikely to survive engagement with reality. Iran's past reports on its military exercises may be propaganda driven, but some of Iran's conventional warfighting exercises do have a strong element of ideology and wishful thinking and a lack of demanding realism. This could lead military officers and civilian decision makers to make serious miscalculations based on the war they want to fight rather than the war they can fight.

Such considerations would have less impact if Iran chose to use proxies or covert means of attack to strike at high-value targets or for the purposes of terrorism and intimidation. The IRGC has conducted the kind of conventional exercise that could be adapted to such ends, and Iran has long supplied conventional weapons to movements like Hezbollah and Hamas.

Any broader Iran military use of chemical weapons would present a number of problems:

- Chemical weapons are not individually lethal enough to have a major impact on ground battles and take time to be effective. They are best suited to relatively static battles, dominated by ground forces that do not have armored and protected vehicles and which cannot mass airpower effectively. This describes Iran and Iraq in 1980–1988. It does not describe the United States or most of Iran's opponents today. Airpower and sea power are largely immune to the kind of chemical attack Iran could launch, with the possible exception of fixed, targetable area targets—many of which could be denied for any significant time only by large numbers of accurate attacks. Rapidly maneuvering ground forces would be a difficult target for Iran's much more static forces. Nations like the United States would have extensive amounts of detection, protection, and decontamination gear. They also would not have large, static, rear area and support operations near the forward edge of the battle area.

- Iranian artillery tends to be slow moving and lacks the ability to rapidly target and switch fires. It relies heavily on static massed fires. This requires relatively short-range engagement against an equally slow-moving or static opponent. In reality, Iran will probably face opponents that maneuver more quickly and have superior intelligence, surveillance, and reconnaissance (IS&R) assets. A repetition of the battlefield conditions of the Iran-Iraq War seems unlikely.

- Chemical weapons could be more effective as area weapons that forced enemy forces to abandon positions, denied the ability to use rear areas, or acted as a barrier to movement. The tactical and maneuver effects were more important in the Iran-Iraq War than using CW as a killing mechanism. They again, however, tend to be most useful against relatively static opponents that do not have air superiority or supremacy.

- Iran has a number of potential long-range artillery rockets and missiles. A single chemical warhead, however, is more a terror weapon than a killing mechanism. Such systems have limited accuracies, and Iran has limited long-range targeting capability against mobile targets. The use of a few chemical rounds would be highly provocative and justify massive escalation by an enemy. As such, it might do more to provoke than terrify, intimidate, or damage. Iran might, however, be able to use persistent nerve and mustard agents to deny the use of a key facility like an air base, key supply facility, mobilization center, oil export facility, or desalination or power plant.

- Effective air strikes require high confidence in the ability to penetrate enemy air defenses and good IS&R assets. In many cases, a chemical weapon would have only marginally greater lethality than a conventional precision-guided weapon or cluster weapon. Again, such use might do more to provoke than terrify, intimidate, or damage.

- The use of chemical weapons against targets at sea presents significant targeting and meteorological problems. These are certainly solvable, but do require exceptional planning and skill. Similarly, firing against coastal targets requires high volumes of CW fire or good meteorological data.

- Covert or proxy use presents serious problems in wartime. Plausible deniability is doubtful, and an opponent simply may not care if it can prove Iran is responsible for any given use of CW.

- Operation lethality is dependent on an opponent's CW defense and decontamination facilities, level of depth, and speed of maneuver. Iran may be dealing with much more sophisticated opponents than the Iraq of the 1980s.

None of these problems and issues mean that Iran could not use chemical weapons effectively under some conditions. They might, however, deter Iran from stockpiling such weapons or using them except under the most drastic conditions. Iran has to understand that their use would tend to make Iran lose the political and information battle and act as a license to its opponent to escalate. While such concerns might well deter Iran under most circumstances, it is also important to understand that wars and drastic crises are not "most circumstances." One inherent problem in any such analysis is that even the most prudent decision maker in peacetime can panic, overreact, or drastically miscalculate in war.

Possible Nuclear Weapons Programs

There is more information available on Iran's nuclear programs than on its chemical and biological programs, but this scarcely eliminates major areas of uncertainty. Estimating Iranian nuclear capabilities is complicated by three key factors:

- First, the United States, the European Union, and the United Nations all agree that Iran has the right to acquire a full nuclear fuel cycle for peaceful purposes under the Nuclear Non-Proliferation Treaty (NPT), but there is no clear way to distinguish many of the efforts needed to acquire a nuclear weapon from such "legitimate" activities or pure research.

- Second, Iran has never denied that it carries out a very diverse range of nuclear research efforts. In fact, it has openly claimed that it is pursuing nuclear technology and has a "national" right to get access to nuclear energy. This has given it a rationale for rejecting Russia's offer to provide Iran nuclear fuel without giving Tehran the technology and the expertise needed to use it for weaponization purposes, and the United States agrees with this position.

- Third, it has never been clear whether Iran does have a "military" nuclear program that is separate from its "civilian" nuclear research. American and French officials have argued that they believe that Iran's nuclear program would make sense only if it had military purposes. Both governments have yet to provide evidence to prove these claims.

If Iran is actively developing nuclear weapons, as now seems steadily more likely, it has shown that it can conduct a skilled program that is capable of hiding many aspects of its program, sending confusing and contradictory signals, exploiting both deception and the international inspection process, rapidly changing the character of given facilities, and pausing and retreating when this is expedient. As Figure 11.1

Figure 11.1 Major Iranian Developments Regarding Iran's Weapons of Mass Destruction Program in 2006 and 2007

- Early January 2006: Iran removed 52 International Atomic Energy Agency (IAEA) seals on Natanz, Pars Trash, and Farayand centrifuge projects.

- February 4, 2006: The IAEA Board of Governors voted to refer Iran to the United Nations Security Council (UNSC).

- IAEA Director General (DG) Report of February 27, 2006: Still tracking enriched uranium activity, status of P-1 centrifuge program uncertain, P-2 centrifuge acquisition uncertain (the P-1 and the P-2 refer to two Pakistani designs for centrifuges), uranium tetrafluoride (UF4) to uranium metal conversion issues, status of plutonium experiments; level of Pu-239 versus Pu-240, still assessing mining, polonium, beryllium, site inspection "transparency" issues (e.g., Lavisan-Shian) dating back to 2004.

- Early March 2006: Twenty cascade machines were reported running at Natanz and Farayand.

- April 2006: The Iranian parliament passed a resolution for Iran to withdraw from the NPT.

- IAEA DG Report of April 28, 2006: No clarification on enrichment, highly enriched uranium (HEU) contamination issues remain, P-1 and P-2 centrifuge issues not addressed; new issues over P-2 designs, new issues over uranium hexafluoride (UF6) to metal and casting of uranium hemispheres (Iran refused to hand over a 15-page document about the casting of enriched and depleted uranium metal into hemispheres), no clarification on plutonium experiments, heavy-water reactor at Arak still under construction, new transparency issues, Iran is building second and third cascades at the Pilot Fuel Enrichment Plant.

- IAEA Director General Mohamed ElBaradei, on May 30, 2006, stated that Iran "does not present an immediate threat."

- Secretary of State Condoleezza Rice on May 31, 2006: Acknowledges right to Iranian civil nuclear energy, supports EU-3 (British, French, German) offer to Iran, offers "new and positive relationship...looks forward to a new relationship," "as soon as Iran fully and verifiably suspends its enrichment and reprocessing activities, the U.S. will come to the table with our EU-3 colleagues and meet with Iran's representatives"; Rice repeats willingness to hold talks on August 29.[1]

- IAEA DG Report of June 8, 2006: No further resolution on contamination, P-1, P-2, or uranium metal and casting, warning Iran has started centrifuge cascade activity for 164-machine cascade and started work on second 164-machine unit (second cascade launched on October 23, 2006, but without UF6 insertion), no improvement in transparency, especially plutonium and heavy-water reactor, new UF6 conversion campaign began in the Isfahan Uranium Conversion Facility (UCF) on June 6, 2006, following up on "Green Salt" project, investigating high explosives testing and design of missile reentry vehicle.

- United Nations Security Council Resolution (UNSCR) 1696 (July 31, 2006): "Serious concern" over IAEA DG reports of February 27, April 28, June 8, "Demands...that Iran shall suspend all enrichment-related and reprocessing activities, including research and development...," Expresses intention (if Iran does not comply by August 31) to adopt appropriate measures under Article 41 of Chapter VII of Charter of UN to "persuade Iran to comply...and underlines that further decisions will be required should such additional measures prove necessary."[2]

- On August 20, Ayatollah Ali Khamenei said in speech in Iran, "The Islamic Republic of Iran has made up its mind based on the experience of the past 27 years to forcefully pursue its nuclear program and other issues it is faced with."[3]

- Mahmoud Ahmadinejad inaugurates Arak heavy-water production plant on August 26.

- Chief nuclear negotiator Larijani rejects UN deadline on August 27. Ahmadinejad says Iran will never abandon purely peaceful program. Repeats rejection of deadline on August 29. Verbally attacks Britain and the United States.

- IAEA DG Report of August 31, 2006: Tested 164-machine cascade to 5-percent enrichment, second 164-centrifuge cascade to start in September (reportedly did start on October 23), limiting access to Natanz, possibly in the future to Arak and Isfahan, no indications of ongoing reprocessing, no resolution of HEU contamination (partly still unaccounted for), P-1, and P-2 issues, machining of uranium remains unresolved, uranium conversion stepping up but is inspected, transparency issues on environmental sampling and missile reentry vehicles (Green Salt) unresolved.

- September 11, 2006: Secretary of State Condoleezza Rice said that a temporary suspension of the uranium enrichment program might be sufficient for holding direct negotiations with Iran.[4]

- October 1: Ahmadinejad announces that Iran is going to construct 100,000 centrifuges.

- IAEA Board of Governors Report November 14, 2006: Testing of the second 164-machine cascade with UF6 was begun; as of November 7, Iran had produced 55 tons of uranium (in the form of UF6) out of the 160 tons of uranium ore it started processing at its Isfahan UCF in June 2006.

- According to the IAEA, between August 13 and November 2, 2006, Iran reported that approximately 34 kilograms of UF6 was fed into the centrifuges and enriched to levels below 5 percent U-235. Iran had reported by August 31 that a total of 6 kilograms of UF6 was fed into the then-single cascade between June 23 and July 8, 2006. This would represent an almost 500-percent increase in the inserted quantity of UF6, which in turn may be an indication of additional and/or more efficient cascades.

- December 23, 2006: The UNSC passes Resolution 1737, which calls on Iran to stop all uranium enrichment activities and heavy-water experiments within 60 days, allow monitoring and verification of its enrichment activities, and imposes sanctions on several Iranian persons and organizations that are believed to be linked to the nuclear program.

- February 19, 2007: Mohamed ElBaradei said that Iran may be six months away from enriching uranium on an industrial scale. He added that according to U.S. and British intelligence, Iran was five to ten years away from developing a nuclear bomb.[5]

- February 22, 2007: The IAEA Board of Governors issued a report (Gov/2007/8) that addressed Iran's compliance with the provisions set forth in UNSCR 1737. The February 22 report concluded that not only had Iran not complied with any of the calls set forth in UNSCR 1737, but it had informed the IAEA that it was installing two additional 164-machine cascades for uranium enrichment. Further, Iran informed the IAEA that it was planning to build a module of 18 164-machine cascades underground by mid-2007. However, by the time IAEA report Gov/2007/8 was issued, apparently no UF6 had been fed into the centrifuges.

- March 15, 2007: The five permanent members of the UN Security Council plus Germany agreed on a draft resolution on further sanctions on Iran. Apparently, the draft contained an arms embargo and broader economic sanctions such as a halt on international loans and freezing assets on individuals connected to the nuclear as well as the ballistic missile development programs. However, by the end of March 2007, the UNSC had not taken up a vote on the matter of further UN sanctions, and it was not clear what the smallest common political denominator at the UNSC would be on the matter.

- April 5, 2007: Iran's head of its Atomic Energy Agency, Ali Larijani, tells a European Union group that, "The Islamic Republic of Iran is ready to negotiate only on non-diversion of its nuclear program for military purposes, and not on its nuclear rights.... Iran will not accept any preconditions or suspension for a time. Nor can suspending enrichment be a precondition or the result of negotiations (with the Permanent Members of the UH Security Council)...[6]

- April 10, 2007: Iranian President Ahmadinejad proclaims that the underground enrichment facility in Natanz is operating 1,300 centrifuges. The IAEA confirmed that 1,300 centrifuges were installed at Natanz.

- May 3, 2007: John Rood, Assistant Secretary at the U.S. Department of State, told a Congressional hearing: "There is also the possibility that Iran could procure a completed system from North Korea as it had done in the past. North Korea possesses ICBM; it is certainly possible that another sale like that could occur in the future. But that would potentially move the date up further beyond 2015 and, depending on the amount of foreign assistance Iran might receive, it might also see that time frame move up."[7]

- May 14, 2007: Inspectors for the IAEA conclude that Iran has solved most of its technical problems in enriching uranium and is doing so on a much larger scale than before. A short-notice inspection of Natanz finds up to 1,300 active centrifuges, with 300 more being tested and another 300 under construction. Iran seems to be capable of installing up to 3,000 centrifuges as early as June 2007 in "cascades" of 164 centrifuges each. Some diplomats speculate that Iran could have as many as 5,000 centrifuges installed by the end of the year, and some estimates go as high as 8,000. There is, however, no data on the efficiency of this effort or its real-world capability to produce given amounts of weapons-grade uranium.[8]

---

indicates, Iran has also shown that denial can be a weapon; by consistently finding an alternative explanation for all its actions, including concealment and actions that are limited violations of the NPT, it can maintain some degree of "plausible deniability" for a long chain of ambiguous actions and events.

PROBLEMS IN ANALYZING IRAN'S WEAPONS OF MASS DESTRUCTION (WMD) PROGRAM: A CASE STUDY

Iran presents major problems in intelligence collection and analysis. The details of U.S., British, and other intelligence efforts to cover Iran remain classified. At the same time, studies of U.S. and British intelligence failures in covering Iraq have provided considerable insights into the difficulties in covering a nation like Iran, and background discussions with intelligence analysts and users reveal the following general problems in analyzing the WMD threat:

- The uncertainties surrounding collection on virtually all proliferation and weapons of mass destruction programs are so great that it is impossible to produce meaningful point estimates. As the Central Intelligence Agency (CIA) has shown in some of its past public estimates of missile proliferation, the intelligence community must first develop a matrix of what is and is not known about a given aspect of proliferation in a given country, with careful footnoting or qualification of the problems in each key source. It must then deal with uncertainty by creating estimates that show a range of possible current and projected capabilities—carefully qualifying each case. In general, at least three scenarios or cases need to be analyzed for each major aspect of proliferation in each country—something approaching a "best," "most likely," and "worst case."[9]

- Even under these conditions, the resulting analytic effort faces serious problems. Security compartmentation within each major aspect of collection and analysis severely limits the flow of data to working analysts. The expansion of analytic staffs has sharply increased the barriers to the flow of data and has brought a large number of junior analysts into the process that can do little more than update past analyses and judgments. Far too little analysis is subjected to technical review by those who have actually worked on weapons development, and the analysis of delivery programs, warheads and weapons, and chemical, biological, and nuclear proliferation tends to be compartmented. Instead of the free flow of data and exchange of analytic conclusions, or "fusion" of intelligence, analysis is "stovepiped" into separate areas of activity. Moreover, the larger staffs get, the more stovepiping tends to occur.

- Analysis tends to focus on technical capability and not on the problems in management and systems integration that often are the real-world limiting factors in proliferation. This tends to push analysis toward exaggerating the probable level of proliferation, particularly because technical capability is often assumed if collection cannot provide all the necessary information.

- Where data are available on past holdings of weapons and the capability to produce such weapons—such as data on chemical weapons feedstocks and biological growth material—the intelligence effort tends to produce estimates of the maximum size of the possible current holding of weapons and WMD materials. While ranges are often shown, and estimates are usually qualified with uncertainty, this tends to focus users on the worst case in terms of actual current capability. In the case of Iraq, this was compounded by some 12 years of constant lies and a disbelief that a dictatorship obsessed with record keeping could not have records if it had destroyed weapons and materials. The end result, however, was to assume that little or no destruction had occurred whenever the United Nations Special Commission, the United Nations

Monitoring, Verification and Inspection Commission, and the IAEA reported that major issues still affected Iraqi claims.

- Intelligence analysis has long been oriented more toward arms control and counterproliferation rather than warfighting, although the Defense Intelligence Agency and the military services have attempted to shift the focus of analysis. Dealing with broad national trends and assuming capability is not generally a major problem in seeking to push nations toward obeying arms control agreements or in pressuring possible suppliers. It also is not a major problem in analyzing broad military counterproliferation risks and programs. The situation is very different in dealing with warfighting choices, particularly issues like preemption and targeting. Assumptions of capability can lead to preemption that is not necessary, overtargeting, inability to prioritize, and a failure to create the detailed collection and analysis necessary to support warfighters down to the battalion level. This, in turn, often forces field commanders to rely on field teams with limited capability and expertise and to overreact to any potential threat or warning indicator.

- The intelligence community does bring outside experts into the process, but often simply to provide advice in general terms rather than a cleared review of the intelligence product. The result is often less than helpful. The use of other cleared personnel in U.S. laboratories and other areas of expertise is inadequate and often presents major problems because those consulted are not brought fully into the intelligence analysis process and given all of the necessary data.

- The intelligence community does tend to try to avoid explicit statements of the shortcomings in collection and methods in much of its analysis and to repeat past agreed judgments on a lowest common denominator level—particularly in the form of the intelligence products that get broad circulation to consumers. Attempts at independent outside analysis or "B-Teams," however, are not subject to the review and controls enforced on intelligence analysis; the teams, collection data, and methods used are generally selected to prove given points rather than to provide an objective counter-point to finished analysis.[10]

- There often is no reliable methodology for estimating capability at the technical level. Models for estimating missile range-payload, accuracy, and reliability are extremely uncertain unless based on observation of actual missile testing and access to classified national data or telemetry. There is no way to reliably estimate the amount of weapons-grade material a given country needs for a functioning warhead or bomb, or its level of progress in design for fission, boosted, and fusion weapons. Estimates of reactor and centrifuge production of weapons-grade material are extremely uncertain, and estimates of the timelines to use such devices to produce given numbers of nuclear weapons are often worst-case speculations. On the other hand, many analyses of such capabilities can be overconservative because they assume an unrealistic emphasis on reliability or conventional production techniques and/or that a nation cannot "leapfrog" into weapons designs using minimal amounts of weapons-grade material.

Few of these problems have been explicitly addressed in open-source reporting on Iran, and it is uncertain from the reporting on past intelligence failures in the intelligence analysis of Iraq before the 2003 invasion that the intelligence community has covered them at the classified level.

Part of the problem lies with the user. Policy-level and other senior users of intelligence tend to be intolerant of analysis that consists of a wide range of qualifications and uncertainties even at the best of times, and the best of times do not exist when urgent policy and warfighting decisions need to be made. Users inevitably either force the intelligence process to reach something approaching a definitive set of conclusions or else they make such estimates themselves.

Intelligence analysts and managers are all too aware of this fact. Experience has taught them that complex intelligence analysis—filled with alternative cases, probability estimates, and qualifications about uncertainty—generally go unused or make policy makers and commanders impatient with the entire intelligence process. In the real world, hard choices have to be made to provide an estimate that can actually be used and acted upon, and these choices must be made either by the intelligence community or by the user.[11]

Uncertainty and Credibility of Sources

If one looks at other sources of reporting on Iran, there have been many claims from many corners. First, one source is from opposition groups that are largely associated with MEK. Their information has proven to be useful at times, yet some of the data they provided have been "too good to be true." Revelations by the National Council of Resistance of Iran (NCRI) about Iran's secret nuclear program did prove to be the trigger point in inviting the IAEA into Tehran for inspections, but their claims about "5,000 centrifuges" were seen by many as an exaggeration or at least an unconfirmed allegation.[12]

The source of such claims must be taken into account. Mr. Alireza Jafarzadeh is the former President of NCRI, which is associated with Mujahadeen-e-Khalq—an organization that is considered by the U.S. Department of State as a terrorist organization. Its motives are well known, and its information must be considered with a certain level of skepticism. As a former CIA counterintelligence official said, "I would take anything from them with a grain of salt."[13]

The NCRI claimed that it relied on human sources, including scientists and civilians working in the facilities or locals who live near the sites. In addition, the NCRI claimed at times that their sources are inside the Iranian regime and added, "Our sources were 100 percent sure about their intelligence."[14] The NCRI did not provide any confirmation about their sources, and their information is considered by some in the U.S. and European governments as less than credible. Another example was the NCRI's claim in September 2004 that Tehran allocated $16 billion to build a nuclear bomb by mid-2005. This again was proven inaccurate.[15]

Second, U.S. officials have cited "walk-in" sources to prove the existence of an Iranian nuclear program. It is unclear who those sources are, but the United States insisted that they were not associated with the NCRI. In November 2004, U.S. officials claimed that a source provided U.S. intelligence with more than 1,000 pages worth of technical documents on Iranian "nuclear warhead design" and missile modifications to deliver an atomic warhead. In addition, it was reported that the documents also included "specific" warhead design based on implosion and adjustments, which was thought to be an attempt at fitting a warhead to Iranian ballistic missiles.[16]

According to the *Washington Post*, the walk-in source that provided the documents was not previously known to U.S. intelligence. In addition, it was not clear if this source was connected to an exile group. The same source was, apparently, the basis for the comments by then Secretary of State Colin Powell on November 17, 2004, when he said, "I have seen some information that would suggest that they have been actively working on delivery systems...You don't have a weapon until you put it in something that can deliver a weapon...I'm not talking about uranium or fissile material or the warhead; I'm talking about what one does with a warhead."[17]

Press reports indicate that walk-in documents came from one source and were without independent verifications. The uncertainty about this source, reportedly, stopped many in the U.S. government from using the information, and some expressed their surprise when Secretary Powell expressed confidence in the information provided. Some saw it as a reminder of the problems in his presentation to the UN regarding Iraqi WMD and hoped that he had not made those remarks before they were confirmed. Some U.S. officials even went as far as saying that Powell "misspoke" when he was talking about the information.[18]

Other U.S. officials described the intelligence as "weak."[19] Other press reports claimed that the source, who was "solicited with German help," provided valuable intelligence that referred to a "black box," which U.S. officials claim was a metaphor to refer to nuclear warhead design. One U.S. official was quoted by the *Wall Street Journal* as saying the documents represented "nearly a smoking gun," yet the same official claimed that this was not a definitive proof.[20]

Third, there are sources within Iran that have cooperated with the IAEA. According to IAEA reports, Iranian nuclear scientists were interviewed on specific questions. For example, in November 2003, the Agency requested clarification on the bismuth irradiation. The IAEA reported that in January 2004, it "was able to interview two Iranian scientists involved in the bismuth irradiation. According to the scientists, two bismuth targets had been irradiated, and an attempt had been made, unsuccessfully, to extract polonium from one of them."[21]

The credibility of these scientists depends on how much freedom they have to talk about specific issues, their level of involvement, and the nature of the questions posed to them. The nature of access and the type of information provided to the IAEA by Iranian scientists remain uncertain.

Fourth, independent intelligence gathered by the United States, the European Union, and regional powers have no obvious substitute. The IAEA and the UN do not have their own intelligence and have to rely on member states to provide them with the necessary information. These include satellite images, electronic intercepts, human intelligence, and various forms of information gathering and intelligence analysis. The history of the U.S. and the U.K. intelligence provided to UN inspectors in Iraq, however, showed the limited ability of many intelligence agencies to get a full picture of a country's nuclear, biological, chemical, and missile programs.

Key Uncertainties in Iran's Nuclear Developments

While Iran and Iraq are very different cases, much the same level of uncertainty exists. Almost no one believes that Iran has nuclear weapons, is so close to acquiring them, or presents a time-urgent threat. Many believe, however, that it is a matter of when rather than if before Tehran acquires nuclear weapons. That is, once Iran gets the capability to produce the materials necessary to closing the nuclear cycle, Iran would acquire the capabilities to produce nuclear weapons.

The previous history has also revealed Iran's attempts to acquire nuclear technology long before the 1979 Revolution. It is also clear from IAEA discoveries that Iran has pursued two key tracks: uranium enrichment and production of plutonium.[22] Both of these tracks can produce the materials that can be used for nuclear reactors and for nuclear weapons. The IAEA, however, does not believe that Iran has yet been successful in achieving either goal. Mohamed ElBaradei, the Director General of the IAEA, was quoted saying, "To develop a nuclear weapon, you need a significant quantity of highly enriched uranium or plutonium, and no one has seen that in Iran."[23]

As of summer 2006, U.S. intelligence estimates still projected that Iran was five to eight years away from a bomb.[24] Israeli estimates in early 2007, however, indicated that Iran might acquire a nuclear device as early as 2009. This Israeli timeline gathered new credibility in the spring of 2007, when Iran claimed that it had succeeded in deploying some 1,312 centrifuges and would have 3,000 by the summer of 2007.

Under optimal—if unlikely—conditions, a fully functional capacity of 3,000 P-1 class centrifuges could give Iran enough material for one fission device in 18–27 months, and some private experts by the worst case figure in as at little as 12 months—some point to 2008. No one knows the actual current or final design output of Iran's P-1 centrifuges or the efficiency of its cascades and overall production systems. Some speculate, however, that the annual output of each P-1 could be 2.5 separative work units (SWUs), or some 0.013 kilograms of HEU a year (European P-2 centrifuges are about twice as efficient and produce 5 SWU a year). Under some conditions, a total system of 3,000 Iranian P-1s could produce as much as 7,500 SWU per year or enough to provide 40 kilograms of HEU per year. This would be enough for one weapon a year and possibly two. [25]

Mohamed ElBaradi discounted such Iranian claims, however, and felt Iran had far less than 3,000 centrifuges, and other experts put the maximum number of functional units at around 650 actually operating in series. They felt many of these were still running empty, although IAEA experts felt some were now running UF6 at low pressure.[26] It should also be noted that some experts speculate Iran may face a special problem because its uranium ore is contaminated with heavy metals like molybdenum and that this would limit enrichment to 20 percent without outside technical aid from an advanced power like Russia.[27]

PLUTONIUM PRODUCTION

Tehran has followed two different tracks to achieve the capacity to produce plutonium. First, it is building heavy-water production plants, which U.S. officials claim that their only purpose is to supply heavy water that is optimal for producing weapons-grade plutonium. The Iranian government, on the other hand, has claimed that their purpose is for isotope production for its civilian nuclear energy program.[28]

The second track followed the production of light-water power reactors. The main reactor is at Bushehr, which is designed to produce civilian nuclear technology. Bushehr is also the reactor that Russia agreed to supply its fuel and recover the spent fuel from the reactor. According to an agreement between Russia and Iran dating from September 2006, Russia agreed to provide low-enriched uranium for the reactor by March 2007, regardless of UN sanctions.[29] The U.S. Under Secretary for Arms Control and International Security, John R. Bolton, claimed that Bushehr would produce enough plutonium per year to manufacture nearly 30 nuclear weapons.[30]

The following chronology by the IAEA shows the history of Iran's plutonium separation experiments:[31]

- **1987–1988:** The separation process was simulated using imported unirradiated uranium dioxide (UO2) [DU (depleted uranium)]; dissolution and purification took place in the Shariaty Building at TNRC (Tehran Nuclear Research Center); pressed and sintered pellets were manufactured using imported UO2 (DU) at Fuel Fabrication Laboratory (FFL); the UO2 pellets were further manipulated into aluminum and stainless steel capsules at FFL.

- **1988–1993:** The capsules (containing a total of 7 kilograms of UO2 in the form of powder, pressed pellets, and sintered pellets) were irradiated in Tehran Research Reactor (TRR).

- **1991–1993:** Plutonium was separated from some of the irradiated UO2 targets in the capsules (about 3 kilograms of the 7 kilograms of UO2) and plutonium solutions produced; these activities were carried out at the Shariaty Building and, after the activities were transferred in October/November 1992, at the Chamaran Building at TNRC; the research and development related irradiation and separation of plutonium were terminated in 1993.

- **1993–1994:** The unprocessed irradiated UO2 was initially stored in capsules in the spent fuel pond of TRR and later transferred into four containers and buried behind the Chamaran Building.

- **1995:** In July, purification of the plutonium solution from the 1988–1993 period was carried out in the Chamaran Building; a planchet (disk) was prepared from the solution for analysis.

- **1998:** In August, additional purification of plutonium from the 1988–1993 period was carried out in the Chamaran Building; another planchet (disk) was prepared from the solution for analysis.

- **2000:** The glove boxes from the Chamaran Building were dismantled and sent to ENTC (Esfahan Nuclear Technology Center) for storage; one glove box was moved to the Molybdenum Iodine Xenon Facility.

- **2003:** Due to construction work being carried out behind the Chamaran Building, two containers holding the unprocessed irradiated UO2 were dug up, moved, and reburied.

- **2003:** Iran in February confirmed that it was building a heavy-water production plant at Arak.

- **2003:** The IAEA DG report of November 10 (GOV/2003/71) asserts that "between 1992 and 1998 it [Iran] had irradiated 7 kg of UO2 targets and extracted small quantities of plutonium."

- **2003:** John Bolton, U.S. Under Secretary of State for Arms Control and International Security, stated at a conference on December 2: "In what can only be an attempt to build a capacity to develop nuclear materials for nuclear weapons, Iran has enriched uranium with both centrifuges and lasers, and produced and reprocessed plutonium... Iran is trying to legitimize as 'peaceful and transparent' its pursuit of nuclear fuel cycle capabilities that would give it the ability to produce fissile material for nuclear weapons. This includes uranium mining and extraction, uranium conversion and enrichment, reactor fuel fabrication, heavy water production, a heavy water reactor well-suited for plutonium production, and the 'management' of spent fuel—a euphemism for reprocessing spent fuel to recover plutonium."[32]

- **2004:** The IAEA in its March 17 Board of Governors Resolution (GOV/2004/21) stated that the nature and the scope of Iranian research into laser isotopic enrichment and the question of experiments in the production of polonium-210 remained not satisfactory disclosed.

- **2004:** IAEA DG report (GOV/2004/82) from November 15: "Between 1988 and 1993, Iran carried out plutonium separation experiments at TNRC. The shielded glove boxes in which these experiments were carried out were dismantled in 1993, relocated to JHL (Jabr Ibn Hayan Multipurpose Laboratories) and used for other purposes...In its letter of 21 October 2003, Iran acknowledged the irradiation of depleted UO$_2$targets at TRR and subsequent plutonium separation experiments in shielded glove boxes in the Nuclear Safety Building of TNRC. Neither the activities nor the separated plutonium had been reported previously to the Agency...Iran stated that the Am-241 had been imported from abroad prior to the Iranian revolution in 1979, and explained that, in 1990, the glove box that had been used in connection with the Am-241 had been transferred to the building where the plutonium separation took place, but that it had been used for training purposes and not for plutonium experiments... In addition, while Iran has provided preliminary design information on the IR-40 heavy water research reactor, the construction of which should commence in 2004, the Agency has raised some questions regarding Iran's attempts to acquire manipulators and lead glass windows for the hot cells. With respect to the latter issue, in October and November 2004, Iran provided some clarifications, which are now being assessed."[33]

- **2005:** In June, Iran admitted that it conducted small-scale experiments to produce plutonium. Iran had declared to the IAEA that it ended certain plutonium experiments in 1993, but disclosed to the IAEA that those experiments were still being undertaken in 1998.

In September 2005, the IAEA analysis of Iran's plutonium separation experiments concluded that the solutions that were tested were 12–16 years old, which seemed to corroborate Iran's claims. In addition, the IAEA carried out verification tests for unprocessed irradiated UO2 targets stored in four containers, and these results also conformed to Iranian claims, although the IAEA argued that the number of targets provided by Iran was much lower than the actual ones it has.

The IAEA reported in September 2005, "A final assessment of Iran's plutonium research activities must await the results of the destructive analysis of the disks and targets."[34]

Much depends, however, on Iranian progress in replacing or supplanting its small, 35-year-old research reactor in Tehran, with a more modern, 40-megawatt, thermal-cooled, heavy-water reactor, at Arak. Some outside experts feel that Iran's IR-40 heavy reactor could be operational by 2011 and allow Iran to begin producing significant amounts of weapons-grade material by 2014. Such a reactor could be used to produce up to 8 kilograms of weapons-grade plutonium a year—enough for one to two weapons a year. Iran might also need far less weapons-grade plutonium per weapon than uranium. One outside expert quotes a figure of 5 kilograms for plutonium versus 25 kilograms of uranium—although such calculations are based on nominal figures used for arms control purposes that have little relevance to actual weapons designs employed since the 1960s.[35]

Uranium Enrichment

Many weapons experts believe that the Iranian uranium enrichment program is much more advanced and does not rely on Iran's nuclear reactors. The former Chief UN weapons inspector in Iraq, Hans Blix, has said that Tehran's plans to build a 1,000-megawatt power reactor at Bushehr, which is considered Iran's main plutonium production facility, should not be the main concern. He argued that the light-water reactor used only low-enrichment (3.5 percent) uranium and is scarcely ideal for plutonium production.

He added, "What is uncomfortable and dangerous is that they have acquired the capacity to enrich uranium of their own uranium that they dig out of the ground... If you can enrich to five percent you can enrich it to 85 percent."[36] Others note, however, that the reactor will use some 103 tons of uranium contained in 193 fuel assemblies and still generate some 250 kilograms of plutonium a year. They speculate that there would be enough plutonium in every four irradiated fuel assemblies to produce a single nuclear weapon, and if Iran broke its fuel agreement with Russia and dedicated the reactor to weapons production, it could provide enough plutonium for 40–50 weapons a year. Given Iran's stated plans to acquire a total of six 1,000-megawatt reactors, it is hard to dismiss these concerns.[37]

These concerns were further exacerbated following Mahmoud Ahmadinejad's announcement on April 11, 2006, that Iran was successful at enriching uranium. "At this historic moment, with the blessings of God almighty and the efforts made by our scientists, I declare here that the laboratory-scale nuclear fuel cycle has been completed and young scientists produced enriched uranium needed to the degree for nuclear power plants [on April 9]." The head of the Atomic Energy Agency of Iran (AEOI) and Iran's Vice President, Gholamreza Aghazadeh, and Iranian nuclear scientists stated Iran's accomplishments and/or goals as follows:[38]

- Started enriching uranium to a level—3.5 percent—needed for fuel on a research scale using 164 centrifuges, but not enriched enough to build a nuclear bomb;
- Produced 110 tons of uranium hexafluoride (UF6)—this amount is nearly double the amount that Iran claimed to have enriched in 2005;
- Aim[s] to produce a gas high with an increased percentage of U-235, the isotope needed for nuclear fission, which is much rarer than the more prevalent isotope U-238; and
- Plan[s] to expand its enrichment program to be able to use 3,000 centrifuges at the nuclear center at Natanz by the end of 2006.

According to one report, Iran commenced its uranium enrichment just after the oil crisis of 1974.[39] In October 2003, during negotiations with the EU-3, Iran agreed to suspend its uranium enrichment program, most likely because it feared an escalation of the issue with interference by the UN Security Council. Two months later, Iran also signed the IAEA Model Additional Protocol.

It is likely that work on uranium enrichment was conducted between 1974 and 2003; however, it is not known to what extent. Reportedly, Iran resumed enrichment activities in 2004, but then agreed to suspension again in 2005, after facing referral to the United Nations Security Council again. In August 2005, the EU-3 proposal failed and Iran began enrichment activities anew.

The Centrifuge Challenge

This time, Iran showed political determination to continue the enrichment program even though it faced referral to the UN Security Council, which eventually took place in February 2006. Mohammad Saeedi, Iran's Deputy Nuclear Chief, reiterated that Iran aimed to expand uranium enrichment to industrial scale at Natanz. In addition to installing 3,000 centrifuges at Natanz by 2006, Saeedi claimed that Iran aims at expanding the total number of centrifuges to 54,000, which would be used to fuel a 1,000-megawat nuclear power plant.[40] Iran's Deputy Foreign Minister Mohammad Reza Bagheri pointed out Iran's stance on giving up the uranium enrichment program: "It is our red line. We will never do it."[41]

While some believe that Iran's claims are credible, others speculated that Iran made the announcement to send a message that military strikes or sanctions would not deter Iran from achieving a full nuclear cycle. Much depends on what the announcement really meant. Iran had previously obtained at least 2-percent enrichment from the experimental use of centrifuges and possibly significantly higher levels. The IAEA had previously made it clear that it lacked the data to determine how far Iran had actually progressed. Iran also had reached enrichment levels as high as 8 percent making experimental use of laser isotope separation, although it seemed far from being able to scale such efforts up beyond laboratory tests.

The Iranian statements also said nothing about how efficient the claimed use of a small 164-centrifuge chain was at the time it became public, what its life cycle and reliability was, and about the ability to engineer a system that could approach weapons-grade material. It is at best possible to speculate on how many centrifuges of the P-1-type centrifuge derivative involved Iran would need to get a nuclear device and then move on to develop a significant weapons-production capability. It would, however, probably be in the thousands in terms of continuously operating machine equivalents to slowly get the fissile material for a single device or "bomb in the basement," and tens of thousands to support a serious nuclear weapons-delivery capability.

One thing was already clear long before these Iranian claims. There was nothing the UN or the United States could do to deny Iran the technology to build a nuclear weapon. The IAEA's discoveries had made it clear Iran already had functioning centrifuge designs, reactor development capability, and plutonium separation capability. It had experimented with polonium in ways that showed it could make a neutron initiator, had the technology to produce high-explosive lenses and beryllium reflectors, could machine fissile material, and had long had a technology base capable of performing the same nonfissile of actual weapons designs used by Pakistan in its nuclear weapons-design efforts. Revati Prasad and Jill Marie Parillo state that the AEOI purchased designs and components for the P-1 centrifuges through the A.Q. Khan network in 1987.[42] It also seemed highly likely that it had acquired P-2 centrifuge designs and the same basic Chinese design data for a fissile weapon suitable for mounting on a ballistic missile that North Korea had sold to Libya.

As a result, both the claims of Iranian President Ahmadinejad that Iran had made a major breakthrough and President George W. Bush's responding statement that Iran would not be allowed to acquire the technology to build a nuclear weapon seemed to be little more than vacuous political posturing. Ahmadinejad's statement seemed to be an effort to show the UN that it could not take meaningful action and exploit Iranian nationalism. The Bush statement was a combination of basic technical ignorance on the part of his speechwriters and an effort to push the UN toward action and to convince Iran that it could face the threat of both serious sanctions and military action if diplomacy and sanctions failed. It effectively ignored the fact that Iran not only already had the technology, but could disperse it to the point where it was extremely unlikely that any UN inspection effort could find it, even if Iran allowed this, or any military option could seriously affect Iran's technology base—as distinguished from its ability to create survivable large-scale production facilities and openly deploy nuclear-armed delivery systems.

In reality, such developments were at most evolutionary and had been expected. Diplomats and officials from the IAEA were quick to point out that the announcement by Iran should not be a sign of concern and that Iran may face many technical hurdles before it can enrich enough quantities of uranium at high levels to produce a nuclear weapon. One European official said that while the 164-machine centrifuges were more industrial, "it's not like they haven't come close to achieving this in the past." This assessment has been reflected in reports by the IAEA, which argues that Iran has used centrifuges and laser to enrich uranium throughout the 1990s and even before.[43]

To put such rhetoric in context, most of Tehran's uranium conversion experiments took place between 1981 and 1993 at the TNRC and at the ENTC. One source reports that uranium enrichment in centrifuges began in 1985.[44] In this case, however, it is clear that some of these activities continued throughout 2002. According to the IAEA, Iran's uranium enrichment activities also received some foreign help in 1991. The IAEA outlined its findings regarding Tehran's uranium enrichment as follows:

> In 1991, Iran entered into discussions with a foreign supplier for the construction at Esfahan of an industrial scale conversion facility. Construction on the facility, UCF, was begun in the late 1990s. UCF consists of several conversion lines, principal among which is the line for the conversion of UOC to UF6 with an annual design production capacity of 200 t uranium as UF6. The UF6 is to be sent to the uranium enrichment facilities at Natanz, where it will be enriched up to 5% U-235 and the product and tails returned to UCF for conversion into low enriched UO2 and depleted uranium metal. The design information for UCF provided by Iran indicates that conversion lines are also foreseen for the production of natural and enriched (19.7%) uranium metal, and natural UO2. The natural and enriched (5% U-235) UO2 are to be sent to the Fuel Manufac-turing Plant (FMP) at Esfahan, where Iran has said it will be processed into fuel for a research reactor and power reactors....
>
> In March 2004, Iran began testing the process lines involving the conversion of UOC into UO2 and UF4, and UF4 into UF6. As of June 2004, 40 to 45 kg of UF6 had been produced. A larger test, involving the conversion of 37 t of yellowcake into UF4, was ini-tiated in August 2004. According to Iran's declaration of 14 October 2004, 22.5 t of the 37 t of yellowcake had been fed into the process and that approximately 2 t of UF4, and 17.5 t of uranium as intermediate products and waste, had been produced. There was no indication as of that date of UF6 having been produced during this later campaign.[45]

The IAEA inspections found traces of contamination from advanced enrichment effects at Natanz. Iran claimed that these contaminations were from equipment it purchased in the 1980s from abroad (presumably from Pakistan). Reports by the IAEA, however, showed that Iran may have started its enrichment program in the 1970s and that the Iranians were already partially successful at uranium conversion.

Iran has tried two different methods to enrich uranium ever since the time of the Shah. First, Iran's nuclear research has facilities that are dedicated to manufacturing and testing centrifuges. This includes its ultimate goal of producing 50,000 centri-fuges in Natanz. Second, Iran also pursued enriching uranium through laser enrich-ment. According to Mohamed ElBaradei, the Director General of the IAEA, Iran was able to enrich uranium up to 1.2 percent using centrifuges and up to a peak enrich-ment grade of 13 percent using lasers.[46]

Some of Iran's gas centrifuge program depended on help Tehran received from Pakistan. Although reports by the Director General of the IAEA do not mention Pakistan by name, Iran's gas centrifuges could be traced back to the mid-1990s when A. Q. Khan approached an Iranian company and offered it P-1 documentation and components for 500 centrifuges. Iran claimed that it received only the P-1 and not the P-2 design. Both Iran and Pakistan would later admit to this transaction and pro-vide the documents to support these allegations.[47]

According to the IAEA, Tehran received P-1 components and documentation in January 1994. Tehran, however, claimed that it did not receive the first of these com-ponents until October 1994. Regardless of the month of delivery, there is one more important element that remains unresolved. The IAEA refers to this as the "1987 offer," which reportedly provided Iran with a sample machine, drawings, descrip-tions, and specifications for production and material for 2,000 centrifuge machines.[48]

In addition, Iran received the P-2 design in 1994/1995 from Pakistan, but all of its components were designed and manufactured in Iran. According to Iran's official statements, the AEOI awarded a contract to a company in Tehran to build P-2 cen-trifuges.[49] Furthermore, Iran claimed that it did not pursue any work on the P-2 design between 1995 and 2002 due to shortages in staff and resources at the AEOI and that Tehran focused on resolving outstanding issues regarding the P-1 design. The IAEA, however, was not convinced that Iran did not pursue further develop-ment of the P-2 design and called on Iran in September 2005 to provide more infor-mation on the history of its P-2 development.[50]

This helps explain why experts have argued that Iran's goal of producing 50,000 centrifuges in Natanz should be considered a sign of serious concern for the international community. As far as the future development of Natanz is concerned, Iran established its additional cascades underground, and the IAEA GOV/2007/8 confirms that Iran moved about ten tons of unenriched uranium into the cavernous halls in Natanz.

Furthermore, David Albright and Corey Hinderstein of the Institute for Science and International Security (ISIS) argued that Iran planned in January 2006 to install centrifuges in modules of 3,000 machines that were designed to produce low enriched uranium for civilian power reactors. If half of these machines, however, were to be used to create HEU, they could produce enough HEU for one nuclear weapon a year. Furthermore, if the Iranians do achieve their ultimate goal of 50,000 centrifuges, Albright and Hinderstein argued, "At 15–20 kilograms per weapon that would be enough for 25–30 nuclear weapons per year."[51]

Natanz is the primary uranium enrichment site in Iran. It contains installations both above and below ground and covers an area of about 100,000 square meters.[52] The commercial enrichment plant reportedly is buried underground and is located in three structures that are to be capable of housing 50,000 cascades.

Until early 2007, Iran was believed to have two 164-cascade machines running in its Natanz facility. In February 2007, however, the IAEA reported that Iran installed four additional cascades underground, which would equal a total of 1,018 centri-fuges in Natanz, most of them underground. IAEA report GOV/2007/8 described the situation as follows:

> During the design information verification (DIV) carried out at FEP (Fuel Enrichment Plant) on 17 February 2007, Agency inspectors were informed that two 164-machine

cascades had been installed and were operating under vacuum and that another two 164-machine cascades were in the final stages of installation. In light of this, in a letter dated 19 February 2007, the Agency requested that arrangements be made for the relocation of cameras into the cascade hall during the Agency's next visit to FEP, which is scheduled to take place between 3 and 5 March 2007. The issue of remote monitoring remains to be resolved.[53]

This meant that in addition to the two cascade machines with 164 centrifuges each that were confirmed to be running in the Natanz pilot plant, Iran had installed another two machines with 164 cascades each. As of the time of the report, 656 cascades were reported by the IAEA to be running, half of them under vacuum. It also meant that if Iran installed yet another two "chains," "cascades," or "links" of 164 centrifuges, the total number of running cascades would amount to 984.

The IAEA gave no indication in this report when any additional chains of centrifuges would be operational. A report by David Albright and Jacqueline Shire from November 14, 2006, had expressed doubt about how quickly this could happen.[54] It then became clear, however, that Iran fed an unexpectedly large amount of UF6 into its cascades in late 2006 and 2007. An ISIS report by Jacqueline Shire and David Albright dated March 15, 2007, concluded that Iran fed about 100 kilograms of UF6 into its cascades at the Natanz plant between mid-August 2006 and mid-February 2007. It should be noted that by March 2007, Iran had reached its highest rate of UF6 insertions, a trend that had continually grown since Iran agreed to resume uranium enrichment in early 2006.

The authors of the ISIS report also computed that at that rate of enrichment activity, Iran could feed about 613 kilograms of UF6 into its existing centrifuges. The uranium, according to Iranian estimates, was enriched to a 5-percent enrichment level. Shire and Albright conclude that Iran operated its centrifuges for an average of about five hours a day.

David Albright noted Iran's potential difficulties in mastering, i.e., linking, all its centrifuge cascades. According to Albright, there are four likely reasons Iran has problems:

- The centrifuges have experienced an unknown technical problem that prevents continuous operation;
- Iran is slowing its program down so as not to alarm the international community;
- Iran is already competent in operating cascades to enrich uranium, but that competency is being hidden. For example, Iran may have received undeclared assistance from the Khan network in this area; or
- Iran is simply implementing its own plan for cascade installation that includes its own method to become proficient, according to its own timetable, and has chosen not to share it with the IAEA or the outside world.[55]

Shire and Albright acknowledged in March 2007, however, that Iran's centrifuges were running better than commonly expected by most observers.[56] Moreover, in

April 2007, Iran claimed that it had succeeded in deploying some 1,312 centrifuges and would have 3,000 by the summer of 2007. As has been noted earlier, a fully functional capacity of 3,000 P-1 class centrifuges could give Iran enough material for one fission device in 18–27 months under optimal—if unlikely—conditions.

The problem in making such estimates is there are no data on the operational status and efficiency of Iran's units. Mohamed ElBaradei discounted Iranian claims in April 2007, for example, and felt Iran had far less than 3,000 centrifuges, and other experts put the maximum number of functional units at around 650 actually operating in series. They felt many of these were still running empty, although IAEA experts felt some were now running UF6 at low pressure.[57]

Rather, the IAEA confirmed on April 18, 2007, that Iran had started feeding UF6 into some of its approximately 1,300 centrifuges installed at Natanz. The U.S. Department of State concluded that the IAEA assessment was in line with its own estimates, disputed the claim, however, that Iran was already feeding UF6 into the centrifuges.[58] On April 20, Gholamreza Aghazadeh, head of the Atomic Energy Organization of Iran, said that Iran had reached enrichment capabilities at an industrial scale but would seek the operation of 50,000 centrifuges, which, according to Aghazadeh, would take "several years."[59] In mid-May 2007, IAEA officials confirmed that Iran was operating up to 3,000 centrifuges at its Natanz plant.[60]

At the same time, a smaller facility might be adequate. A study by Frank Barnaby for the Oxford Research Group estimates Iran's current centrifuges could produce about 2.5 SWUs a year, with a range of 1.9–2.7 SWUs. If Iran had the P-2, each centrifuge would produce roughly 5 SWUs a year. A fully operational 3,000-centrifuge facility could then produce some 7,500 SWUs or about 40 kilograms of HEU a year, and it would probably take a total capacity of 5,000 machines to keep 3,000 online at all times.[61] As is discussed later, the 1,500-centrifuge pilot facility that Iran is now seeking to operate could conceivably produce a single weapon in two to three years.

Laser Isotope Separation

As for the other enrichment route, Iran acknowledged it had started a laser enrichment program in the 1970s. Iran claimed that it used two different tracks in using laser enrichment: (1) atomic vapor laser isotope separation (AVLIS) and (2) molecular isotope separation (MLIS). Iran, however, depended on key contracts with four (unnamed) different countries to build its laser enrichment program. The following chronology was presented by the IAEA:[62]

- **1975:** Iran contracted for the establishment of a laboratory to study the spectroscopic behavior of uranium metal; this project was abandoned in the 1980s as the laboratory did not function properly.
- **Late 1970s:** Iran contracted with a second supplier to study MLIS, under which four carbon monoxide lasers and vacuum chambers were delivered, but the project was

ultimately terminated due to the political situation before major development work was begun.

- **1991:** Iran contracted with a third supplier for the establishment of a "Laser Spectroscopy Laboratory" (LSL) and a "Comprehensive Separation Laboratory" (CSL), where uranium enrichment would be carried out on a milligram scale based on the AVLIS process. The contract also provided for the supply of 50 kilograms natural uranium metal.

- **1998:** Iran contracted with a fourth supplier to obtain information related to laser enrichment and the supply of relevant equipment. However, due to the inability of the supplier to secure export licenses, only some of the equipment was delivered (to Lashkar Ab'ad).

The IAEA seems to be more confident about its findings regarding Iran's laser enrichment developments than gas centrifuges. This is largely due to Iranian co-operation, but it also stems from the fact that Iran had nothing to hide since its foreign contractors failed to deliver on the four contracts Tehran signed between the 1970s and the 1990s.

According to the IAEA, Iran claimed that the laser spectroscopy laboratory and the MLIS laboratory (the first two contracts) were never fully operational.

As for the third contract, the IAEA estimated the contract was finished in 1994, but that CSL and LSL had technical problems and were unsuccessful between 1994 and 2000. Iran responded by claiming that the two labs were dismantled in 2000. In addition, the IAEA concluded, "As confirmed in an analysis, provided to the Agency, that had been carried out by the foreign laboratory involved in the project, the highest average enrichment achieved was 8%, but with a peak enrichment of 13%."[63]

Finally, the fourth contract was signed in 1998, but failed due to the supplier's inability to obtain export licenses. Tehran claimed that it attempted to procure these equipment and parts, but it was unsuccessful.[64]

These failures almost certainly did strain Tehran's ability to effectively use the laser enrichment track to advance its uranium enrichment activities. This may explain why Iran did less to try to conceal its laser enrichment program than conceal the details of its centrifuge program. According to the IAEA, Tehran's declarations largely tracked with the IAEA inspectors' findings. For example, Iran claimed that its enrichment level was 0.8 percent U235, and the IAEA concluded that Iran reached an enrichment level of 0.99 percent ± 0.24 percent U235.[65]

The IAEA findings regarding this aspect of Tehran's enrichment program are summarized in the following two paragraphs:

The Agency has completed its review of Iran's atomic vapor laser isotope separation (AVLIS) program and has concluded that Iran's descriptions of the levels of enrichment achieved using AVLIS at the Comprehensive Separation Laboratory (CSL) and Lashkar Ab'ad and the amounts of material used in its past activities are consistent with information available to the Agency to date. Iran has presented all known key equipment, which has been verified by the Agency. For the reasons described in the Annex to this report, however, detailed nuclear material accountancy is not possible.

It is the view of the Agency's AVLIS experts that, while the contract for the AVLIS facility at Lashkar Ab'ad was specifically written for the delivery of a system that could achieve 5 kg of product within the first year with enrichment levels of 3.5% to 7%, the facility as designed and reflected in the contract would, given some specific features of the equipment, have been capable of limited HEU production had the entire package of equipment been delivered. The Iranian AVLIS experts have stated that they were not aware of the significance of these features when they negotiated and contracted for the supply and delivery of the Lashkar Ab'ad AVLIS facility. They have also provided information demonstrating the very limited capabilities of the equipment delivered to Iran under this contract to produce HEU (i.e. only in gram quantities).[66]

The accuracy of such findings is critical because isotope separation is far more efficient than centrifuge separation, much less costly once mature, uses far less power, and is much harder to detect.[67]

Other Aspects of Iranian Activity

Other aspects of Iranian activity were less reassuring. Following Iran's announcement that it converted 37 tons of yellowcake into UF4 in May 2005, experts believed that this amount of uranium could "theoretically" produce more than 200 pounds of weapons-grade uranium, which would be enough to produce five to six crude nuclear weapons. The head of Iran's Supreme National Security Council, Hasan Rowhani, was quoted in 1995 saying, "Last year, we could not produce UF_4 and UF_6. We didn't have materials to inject into centrifuges to carry out enrichment, meaning we didn't have UF_6...But within the past year, we completed the Isfahan facility and reached UF_4 and UF_6 stage. So we made great progress."[68]

In February 2006, ahead of the IAEA board meeting, it was reported in the press that a report was circulated to IAEA member states regarding what press reports called "the Green Salt Project." The report largely used information provided by U.S. intelligence. The project name was derived from "green salt," or uranium tetra-fluoride. The materials are considered intermediate materials in uranium conversion ore into uranium hexafluoride, UF4, which is central to producing nuclear fuel.[69]

This project was reportedly started in the spring of 2001 by an Iranian firm, Kimeya Madon, under the auspices of the IRGC. U.S. officials believe that Kimyea Madon completed drawings and technical specifications for a small uranium conversion facility (UCF), and they argue that the drawings provide "pretty compelling evidence" for Iran's clandestine uranium conversion program. In addition, there was evidence that the Iranians envisioned a second UCF. It remains uncertain why the operation of Kimeya Mado stopped in 2003. Some speculated that this was a plan to replace Isfahan in case of a military strike against it. Another view is that Iran scratched the plan after it was revealed that the new UCF was not "as good as what they had" at Isfahan.[70]

Another important development in Iranian activities was the IAEA's discovery of "a document related to the procedural requirements for the reduction of UF6 to metal in small quantities, and on the casting and machining of enriched, natural and depleted uranium metal into hemispherical forms," as the IAEA February 4, 2006, resolution emphasized.[71]

The description of this document first appeared in the IAEA November 15, 2005, reports. This "one-page document" apparently was related to the Pakistani offer in 1987, and the IAEA made the following assessment:[72]

As previously reported to the Board, in January 2005 Iran showed to the Agency a copy of a hand-written one-page document reflecting an offer said to have been made to Iran in 1987 by a foreign intermediary for certain components and equipment. Iran stated that only some components of one or two disassembled centrifuges, and supporting drawings and specifications, were delivered by the procurement network, and that a number of other items of equipment referred to in the document were purchased directly from other suppliers. Most of these components and items were included in the October 2003 declaration by Iran to the Agency.

The documents recently made available to the Agency related mainly to the 1987 offer; many of them dated from the late 1970s and early to mid-1980s. The documents included: detailed drawings of the P-1 centrifuge components and assemblies; technical specifications supporting component manufacture and centrifuge assembly; and technical documents relating to centrifuge operational performance. In addition, they included cascade schematic drawings for various sizes of research and development (R&D) cascades, together with the equipment needed for cascade operation (e.g. cooling water circuit needs and special valve consoles). The documents also included a drawing showing a cascade layout for 6 cascades of 168 machines each and a small plant of 2000 centrifuges arranged in the same hall. Also among the documents was one related to the procedural requirements for the reduction of UF6 to metal in small quantities, and on the casting and machining of enriched, natural and depleted uranium metal into hemispherical forms, with respect to which Iran stated that it had been provided on the initiative of the procurement network, and not at the request of the Atomic Energy Organization of Iran (AEOI).

As noted earlier, the foreign intermediary is believed to have been A.Q. Khan, the Pakistani nuclear scientist. The United Kingdom argued that the document, on casting uranium into hemispheric form, had no other application other than nuclear weapons. Experts agreed with this assessment.[73] IAEA officials, however, were more cautious. One senior IAEA official was quoted as saying that the document "is damaging," but he argued that the handwritten document was not a blueprint for making nuclear weapons because it dealt with only one aspect of the process.[74]

Many experts believe that in order to understand Iran's nuclear program, one must understand its gas centrifuge program—particularly whether Tehran's ability to establish a test run of 1,500 centrifuges at Natanz would give Iran enough capacity to produce HEU. David Albright and Corey Hinderstein of the ISIS argued that Iran may well be on its way to achieving this capacity:

Each P1 centrifuge has an output of about 3 separative work units (swu) per year according to senior IAEA officials. From the A. Q. Khan network, Iran acquired drawings of a modified variant of an early-generation Urenco centrifuge. Experts who saw these drawings assessed that, based on the design's materials, dimensions, and tolerances, the P1 in Iran is based on an early version of the Dutch 4M centrifuge that was subsequently modified by Pakistan. The 4M was developed in the Netherlands in the mid-1970s and was more advanced than the earlier Dutch SNOR/CNOR machines. Its rotor assembly has four aluminum rotor tubes connected by three maraging steel bellows.

With 1,500 centrifuges and a capacity of 4,500 swu per year, this facility could produce as much as 28 kilograms of weapon-grade uranium per year, assuming a tails assay of 0.5 percent, where tails assay is the fraction of uranium 235 in the waste stream. This is a relatively high tails assay, but such a tails assay is common in initial nuclear weapons programs. As a program matures and grows, it typically reduces the tails assay to about 0.4 percent and perhaps later to 0.3 percent to conserve uranium supplies.

By spring 2004, Iran had already put together about 1,140 centrifuge rotor assemblies, a reasonable indicator of the number of complete centrifuges. However, only about 500 of these rotors were good enough to operate in cascades, according to knowledgeable senior IAEA officials. The November 2004 IAEA report stated that from the spring to October 10, 2004, Iran had assembled an additional 135 rotors, bringing the total number of rotors assembled to 1,275. As mentioned above, a large number of these rotors are not usable in an operating cascade.

Iran is believed to have assembled more centrifuges prior to the suspension being re-imposed on November 22, 2004. Without more specific information, it is assumed that Iran continued to assemble centrifuges at a constant rate, adding another 70 centrifuges, for a total of 1,345 centrifuges. However, the total number of good centrifuges is estimated at about 700.[75]

These developments also led some observers to question whether Iran received more help from Pakistan than it admitted. Some experts argued that the A. Q. Khan network tended to hand over the "whole package" as was the case with Libya, and they question whether Iran received only the few pages that it shared with the IAEA.[76] These revelations showed how little is known about how advanced Iran's uranium enrichment program is.

Most experts, however, believe that Iran's uranium enrichment program is far more dangerous and far more advanced than its plutonium production activities. They argue that the danger of the enrichment program is that regardless of how high Iran's enrichment level of uranium is, if Iran were able to enrich it at a low level, Iran will have the know-how to enrich it at higher levels and produce the weapons-grade uranium to produce nuclear weapons.[77]

In addition, experts are concerned that Iran may acquire uranium from other nations. For example, during a visit by Iranian Parliament Speaker Gholam Ali Haddad-Adel in early 2006, Iran and Venezuela signed a deal that allowed Iran to explore Venezuela's strategic minerals. Venezuelan opposition figures to President Hugo Chávez claimed that the deal could involve the production and transfer of uranium from Venezuela to Iran. The United States, however, downplayed such reports. A Department of State official was quoted as saying, "We are aware of reports of possible Iranian exploitation of Venezuelan uranium, but we see no commercial activities in Venezuela."[78]

Iranian Commitment to Nuclear Power Programs

It is not clear how future Iranian leaders will treat either Iran's nuclear weapons programs or the issue of nuclear power. Iran did, however, express an interest in acquiring two more nuclear power reactors in April 2007, and its statements in reaction to both the new Security Council sanctions passed in early 2007 and the announcement in April 2007 that it was scaling up its centrifuge program provide at least some indication of how deep Iran's commitment may be.

The following quotes all come from Iranian statements made on Iran's "Nuclear Day" on April 10, 2007, and show little sign of giving way to international pressure:[79]

- **President Mahmoud Ahmadinejad, speaking on Iran's Nuclear Day, April 10, 2007:** "I declare today, in all pride, that from this day, Iran is among the countries producing nuclear fuel on an [industrial] scale...Today, Iran's enemies are embarrassed by Iran's progress in various areas...According to a pre-set program, the Iranian government is determined to produce at least 20,000 megawatts of nuclear electricity according to a specific timetable...We warmly shake the hands of all governments interested in holding talks with us and in cooperating with us in this area.

    I [address] the governments that have so far refused to come to terms with today's reality and with the Iranian people's right [to develop nuclear technology], and demand that they stop acting aggressively, illogically, hostilely, and in violation [of the law] towards Iran. [They had better realize] that every member of the Iranian people stands fast behind its leaders, out of knowledge, faith, and absolute unity, and [that the Iranian people] will defend its right to the end...The [Western countries] should know that the path of the progress of the Iranian people is irreversible...They must pay attention, and do nothing to cause this brave and great people to reconsider the way it deals with them. [Western countries] have tried this [hostile] approach several times, and have seen that this [Iranian] people is capable of [reconsidering its approach towards them]..."[80]

- **Ali Larijani, Iran's chief Nuclear Negotiator, April 10, 2007:** "[The Western countries] must in any event accept a nuclear Iran...We are moving vigorously along the path of obtaining...54,000 centrifuges...The sanctions against us [UN Resolution 1747] have had no effect, and will have no effect, on our government towards this goal [in the future]...The number of centrifuges doesn't matter. But we have a work output of 3,000 centrifuges. This level and above is considered industrial..."[81]

- **Gholam Reza Aghazadeh, Vice President for Atomic Energy of the Islamic Republic of Iran and President of the Atomic Energy Organization of Iran, April 10, 2007:** "Iran's program is not to install and operate only 3,000 centrifuges at the Natanz uranium enrichment facilities, but 50,000...We planned and invested for [the installation of] 50,000 centrifuges. The infrastructure that has been established— including equipment for air filtering, electricity, a new air supply, and everything required for this industry—was for 50,000 centrifuges...I intentionally did not indicate any number [in my speech at the Natanz celebrations]...because I wanted no misunderstandings in the foreign media, [and I did not want] them to think that Iran's [nuclear program] included [only] 3,000 centrifuges.

[The situation is] quite the opposite. As we enter the industrial stage, the installation of the centrifuges will be carried out on an ongoing basis, until all 50,000 [centrifuges] are installed...Our declaration that we have entered the stage [of producing nuclear fuel] on an industrial [scale means] that there is no turning back."

At the Natanz celebrations, Aghazadeh stressed that "despite the commitments we have received from [various] countries, no expert of [any external] company has stood by us...but despite these challenges, obstacles, and problems, Iran was determined to realize, by means of its creative young people, its nuclear program—which includes peaceful purposes, with the first priority being to produce a nuclear fuel cycle as supreme science in nuclear technology...and in the past year, our young scientists have managed to produce 270 tons of UF^6. Not long ago, [producing] this important substance was far from the imagination of our country's nuclear researchers and scientists. But finally, we managed to attain [enrichment of] uranium, at [a level of] 3.5% to 5%.....Now, as we enter mass production of centrifuges and begin to produce [nuclear fuel] on an industrial [scale], we are taking one more step towards the flowering of Iran...

Now that Iran has entered into production of nuclear fuel on an industrial [scale], there will be no limit on the production of nuclear fuel in Iran...This is the accomplishment of some 3,000 expert scientists and the best of the forces that worked in the best year night and day at the Natanz facility."[82]

- **Keyhan editorial, "The West Must Expect a Shock from Iran at Any Moment, April 10, 2007:** "Under the current threatening and unjust conditions, Iran has decided to employ a strategy of ambiguity. Since Iran's nuclear dossier was illegally returned to the UN Security Council, the eyes of the IAEA—the intelligence agency of the West—are finding it more difficult every day [to monitor Iran's activities]. When [the IAEA] reported on [Iran's nuclear dossier] to the Security Council last winter, Iran announced that it would no longer be implementing the Additional Protocol. A few months later, when sanctions resolution 1737 was issued, Iran began to install 3,000 centrifuges in Natanz...When sanctions resolution 1747 was passed, Iran further reduced IAEA access [to its nuclear facilities] by stopping the implementation of the agreements connected to the 'Safeguards Agreement.'"

- **Keyhan editorial, "Duel with an Unloaded Gun," April 11, 2007:** "Now America has expended all the bullets in its clip. Now, it is Iran that will decide, in the face of the shocked world, on the 'news' and the 'event' with which it will strike the superpowers at their weak points and their Achilles heel. Iran still has great wisdom in its clip—each bullet of wisdom prepares the ground for new opportunities, and makes Iran's hands more skilled...America is now dealing with the deadly hail of Iran's wisdom..."

A CONTINUING PROCESS OF DISCOVERY

It is also clear that there is still much more to learn. As noted earlier, in early 2006, the *New York Times* reported on new U.S. intelligence estimates that suggested Iran's "peaceful" program included a "military-nuclear dimension." This assessment was reportedly based on information provided by the United States to the IAEA and referred to a secret program called the Green Salt Project. This project was started to work on uranium enrichment, high explosives, and on adapting nuclear warheads to Iranian missiles. The report suggested that there was evidence of "administrative interconnections" between weaponization and nuclear experts in Iran's nuclear program. Tehran argued that these claims were "baseless" and promised to provide further clarifications on the matter.[83]

The IAEA report on Iran's nuclear activities in August 2006 made it clear, however, that Iran was not clarifying any major issues raised relating to its nuclear activities, and this raised new questions about Iran's activities in highly enriching uranium that could not be linked to any contamination of centrifuges imported from Pakistan.

Claims that there was a link between Iran's civilian and military nuclear tracks seem to support the comments made by then Secretary of State Colin Powell in November 2004, yet it remains uncertain if the sources of intelligence were the same. Mr. Powell argued that the U.S. intelligence had information that showed Iranian efforts to adapt their nuclear research to fit their Shahab-3 missile. He argued that it made no sense that Iran would work on advancing its delivery systems unless it were also working on the warheads. Other U.S. officials, however, argued that the information Colin Powell used came from unconfirmed sources with uncertain information and should not be seen as a definitive proof.[84]

The source for this information seems to be a stolen laptop computer, which contained designs of a small-scale uranium gas production facility by Kimeya Madon, an Iranian company. In addition, the documents contained modification to the Shahab-3 missile in a way, U.S. officials believe, to fit a nuclear warhead. U.S. intelligence experts, reportedly, believe that the files on the computer were authentic, but they argue that there was no way to prove it. They argue that while there was the possibility that the document was forged by Iranian opposition groups or fabricated by a third country like Israel, it was unlikely. In addition, the authenticity of the document also seemed to have been confirmed by British intelligence.[85]

What concerns U.S. officials is that while there was no mention of the word "nuclear" on the laptop, the documents mentioned the names of military officers that were linked to Mohsen Fakhrizadeh, who is believed to direct "Project 111." U.S. intelligence believes that this project has been responsible for weaponizing Iran's nuclear research efforts and missile developments. In addition, the United States believes that this project is the successor to Project 110, which used to be the military arm of Iran's nuclear research program. These revelations, however, are "cloaked" with uncertainty, and the United States believes that the only way to know is if Fakrizadeh cooperates with IAEA inspectors.[86]

These concerns about Iranian weaponization efforts were exacerbated by the IAEA's discovery of a document relating to the requirement of reducing UF6 to small quantities of metal as well as casting enriched and natural depleted uranium into hemispherical forms.[87] This is believed to be the first link the IAEA has shown between Iran's military and civilian nuclear program. Many argue that this discovery was the turning point in the IAEA negotiation efforts with Tehran and that the failure to disclose this document early in the inspections was a cause for concern for the Agency.

Press reports have also claimed that there was further evidence of Iran's effort to weaponize its nuclear research. A U.S. intelligence assessment was leaked to the *Washington Post*. According to U.S. officials, Iran's nuclear researchers have completed the drawing of "a deep subterranean shaft." The drawings outlined the plans for a 400-meter underground tunnel with remote-controlled sensors to measure pressures and temperatures. U.S. experts believed that the tunnel was being prepared for an underground nuclear test. One U.S. official was quoted saying, "The diagram is consistent with a nuclear test-site schematic." This assessment was based on the fact that the drawings envisioned a test control team to be so far away—ten kilometers—from the test site, but the United States believes that the tunnel was still in the drawing stage and no developments have taken place. The evidence for this tunnel and Iranian weaponization efforts were the closest thing to a smoking gun in proving Iranian nuclear weapons program.[88]

This illustrates the point that Iran can gain as much from concealing and obfuscating its weaponization activities as from hiding or obfuscating the nature of its nuclear program. As long as Iran does not actually test a full nuclear explosion, it can develop and test potential weapons and warhead designs in a wide range of ways. It can also prepare for underground testing and test simulated weapons underground to validate many aspects of the test system—including venting—without exploding a bomb until it is ready for the international community to know it has actually tested a weapon.

It can develop and deploy its missile program with conventional warheads and create considerable confusion over the nature of its warhead and bomb tests, concealing whether it has carried out extensive research on CBRN weaponization as part of what it claims is the testing of conventional weapons. Telemetry can be encrypted, avoided, and made deliberately misleading. The same is true of static explosive testing or the use of air-delivered warheads and bombs. So far, for example, the international community and outside experts have generally failed to explore the rationale for Iran's missile efforts and other weaponization activities. The IAEA and the Chemical Weapons Convention lack any clear mandate for inspection and analysis of such activities, and the Biological Weapons Convention does not address the issue.

Iran's Strategic Capabilities and the Possible Response

In the introduction to this book, it is suggested that Iran's military capabilities should be evaluated in terms of five major kinds of current and potential threats:

- *As a conventional military power.* Iran has limited capabilities today, but it could become a much more threatening power if it modernized key elements of its forces and its neighbors did not react.

- *As an asymmetric threat that can seek to intimidate or attack using unconventional forces.* Iran has established a large mix of unconventional forces that can challenge its neighbors in a wide variety of asymmetric wars, including a low-level war of attrition.

- *In terms of the ways Iran's asymmetric and unconventional capabilities give it the ability to use proxies and partners in the form of both state and nonstate actors.* Iran's support of Shi'ite militias in Iraq, ties to elements in the Iraqi government, partnership with Syria, and ties to Hezbollah in Lebanon are all practical examples of such activities.

- *As a potential nuclear power armed with long-range missiles.* Iran is a declared chemical weapons power. Its biological weapons efforts are unknown, but it seems unlikely that it remained passive in reaction to Iraq's efforts. It has openly made the acquisition of long-range missiles a major objective, and its nuclear research and production programs almost certainly are intended to produce nuclear weapons.

- *And, in terms of the threat Iran presents as a potential religious and ideological threat in a region and Islamic world polarized along sectarian lines.* For all of the talk about a clash between civilizations, the potential clash within Islam seems far more dangerous. The risk that Sunni and Shi'ite extremists can provoke a broader split between sects and nations could push Iran into a more aggressive religious and ideological struggle.

The preceding analysis has shown Iran's potential strengths and weaknesses in each of these areas and the tools its leaders have on hand and are seeking to develop. No one can predict events that could lead Iran to try to use these tools in new and unanticipated ways, but it is possible to sum up Iran's capabilities in broad terms.

IRAN'S CONVENTIONAL WEAKNESSES AND STRENGTHS

No one can ignore the fact that Iran does have a large, if divided force structure. It currently has some 545,000 actives and 350,000 army reserves, not counting the Basij. Its army has an active strength of around 350,000 men, although 220,000 are low-grade conscripts and its corps of technicians and noncommissioned officers is poorly trained and given limited initiative. Iranian training and doctrine have slowly improved over time, although Iran has little practical experience with advanced command and control, targeting, intelligence, surveillance, and reconnaissance (IS&R), and electronic warfare capability; and its efforts to improve its capability in joint operations and sustainability have had only limited success.

Iran's Limited Conventional Offensive Capabilities

The Iranian Army has considerable mass and ability to operate in relatively static defensive roles. It is not, however, a modern maneuver force by any means. Only a third of its main battle tanks are modern enough to have moderate capability and most of its other tanks, other armored fighting vehicles, and armored personnel carriers are worn and obsolete. It is reliant on towed artillery forces with weak to poor targeting and fire control, and its 50-odd remaining attack helicopters are worn and have limited operational capability. Its short-range air defenses are ineffective against modern attack aircraft with long-range targeting and precision fire capability. Most of its conventionally armed MRLSs (Multiple Rocket Launcher Systems) and surface-to-surface weapons seem to have some cluster warheads, but are too inaccurate and lacking in lethality to use against anything other than static forces and area targets and then are more likely to produce harassment effects than kills.

There is an additional 100,000 men in the land/air branch of the Iranian Revolutionary Guards Corps (IRGC), but this too is a largely conscript force organized into many small formations with grandiose unit designations like "division." It has some armor and artillery, but is largely an infantry force. Only selected elements trained in missions like operating Iran's longer-range surface-to-surface missiles, operating as advisors and embedded forces in other armies or militias, special missions, and unconventional warfare have moderate to high capability. The IRGC can, however, potentially draw upon 100,000s of young men in the Basij for local defense missions.

The 35,000-man-plus Iranian Air Force has shown considerable skill in keeping its fleet of aircraft operating, modernizing some subsystems and avionics, and adapting new weapons to aging platforms. Its core electronic warfare, IS&R, and command, control, communications, computers, and intelligence (C4I)/battle management systems, however, have low to moderate capability and are severely limited by the age and inherent limitations to the avionics on its aircraft.

It has some 260+ combat aircraft, but operational availability is about 50–60 percent for U.S. supplied types, all of which are now three decades old or older, and none of which have had access to generations of U.S. upgrades. Operational readiness for its Russian and People's Republic of China (PRC)-supplied aircraft may be 75–80 percent, but only some 10–12 Su-25Ks, 18–23 MiG-29As, and 20–25 Su-24MKs represent anything approaching modern aircraft, and all are export versions of Russian fighters with limited avionics. Even with the addition of some 18–22 operational F-14s and 30–50 operational F-4Es, this is a limited force of less than 100 combat aircraft with moderate modern warfighting capability, and it would have severe problems in generating and sustaining high numbers of sorties.

The Iranian Air Force does have some modern air-to-air and air-to-ground missiles, although much of its inventory is aging severely and has limited capability. It still operates five P-3MP Orions with airborne warning, air control, maritime patrol, and remote anti-ship missile targeting capability, but their operational status is unclear and their electronic warfare capabilities are limited. Overall reconnaissance, electronic warfare, battle management, and targeting capabilities are poor to moderate. The Iranian Air Force remains severely equipment limited.

There are some 15,000 men assigned to land-based air-defense forces. Iran's main surface-to-air (SAM) missile defenses include roughly 150 Improved Hawk (I-Hawk) surface-to-air missile launchers, 45 SA-2s and additional PRC-clone launchers, and 10 obsolescent long-range SA-5 launchers. It has some operational FM-80 Crotale, 20–30 Rapiers, and 3–15 Tigercat shorter-range systems. It also has large numbers of man-portable surface-to-air missiles (some modern) and anti-aircraft guns.

Iran has found some ingenious ways to modernize the sensors, battle management, and electronic warfare systems supporting this force, and to improvise a crude form of netting to integrate some fire units. The new TOR-M1 surface-to-air missiles it is importing from Russia reportedly were delivered and test-fired in January 2007; they are the first truly modern systems it has received since the fall of the Shah and they are best suited for short- to medium-range point defense. Barring massive deliveries of Russian S-300 or S-400 surface-to-air missiles, sensors, and battle management systems, the Iranian system is vulnerable and largely obsolete.

The 16,000–20,000 man Iranian Navy has many limitations. It has learned how to keep its three Kilo-class submarines operational, but its larger surface ships (three aging missile frigates and two aging gun corvettes) are obsolete; it has limited amphibious capability for anything other than raids or Special Forces missions against exposed targets in the Gulf, and its amphibious exercises are largely set piece shams. (It has three landing ships, medium with a total lift capacity of around 300–350 troops and 30 major armored weapons.)

The navy does have significant numbers of mine vessels, smaller patrol ships (some armed with anti-ship missiles), and maritime patrol aircraft and mine-laying helicopters. In overall terms, however, it is now far less capable of fighting a conventional battle at sea than it was when it was decisively defeated by the U.S. Navy in the "tanker war" of 1987–1988.

Iran as a Defensive Power

This force mix scarcely makes Iran any kind of regional military "hegemon," and the region would have years of warning before Iranian forces could acquire and absorb major numbers of new weapons. Iran can certainly improve its defensive capabilities and the attrition it can impose on an attacker, but it would virtually require the United States to abandon the Gulf for Iran to be able to win a regional arms race that would give it the air and naval capabilities to gain serious offensive capabilities in conventional war, and even then, a cohesive response by the Gulf Cooperation Council (GCC) would seriously challenge any capability that Iran could develop.

Geography is also a critical factor. Iran would virtually have to be invited in to cross the Gulf with significant forces. It has little or no foreseeable incentive to strike at most of its other neighbors, and many of the border areas it might advance into present other geographic problems as well as offer little or no strategic advantage. Iran certainly has the ability to wage war, but it does not have the capability to win most wars in ways that give it any advantage.

The two exceptions that must be kept clearly in mind are the defense of its own territory and Iraq. Iran is a highly populated country of over 65 million people with centrally located cities, and its forces are strong enough to make it anything but a defensive "weakling." As the Iran-Iraq War and Gulf Wars show, much depends on popular support, but any invasion of Iran that produced a strong nationalist response, rather than a broad-based uprising against the regime, would almost certainly turn into a bloody and pointless war of attrition.

This would be the kind of war where even major tactical victories against Iran would not offer lasting strategic advantage and would tie the attacker down in exposed positions. As will be discussed shortly, the defeat or large-scale destruction of Iran's conventional forces also would not deprive it of the ability to retaliate using unconventional forces, proxies, or partners. It also might drive Iran to respond over time with far larger efforts to acquire nuclear weapons.

Iran's Conventional Forces and Iraq

It is also important to point out that Iran does have the ability to rapidly deploy a large mix of conventional and unconventional forces into Iraq. Iraq's current military forces are divided and extremely weak and Shi'ite and Kurdish dominated. If Iran was invited in following a U.S. and British withdrawal by a Shi'ite-dominated government, and had popular support from most of Iraq's Shi'ite Arabs, it could quickly dominate most areas with a Shi'ite majority, defeat insurgent or Sunni resistance in most areas outside Anbar and Mosul, and defeat Kurdish forces in any clash over Kirkuk.

Iraq would now become a virtual military power vacuum if U.S. forces were not present. If Iran and Iraq cooperated to secure a Shi'ite dominated "federation," Iran could play a major offensive role with only limited warning and preparation. Much would depend on the Iraqi government and Iraq Arab Shi'ite support in such a scenario, however, and on the willingness of the United States to permit the movement of Iranian conventional forces.

It should also be noted, however, that no Sunni Arab state is now organized to project large ground force contingents into most of the populated areas of Iraq, although Jordan and Syria could project significant ground forces into the West. Turkey could project a corps-sized force into northern Iraq (and did so at the time of Saddam Hussein), but its fears of the Kurds are unlikely to make it intervene on the part of the Arabs even if invited.

IRAN AS AN ASYMMETRIC THREAT

As nations even as powerful as the United States have learned to their cost, the conventional balance is only one balance in modern warfare. Iran has responded to its conventional weaknesses by seeking three different forms of asymmetric capability that it can try to use to intimidate or attack:

- The creation of its own regular and IRGC forces for unconventional warfare.
- The development of long-range strike systems and weapons of mass (WMD) destruction.
- The creation of ties to proxies and partners it can join or use in asymmetric conflicts.

The Iranian Threat in the Gulf

Iran has built up a large mix of unconventional forces in the Gulf that can challenge its neighbors in a wide variety of asymmetric wars, including low-level wars of attrition. These include a wide range of elements in the regular forces and IRGC as well as some elements in the Ministry of Intelligence and Security (MOIS), or Vezarat-e Ettela' at va Aminat-e Keshvar, which was installed following the Revolution to replace the now-disbanded National Organization for Intelligence and Security. In 2006, the MOIS employed about 15,000 civilian staff. Its major tasks included intelligence collection and operations in the Middle East and Central Asia domestic intelligence and monitoring of clerical and government officials, as well as work on preventing conspiracies against the Islamic republic.

Its air forces remain vulnerable in any form of mission, but are less vulnerable near Iranian bases, sensor coverage, and SAM coverage. Its naval forces include its three Kilo-class submarines, which can harass or seek to interdict ships moving in and out of the Gulf, a wide range of mines and vessels that can be used as minelayers, or to release free-floating mines.

They also include roughly 140 light patrol and coastal combatants, including 11 French-designed Kaman-class missile patrol boats with 2-4 CSS-N-4/YJ-1/ "Sardine" anti-ship missiles each. These are sea-skimming, solid-fueled missiles with a 42- to 50-kilometer range, 165-kilogram warheads, INS (Inertial Navigation System) and active radar similar to the Exocet, and can be used to harass civil shipping and tankers, and offshore facilities, as well as attack naval vessels. Iran may well have far more advanced Russian- and Chinese-supplied missiles as well and claims to be developing advanced anti-ship and anti-fixed target missiles of its own.

Iran made claims in the spring of 2006 that it was testing more advanced weapons for such forces. These included a sonar-evading anti-ship missile that can be fired from submarines as well as surface combatants that IRGC Rear Admiral Ali Fadavi claimed no enemy warship could detect, and "no warship could escape because of its high velocity." Iran also claimed to be testing a new missile called the Kowsar with a very large warhead and extremely high speed to attack "big ships and submarines" that it claimed could evade radar and anti-missile missiles. While such tests may have been real, Iran has made so many grossly exaggerated claims about its weapons developments in the past, it seems they were designed more to try to deter U.S. military action and/or reassure the Iranian public than truly being serious real-world capabilities. It followed these actions up in the late summer of 2006 by testing new submarine launched anti-ship missiles.

It has a 20,000 man naval branch in the IRGC that includes some 5,000 marines. This branch of the IRGC has ten Houdong missile patrol boasts with CSS-N-8/C-802/YJ-2 missiles with 165-kilogram warheads, active and inertial guidance, and maximum ranges of 120 kilometers. It operates mobile land-based CSS-C-3/HY-2/Sea Eagle/Seersucker anti-ship missiles that can be rapidly emplaced on the Iranian coast or islands in the Gulf shipping channel. These systems have ranges of 95–100 kilometers, very large warheads, and autocontrol and radar-homing guidance. They can be targeted by a remote air link, and the exact level of upgrading of these missiles since their initial delivery during the Iran-Iraq War is unknown.

The IRGC has large numbers of Boghammar and other patrol boats with recoilless rifles, rocket launchers, man-portable surface-to-air missiles, and anti-armor guided weapons. The IRGC routinely uses small civilian ships and vessels in unconventional operations in various exercises, including minelaying and raids on offshore facilities. This force has facilities at Bandar Abbas, Khorramshar, and on the islands of Larak, Abu Musa, Al Farsiyah, Sirrir, and the Halul oil platform. It can make use of additional facilities at Iran's main naval bases at Bandar Abbas, Bushehr, Kharg Island, Bandar Anzali, Bandar Khomeini, Bandar Mahshahr, and Chah Bahar. These forces can rapidly disperse and shelter in caves and hardened sites. Small ships can be very hard to detect with most radars even in a normal sea state, and civilian ships can easily change flags and meld in with commercial traffic.

According to one Israeli source, Iran plans to defeat the United States by attrition, trying to exploit perceived American psychological vulnerabilities for a high number of casualties. Further, the report states, "Iran's military acquisitions reveal a rather defensive mindset with an intention to deter against an attack rather than to win a war by overwhelming force."[1]

"Closing the Gulf?"

These light naval forces have special importance because of their potential ability to threaten oil and shipping traffic in the Gulf and the Gulf of Oman, raid key offshore facilities, and conduct raids on targets on the Gulf coast. Many Gulf energy facilities are extremely vulnerable, and the GCC states are extremely vulnerable to any form of attack on their desalination and coastal power facilities, and precision strikes on critical high-capacity, long-lead time replacement items in energy facilities and power grids. This vulnerability might also allow Iran to carry out very successful air attacks in a surprise raid with precision weapons, using IRGC "suicide" aircraft, and future unmanned aerial vehicles (UAVs) and precision cruise missiles. It is also possible that Iran could conduct coastal raids with IRGC and/or Special Forces that went deeper into southern Gulf territory.

Iran could not "close the Gulf" for more than a few days to two weeks even if it was willing to sacrifice all of these assets, suffer massive retaliation, and potentially lose many of its own oil facilities and export revenues. Its chronic economic misman-agement has made it extremely dependent on a few refineries, product imports, and food imports. It would almost certainly lose far more than it gained from such a "war," but nations often fail to act as rational bargainers in a crisis, particularly if attacked or if their regimes are threatened.

Even sporadic, low-level attacks on Gulf shipping and facilities, however, could allow Iran to wage a war of intimidation in an effort to pressure its neighbors. As a recent International Energy Agency study shows, the current and future volume of oil export traffic through the Gulf is steadily increasing and presents a target of global strategic importance that will grow steadily in the coming years even if one exempts growing the growth in tanker shipments of liquefied petroleum gas (see Figure 12.1). This will make any threat that sharply raises oil prices, deters smooth tanker flows and deliveries, and otherwise interferes with energy exports of great importance, par-ticularly in a world where every developed economy is critically dependent on global trade and the continuing flow of Asian heavy manufactures that are steadily more de-pendent on Gulf oil.

It should be noted, however, that Iran is acutely dependent on oil revenues and that attacks on its refineries and power plants could do immense retaliatory damage. In mid-September of 2006, reports also surfaced that the U.S. Navy was reconsider-ing older plans for blocking two Iranian oil ports near the Straits of Hormuz. This apparently was accompanied by a "prepare-to-deploy" order for several mine-warfare vessels.[2] In February 2007, a second aircraft-carrier group was deployed to the Persian Gulf, and reportedly plans to send a third one were considered.[3] Iran is also as vulnerable to attacks on its oil platforms and loading facilities in the Gulf as the southern Gulf States.[4]

Other Contingencies

At the same time, as the previous discussion has shown, Iran could use its entire mix of forces in unconventional and asymmetric defenses of its own territory and in conducting deep penetration and border raids and attacks on its neighbors. Iran's material and resource limits may affect its major weapons systems and military sophistication and modernization. Its internal division may delay or limit some

Figure 12.1   The Importance of Gulf Oil Exports

Area of Export Flow	Current Flow in MMBD*	Share of World Oil Demand in Percent		
		In 2004	In 2030	In 2030
Strait of Hormuz	17.4	21.2	28.1	19.4
Straits of Malacca/Far East	13	15.8	23.7	23.3
Bab el-Mandab	3.5	4.3	4.5	4.9
Suez	3.9	4.7	4.8	5.3

*   MMBD = million barrels per day.

Source: Adapted by Anthony H. Cordesman from material provided by Ambassador William C. Ramsay, Deputy Executive Director, International Energy Agency, February 6, 2007.

aspects of its military coordination and effectiveness, as does its dependence on conscripts. It is clear from Iran's military literature, however, that it keenly studies both asymmetric warfare techniques and asymmetric vulnerabilities and opportunities, and while its exercises are of patchy quality, some elements of the Iranian forces are highly effective in testing asymmetric methods of operation.

IRAN'S USE OF STATE AND NONSTATE ACTORS AS PROXIES AND PARTNERS

Iran also can make use of both state and nonstate actors. Iran's support of Shi'ite militias in Iraq, ties to elements in the Iraqi government, partnership with Syria, ties to Hezbollah in Lebanon, support of Shi'ite Afghan elements, and arms supply and training of elements of Hamas and the Palestinian Islamic Jihad (PIJ) are all practical examples of such activities. So are past efforts to destabilize the Hajj and support Shi'ite unrest in Bahrain and Saudi Arabia.

As has been discussed earlier, Iran has developed a special element in the IRGC called the Al-Quds Force that is often associated with Iranian efforts to arm, train, and advise foreign states and nonstate actors. This Force has been active in countries like Lebanon and Iraq and has operated in cells in other countries. Iranian intelligence is also involved in supporting such efforts. Iran carries out activities under diplomatic cover, uses commercial entities and dummy corporations, and sometimes uses elements of Iran's regular forces. This is scarcely a unique mix of operations, and one adopted by many other countries, but Iran has become far more skilled in such operations than most countries.

"Proxies" and "Partners"

The use of state and nonstate actors can involve both "proxies"—foreign forces directly under Iranian control—and "partners"—forces that cooperate with Iran to their own or a common advantage. The issue of who is using whom is largely moot if all the actors involved are willing to cooperate and feel they benefit from such cooperation.

The use of allies and proxies is generally cheap, reduces risk, and acts as a force multiplier. It also provides some degree of deniability—plausible or implausible—and this is a major reason for both the complexity of some efforts and consistent efforts to deny the nature or scale of such efforts and Iran's attempts at concealment.

The Strengths and Weaknesses of Such Operations

Like direct forms of asymmetric operations, the use of foreign actors can be both defensive and offensive. It can also serve ideological and religious causes. It also is extremely difficult to establish a motive and the scale of such efforts under many conditions, particularly since they can be conducted without attribution to Iranian government support (false flags) or under conditions where the Iranian government can claim any document incident was a rogue operation it did not authorize. A sophisticated effort can take on the character of a three-dimensional chess game in which most of the one side's players are truly what they seem and that player keeps changing the rules without announcing the changes.

The problem Iran faces in most such operations is that they can harass or "spoil," but rarely achieve decisive strategic results. The end result is a "spoiler" operation that may damage an opponent, or cause local or regional instability, but does not really benefit Iran. Iranian influence also does not give Iran control.

The Hezbollah operation against Israel, and Israel's destruction of most of the medium- and long-range rocket forces Iran and Syria had laboriously built up, is a case in point. Supporting anti–U.S. elements in Iraq does not necessarily benefit Iran in the long run. Implausible deniability provokes direct or indirect hostile responses, and Iran can find itself dragged into a far more serious conflict or crisis than it intends through the acts of its "partner."

Much depends on the specific case and the skill with which Iran acts. Sheer distance, and the tactical buffer caused by the need to bypass or overfly Arab states, gives Iran some freedom of action in supporting Hezbollah, Hamas, and the PIJ. This also allows Iran to build up its capabilities and influence by appearing to take the Arab side—although not if its efforts in nations like Lebanon provoke Arab states to see such actions as threatening their security or it provokes Israel to the point where its tenuous restraint turns into hostile action.

Low-level operations that intimidate a Gulf State or other neighbor without making it react in hostile ways can also succeed, although they involve careful balance and judgment. Simply building up military and security relations can provide both a defensive option and a potential threat to other powers without being a direct provocation.

If there are strategic options where such methods could play a direct role, they seem to lie in three areas, two of which are marginal. Iran could seek to attack the United States or any other power by using nonstate actors, particularly if they seemed at least partially hostile to Iran. Iran may have supported Al Qa'ida in Iraq for precisely this reason. Supporting Shi'ite elements in Afghanistan would be another way of securing its interests against any resurgence of the Taliban, and Iran could do so without having to confront the United States or NATO (North Atlantic Treaty Organisation).

The Iraq Option

The most serious opportunity Iran has in conducting such operations is in Iraq, for all of the reasons already touched upon earlier in this analysis. It is also one of the only two serious opportunities that Iran has to move from a largely defensive power to one that has seriously expanded its power and influence. The other is the effort to acquire long-range missiles and nuclear weapons discussed in the following section.

Iran already plays a major role in the political stability (or instability) of Iraq and may take a more aggressive role in trying to shape Iraq's political future and security position in the Gulf. Some believe that the Iranians have abandoned their efforts to export their "Shi'ite revolution" to the Gulf. This view has changed since the invasion of Iraq. Officials across the Arab world, especially in Saudi Arabia and Jordan, have expressed reservations over the lack of rights of Iraqi Sunnis, Kurdish and Shi'ite dominance over the Iraqi government, and a new "strategic" Shi'ite alliance between Iran and Iraq.

Jordan's King Abdullah II claimed that more than 1 million Iranians have moved into Iraq to influence the Iraqi election. The Iranians, King Abdullah argued, have been trying to build pro-Iranian attitudes in Iraq by providing salaries to the unemployed. The King has also said that Iran's Revolutionary Guards are helping the militant groups fighting the United States in Iraq, and he warned in an interview with the *Washington Post* of a "Shi'ite Crescent" forming between Iran, Iraq, Syria, and Lebanon. He was quoted as saying,

> It is in Iran's vested interest to have an Islamic republic of Iraq.
>
> If Iraq goes Islamic republic, then, yes, we've opened ourselves to a whole set of new problems that will not be limited to the borders of Iraq. I'm looking at the glass half-full, and let's hope that's not the case. But strategic planners around the world have got to be aware that is a possibility.
>
> Even Saudi Arabia is not immune from this. It would be a major problem. And then that would propel the possibility of a Shi'ite-Sunni conflict even more, as you're taking it out of the borders of Iraq.[5]

The same sentiment has been echoed by former interim Iraqi President Ghazi Al-Yawar, a Sunni. "Unfortunately, time is proving, and the situation is proving, beyond any doubt that Iran has very obvious interference in our business—a lot of money, a lot of intelligence activities and almost interfering daily in business and many [provincial] governorates, especially in the southeast side of Iraq." Mr. Al-Yawar, however, asserted that Iraq should not go in the direction of Iran in creating a religious-oriented government. He was quoted in a *Washington Post* interview as saying, "We cannot have a sectarian or religious government... We really will not accept a religious state in Iraq. We haven't seen a model that succeeded."[6]

These comments were rejected by both Iran and Iraqi Shi'ites. Iran called King Abdullah's comment "an insult" to Iraq. Iranian Foreign Ministry Spokesman Hamid Reza Asefi also called on Ghazi Al-Yawar to retract his statement and accused King Abdullah II and Al-Yawar of wanting to influence the election against Iraqi Shi'ites. Asefi said, "Unfortunately, some political currents in Iraq seek to tarnish the trend of election there and cause concern in the public opinion . . . We expect that Mr. al-Yawar takes the existing sensitive situation into consideration and avoids repeating such comments."[7]

What is clear is that Iran has close relations with many Iraqi Shi'ites, particularly Shi'ite political parties and militias. Some Iraqi groups have warned against U.S. military strikes against their neighbors. For example, Moqtada Al-Sadr pledged that he would come to the aid of Iran in the case of a military strike by the United States against Tehran. Al-Sadr pledged that his militia, Al-Mahdi Army, would come to the aid of Iran. According to Al-Sadr, Iran asked him about what his position would be if Iran was attacked by the United States, and he said he pledged that Al-Mahdi Army would help any Arab or neighboring country if it was attacked.[8]

The *London Times* in September 2005 identified at least a dozen active Islamic groups in Iraq with ties to Tehran. Eight were singled out as having considerable cross-border influence:

- **Badr Brigade:** A Shi'ite militia force of 12,000 trained by Iran's Revolutionary Guards and blamed for a number of killings of Sunni Muslims. They are thought to control several cities in southern Iraq.

- **Islamic Dawa Party:** A Shi'ite party that has strong links to Iran. Its leader, Ibrahim al-Jaafari, the present Prime Minister of Iraq, has vowed to improve ties between the two neighbors.

- **Al-Mahdi Army:** Received arms and volunteers from Iran during its battle against U.S. and British troops last year. The group's commander in Basra, Ahmed al-Fartusi, was arrested by British forces in mid-September 2005.

- **Mujahideen for Islamic Revolution in Iraq:** A Tehran-backed militia blamed for the murder of six British Royal Military Police soldiers in Majar el-Kabir in 2003.

- **Thar Allah (Vengeance of God):** An Iranian-backed terror group blamed for killing former members of the ruling Ba'ath Party in Iraq and enforcing strict Islamic law.

- **Jamaat al-Fudalah (Group of the Virtuous):** A paramilitary group that imposes Islamic rules on Shi'ite areas and has attacked shops selling alcohol and music.

- **Al-Fadilah (Morality):** A secret political movement financed by Iran. It is thought to have many members among provincial officials.

- **Al-Quawaid al-Islamiya (Islamic Bases):** An Iranian-backed Islamic movement that uses force to impose Islamic law.[9]

A number of experts believe that Tehran-backed militias have infiltrated Iraqi security forces. In September 2005, Iraq's National Security Adviser, Mouwafak al-Rubaie, admitted that insurgents had penetrated Iraqi police forces in many parts of the country, but he refused to speculate about the extent of the infiltration.[10]

In addition, both the U.S. and British Ministers of Defense have complained that Iran is actively supporting various militias in Iraq, has supplied advanced triggering and motion detector systems for improvised explosive devices, and is using elements of the Al-Quds Force to train death squads and militias.[11] Work by Nawaf Obaid and the Saudi National Security Assessment Project indicates the following:

> Iran is insinuating itself into Iraq. The first is through the activities of the al-Quds Forces, the special command division of the Iranian Revolutionary Guard (IRGC). The second approach is by funding and arming Shi'ite militias, the most prominent of which is the SCIRI's [Supreme Council for the Islamic Revolution in Iraq's] 25,000-strong armed wing, the Badr Organization of Reconstruction and Development. Senior members of the Badr Organization and the al-Quds Forces have a closely coordinated relationship. Intelligence reports have indicated that Iranian officers are directing operations under cover in units of the Badr Organization. The Mahdi Army also receives important Iranian assistance, but on a much smaller scale.
>
> The IRGC Commander is General Yahya Rahim-Safavi and the Deputy Commander is General Mohammad Bager Zulgadr. The al-Quds Forces Commander is General Qassem Soleimani. Generals Zulgadr and Soleimani are two most senior officers responsible for Iran's large covert program in Iraq and have a direct link to the Office of the Leader. Additionally, intelligence estimates have identified four other IRGC generals and nine IRGC colonels that are directly responsible for covert operations in Iraq.
>
> The al-Quds Forces mainly functions as a large intelligence operation skilled in the art of unconventional warfare. Current intelligence estimates puts the strength of the force at 5,000. Most of these are highly trained officers. Within the al-Quds Forces, there is a small unit usually referred to as the "Special Al-Quds Force" which consists of the finest case officers and operatives.
>
> The senior officers attached to this unit conduct foreign covert unconventional operations using various foreign national movements as proxies. The forces operate mainly outside Iranian territory, but maintain numerous training bases inside Iran as well. Al-Quds international operations are divided into geographic areas of influence and various corps. The most important and largest cover Iraq, Saudi Arabia (and the Arabian Peninsula), and Syria/Lebanon. The smaller corps cover Afghanistan, Pakistan/India, Turkey, the Muslim Republics of the former Soviet Union, Europe/North America, and North Africa (Egypt, Tunisia, Algeria, Sudan, and Morocco).
>
> The goal of Iran is to infiltrate all Iraq-based militias by providing training and support to their members. For example, al-Sadr's estimated 10,000-strong Mahdi Army, which gets logistical and financial support from al-Quds, also receives training in IRCG camps in Iran. Moreover, nearly all of the troops in the Badr Organization were trained in these camps as well. In addition, most senior officers acquired their skills in specialized camps under the control of the al-Quds Forces. Intelligence estimates that al-Quds currently operates six major training facilities in Iran, with the main facility located adjacent to Imam Ali University in Northern Tehran. The other most important training camps are located in the Qom, Tabriz, and Mashhad governorates. There are also two similar facilities operating on the Syrian-Lebanese border.

According to a senior general in the Iraqi Defense Ministry and a critic of Iran, the Iranians have set up the most sophisticated intelligence-gathering network in the country, to the extent that they have infiltrated "every major Iraqi ministry and security service." There is also an intelligence directorate that has been set up within the Revolutionary Guard that is under the command of the al-Quds Forces devoted exclusively to monitoring the movements of U.S. and Allied forces in Iraq.

Many members of the newly created police and Iraqi forces are controlled by Shi'ite officers who, in some form or another, previously belonged to SCIRI or other groups affiliated with Iran. Recent intelligence indicates that IRGC officers are currently operating in Iraq in certain Shi'ite militias and actual army and police units. The degree of penetration of these organizations is difficult to assess, and it is virtually impossible to distinguish between Iraqi Shi'ite militias and police units, both of which are profoundly influenced by Iran, and in some cases are under Iranian control.

Iranian manipulation has filtered down to street level as well. Ordinary police and military officers now have a stronger allegiance to the Badr Organization or the Mahdi Army than to their own units. And of course, these organizations are deeply connected to Iran. According to the head of intelligence of an allied country that borders Iraq, "the Iranians have not just pulled off an infiltration, in certain regions in Baghdad and Basra, it's been a complete takeover."[12]

It is not clear just how much Iran is using its security and intelligence forces to destabilize the political situation in Iraq. Iran's political objectives in Iraq remain obscure and partly contradictory. Tehran has stated repeatedly that it supports stability in Iraq. At the same time, several organizations with ties to the Iranian security apparatus are suspected of actively driving a wedge between rivaling factions in Iraq. The IRGC and its affiliates, out of any Iranian government organization, appear to be most strongly involved in assisting terrorist groups in neighboring Iraq.

In December 2004, a group named the Committee for the Commemoration of Martyrs of the Global Islamic Campaign assembled more than 25,000 "martyrdom-seeking volunteers" to fuel the insurgency of Iraqi groups against American forces. The committee maintains close ties to the IRGC from which it probably receives considerable material support. According to Iranian dissident groups, the IRGC is also directly involved in instigating the Iraqi insurgency through its Qods commandos, particularly in southern Iraq. Their number and extent of involvement with Iraqi factions remains unclear, however. Since the beginning of the American military campaign in Iraq, more than 2,000 people—believed to be sponsored directly by Iran—have entered the country to promote militant Islam.[13]

Reports suggest that Iranian sources have tried to establish contact with Moqtada Al-Sadr's organization in Iraq. Al-Sadr in the past spoke out against Iranian influence in Iraq. A relatively close connection between his organization and the Committee for the Commemoration of Martyrs of the Global Islamic Campaign with Iran suggests that destabilizing the political situation in Iraq is an important objective for the Iranian leadership. Apparently, Iranian forces try to gain leverage even over hostile forces in order to further Iraqi factionist politics.

Iran has a strategic interest in a stable Iraqi government. However, at this time, it appears as if Tehran is mobilizing resources to tilt the political climate in its favor, although it understands that this is causing some degree of additional political instability. All of the above concerns could also suddenly become far more serious if Iraq plunges into full-scale civil war or divides along ethnic and sectarian lines. Iran might be virtually forced to intervene on the Shi'ite side, potentially triggering new tensions and conflicts with both Iraq's Sunnis and Sunni states outside Iraq and raising new issues regarding Iran's attitudes toward Iraq's Kurds as well as its own Kurdish minority.

In late August 2006, several reports surfaced that American intelligence had no credible evidence that Iran ordered Hezbollah attacks against Israel, which led to the 34-day war in the summer.[14]

Like all of Iraq's neighbors, Iran has an incentive to avoid direct major military intervention that might well provoke a broad regional conflict, which could trigger large-scale U.S. intervention, and which ultimately might alienate the Iraqi Arabs that Iran came to aid. It does, however, have every incentive to see Iraq come under the effective control of a strong Arab Shi'ite government that would be a reliable partner and at least partially dependent on Iran.

Iran has had strong ties to SCIRI and the Islamic Dawa Party since these exile movements started fighting during the Iran-Iraq War and trained and equipped their forces from the early 1980s to 2004. It has built up some ties to the Sadr's Al-Mahdi militia, in spite of political and religious differences. It actively supports some elements of the Shi'ite leaders in the Iraqi government and can increasingly play on both the sectarian civil conflict in Iraq and Iraqi fears that the United States may withdraw.

There have also been British and American charges that Iran has supported both Shi'ite and Sunni elements hostile to British and U.S. forces and armed them with shaped charge bombs, advanced triggering devices, night sights, and other weapons whose transfer had been traced to the Mandali and Mehran border crossings to the northeast and the southeast of Baghdad. They also charged that Iran had regularly provided money to Shi'ite extremist groups and military training and that this was done by the Al-Quds Force in Iran's Revolutionary Guards, which reported to Iran's Supreme Leader.

On February 11, 2007, for example, U.S. experts gave a background briefing in Baghdad in which they said that Iran had armed Shi'ite militants in Iraq with sophisticated armor-piercing roadside bombs that had killed more than 170 American forces. These weapons included simple systems like mortars, but also included more sophisticated weapons known as "explosively formed penetrators," or EFPs where the "machining process" used in the construction was said to have been traced to Iran. The experts said that the supply trail began with the Al-Quds Force, which had armed Hezbollah, which had begun to use EFP weapons against Israel in the 1990s.

The briefing also included a PowerPoint slide program and sample mortar shells and rocket-propelled grenades that the military officials said were made in Iran after the fall of Saddam Hussein. The EFPs, as well as Iranian-made mortar shells and rocket-propelled grenades, were said to have been supplied to what U.S. experts said were "rogue elements" of the Mahdi Army militia of anti-American Shi'ite cleric Moqtada Al-Sadr, a key backer of Shi'ite Prime Minister Nouri al-Maliki. They did not fully respond to questions as to whether similar weapons had been provided to the Badr Brigade, the military wing of the Supreme Council for the Islamic Revolution in Iraq, but it seemed clear that this was an issue.

A U.S. intelligence analyst stated that Iran was working through "multiple surrogates"—mainly in the Mahdi Army—to smuggle the EFPs into Iraq. He said most of the components are entering the country at crossing points near Amarah, the Iranian border city of Meran, and the Basra area of southern Iraq. The previous week, the United States had announced that Shi'ite lawmaker Jamal Jaafar Mohammed was a key actor in allowing the main conduit for Iranian weapons entering the country.

U.S. officials did say that there was no evidence of Iranian-made EFPs having fallen into the hands of Sunni insurgents who operate mainly in Anbar Province in the west of Iraq, Baghdad, and regions surrounding the capital. They also said that there was no clear evidence that Iran was the source of the SA-7, SA-14, and SA-16 shoulder-fired anti-aircraft missiles in Iraqi insurgent and militia forces, although they provided evidence that Iranian-made Misaq-1 man-portable missiles had been used by insurgents in Baghdad in November and December 2006.

The United States has seized members of the Al-Quds Force operating in Iraq. For example, one of the six Iranians detained in Irbil in January 2007, Mohsin Chizari, was the operational commander of the Al-Quds Force there. Iranian advisors have been found in areas like the Ministry of the Interior, and many of the senior officials in the Iraqi government are former exiles that lived in Iran at some point. All of these events could lead to a major expansion of Iranian influence, particularly if a U.S. withdrawal creates a power vacuum in Iraq or the current low-level sectarian and ethnic civil war makes Iraqi Shi'ites dependent on Iran.

IRAN AS A NUCLEAR POWER ARMED WITH LONG-RANGE MISSILES

Iran's second possible option for making a major increase in its regional influence and power is to acquire weapons of mass destruction. Iran is a declared chemical weapons power. Its biological weapons efforts are unknown, but it seems unlikely that it remained passive in reaction to Iraq's efforts. It has openly made the acquisition of long-range missiles a major objective, and its nuclear research and production programs almost certainly are intended to produce nuclear weapons.

Iran's major long-range missile development program is the Shahab series, which now seems to include both solid- and liquid-fueled intermediate-range ballistic missiles and medium-range ballistic missiles. While Iran claims some of these systems are deployed, it continues to test new variants with ranges of 2,500–3,000 kilometers and improved warhead designs and accuracy. Iran has also obtained long-range Soviet bloc cruise missiles such as the Kh-55 Granit or Kent. This system has a range of 2,500–3,000 kilometers. It has a theoretical circular error probable (CEP) of about 150 meters and a speed of Mach 0.48–0.77, and while Iran may have bought some 12 systems to reverse engineer, it is possible that they could be carried and fired by its Su-24s.

As the previous chapters have made clear, Iran's progress in actually producing usable nuclear weapons and warheads for such systems is uncertain, but U.S. intelligence experts estimate that it is unlikely that Iran will have any form of nuclear device before 2010. Given the accuracy of its longer-range missile systems, it would virtually have to arm them with a nuclear weapon for them to be more than terror weapons, although advanced chemical and biological cluster munitions could be an option.

Iran faces major strategic problems because of an increasingly hostile international reaction to its nuclear enrichment program and failure to fully comply with International Atomic Energy Agency (IAEA) inspections. Iran's nuclear file had become a major issue in the UN Security Council (UNSC) by mid-2006, and the UNSC has since voted twice to impose sanctions on Iran. No one knows how far UN sanctions will go in the future, or how effective they will be, but Iran is likely to face steadily hardening international action if it does not end its nuclear program.

Sanctions and Economic Vulnerability

The UN has already acted to restrict Iranian officials, including President Mahmoud Ahmadinejad, as well as other top officials and clerics, from traveling outside Iran. It has also acted to target Iran's nuclear industry, in particular, components and processes.[15] These sanctions have little impact on the general population, and while their impact is limited, they have sent a message to the Iranian government and the world that the world does not approve of Iran's nuclear weapons.

The problem is that it is far from clear that such sanctions can change the attitudes or actions of the Iranian government and Iranian public attitudes toward acquiring nuclear technology. The Iranian nuclear research program does not depend on the ability of the Iranian president to visit Paris, and Iran has already reached the point where it can probably sustain a nuclear weapons effort with its own capabilities and those it can smuggle in ways UN sanctions cannot prevent.

More drastic sanctions (or attacks) targeting specific parts of the industrial sector might be a different story. Iran has a relatively weak economy that is vulnerable to both sanctions and attack. The problem with some such options, however, is that many could do more to hurt Iran's people or the global economy than force Iran's leaders to change their behavior.

Food imports and agricultural sanctions, for example, do not seem practical. The Central Intelligence Agency estimates that Iran's gross domestic product is generated by an 11.8-percent share of the agricultural sector, a 43.3-percent share of the industry sector, and a 44.9-percent share of the services sector.[16] It would be difficult for the United States, its allies, and members of the UN to justify the use of sanctions or attacks against any aspect of Iran's agricultural products or imports—except possibly certain carefully selected dual-use technologies and fertilizers that can be used in the production of WMD.

Petroleum Sanctions

Although Iran is still a major oil exporter, it badly needs outside investment and technology to modernize its petroleum sector and maintain and expand its oil and gas production. Even sanctions that slow down outside investment and technology transfer have already proven capable of putting continuous pressure on the Iranian economy and leadership.

Iran's economy, particularly its transportation sectors and heavier industries, relies on imports of refined products. Since 1982, Iran's dependence on imports of gasoline have surged due to the fact that its refineries were damaged by the Iran-Iraq War, the mismanagement of these refineries, and the lack of foreign investment in its refinery sector. According to the International Energy Agency, Iran's refining sector is inefficient. For example, only 13 percent of the refinery output is gasoline—which is estimated to be half of what European refineries produce.[17] Iran plans to ease its dependence on product imports by expanding its refinery capabilities, but this will remain an important vulnerability in the near to midterm.[18]

Iran's economy is heavily dependent on energy exports. Revenues from oil and gas exports were around $43 billion in the Iranian year beginning in March 2005 and ending in March 2006. The National Iranian Oil Company (NIOC) estimated oil revenues as reaching nearly $54 billion between March 2006 and March 2007.[19] This estimate is based on a production capacity of 3.8 million barrels per day (MMBD) (Bloomberg Financial Services reached the same estimate; another Western source lists 4 MMBD[20]) of which 2.4 MMBD are exported. The Iranian estimate also means that over 60 percent of Iranian oil gets exported, a claim that is supported by most Western estimates.[21]

The U.S. Energy Information Agency (EIA) estimates that Iran produces approximately 4 million barrels of oil a day—5 percent of global output—and imports about 2.5 million barrels. Iran's oil export revenues represent around 80–90 percent of total export earnings and 40–50 percent of the government budget. It estimates that strong oil prices the past few years have boosted Iran's oil export revenues and helped Iran's economic situation. It estimates that Iran's real gross domestic product increased by around 6.1 percent in 2005, but that inflation officially has reached 16 percent per year and unofficial estimates put inflation as high as 40–50 percent. It also estimates that Iran's oil export revenues have increased, but only from $32 billion in 2004, to $45.6 billion in 2005, with 2006 estimates at $46.9 billion.[22]

The EIA analysis also states,

> Despite higher oil revenues, Iranian budget deficits remain a chronic problem, in part due to large-scale state subsidies on foodstuffs and gasoline. Thus, the country's parliament (the Majlis) decided in January 2005 to freeze domestic prices for gasoline and other fuels at 2003 levels. In March 2006, parliament reduced the government's

gasoline subsidy allocation for FY [fiscal year] 2006/07 to $2.5 billion, compared with a request of $4 billion and costs of over $4 billion for imports last year. As of July 2006, the Iranian government is still debating how to handle gasoline subsidies. NIOC has said it has used nearly all of its $2.5 billion budget for gasoline imports, but legislators have stated their opposition to providing the additional $3.5 billion necessary to pay for imports through the end of the fiscal year, in March 2007 . . .

Another problem for Iran is the lack of job opportunities for the country's young and rapidly growing population. Unemployment in Iran is around 11 percent, but is significantly higher among young people. Iran is attempting to diversify its economy by investing some of its oil revenues in other areas, including petrochemicals production. In 2004, non-oil exports rose by a reported 9 percent. Iran also is hoping to attract billions of dollars worth of foreign investment to the country through creating a more favorable investment climate by reducing restrictions and duties on imports and creating free-trade zones. However, there has not been a great deal of progress in this area. Foreign investors appear to be cautious about Iran, due to uncertainties regarding its future direction under new leadership, as well as the ongoing international controversy over the country's nuclear program . . .

During 2005, Iran produced about 4.24 million bbl/d of total liquids. Of this, 3.94 million bbl/d is crude oil, roughly 5 percent of world crude production. Iran's current sustainable crude oil production capacity is estimated at 3.8 million bbl/d, which is around 310,000 bbl/d below Iran's latest (July 1, 2005) OPEC [Organization of the Petroleum Exporting Countries] production quota of 4.110 million bbl/d. . . . Through the first half of 2006, the EIA places Iran's crude oil production at 3.75 million bbl/d. Iran's domestic oil consumption, 1.5 million bbl/d in 2005, is increasing rapidly as the economy and population grow. Iran subsidizes the price of oil products heavily, which contributes to rising domestic consumption.

Iran's existing oilfields have a natural decline rate estimated at 8 percent onshore and 10 percent per year offshore. The fields are in need of upgrading, modernization, and enhanced oil recovery (EOR) efforts such as gas reinjection. Current recovery rates are just 24–27 percent, compared to a world average of 35 percent. Iran also needs to increase its search for new oil, with only a few exploration wells being drilled in 2005.

With sufficient investment, Iran could increase its crude oil production capacity significantly. The country produced 6 million bbl/d of crude oil in 1974 but has not come close to recovering to that level since the 1978/79 Iranian revolution. Still, Iran has ambitious plans to increase oil production to more than 5 million bbl/d by 2010, and 8 million bbl/d by 2015. The country will require billions of dollars in foreign investment to accomplish this.[23]

Virtually all outside sources agree that Iran's average oil output is decreasing. According to one source, the average Iranian oil production fell by 200,000 barrels per day between 2002 and 2006.[24] Reportedly, Iran's oil output capacity has stagnated for the past ten years; natural declines in oil field reserves have broadly been offset by investments of Western companies that resulted in higher productivity.[25]

The problem with sanctions on Iran's crude exports, however, is obvious—as is the impact of lasting sanctions on Iran's ability to get the capital and technology it needs to maintain and increase oil and gas production. The global supply of oil is meeting steadily increasing demand, and sanctions on Iranian exports would have a major impact on the world's importers and global economy as well as Iran's. One analyst deems broad sanctions against Iran are "no longer feasible" because of fear of rising oil prices around the world, which in return, may have a negative impact on global economic growth.[26] Sanctions on energy resources remain politically difficult. Moreover, the European Union (EU) supports constructing a multi-billion-dollar gas pipeline that would partly be fed by Iranian gas.[27]

Petroleum and Product Sanctions

Sanctions on Iran's imports of product and ability to increase its refinery capability might be a different story (as would precision attacks that temporarily halted all refinery output). Declining production and increasing demand raise growing doubts as to whether Iran can reduce its reliance on imports of refined petroleum products at anything like the schedule it desires. In 2004, Iran imported an estimated 0.160 MMBD of oil equivalent of gasoline (40 percent of its domestic consumption).

Iran's dependence on gasoline imports steadily increased in 2005 and 2006. Iran imported an estimated 0.170 MMBD of gasoline (41 percent of its domestic consumption) in 2005 and 0.196 MMBD (43 percent of its domestic consumption) in 2006. It is equally noteworthy that 60 percent of Iran's gasoline is imported from Europe, 15 percent from India, and the rest from elsewhere (Middle East and Asia).[28]

These trends are likely to continue. The Iranian parliament did vote to ration gasoline in March 2007, starting in May 2007. Even so, Iran's domestic demand for gasoline is estimated to increase at approximately 12 percent per year, and the costs of gasoline imports are also steadily increasing.[29] For example, Iran paid an estimated $2.5–$3.0 billion for its gas imports in 2004 and about $4 billion in 2006.[30] Iran had to import 60 percent of the refined gasoline that it used in 2006.

The Iranian government set aside $2.5 billion for oil imports in its 2006–2007 budgets, but it is not clear if this sum was to cover all refined products.[31] Other experts estimate that the cost of importing refined products was as high as $6 billion or even $10 billion in 2005.[32] This is likely to include jet fuels, diesel, residual oil, kerosene, and other products. While Iran is heavily subsidizing gasoline with funds from the reserve fund for oil revenues, it at the same time must import an increasing share of refined gasoline that it has to buy at world market prices. It is difficult to estimate foregone revenues, but guesses range from $10 billion to $50 billion per year. Further, it is believed that gasoline worth a total of $1 billion is getting smuggled out of Iran every year.[33] Indicators show that in 2006 gasoline subsidies are believed to have increased by 30 percent as compared to the year before.

Iran is planning to spend $16 billion between 2003 and 2030 to expand its refinery capacity from 1.5 MMBD in 2004 to 1.7 MMBD in 2010, 2.2 MMBD in 2020, and 2.6 MMBD in 2030. The director of the state-run Iranian refinery company allegedly revised these goals in early 2007, saying that refinery capacity is to increase from 1.6 MMBD to 2.6 MMBD in 2006. According to the director, this capacity expansion requires investment of $16 billion, $4 billion of which is already secured.

Given that only a quarter of the necessary funds now seems to be available, and reaching the stated objective will depend on the application of modern technology, it appears doubtful that Iran can meet its goal.

The freezing of foreign investment and technology transfer for Iran's oil refineries could, therefore, be a productive target for internationally imposed sanctions.[34] Iran might get around some of the impact of such sanctions through unofficial deals and smuggling, but the price for gasoline and refined products is a sensitive issue because price hikes regularly upset the Iranian population, and, on the other hand, they are likely to lead to higher inflation rates, a long-standing and pervading problem for the Iranian economy. The Iranian parliament's decision to ration gasoline as of May 2007 is already acting to increase gas prices. Subsidized Iranian gasoline sells for 9 cents per liter at the pump, while a liter of imported gasoline costs about 40 cents a liter.[35]

Financial Sanctions

Most of the financial assets held in the West belong to the government or the ruling elite of Iran. The combination of freezing assets held in Westerns banks and travel restrictions can have the least impact on the general population and the maximum amount of pressure on the ruling elites.

While U.S. capital markets have been closed to the Iranian government since the Revolution, Iran had alternative sources. Iran relies on loans particularly from European and Asian banks to finance domestic projects in its energy sector.[36] For example, Iran's shipbuilding and car-making sectors are growing faster than Iranian domestic financial institutions. These industries have relied on European banks for investment loans. Some European banks stopped doing business with Tehran, but many other banks continue to finance projects in Iran including major European banks such as HSBC, BNP Paribas, Deutsche Bank, Commerzbank, Standard Chartered, and Royal Bank of Scotland. Observers have argued that targeting loans from European banks could have a major impact on the Iranian economy, particularly since the Iranian capital market is still small and key industries in Iran cannot survive without investment loans from the outside.[37]

Another option to target Iranian finances is to freeze Iranian assets in European and Asian banks. There are no reliable estimates of how much Iran's hard currency deposits are. It is, however, safe to assume that it is a large amount given the recent surge in oil prices. Some estimates put it at $36 billion in 2005 and $60 billion in foreign exchange reserves in 2006.[38]

The Iranian government also began to react following the IAEA referral of Iran's case to the UNSC. In January 2006, the governor of Iran's Central Bank announced that Iran had started transferring its assets out of European banks. It is unclear where the funds have been moved, but there are indications and an initial admission that they may have been transferred to Southeast Asia.[39]

It has also been reported that Iranian government figures have started to move their money from European financial institutions to Dubai, Hong Kong, Malaysia,

Beirut, and Singapore. Iranian officials were quoted as saying that as high as $8 billion was moved out of Europe.[40]

A further option may be to restrict Western investment in Iran. It already is comparatively low, but it provides some key technology transfers to Iran. According to one source, the Iranian Management and Planning Organization permitted foreign investments worth $27.4 billion between 2000 and 2005, or $4.6 billion on average per year, but only $8.2 billion were carried out.[41] Given that several international organizations estimate the actual amount of foreign investments as between $300 to 700 million, this would equal a $50- to $117-million average inflow of foreign investment per year.

Sanctions can reach beyond European financial institutions to include Asian banks and international nongovernmental organizations such as the World Bank and the International Monetary Fund. This would drain another key source of financial support to the Iranian government. For example, in May 2005, the World Bank approved a $344-million loan to Iran to support the Caspian provinces in managing scarce water resources, $200 million for rebuilding following the Bam earthquake in October 2004, and $359 million in loans to the Government of Iran in order to improve housing, sanitation, and access to clean water in Ahwaz and Shiraz.[42] These loans, however, are focused toward humanitarian projects, but that does not mean that they could not be delayed to force Iran back to the bargaining table.

If Iran Becomes a Serious Nuclear Power

The situation will also change strikingly if Iran goes from developing nuclear weapons and long-range missiles to deploying an effective nuclear strike capability. At this point in time, there is no way to be certain what such a force would look like or how capable it would be, but certainly political-psychological impacts would be enormous. There are many different ways in which Iran can proliferate, deploy nuclear-armed or other chemical, biological, radiological, and nuclear (CBRN) weapons, and use them to deter, intimidate, and strike against other nations. All have only one thing in common: they are all provocative and dangerous to any nation Iran may choose to try to intimidate and target, *and* they are all provocative and dangerous to Iran.

Even Iranian ambiguity will probably lead Israel and the United States—and possibly India, Pakistan, and Russia—to develop nuclear options to deter or retaliate against Iran. Israeli and/or U.S. restraint in striking Iran does not have to stop at the first convincing Iranian threat to use nuclear or highly lethal biological weapons, but it could do so.

As of regional options, Iranian nuclear ambiguity might be enough to trigger Saudi, Egyptian, and Turkish efforts to become nuclear powers and some form of Israeli sea basing to enhance the survivability of its nuclear forces while increasing range and/or yield to strike Iran. Saudi Arabia has already said that it has examined nuclear options and rejected them, but this is no certainty and inevitably depends on Iranian action. The successful deployment of a highly capable Iranian force, and

Israel's existential vulnerability, would almost certainly lead Israel to develop a retaliatory capability to destroy Iran's cities and kill most of its population.

Regional powers might show restraint if the United States could provide convincing ballistic and cruise missile defenses and the same form of extended deterrence it once provided to Germany during the Cold War. But these options are speculative and do not yet exist. Successfully deploying a nuclear warhead is one achievement; second-strike capability is another that must be considered by Iranian decision makers. It borders certainty that Iran's reaching a second-strike nuclear capability will take at least a decade if it will ever be achieved.

Any form of major nuclear confrontation could be a nightmare for all concerned. Iran's effort to limit or control the game will probably end at the first ground zero. Any actual Iranian use of such weapons is likely to provoke a nuclear response and may well provoke one targeted on Iranian cities and its population. Moreover, while Israel may technically be a more vulnerable "one bomb" country, it is highly questionable whether any form of Persian state could emerge from nuclear strikes on Iran's five to ten largest cities.

The end result is the prospect of a far more threatening mix of CBRN capabilities in the Gulf region and the area that most models project as the main source of continued world oil and gas exports beyond 2015. It is also the near certainty of an Israeli-Iranian nuclear arms race that means crossing Arab territory, U.S. nuclear targeting of Iran in some form of extended deterrence, and the threat of more polarization between Sunni and Shi'ites and broader regional tensions and actions that spill over out of the confrontation over Iran's nuclear activities. None of these prospects are pleasant.

IRAN AS A RELIGIOUS AND IDEOLOGICAL THREAT IN A REGION AND AN ISLAMIC WORLD POLARIZED ALONG SECTARIAN LINES

For all of the talk about a clash between civilizations, the potential clash within Islam seems far more dangerous. It already is a serious problem in Afghanistan, Algeria, much of Central Asia, Egypt, Pakistan, Saudi Arabia, and Yemen. Hard-line Neo-Salafi Islamist elements exist in most non-Western countries with a major Islamic population and in virtually every Arab state. In many cases—such as Iran, Pakistan, and Yemen—these extremists also treat Shi'ites as being apostates to Islam and have already encouraged serious violence between sects. In far too many areas, they are helping to polarize Muslims in ways that could lead to other acts of sectarian violence and "cleansing."

The struggle between Sunnis and Shi'ites is not new in the Gulf, but statements and actions by Al Qa'ida leaders such as Abu Musab al-Zarqawi have led many Shi'ites to see neo-Salafi groups as a key threat. As noted earlier, Iran has not suffered from the threat of terrorism, but Arab Sunni groups could become a threat to Iran's internal stability.

The threat from such groups also does not have to be direct. An escalation of the attacks that took place in Iraq against Shi'ite holy sites, religious rituals, or leaders that spill over into neighboring states may force Iran to get involved to protect Shi'ites and their holy shrines against such attacks. This has led some Sunni states—notably Egypt, Jordan, and Saudi Arabia—to become steadily more concerned about a Shi'ite crescent of expanding Iranian influence that would include Iran, Iraq, Syria, and Lebanon.

While Iran has evidently ceased to attempt to export its Islamic revolution to neighboring states since the mid-1990s, many Arab Gulf States fear that Iran is seeking hegemony in the Gulf, and/or that its expansion of its capabilities for asymmetric warfare in the Gulf and its ability to threaten Gulf shipping and energy facilities is a serious threat. Bahrain is concerned over Iran's relations with Bahrain's restive Shi'ite population. Saudi Arabia is concerned over its Shi'ite population in its oil-rich Eastern Province. Qatar and Kuwait are concerned over Iranian energy claims, and the United Arab Emirates is concerned over the issue of Abu Musa and the Tunbs.

The risk that Sunni and Shi'ite extremists can provoke a broader split between sects and nations could push Iran into a more aggressive religious and ideological struggle. One of the unfortunate aftermaths of "9/11" is that Arab and Islamic states have tended to deal with movements like Al Qa'ida as internal security threats and avoid the broader issue of ensuring that Islamist extremism does not polarize and divide Islam and the Middle East. Arab, Iranian, and non-Arab Muslim intellectual and religious leaders have also done more to defend their own cultures and Islam in dealing with the West than show they will deal directly with the threat such extremism can present.

Afghanistan, Algeria, Bahrain, Iraq, Lebanon, and Saudi Arabia, however, are just some of the warnings of what happens when Islamist extremists threaten to take power, Sunni and Shi'ite Islamists turn upon each other, and other sectarian tensions and discrimination are not dealt with and put to an end. It is also worth noting that much of the vaunted religious tolerance within Western culture was forced upon that largely Christian culture by some of the bloodiest wars in its history during the Protestant Reformation and the Counter-Reformation and just how consistently horrifying the results of anti-Semitism were during the long centuries before it reached its apogee in the Holocaust.

Iran is scarcely free of its own form of Shi'ite extremists, but has scarcely been dominated by them. As was the case in Bosnia and Kosovo, the collapse of the existing power structure in Iraq without any stable replacement has been the source of open religious warfare, and this has been driven largely by Sunni, not Shi'ite, extremism. At the same time, Iran has been opportunistic in dealing with events in Iraq, in exploiting its ties to Syria's Alewite regime, and in dealing with the Shi'ite Hezbollah in Lebanon. It has supported Shi'ite separatists in Bahrain and Shi'ite unrest in Saudi Arabia's Eastern Province in the past.

The idea of a Shi'ite crescent may be more an unfounded fear than a clear possibility, but growing divisions that divide Sunni, Shi'ite, and the other sects of Islam in ways where Iran is virtually forced to play an opportunistic role are all too credible. The potential cost is also indicated by the fact that while more than 85 percent of the world's Muslims are Sunni, Shi'ites are the majority of the population in

Azerbaijan, Bahrain, Iran, and Iraq. They are about 30 percent of the population in Kuwait, about 15 to 20 percent in Pakistan, and about 25 percent in Yemen.

The problem could go beyond differences between Sunnis and Shi'ite "twelvers." Some other sects of Islam, like the Ibadis, differ with Sunnis but differ significantly with Shi'ites as well. Some modern Alawites identify themselves as close to Shi'ite twelvers, but differ sharply in the details of their beliefs in regard to the status of Ali and in many other Gnostic and syncretistic beliefs, particularly a belief a metempsychosis. Ahmadi Muslims depart strikingly from other Muslims in their belief in Mirza Ghulam Ahmad as the Mujaddid (Renewer) of Islamic Ismailism, which presents other problems in establishing Islamic identity because of the diversity of interpretations.

Even without a major Sunni-Shi'ite clash, Islamic extremism could lead to a wide range of asymmetric struggles and partner and proxy conflicts. If there is one area where dialogue, negotiation, and common efforts to promote tolerance and common understanding are truly critical, it lies in doing everything possible to prevent this possibility from becoming real.

LIMITING IRAN'S CURRENT AND FUTURE OPPORTUNITIES FOR OPPORTUNISM

Most of the threats Iran poses can be contained with the right choice of policies and military actions. Barring major shifts in its regime, Iran not only is deterrable, but is a nation that will probably respond to the proper security incentives over time. The real issue may well be whether Iran's neighbors, the United States, the EU, and other outside nations provide the right mix of deterrence and incentives, not Iran's current and potential capabilities.

There is no space in an analysis of Iran's military capabilities to fully discuss all of the problems in Iran's relations with its neighbors or to indulge in the region's obsession with using history to produce self-inflicted wounds. There is equally little space to discuss America's and Israel's mistakes in demonizing what are often real problems in Iran's behavior. The same is equally true of the tendency of other nations, and private organizations and individuals, to confuse mere dialogue with actual negotiation.

Actions by the United States, the EU, Other Outside Powers, and the UN

The United States has already moved away from hollow charges that Iran is part of the "axis of evil" and has given a deserved low priority to futile outside efforts at regime change. Senior U.S. officials have repeatedly said that they will not take military options to deal with Iranian proliferation off the table or ignore Iranian support of militias and insurgents in Iraq. At the same time, they have stressed that the United States has no immediate interest in military intervention inside Iran and is actively pursuing diplomatic options with its European allies and within the context of the UN Security Council. The United States has also shown that it is willing to engage in dialogue with Iran and has done so—albeit at arms length in meetings over the future of Iraq.

Engagement and negotiation are critical tools for U.S. action. Simply threatening, sanctioning, or even attacking Iran is not going to produce the kind of change in Iranian behavior. It is more likely to lead to broader direct or proxy conflicts, Iranian overreaction and extremism, and help hard-liners in Iran discredit more moderate elements on the ground of disloyalty. Exaggerated American rhetoric and political posturing have much the same effect and also alienate international support the United States badly needs.

The United States also needs to fully accept the fact that encouraging weak and sometimes repellant Iranian exile groups is not going to change the regime, and neither are TV problems and broad U.S.-sponsored information operations. Iran is deeply divided, but that does not mean the United States will be any more successful in exploiting Iran's fracture lines than it was in Iraq. What the United States can do is find subtler ways to encourage Iran's moderates and reformers. Exchanges, second track meetings and dialog, visits and scholarships, and all of the other ways of improving contacts that show the United States wants Iranian success on peaceful terms are key steps. Backing human rights movements, forcing transparency as to the nature of the Iranian regime's actions, and repeatedly and constantly making it clear that the United States wants good relations are additional steps. Only Iranians in Iran can accomplish real regime change, but the United States can do far more to have a positive rather than a negative influence.

At the same time, Europe, Russia, China, and other key elements of the UN cannot be too soft. The problem is to find the right international balance of pressure and incentives that might gradually change Iran's behavior and ensure it does not see exaggerated threats or find "windows of opportunism" it will not resist attempting to explore. This requires all of the nations involved, not just the United States, to move toward a new degree of realism. Europe needs to understand that dialogue and negotiation are only means to an end, not ends in themselves. All carrots and no sticks are just as dangerous and ineffective as all sticks and no carrots.

The slow escalation of UN sanctions, in a step-by-step response to Iranian nuclear noncompliance, is an example of the right course to follow. The question is whether the key members of the Security Council will have the courage to take more decisive action if Iran does not eventually respond. The previous chapters also strongly indicate that the going will get tougher for some years, even if it does get much easier in the long run.

The United States also cannot ignore the unique security role that only it can perform in the region. Russia can still influence some of Iran's neighbors, but the United States still can play a unique role in working with Turkey, Afghanistan, Pakistan, and Iraq. Seeking regional action to both give Iran incentives for good behavior and clear collective deterrents to opportunism is going to be just as critical as broader international action.

The United States is also the only power that can—in the near to midterm—deter and defend against some forms of Iranian military threat. Turkey and Pakistan are largely immune, but Iraq, Afghanistan, and the southern Gulf States are not. The United States needs to maintain the kind of military presence in the Gulf that makes it clear to Iran that it cannot take military action without the fear or reality of an American response. The United States must play a critical role in deterrence and containment.

The United States also cannot leave a power vacuum in Iraq. It is easy to talk about "withdrawing," but Iraq is not Vietnam. Its location and global dependence on Gulf energy exports will make it a critical U.S. strategic interest indefinitely into the future. It may no longer be able to "win" in Iraq—although this is far from certain—but it can still use aid, advice, and security assistance as key tools to influence Iraq's future and build it up as a state and military force that can stand on its own.

War may have to be the ultimate choice, but this is now far from clear, as is the ability of the United States to use military options to achieve lasting strategic effects, as distinguished from tactical victories that lead to worse outcomes in the future. The United States truly does need to keep the military option constantly up-to-date, work with its allies to prepare, and maintain the necessary capabilities and strength. At the same time, solidly founded regional defense options ranging from missile defense to anti-mine warfare, and even the threat and reality of extended deterrence are possible substitutes for preventive or preemptive attacks.

The United States needs to carefully and collectively develop all of the proper military options, ensuring that Iran cannot block the flow of Gulf oil for more than a few days or weeks, be ready for limited action against any low-level Iranian adventures, be able to act quickly enough to prevent clashes from becoming war, and build up its regional allies. In the right political and strategic context, military containment and deterrence are both carrots *and* sticks. They deter without threatening, and they make diplomatic and economic incentives more attractive.

The United States also needs to clearly separate its alliance with Israel, and support for the Arab-Israel peace process, from any apparent "green light" for Israel military action. Alliance never means identity of interest, and this is particularly true given the currently weak nature of Israel's political situation, its tendency to exaggerate and overreact, and the danger the United States could suddenly be pressured to finish what Israeli forces start. Either a U.S. attack is necessary in the U.S. national interest, or the United States should clearly oppose Israeli action. Israel is simply too weak a power, and too divisive in terms of regional politics, to be either a useful alternative or a proxy.

The United States should not, however, leave Israel vulnerable or discourage it from quietly proving to Iran that any Iranian nuclear option directed at Israel would be suicidal. In fact, the United States should strongly consider making extended deterrence an option that covers the entire Middle East, including Israel, and do so in ways that leave Iran in no doubt as to the prospect of U.S. retaliation. Hopefully, Iran will never choose to really play the nuclear card. If it does, it must be certain that if it does play the game, the consequences will be suicidal. It must know long in advance that it will lose in ways from which it can never recover.

Actions by Iran's Neighbors

Given Iran and the region's recent history, there are several steps that Iran's Arab neighbors clearly need to take to structure the best mix of deterrence and incentives for Iran and to do so in the context of a broader effort to bring regional security:

- *Rely on actions not words.* If the Arab world has not yet succeeded in talking itself to death, it is not for the want of trying. Iran's rhetoric, however, has been far more extreme and much less productive, and the same has often been true of the United States. Presidential and Congressional rhetorical excess and empty gestures have provoked Iran without changing it ways that have become a self-inflicted wound. Israel has done almost as good a job in provoking Iran while exaggerating its importance. Demonstrating a serious mix of deterrent capabilities, tied to a clear pattern of actions that do not threaten Iran or its regime if it is not aggressively opportunistic, is far better than provocative rhetoric or empty promises on any side.

- *Abandon efforts at active Iranian regime change without abandoning efforts to influence evolutionary change:* The Gulf and Islamic world do not need another example of the dangers of attempting regime change from the outside and empowering incapable exile groups. Iran's political and economic structure badly need modernization, liberalization, and reform for the good of the Iranian people, but this should be encouraged peacefully and by quietly supporting internal Iranian reformers.

- *Create truly effective deterrent forces with a strong and unified local component.* It may well be a decade or more before the Cooperation Council for the Arab States of the Gulf (CCASG) can provide a strong mix of regional security and deterrent capabilities on its own. There is, however, a serious danger in simply going on with separate Gulf national efforts, many of which have limited real-world mission capability and deterrent value. There is no reason for the CCASG state not to rely on the United States, but the more they do for themselves, the less direct and provocative that reliance will be.

- *Resolve strategically unimportant disputes and seek clearly defined mutual agreements.* Many of the current tensions between Iran and its neighbors are over border, riverine, island, and dividing line issues that either have no strategic importance or where both sides would benefit from arbitration, mediation, or turning the issue over to the World Court. As Bahrain and Qatar have shown, persistent efforts to resolve issues on this basis may take years to initiate and complete, but can ultimately be successful.

- *Support negotiating efforts to have Iraq comply with the IAEA and the UN. However, make it unambiguously clear to Iran that seeking nuclear armed missile forces will trigger a major defensive reaction, and the risk of retaliation and/or preemption is far more dangerous than the exercise is worth.* It may be years before Iran can develop a serious nuclear threat to its neighbors or one that could trigger a regional conflict, but it should be made clear to Iran now that the most dangerous military action it can take will steadily endanger its security, if not its existence.

- *Understand that the failure to deal with regional disputes and equity for Shi'ites empowers Iran.* Iran is only as strong in its ability to manipulate most state and nonstate actors as partners and proxies as the Arab world is weak or indifferent in resolving its own internal disputes. One key to success is a collective effort to aid Bahrain's "post-oil" economy and its Shi'ites, another is social and economic equity for Saudi Arabia's Shi'ites, and another is broad-based aid to the development of Lebanon.

- *Do not give up on Iraq.* The most important single key to both offering Iran security and limiting its opportunism will be creating a stable, independent Iraq. It is doubtful that outside powers can produce Iraqi consensus, but they may well be able to offer aid and incentives that will limit forced migration, help bridge over ethnic and sectarian differences, and keep a Shi'ite-dominated Iraq from tilting toward Iran. There will be a competition for influence, and if Arab Sunni states take the side of Iraqi Sunnis, they will play into Iranian hands.

- *Persist in the Arab League Effort to Reach a Full Arab-Israeli Peace and King Abdullah's Peace Plan.* The Israeli-Palestinian conflict and Israeli-Lebanese/Syrian conflicts are additional keys to Iran's ability to create regional problems. This is only one reason to persist in current Arab peace efforts in spite of the frustrations in dealing with Israel, the United States, and the Palestinians. The cause is simply too important to abandon.

- *Talk to Turkey, Syria, and Pakistan; Seek Influence in Afghanistan and Turkmenistan.* Do not ignore Russia. This is a regional game in terms of influence, not a Gulf game. It needs to be played as such.

- *Redefine GCC relations with the United States. to Create a True Partnership:* The United States needs to pay far more attention to its regional friends and allies in shaping its polices toward Iran and its overall security posture in the Gulf, particularly in light of the uncertainties surrounding Iraq and the need for consensus in dealing with Iraq. Gulf States, however, need to both take more responsibility and stop acting in a fragmented and sometimes divisive way. Iran is only one of the catalysts that should make the United States and the GCC states seriously think out the need to develop a coordinated approach to seeking Gulf security, and one based on pragmatism and military realities.

- *Accept the seriousness of the danger posed by both Shi'ite and Sunni religious extremists.* The moderate Arab states, and religious and intellectual leaders of the Arab world, need to work together to meet the challenge posed by extremists in both sects. A clash between civilizations has always been more of a myth than a reality, but allowing Islam to become the scene of a steadily accelerating struggle between Sunnis and Shi'ites, dragging in both state and nonstate actors, poses a threat that goes far beyond Iran, the Gulf, and the risk of some Shi'ite crescent.

THE WORST CASE: ISRAELI AND U.S. COUNTER-NUCLEAR STRIKES ON IRAN

If these options for negotiation, containment, and deterrence fail it is not likely to be over Iran's use of its conventional forces, asymmetric warfare, or allied/proxy forces. These may produce clashes or localized, low-level conflicts like the "Tanker War" of 1987-1988. They are very unlikely to explode into more serious conflicts. Iran may choose to test the seriousness of U.S. and regional willingness to fight under such conditions and may even "win" some encounters, but limited stakes in limited wars are problems that outside nations can deal with.

Iran's nuclear programs are a different story, and while the previous analysis has recommended a focus on negotiation, containment, and deterrence, it is already clear that the United States and Israel have at least examined preventive and/or preventive attack options. Israel and the United States do differ over the timing and level of risk posed by Iran's nuclear efforts. The United States sees a mature or serious Iranian nuclear threat as coming well after 2010. Israel claims to see it as coming as early as 2009—although much of this may be Israeli hype designed to push the United States into diplomatic action, and military action if that fails.

Official U.S. policy is to leave all options on the table and to emphasize diplomatic activity through the EU3 (France, Germany, and Great Britain) and the UN. The U.S. estimates of timelines for Iran's nuclear and missile efforts also leave at least several years in which to build an international consensus behind sanctions and diplomatic pressure, and a consensus behind military options if diplomacy fails. The United States would also have the potential advantage of finding any Iranian "smoking gun," improving its targeting and strike options, and being able to strike targets in which Iran had invested much larger assets. The fact Iran can exploit time as a weapon in which to proliferate does not mean that the United States cannot exploit time as a weapon with which to strike Iran.

Israel, on the other hand, sees Iran as an existential threat. A single strike on Tel Aviv and/or Haifa would raise major questions about Israel's future existence.

The Problem of Targeting

There are no risk-free military options for Israel, the United States, or neighboring states. Tehran's known nuclear research facilities are dispersed around the country, generally large, and have constant new construction. There are six major complexes in Iran's public program; six more suspect facilities are under construction. Unclassified satellite photos show over 100 buildings in the six major complexes, although many seem to be small service facilities, and there is no way to know the level of knowledge the Israeli or U.S. intelligence community has, or the quality of their targeting data. Work by Frank Barnaby and Global Security have identified the following confirmed and potential nuclear centers, many of which are also potential major target complexes:[43]

- *Saghand:* Uranium mine (200 kilometers, 125 miles from Yazd) from 350 meters (1,160 feet) deep.

- *Gchine:* Uranium mine in the south of Iran, near Bandar Abbas, with co-located mill. Low but variable grade uranium ore found in near-surface deposits will be open-pit mined and processed. Global Security indicates that the estimated production design capacity is 21 tons of uranium per year. Iran has stated that, as of July 2004, mining operations had started and the mill had been hot tested, during which testing a quantity of about 40 to 50 kilograms of yellowcake was produced.

- *Ardekan near Yazd:* Yellowcake preparation at a site known as Ardekan Nuclear Fuel Unit.

- *Bonab:* Atomic energy research center in northwest Iran.
- *Gorgon:* Nuclear research facility in north-central Iran.
- *Damavand:* Plasma physics research center.
- *Tehran Nuclear Research Center:* Tehran Research Reactor (operating). Molybdenum, Iodine and Xenon Radioisotope Production Facility (constructed, but not operating). Jabr Ibn Hayan Multipurpose Laboratories (JHL) (operating). Waste Handling Facility (operating).
- *Tehran:* Kalaye Electric Company: Dismantled pilot enrichment facility.
- *Bushehr Nuclear Power Plant:* (Under construction).
- *Esfahan Nuclear Technology Center:* Miniature Neutron Source Reactor (operating). Light Water Sub-Critical Reactor (operating). Heavy Water Zero Power Reactor (operating). Fuel Fabrication Laboratory (operating). Uranium Chemistry Laboratory (closed down?) Uranium Conversion Facility (UCF) (under construction, first process units being commissioned for operation). Graphite Sub-Critical Reactor (decommissioned). Fuel Manufacturing Plant (in detailed design stage, construction to begin in 2004).
- *UCF Facility in Isfahan site:* At the UCF in Isfahan, using the yellowcake prepared in the Ardekan, a number of by-products including uranium hexofloride (UF6), metallic uranium, and uranium oxide are produced. These are later used for uranium enrichment.
- *Natanz:* Pilot Fuel Enrichment Plant (operating). Fuel Enrichment Plant (under construction). Uses yellowcake and the products of the Isaheur UCF unit to enrich uranium using the centrifuge equipment.
- *Karazj:* Radioactive Waste Storage (under construction, but partially operating).
- *Koloduz:* possible nuclear-related facility located about 14 kilometers west of Tehran; the plant is reportedly concealed within a large military complex. National Imagery and Mapping Agency's (NIMA's) only rendering of this name is Kolah Duz, but the name of this facility is also transliterated as Kolahdouz, Kolahdooz, or Kolahdoz.
- *Lashkar Ab'ad:* Pilot Uranium Laser Enrichment Plant (dismantled).
- *Arak:* Iran Nuclear Research Reactor (IR-40) 40-megawatt heavy-water reactor (in detailed design phase). Hot cell facility for production of radioisotopes (in preliminary design stage). Heavy Water Production Plant (HWPP) (under construction; not subject to Safeguards Agreement). There are claims there is also a secret nuclear facility located at the Qatran Workshop near the Qara-Chai River in the Khondaub/Khondab region, in Central Iran, 150 miles south of Tehran.
- *Anarak:* Waste storage site (waste to be transferred to JHL).
- *Chalus:* Reported to be an underground nuclear weapons developoment facility located inside a mountain south of this coastal town. Variously reported as being staffed by experts from Russia, China, and North Korea.
- *Darkhovin, also variously referred to as Ahvaz, Darkhouin, Esteghlal, and Karun:* Located on the Karun River south of the city of Ahvaz. A facility at this location is reportedly under the control of the Islamic Revolution Guard Corps and is said to be suspected of being an underground nuclear weapons facility of unspecified nature.

• *Tabas:* Reported as a possible site of a nuclear reactor of North Korean orgin. This is probably an unfounded speculation.

Many key sites are underground and many others may be unknown or are not identifiable. IAEA inspections have identified at least 18 sites, but others argue that there might be more than 70. A great deal of the equipment other than major centrifuge facilities is also easy to move or relocate. Iran may already be playing a shell game with key research facilities and equipment, constantly changing the targeting pattern.

Tehran has had a quarter of a century to learn from the experience of Israel's attack on Iraq in 1981. Iran may have built redundant sites, underground facilities, and constructed a high level of protection around its known nuclear research centers. Others have argued that Iranian nuclear sites may have been deliberately built near populated areas or in facilities with many other "legitimate" purposes so Israel and the United States would be confronted with the problem of collateral damage or being charged with having hit an "innocent target." The previous chapters have also strongly suggested that many of Iran's research, development, and production activities are almost certainly modular and can be rapidly moved to new sites, including tunnels, caves, and other hardened facilities.

U.S. and Israeli officials have publicly identified key nuclear research sites that may have been placed underground to shield them against airborne assaults. For example, the United States identified the Parchin military complex, located south of Tehran, as a "probable" location for nuclear weaponization research. This site alone has many sections, hundreds of bunkers, and several tunnels. It is also a site that is being used to manufacture conventional armaments and Iranian missiles. This is one possible site that could be attacked, but even the evidence linking this to military nuclear weapons manufacturing was ambiguous. The site has civilian and conventional military use. The IAEA's initial assessment was that the site was not linked to nuclear weapons manufacturing, but most agree that there was not definitive proof.

It is equally important to note that Iran had increased its protection of sites against possible U.S. or Israel air strikes. It has been reported that the IRGC launched a program to protect major nuclear facilities. The program was recommended by the Nuclear Control Center of Iran and endorsed by Iran's Supreme Leader, Ali Khamenei. The program's mission was to build a defense infrastructure for Iran's nuclear research facilities.

This program, reportedly coordinated with North Korea, is to build underground halls and tunnels at the cost of "hundreds of millions of dollars." Some key sites such as Isfahan and Natanz are high on the list of the program to protect. The Isfahan facility, which reached fully operational status in February 2006, is most likely the primary source for converting yellowcake into UF6. The logistic defense infrastructure would include natural barriers (tunnels into mountains and cliffs), manufactured barricades (concrete ceilings and multiple floors), and camouflage activities around key sites. The construction, a joint venture between Iranian and North Korean companies, was estimated to finish by June 1, 2006.

Israeli Options

A number of Israeli officers, officials, and experts have said that Israel must not permit the Iranians to acquire nuclear capabilities, regardless of Tehran's motivations. Some have called for preemptive strikes by Israel. Ephraim Inbar, the President of the Jaffee Center for Strategic Studies, said, "For self-defense, we must act in a pre-emptive mode."

Senior U.S. officials have warned about this capability. Vice President Richard Cheney suggested on January 20, 2005, "Given the fact that Iran has a stated policy that their objective is the destruction of Israel, the Israelis might well decide to act first, and let the rest of the world worry about cleaning up the diplomatic mess afterwards."

General Moshe Ya'alon, the Israeli Chief of Staff, was quoted as saying in August 2004 that Iran must not be permitted to acquire nuclear weapons. He added that Israel must not rely on the rest of the world to stop Iran from going nuclear because he said a nuclear Iran would change the Middle East where "Moderate States would become more extreme."

Israeli military officials were quoted in press reports in January 2006 as saying that the Israel Defense Forces (IDF) got the order to get ready for a military strike against Iranian nuclear sites by March 2006. It is unclear what type of military strikes Israel may chose, if it decides to respond preemptively. Some have argued that Israel may declare its nuclear weapons and establish a "mutually assured destruction: deterrence." While the impact of an Israeli declaration remains uncertain, it is likely to have little impact on Israel's strategic posture in the region, since most states factor Israel's nuclear weapons into their strategic thinking.

Possible Methods of Israeli Attack

Some experts argue that Israel does not have viable military options. They argue it does not have U.S. targeting capability and simply cannot generate and sustain the necessary number of attack sorties. Some argue that Israel might do little more than drive Iranian activity further underground, provoke even more Iranian activity, make it impossible for diplomatic and UN pressure to work, and make Israel into a real, rather than a proxy or secondary, target.

In April 2005, it was reported that a senior Israeli Air Force (IAF) officer dismissed plans to strike Iran's nuclear facilities because it was too risky and too complex both in terms of executing the mission as well as in long-term consequences, although he did not rule out the feasibility of military action against Iran. The officer further said that the most critical targets were concentrated near Tehran and 150 kilometers to the south of the city. He also noted that Iran possesses only 20 ballistic missile launchers, which should not present insurmountable difficulties when planning attacks.[44] These remarks came one month after Israel held large-scale exercises together with the United States that simulated a missile attack on Iran. This was widely interpreted as a contingency plan to prepare for potential consequences after an attack on Israel.

There is no doubt that such a strike would face problems. Israel does not have conventional ballistic missiles or land-/sea-based cruise missiles suited for such a mission. The shortest flight routes would be around 1,500–1,700 kilometers through Jordan and Iraq, 1,900–2,100 kilometers through Saudi Arabia, and 2,600–2,800 kilometers in a loop through Turkey.

There have been reports that Israel approached the United States in order to obtain permission for overflying Iraq in case of a contingency.[45] Another report has stated that Israeli forces have obtained U.S. permission to establish a military base in Iraq near the Iranian border. None of these reports seem accurate or founded on more than speculation.

There are many other problems in launching such a strike. Even if Israel had the attack capabilities needed for the destruction of the all elements of the Iranian nuclear program, it is uncertain whether Israel has the kind of intelligence needed to be certain that all the necessary elements of the program were traced and destroyed fully. Israel has good photographic coverage of Iran with the Ofeq series of reconnaissance satellites, but being so distant from Iran, one can assume that other kinds of intelligence coverage are rather partial and weak.

Retired Brigadier General Shlomo Brom has argued that Israel's capabilities may not be enough to inflict enough damage on Iran's nuclear program:

> [A]ny Israeli attack on an Iranian nuclear target would be a very complex operation in which a relatively large number of attack aircraft and support aircraft (interceptors, ECM [electronic countermeasures] aircraft, refuelers, and rescue aircraft) would participate. The conclusion is that Israel could attack only a few Iranian targets and not as part of a sustainable operation over time, but as a one time surprise operation.

All that said, this does not mean that Israel and the United States cannot target and strike much or most of Iran's capabilities. One great danger in open-sourced analysis is that it is not targeting intelligence and cannot provide a meaningful picture of what the United States or other potential attackers know at the classified level. It is also dangerous, if not irresponsible, for analysts with no empirical training and experience in targeting and modern weapons effects to make sweeping judgments about strike options. They simply lack basic professional competence and even minimal credibility.

Israel could launch and refuel two to three full squadrons of 36 to 54 combat aircraft for a single set of strikes with refueling. It could use either its best F-15s (28 F-15C/D, 25 F-15I Ra'am) or part of its 126 F-16CDs and 23 F-16I Sufas. It has at least three specially configured squadrons with conformal fuel tanks specially designed for extended range use. It could add fighter escorts, but refueling and increased warning and detection would be major problems.

For the purposes of guessing how Israel might attack, its primary aircraft would probably be the F-15I, although again this is guesswork. Global Security has excellent reporting on the F-15I:

The key aspects are that Boeing's (formerly McDonnell Douglas) F-15E Strike Eagle entered service with the IDF/Heyl Ha'Avir (Israeli Air Force) in January of 1998 and was designated the F-15I Ra'am (Thunder). The F-15E Strike Eagle is the ground attack variant of the F-15 air superiority fighter, capable of attacking targets day or night, and in all weather conditions.

The two seat F-15I, known as the Thunder in Israel, incorporates new and unique weapons, avionics, electronic warfare, and communications capabilities that make it one of the most advanced F-15s. Israel finalized its decision to purchase 25 F-15Is in November 1995. The F-15I, like the U.S. Air Force's F-15E Strike Eagle, is a dual-role fighter that combines long-range interdiction with the Eagle's air superiority capabilities. All aircraft are to be configured with either the F100-PW-229 or F110-GE-129 engines by direct commercial sale; Night Vision Goggle compatible cockpits; an Elbit display and sight helmet (DASH) system; conformal fuel tanks; and the capability to employ the AIM-120, AIM-7, AIM-9, and a wide variety of air-to-surface munitions.

Though externally the Ra'am looks similar to its USAF [United States Air Force] counterpart, there are some differences, mainly in the electronic countermeasures gear and the exhaust nozzles. The Ra'am has a counterbalance on the port vertical stabilizer instead of the AN/ALQ-128 EWWS (Electronic Warfare Warning System) antenna found on USAF Strike Eagles. The Ra'am uses two AN/ALQ-135B band 3 antennas, one mounted vertically (starboard side) and one horizontally (port side). These are located on the end of the tail booms. They are distinguished by their chiseled ends, unlike the original AN/ALQ-135 antenna, which is round and located on the port tail boom of USAF Eagles.

The Ra'am utilizes extra chaff/flare dispensers mounted in the bottom side of the tail booms. Unlike USAF Eagles, the Ra'am still use engine actuator covers (turkey feathers) on their afterburner cans. The U.S. Air Force removed them because of cost and nozzle maintenance, though curiously, USAF F-16s still have their actuator covers installed. Israeli Strike Eagles and some USAF Eagles based in Europe use CFT air scoops. These scoops provide extra cooling to the engines.

The 25 F-15Is operational since 1999 [and the 100 F-16Is] were procured first and foremost to deal with the Iranian threat. In August 2003 the Israeli Air Force demonstrated the strategic capability to strike far-off targets such as Iran [which is 1,300 kilometers away], by flying three F-15 jets to Poland 1,600 nautical miles away. After they celebrated that country's air force's 85th birthday, on their return trip, the IAF warplanes staged a fly-past over the Auschwitz death camp.[46]

Israeli aircraft would probably need to carry close to their maximum payloads to achieve the necessary level of damage against most targets suspected of WMD activity, although any given structure could be destroyed with one to three weapons. (This would include the main Bushehr reactor enclosure, but its real-world potential value to an Iranian nuclear program is limited compared to more dispersed and/or hardened targets.) At least limited refueling would be required, and backup refueling and recovery would be an issue.

They key weapon to be used against hard targets and underground sites like Natanz might be the GBU-28, although the United States may have quietly given Israel much more sophisticated systems or Israel may have developed its own, including a nuclear armed variant.

The GBU-28 is carried by the F-15I. It is a "5,000-pound" laser-guided bomb with a 4,400-pound earth-penetrating warhead that can be upgraded by the IAF to use electro-optical or global positioning system (GPS) targeting. It is a vintage weapon dating back to the early 1990s, and the IAF is reported to have bought at least 100. It has been steadily upgraded since 1991, and the USAF ordered an improved version in 1996. It looks like a long steel tube with rear fins and a forward guidance module. It can glide some three to seven miles depending on the height of delivery. It is 153 inches long by 14.5 inches in diameter.[47]

Multiple strikes on the dispersed buildings and entries in a number of facilities would be necessary to ensure adequate damage without restrikes—which may not be feasible for Israel given the limits to its sortie generation capability over even Iranian soft targets. As for hardened and underground targets, the IAF's mix of standoff precision-guided missiles—such as Harpoon or Popeye—would not have the required lethality with conventional warheads, and Israel's use of even small nuclear warheads would cause obvious problems.

Israel may have specially designed or adapted weapons for such strikes and bought 500 bunker busters from the United States in February 2005. Experts speculated whether the purchase was a power projection move or whether Israel was, in fact, planning to use these conventional bombs against Iranian nuclear sites. These speculations were further exacerbated when Israeli Chief of Staff Lieutenant General Dan Halutz was asked how far Israel would go to stop Iran's nuclear program; he said, "2,000 kilometers."

The hard-target bombs it has acquired from the United States are bunker busters, however, not systems designed to kill underground facilities. They could damage entrances, but not the facilities. What is not known is whether Israel has its own ordnance or has secretly acquired the more sophisticated systems described later.

Its main problem would be refueling—its 5 KC-130H and 5 B-707 tankers are slow and vulnerable and would need escorts—and its ordinary B-707 Airborne Early Warning (AEW), electronic intelligence (ELINT), and electronic warfare aircraft are also slow fliers, although the new G-550 Shaved ELINT aircraft is a fast flier and the IAF has some long-range unmanned aerial vehicles (UAVs) that could support its aircraft, before, during, and after such missions.

The big manned "slow fliers" would have serious problems penetrating and surviving in Iranian air space. Israel has, however, specially configured some of its F-15s and F-16s with targeting, EW, SAM-suppression aids, and ELINT for this kind of mission. The full details of such capabilities are unknown.

Repeated strikes would be a problem because Israel could probably get away with going through Jordan and then through Saudi Arabia/Gulf or Iraq once, but any repeated effort would be too politically dangerous for Arab governments to easily tolerate. Israel has also had problems with its intelligence satellites, and its battle damage assessment and time-urgent retargeting capabilities for precision strikes with a target mix as complex as Iran's could be a major problem.

Much would depend on just how advanced Israel's long-range UAV capabilities really are and whether Israel could get access to U.S. intelligence and IS&R capabilities for both its initial targeting and restrikes, but confirming the actual nature of damage, carrying out restrikes, and sending a clear signal that Israel can repeat its strikes if Iran rebuilds or creates new facilities would be a problem. Israel has kept the details of such programs classified, along with those of its long-range cruise missile and ballistic missile booster developments. Enough has leaked into the press, however, to indicate that the IDF has made very substantial progress in developing the long-range UAVs it would need for such missions.

The radars in the countries involved would probably detect all IAF and U.S. missions relatively quickly, and very low-altitude penetration profiles would lead to serious range-payload problems. The countries overflown would be confronted with the need to either react or have limited credibility in claiming surprise. An overflight of Iraq would be seen in the region as having to have had a U.S. "green light."

Iran would almost certainly see Jordanian, Turkish, and/or Saudi tolerance of such an IAF strike as a hostile act. It might well claim a U.S. green light in any case in an effort to mobilize hostile Arab and Muslim (and possibly world) reactions.

Many have compared current Israeli military options with Iran to that of the 1981 attack against Iraq's Osiraq reactor and have noted the conditions are very different. For example, Peter Brookes, a military expert, argued that Israel has several options including satellite-guided Joint Direct Attack Munition (JDAM) bombs, cruise missiles on submarines, and Special Operation Forces. He, however, argued that attacking Iranian nuclear facilities are "much tougher" to target given the nature of the Iranian nuclear facilities and the strategic balance in the region.

Covert action demands different kinds of operational capabilities and intelligence. There is no indication that Israel has capabilities of covert operations in Iran. The recent information about the development of the Iranian program indicated that it reached a status of being independent of external assistance. Moreover, the assistance Iran got was mostly from Pakistan, another place that is not a traditional area of operations for the Israeli Secret Services, like Europe or South America. It seems that there is no real potential for covert Israeli operations against the Iranian nuclear program.

Reports have surfaced, however, about more drastic Israeli strike options. One recent report, dating from early 2007, states that Israel has created plans to strike Iran with nuclear bunker-buster bombs. This would apparently be used if the United States fails to neutralize Iran's nuclear facilities. The three prime targets in this plan include the enrichment facility in Natanz, the uranium conversion in Isfahan, and the heavy-water reactor in Arak.[48] Other, possibly longer term, options include deploying Israeli submarines in the Gulf or Gulf of Oman, which could respond to lower-level Iranian attacks on Israel by attacking Iran's oil exports, and eventually being armed with nuclear cruise missiles to preempt or retaliate to an Iranian nuclear strike on Israel.

Iranian Defense against Israeli (and U.S.) Strikes

Iran would find it difficult to defend against U.S. forces using cruise missiles, stealth aircraft, standoff precision weapons, and equipped with a mix of vastly superior air combat assets and the IS&R assets necessary to strike and restrike Iranian targets in near real time. Iran might be able to incept Israeli fighters, Iran has "quantity," but the previous chapters have shown that its air defenses have little "quality." It has assigned some 12,000-15,000 men in its air force to land-based air-defense functions, including at least 8,000 regulars and 4,000 IRGC personnel. It is not possible to distinguish clearly between the major air-defense weapons holdings of the regular air force and of the IRGC, but the air force appeared to operate most major surface-to-air missile systems.

Although Iran has made some progress in improving and updating its land-based air-defense missiles, sensors, and electronic warfare capability—and has learned much from Iraq's efforts to defeat U.S. enforcement of the "no-fly zones" from 1992–2003—its defenses are outdated and poorly integrated. All of its major systems are based on technology that is now more than 35 years old, and all are vulnerable to U.S. use of active and passive countermeasures.

Iran's land-based air-defense forces are too widely spaced to provide more than limited air defense for key bases and facilities, and many lack the missile launcher strength to be fully effective. This is particularly true of Iran's SA-5 sites, which provide long-range, medium-to-high altitude coverage of key coastal installations. Too few launchers are scattered over too wide an area to prevent relatively rapid suppression. Iran also lacks the low-altitude radar coverage, overall radar net, command and control assets, sensors, resistance to sophisticated jamming and electronic countermeasures, and systems integration capability necessary to create an effective air-defense net.

Most Iranian squadrons can perform both air-defense and attack missions, regardless of their principal mission—although this does not apply to Iran's F-14 (air defense) and Su-24 (strike/attack) units. Iran's F-14s were, however, designed as dual-capable aircraft, and the Iranian Air Force has not been able to use its Phoenix air-to-air missiles since the early 1980s. Iran has claimed that it is modernizing its F-14s by equipping them with Improved Hawk missiles adapted to the air-to-air role, but it is far from clear that this is the case or that such adaptations can have more than limited effectiveness. In practice, this means that Iran might well use the F-14s in nuclear strike missions. They are capable of long-range, high-payload missions and would require minimal adaptation to carry and release a nuclear weapon.

Iran's air forces are only marginally better able to survive in air-to-air combat than Iraq's were before 2003. Its land-based air defenses must operate largely in the point defense mode, and Iran lacks the battle management systems and data links are not fast and effective enough to allow it to take maximum advantage of the overlapping coverage of some of its missile systems—a problem further complicated by the problems in trying to net different systems supplied by Britain, China, Russia, and the United States. Iran's missiles and sensors are most effective at high-to-medium altitudes against aircraft with limited penetrating and jamming capability.

Iranian Retaliation against Israel

For all the reasons outlined earlier in this chapter, however, Iran has other capabilities to strike back against Israel. In fact, it has threatened retaliation if attacked by Israel. Iranian Foreign Minister Manouchehr Mottaki was quoted as saying that an attack by Israel or the United States would have "severe consequence," and he threatened that Iran would retaliate "by all means" at its disposal. Mottaki added, "Iran does not think that the Zionist regime is in a condition to engage in such a dangerous venture and they know how severe the possible Iranian response will be to its possible audacity...Suffice to say that the Zionist regime, if they attack, will regret it."

Iran has several options in responding to an Israeli attack:

- Multiple launches of Shahab-3 including the possibility of CBR warheads against Tel Aviv, Israeli military and civilian centers, and Israeli suspected nuclear weapons sites.

- Escalate the conflict using proxy groups such Hezbollah or Hamas to attack Israel proper with suicide bombings, covert CBR attacks, and missile attacks from southern Lebanon and Syria.

- Covert attacks against Israeli interests by its intelligence and IRGC assets. This could include low-level bombings against Israeli embassies, Jewish centers, and other Israeli assets outside and inside Israel.

In addition, any Israeli military option would have to include an air strike that involved overflights of Arab territory that might seriously complicate Israel's fragile relations with Jordan and may provoke Saudi Arabia to respond. An Israeli strike against Iranian nuclear facilities may also strengthen the Iranian regime's stance to move toward nuclear capabilities and drive many neighboring states to support Iran's bid for nuclear weapons. In addition, it could lead to further escalation of the Iraqi insurgency and increase the threat of asymmetric attacks against American interests and allies in the region.

On the other hand, Israeli officials have expressed the concern that if Iran acquires nuclear weapons and the means to deliver them, this may spark further proliferation in the region. This would spread WMD capabilities around the Middle East and greatly increase the threat of CBRN attacks against Israel and the entire region. Waiting also has its penalties.

U.S. Options against Iran

A power as large as the United States would have far more capability than Israel. It could strike at possible targets as well as confirm targets. The problem with a shell gamer is that it virtually provokes strikes at all the shells.

The United States also could strike at a wide range of critical Iranian military facilities, including its missile production facilities. Most are soft targets and would be extremely costly to Iran. Even if many of Iran's nuclear facilities did survive U.S. strikes, Iran would be faced with either complying with the EU3 and UN terms or taking much broader military losses—losses its aging and limited forces can ill afford.

Possible U.S. Strike Methods

The United States has a wide range of attack assets it could use, including cruise missiles, standoff precision-guided weapons, and stealth aircraft. Military operations against Iran's nuclear, missile, and other WMD facilities and forces would still be challenging, however, even for the United States. Iran would find it difficult to defend against U.S. forces using cruise missiles, stealth aircraft, standoff precision weapons, and equipped with a mix of vastly superior air combat assets and the IS&R assets necessary to strike and restrike Iranian targets in near real time.

For example, each U.S. B-2A Spirit stealth bomber could carry eight 4,500-pound enhanced BLU-28 satellite-guided bunker-busting bombs—potentially enough to take out one hardened Iranian site per sortie. Such bombers could operate flying from Al Udeid air base in Qatar, Diego Garcia in the Indian Ocean, RAF Fairford in Gloucestershire, United Kingdom, and Whiteman USAF Base in Missouri.

The United States has a wide range of other hard-target killers, many of which are in development or classified. Systems that are known to be deployed include the BLU-109 Have Void "bunker busters," a "dumb bomb" with a maximum penetration capability of four to six feet of reinforced concrete. An aircraft must overfly the target and launch the weapon with great precision to achieve serious penetration capability. It can be fitted with precision guidance and converted to a guided glide bomb.

There seems to be a follow-on version of the 2,000-pound BLU-109, with an advanced unitary penetrator that can go twice as deep as the original BLU-109. Newest development is the 5,000-pound BLU-122, which is supposed to be operational in 2007. Further, there is the Massive Ordnance Penetrator (MOP), weighing almost 30,000 pounds, carrying 5,300 pounds of explosives. According to some estimates optimum penetrating distance is up to 200 feet. A possible alternative is directed energy and high-power microwave (HPM) testing phase.

The JDAM GBU-31 version has a nominal range of 15 kilometers with a CEP of 13 meters in the GPS-aided Inertial Navigation System (INS) modes of operation and 30 meters in the INS-only modes of operation.

More advanced systems that have been publicly discussed in the unclassified literature include the BLU-116 Advanced Unitary Penetrator, the GBU-24 C/B (USAF), or the GBU-24 D/B (U.S. Navy), which has about three times the penetration capability of the BLU-109. The United States is investing in weapons that are supposed to destroy targets that are buried under more than 20 meters of dirt and concrete.

The newest development in the BLU-series that has been open reported is the 5,000-pound BLU-122, which is supposed to be operational in 2007. Further, there is the Massive Ordnance Penetrator (MOP), weighing almost 30,000 pounds and able to carry 5,300 pounds of explosives. According to some estimates the optimum penetrating distance for the MOP is up to 200 feet. A possible alternative to these weapons are directed-energy and high-power microwave (HPM) weapons, none of which are currently beyond the testing phase.

It is not clear whether the United States has deployed the AGM-130C with an advanced earth penetrating/hard-target kill system. The AGM-130 Surface Attack Guided Munition was developed to be integrated into the F-15E, so that the F-15E could carry two such missiles, one on each inboard store station. The AGM-130 is a retargetable, precision-guided standoff weapon using inertial navigation aided by GPS satellites and has a 15-40-nautical mile range.

The United States also has a number of other new systems that are known to be in the developmental stage and can probably deploy systems capable of roughly twice the depth of penetration with twice the effectiveness of the systems known from its attacks on Iraq in 1991. The nature and characteristics of such systems are classified,

It is not clear whether any combination of such weapons could destroy all of Iran's most hardened underground sites, although it seems likely that the BLU-28 could do serious damage at a minimum and might well collapse enough of them to make them unusable. Much depends on the accuracy of reports that Iran has undertaken a massive tunneling project with some 10,000 square meters of underground halls and tunnels branching off for hundreds of meters from each hall.

Iran is reported to be drawing on North Korean expertise and to have created a separate corporation (Shahid Rajaei Company) for such tunneling and hardening efforts under the IRGC, with extensive activity already under way in Natanz and Isfahan. The facilities are said to make extensive use of blast-proof doors, extensive divider walls, hardened ceilings, 20-centimeter-thick concrete walls, and double concrete ceilings with earth filled between layers to defeat earth penetrates. Such passive defenses could have a major impact, but reports of such activity are often premature, exaggerated, or report far higher construction standards than are actually executed.

At the same time, the B-2A could be used to deliver large numbers of precision-guided 250- and 500-pound bombs against dispersed surface targets or a mix of light and heavy precision-guided weapons. Submarines and surface ships could deliver cruise missiles for such strikes, and conventional strike aircraft and bombers could deliver standoff weapons against most suspect Iranian facilities without suffering a high risk of serious attrition. The challenge would be to properly determine what targets and aim points were actually valuable, not to inflict high levels of damage.

One analyst projects that strikes against some 400 targets would be necessary to dismantle the program. According to other reports, the U.S. Department of Defense is considering both conventional and nuclear weapons to use against reinforced underground targets and would strike at Iran's other WMD facilities, missiles and missile production facilities, and create an entry corridor by destroying part of Iran's air-defense system. This could easily require 800–1,200 sorties and cruise missile strikes.

One expert (Lieutenant General Thomas McInerny, the former retired Assistant Vice Chief of the USAF) speculates that this could require an initial strike force of 75 stealth aircraft, including B-2s, F-117s, and F-22s; and 250 nonstealth aircraft, including F-15s, F-16s, B-52s, and B-1s, It might include three carrier task forces with 120 F-18s, and large numbers of cruise missiles, supported by a large array of intelligence platforms, support aircraft, and UAVs.

More generally, the United States could cripple Iran's economy by striking at major domestic gas production and distribution facilities, refineries, and electric power generations. There are no rules that would preclude the United States from immediate restrikes or restrikes over time. If the United States chose to strike at the necessary level of intensity, it could use conventional weapons to cripple Iran's ability to function as a nation in a matter of days with attacks limited to several hundred aim points.

Possible U.S. War Plans: Attacking, Delaying, and Waiting Out

If the U.S. does choose to respond militarily, it has several major types of military and strategic options. These options are summarized in Figure 12.2. Each of these options might have many of the following broad characteristics, although it should be stressed that these are only rough outlines of U.S. options and are purely speculative and illustrative points. They are more warnings than recommendations, and they are not based on any inside knowledge of actual U.S. war plans and calculations. Those who argue strongly for and against such options should note, however, that there are many different ways in which the United States could act. There are no rules or certainties that say such attacks either could not succeed or that they would.

Iran's ride out option is one that many commentators need to consider in more depth, particularly as long as Iran's capital investment is limited, its programs are not fully mature, the United States cannot be sure of destroying a target mix Iran cannot replace, and the United States does not have broad international support for its attacks. Unless the United States does find evidence of an imminent Iranian threat—which at this point might well require Iran to find some outside source of nuclear weapons or weapons-grade material—the United States may well simply choose to wait. Patience is not always a virtue, but it has never been labeled a mortal sin.

Iranian Retaliation against U.S. Strikes

It is not easy or desirable for the United States to exercise its military options. U.S. forces are preoccupied in Iraq, and some believe that the lack of security in Iraq makes a full military attack against Iran all too unlikely. U.S. military options are

Figure 12.2   U.S. Strike Options against Iran

Demonstrative, Coercive, or Deterrent Strikes

1. Conduct a few cruise missile or stealth strikes simply as a demonstration or warning of the seriousness of U.S. intentions if Iran does not comply with the terms of the EU3 or UN.

2. Hit at least one high-value target recognized by the IAEA and EU3 to show credibility to Iran, minimize international criticism.

3. Might strike at new sites and activities to show Iran cannot secretly proceed with, or expand its efforts, by ignoring the UN or EU3.

4. Could carrier base; would not need territory of Gulf ally.

5. International reaction would be a problem regardless of the level of U.S. action.

6. Might trigger Iranian counteraction in Iraq, Afghanistan, and dealing with Hezbollah.

Limited U.S. Attacks:

1. A limited strike would probably take 16-20 cruise missile and strike sorties. (Total sorties in the Gulf and the area would probably have to total 100 or more including escorts, enablers, and refuelers.)

2. Might be able to combine B-2s and carrier-based aircraft and sea-launched cruise missiles. Might well need land base(s) in the Gulf for staging, refueling, and recovery.

3. Goal would be at least 2-3 of the most costly and major facilities critically damaged or destroyed.

4. Hit at high-value targets recognized by the IAEA and EU3 to show credibility to Iran, minimize international criticism.

5. Might strike at new sites and activities to show Iran cannot secretly proceed with, or expand its efforts, by ignoring the UN or EU3.

6. Might slow down Iran if used stealth aircraft to strike at hard and underground targets, but impact over time would probably still be more demonstrative than crippling.

7. Hitting hard and underground targets could easily require multiple strikes during mission and follow-on restrikes to be effective.

8. Battle damage would be a significant problem, particularly for large buildings and underground facilities.

9. Size and effectiveness would depend very heavily on the quality of U.S. intelligence, and suitability of given ordnance, as well as the time the United States sought to inflict a given effect.

10. Iran's technology base would survive; the same would be true of much of the equipment even in facilities hit with strikes. Little impact, if any, on pool of scientists and experts.

11. Iranian response in terms of proliferation could vary sharply and unpredictably: deter and delay versus mobilize and provoke.

12. Likely to produce cosmetic Iranian change in behavior at best. Would probably make Iran disperse program even more and drive it to deep underground facilities. Might provoke to implement (more) active biological warfare program.

13. Any oil embargo likely to be demonstrative.

14. Would probably trigger Iranian counteraction in Iraq, Afghanistan, and dealing with Hezbollah.

15. International reaction could be a serious problem; United States might well face same level of political problems as if it had launched a comprehensive strike on Iranian facilities.

Major U.S. Attacks on Iranian CBRN and Major Missile Targets:

1. Period of attacks could extend from three to ten days with 200-600 cruise missiles and strike sorties; would have to be at least a matching number of escorts, enablers, and refuelers.

2. Hit all suspect facilities for nuclear, missile, BW, and related C4IBM.

3. Knock out key surface-to-air missile sites and radars for future freedom of action.

4. Would need to combine B-2s, carrier-based aircraft, and sea-launched cruise missiles and use land base(s) in Gulf for staging, refueling, and recovery.

5. Threaten to strike extensively at Iranian capabilities for asymmetric warfare and to threaten tanker traffic, facilities in the Gulf, and neighboring states.

6. Would take at least seven to ten days to fully execute and validate.

7. Goal would be at least 70–80 percent of the most costly and major facilities critically damaged or destroyed.

8. Hit at all high-value targets recognized by the IAEA and EU3 to show credibility to Iran, minimize international criticism, but also possible sites as well.

9. Strike at all known new sites and activities to show Iran cannot secretly proceed with, or expand its efforts, unless hold back some targets as hostages to the future.

10. Impact over time would probably be crippling, but Iran might still covertly assemble some nuclear device and could not halt Iranian biological weapons effort.

11. Hitting hard and underground targets could easily require multiple strikes during mission and follow-on restrikes to be effective.

12. Battle damage would be a significant problem, particularly for large buildings and underground facilities.

13. Size and effectiveness would depend very heavily on the quality of U.S. intelligence and suitability of given ordnance, as well as the time the United States sought to inflict a given effect.

14. Much of Iran's technology base would still survive; the same would be true of many equipment items, even in facilities hit with strikes. Some impact, if any, on pool of scientists and experts.

15. Iranian response in terms of proliferation could vary sharply and unpredictably: deter and delay versus mobilize and provoke.

16. A truly serious strike may be enough of a deterrent to change Iranian behavior, particularly if coupled to the threat of follow-on strikes in the future. It still, however, could as easily produce only a cosmetic Iranian change in behavior at best. Iran might still disperse its program even more and shift to multiple, small, deep underground facilities.

17. Might well provoke Iran to implement (more) active biological warfare program.

18. An oil embargo might be serious.

19. Iranian government could probably not prevent some elements in Iranian forces and intelligence from seeking to use Iraq, Afghanistan, support of terrorism, and Hezbollah to hit back at the United States and its allies if it tried; it probably would not try.

20. International reaction would be a serious problem, but the United States might well face the same level of political problems as if it had launched a small strike on Iranian facilities.

Major U.S. Attacks on Military and Related Civilian Targets:

1. Would take 1,000–2,500 cruise missiles and strike sorties.

2. Hit all suspect facilities for nuclear, missile, BW, and C4IBM, and potentially "technology base" targets including universities and dual-use facilities.

3. Either strike extensively at Iranian capabilities for asymmetric warfare and to threaten tanker traffic, facilities in the Gulf, and neighboring states or threaten to do so if Iran should deploy for such action.

4. Would require a major portion of total U.S. global assets. Need to combine B-2s, other bombers, and carrier-based aircraft and sea-launched cruise missiles. Would need land base(s) in the Gulf for staging, refueling, and recovery. Staging out of Diego Garcia would be highly desirable.

5. Would probably take several weeks to two months to fully execute and validate.

6. Goal would be 70–80-percent-plus of the most costly and major CBRN, missile, and other delivery systems, key conventional air and naval strike assets, and major military production facilities critically damaged or destroyed.

7. Hit at all high-value targets recognized by the IAEA and EU3 to show credibility to Iran, minimize international criticism, but also possible sites as well.

8. Strike at all known new sites and activities to show Iran cannot secretly proceed with, or expand its efforts, unless hold back some targets as hostages to the future.

9. Hitting hard and underground targets could easily require multiple strikes during mission and follow-on restrikes to be effective.

10. Impact over time would probably be crippling, but Iran might still covertly assemble some nuclear device and could not halt Iranian biological weapons effort.

11. Battle damage would be a significant problem, particularly for large buildings and underground facilities.

12. Size and effectiveness would depend very heavily on the quality of U.S. intelligence and suitability of given ordnance, as well as the time the United States sought to inflict a given effect.

13. Much of Iran's technology base would still survive; the same would be true of many equipment items, even in facilities hit with strikes. Some impact, if any, on pool of scientists and experts.

14. Iranian response in terms of proliferation could vary sharply and unpredictably: deter and delay versus mobilize and provoke.

15. Such a series of strikes might be enough of a deterrent to change Iranian behavior, particularly if coupled to the threat of follow-on strikes in the future. It still, however, could as easily produce only a cosmetic Iranian change in behavior at best. Iran might still disperse its program even more, and shift to multiple, small, deep underground facilities.

16. Might well provoke Iran to implement (more) active biological warfare program.

17. An oil embargo might be serious.

18. Iranian government could probably not prevent some elements in Iranian forces and intelligence from seeking to use Iraq, Afghanistan, support of terrorism, and Hezbollah to hit back at the United States and its allies if it tried; it probably would not try.

19. International reaction would be a serious problem, and far greater than strikes that could be clearly associated with Iran's efforts to proliferate.

Delay and Then Strike:

1. The United States could execute any of the above options and wait until after Iran provided proof it was proliferating. Such a "smoking gun" would create a much higher chance of allied support, and international tolerance or consensus.

2. Iran will have committed major resources and created much higher value targets.

3. The counter-risk is an unanticipated Iranian breakout: some form of Iranian launch on warning, launch under attack, or survivable "ride out" capability.

4. Iranian dispersal and sheltering may be much better.

5. Iran might have biological weapons as a counter.

6. Allied and regional reactions would be uncertain. Time tends to breed tolerance of proliferation.

Ride Out Iranian Proliferation:

1. Announce or quietly demonstrate U.S. nuclear targeting of Iran's military and CBRN facilities and cities.

2. Tacitly signal U.S. "green light" for Israeli nuclear retaliation or preemption.

3. Deploy anti-ballistic and cruise missile defenses, and sell to Gulf and neighboring states.

4. Signal U.S. conventional option to cripple Iran by destroying its power generation, gas, and refinery facilities.

5. Provide U.S. guarantees of extended deterrence to Gulf states.

6. Tacitly accept Saudi acquisition of nuclear weapons.

7. Maintain preventive/preemptive option at constant combat readiness. Act without warning.

8. Encourage Israel to openly declare its strike options as a deterrent.

9. Announce doctrine that any Iranian use of biological weapons will lead to nuclear retaliation against Iran.

---

not risk-free, and the consequences of U.S. strikes are enormous. As is the case with Israeli attacks on Iran, Tehran has several retaliatory options:

- Retaliate against U.S. forces in Iraq and Afghanistan overtly using Shahab-3 missiles armed with CBR warheads.
- Use proxy groups including al-Zarqawi and Sadr in Iraq to intensify the insurgency and escalate the attacks against U.S. forces and Iraqi Security Forces.
- Turn the Shi'ite majority in Iraq against the U.S. presence and demand the U.S. forces to leave.
- Attack the U.S. homeland with suicide bombs by proxy groups or deliver CBR weapons to Al Qa'ida to use against the United States.
- Use its asymmetric capabilities to attack U.S. interests in the region, including soft targets, e.g., embassies, commercial centers, and American citizens.
- Attack U.S. naval forces stationed in the Gulf with anti-ship missiles, asymmetric warfare, and mines.
- Attack Israel with missile attacks possibly with CBR warheads.
- Retaliate against energy targets in the Gulf and temporarily shut off the flow of oil from the Strait of Hormuz.
- Stop all of its oil and gas shipments to increase the price of oil and inflict damage on the global and U.S. economies.

Iran has close relations with many Iraqi Shi'ites, particularly Shi'ite political parties and militias. Some Iraqi groups have warned against U.S. military strikes against their neighbors. For example, Moqtada Al-Sadr pledged that he would come to the aid of Iran in the case of a military strike by the United States against Tehran. Sadr pledged that his militia, the Al-Mahdi Army, would come to the aid of Iran. According to Sadr, Iran asked him about what his position would be if Iran was attacked by the United States and he pledged that the Al-Mahdi Army would help any Arab or neighboring country if it were attacked.

Many observers argue that a military strike against Iran can add to the chaos in Iraq and may further complicate the U.S. position in Iraq. While the consequences of U.S. military attacks against Iran remain unclear, the Shi'ite majority in Iraq can (1) ask the United States forces to leave Iraq, (2) instigate Shi'ite militia groups to directly attack U.S. forces, and/or (3) turn the new Iraqi security and military forces against U.S. forces in Iraq.

As has been described in earlier chapters, Iran has extensive forces suited to asymmetric warfare. It could not close the Strait of Hormuz, or halt tanker traffic, but it could threaten and disrupt it and create a high-risk premium and potential panic in oil markets. Iran could potentially destabilize part of Afghanistan and use Hezbollah and Syria to threaten Israel.

Iran can also use its IRGC asymmetric warfare assets to attack U.S. interests in the region. Iranian officials do not hide the fact that they would use asymmetric attacks against U.S. interests. For example, a Brigadier General in the IRGC and the commander of the "Lovers of Martyrdom Garrison," Mohammad-Reza Jaafari, threatened U.S. interests with suicide operations if the United States were to attack Iran:

> Now that America is after gaining allies against the righteous Islamic Republic and wants to attack our sanctities, members of the martyrdom-seeking garrisons across the world have been put on alert so that if the Islamic Republic of Iran receives the smallest threat, the American and Israeli strategic interests will be burnt down everywhere.
>
> The only tool against the enemy that we have with which we can become victorious are martyrdom-seeking operations and, God willing, our possession of faithful, brave, trained and zealous persons will give U.S. the upper hand in the battlefield...
>
> Upon receiving their orders, our martyrdom-seeking forces will be uncontrollable and a guerrilla war may go on in various places for years to come...
>
> America and any other power cannot win in the unbalanced war against us.

Iran could seek to create an alliance with extremist movements like Al Qa'ida in spite of their hostility to Shi'ites. It can seek to exploit Arab and Muslim anger against U.S. ties to Israel and the invasion of Iraq on a global level, and European and other concerns that the United States might be repeating its miscalculation of the threat posed by Iraq and striking without adequate cause. Unless Iran is far more egregious in its noncompliance, or the United States can find a definitive smoking gun to prove Iran is proliferating, Iran would be certain to have some success in such efforts.

Iran's energy resources are another potential weapon. Shutting off exports would deeply hurt Iran but would also have an impact on global markets.[49] As Iraq found, energy deals can also sharply weaken support for even diplomatic options, and Russia and China might well oppose any kind of U.S. military strike, regardless of the level of justification the United States could advance at the time.

NO SHORT OR EASY ROAD

One thing is certain: Effective action to deal with Iran's capabilities and possible future intentions has to be complex, nuanced, and sustained. It cannot be accomplished either by threats or by calls for dialogue and grand bargains. It must be done in the context of finding broader solutions to regional security and in the context of military realities rather than in hopes and good intentions.

It is equally clear that Iran cannot dismiss "worst case" attacks on its WMD and missile facilities and bases by either Israel or the United States, but that such attacks involve uncertain and high-risk options for the attacker. It is easy to call for war and to initiate it. The problem lies in achieving a lasting grand strategic outcome at a cost lower than the alternative options. The United States seems committed to playing out the diplomatic option as long as possible, and this seems the wisest course of action.

At the same time, Iran should understand that the fact U.S. strike options are difficult and involve risk in no way means that they will not eventually be exercised. Moreover, Iran needs to be equally clear about the risk of actually deploying effective nuclear strike options if Israel and the United States do not launch preventive or preemptive strikes. One way or another Iran is almost certain to provoke potentially suicidal nuclear retaliatory targeting of Iran, and any actual Iranian use of nuclear weapons might well be suicidal. The world may need Iranian oil, but no one needs Iran. The only way Iran can really win such a "war game" is not to play it.

Notes

CHAPTER 1

1. The CIA notes that Supreme Leader Ali Hoseini-Khamenei (since June 4, 1989) also has authority over the law enforcement system and de facto control over the media. The head of government, President Mahmud AhmadiI-Nejad (since August 3, 2005), and First Vice President Parviz Davudi (since September 11, 2005) have their powers further limited by the fact their cabinet or Council of Ministers is selected by the president but requires legislative approval and the Supreme Leader has control over appointments to the more sensitive ministries. The Supreme Leader, head of the IRGC, and the head of the Vevak (or their representatives) are all members of the Iranian National Security Council.

The Executive branch of government is also limited and influenced by three oversight bodies:

1) Assembly of Experts, a popularly elected body of 86 religious scholars constitutionally charged with determining the succession of the Supreme Leader, reviewing his performance, and deposing him if deemed necessary;

2) Expediency Council or Council for the Discernment of Expediency is a policy advisory and implementation board consisting of permanent and temporary members representing all major government factions, some of whom are appointed by the Supreme Leader; the Council exerts supervisory authority over the executive, judicial, and legislative branches and resolves legislative issues on which the Majles (parliament) and the Council of Guardians disagree;

3) Council of Guardians or Council of Guardians of the Constitution is a 12-member board of clerics and jurists serving six-year terms that determines whether proposed legislation is both constitutional and faithful to Islamic law; the Council also vets candidates for suitability and supervises national elections.

2. Reporting on the structure of the Iranian government varies somewhat by source. This description is adapted from the CIA analysis in the 2007 edition of the *World Factbook*, https://www.cia.gov/library/publications/the-world-factbook/geos/ir.html.

3. "Iran," https://www.cia.gov/library/publications/the-world-factbook/geos/ir.html.

4. For a short overview of the problems in determining who is in charge of Iran's national security apparatus, see Hesham Sallam, Anrew Mandelbaum, and Robert Grace, "Who Rules Ahmadinejad's Iran?" *USIP Peace Briefing*, April 2007. The works of Sharam Chubin cover this subject in depth. See *Iran's Nuclear Ambitions*, October 2006, and *Wither Iran? Reform, Domestic Politics, and National Security*, Adelphi Papers 342 (London: Institute of Strategic Studies, April 2002). Also see Ray Takeyh, *Hidden Iran: Paradox and Power in the Islamic Republic* (New York: CFR Book/Times Books/Henry Holt, October 2006); Steven R. Ward, "The Continuing Evolution of Iran's Military Doctrine," *Middle East Journal*, 59, no. 4 (Autumn 2005); and Michael Connell, "The Influence of the Iraq Crisis on Iranian Warfighting Doctrine and Strategy" (Alexandria, VA: CNA Corporation, April 2007).

5. Agence France-Presse (AFP), "Iran Threatens 'Longer Stride' for Nuclear Drive," June 21, 2007.

6. AFP, "Iran 'Invincible' in Nuclear Standoff: Ahmadinejad," June 3, 2007.

7. AFP, "Iran Vows 'No Retreat' on Atomic Drive," May 24, 2007.

8. BBC Monitoring International Reports, "Use of Nuclear Weapons 'Thing of the Past'—Iran's President," April 23, 2007.

9. BBC Monitoring International Reports, "Installation of Centrifuges Continues in Natanz—IRAN Nuclear Official," April 17, 2007.

10. BBC Monitoring International Reports, "Iranians Will not Back Down 'Even One Step," President, April 17, 2007.

11. AFP, Tehran, April 5, 2007.

12. Borzou Daragahi and Ramin Mostaghim, "US Strategy on Iran May Have Backfired," *Los Angeles Times*, April 3, 2007.

13. Ibid.

14. BBC News Middle East, "Iran Willing to Act Illegally," March 21, 2007.

15. "Iran Army Vows to Defend Nuclear Program," *New York Times*, March 18, 2007, p. 18.

16. BBC Monitoring Middle East, "Iranian President Warns 'Enemies' not to Make Mistake, March 14, 2007.

17. Ali Akbar Dareini, "Iranian Conservatives, Reformers Denounce Ahmadi-Nejad's Harsh Rhetoric on Nuclear Program," *Associated Press Worldstream*, February 27, 2007.

18. Nasser Karimi, "No 'Brakes' on Iran Nuclear Effort," *Washington Post*, February 26, 2007.

19. Ali Akbar Dareini, "Iran Says U.S. Is not in a Position to Take Military Action Against," *Associated Press*, February 24, 2007.

20. Cnn.com, "Iran Vows not to 'Retreat One Iota' in Nuclear Pursuit," February 21, 2007.

21. "Iranian Guard's Mission Evolves," *Washington Times*, March 19, 2007, p. 1.

22. Bernard Guetta, "Nucléaire iranien: 'Il n'y a pas de limitation à la négociation,'" *Libération*, February 14, 2007.

23. Nazila Fathi, "Iran Vows to Hit U.S. Worldwide if Attacked," *International Herald Tribune*, February 9, 2007.

24. Nazila Fathi, "Iran Leader Calls Nuclear Sanctions Ineffective," *New York Times,* February 2, 2007.

25. "Iranian Guard's Mission Evolves."

26. BBC Monitoring International Reports, "Iran Says Prepared for Any American Move in Region," January 24, 2007.

27. Xinhua General News Service, "Iran Vows to Continue Installing at Least 3,000 Centrifuges," January 15, 2007.

28. Nazila Fathi, "Iranian Leader Vows to Resist U.N. Sanctions, *New York Times,* January 9, 2007.

29. FT.com. December 27, 2006.

30. BBC Monitoring International Reports, "Iranian Press Dismissive of UN Nuclear Resolution," December 25, 2007.

31. Najmeh Bozorgmehr, "Iran 'Revises' Co-operation with IAEA, *Associated Press Worldstream,* December 5, 2006.

32. BBC Monitoring Middle East, *Iran's Guard Commander Comments on Tehran's Missile Power,* November 12, 2006.

33. Vision of the Islamic Republic of Iran, Net Work 2, 1915 GMT, November 12, 2006. (Drawn from work by Michael Connell of CNA.)

34. Kim Murphy, "Iran Warns U.N. against Sanctions," *Los Angeles Times,* November 11, 2006.

35. Ali Akbar Dareini, "Ahmadi-Nejad warns EU against Backing UN Steps on Iran, Threatens to Retaliate," *Los Angeles Times,* November 11, 2006.

36. AFX—Asia, "Iran Warns U.N. on Sanctions; Implying It Might Block Nuclear Inspections, It Promotes Russia's Tack," October 10, 2006.

37. "Iran Proposes that France Enrich Tehran's Uranium," *Houston Chronicle,* October 3, 2006.

38. Associated Press Worldstream, *Khamenei Vows Iran Will Press ahead with Nuclear Programme,* September 22, 2006.

39. Nasser Karimi, "Iranian VP Says Country's Supreme Leader Forbids Use of Nuclear Weapons," *Fed News,* September 20, 2006.

40. AFP, "Chavez, Ahmadinejad Solidify Iran-Venezuela Ties," September 18, 2006.

41. Barbara Slavin, "U.S., Iran Share Interests in Iraq, Khatami Says," *Today,* September 5, 2006.

42. Ali Akbar Dareini, "Iran Tests Submarine-to-Surface Missile," *washingtonpost.com,* August 27, 2006; Ewen MacAskill, "Iran Fires Missile from Submarine as Deadline Nears," *The Guardian,* August 28, 2006.

43. Author unknown, "Khamenei Vows Iran will Keep Nukes," *Hobart Mercury,* August 23, 2006.

44. Nazila Fathi, "Iran Won't Give up Right to Use Atomic Technology, Leader Says," *New York Times,* June 28, 2006.

45. Alissa J. Rubin, "Iran Builds Support for Right to Nuclear Power," *Los Angeles Times,* June 28, 2006.

46. Vision of the Islamic Republic of Iran, Esfahan Provincial TV, 1721 GMT, May 11, 2006. (Drawn from work by Michael Connell of CNA.)

47. Vision of the Islamic Republic of Iran Network 1, 1834 GMT, March 5, 2005. (Drawn from work by Michael Connell of CNA.)

48. *Aftab-e-Yazd,* January 25, 2005 edition.

49. Brigadier General Sa'id Amiri, "Guerilla Warfare Is the Best Method for Fighting the Enemy," *Saff,* April 20, 2004, pp. 16–17.

50. United Press International, "Iran to Hold Military Exercises," July 19, 2007.

51. "Iran Port Bustles in Shadow of War," *Washington Times,* March 14, 2007, p. 17.

52. BBC Monitoring Middle East, *Paramilitary Forces Begin "Persian Gulf 3" Exercise in Iran's Sistan-Baluchestan,* February 25, 2007.

53. BBC Monitoring Middle East, *Coverage of Manoeuvres by Iran's Sistan-Baluchestan TV,* February 22, 2007.

54. BBC Monitoring Middle East, *Persian Press: Commanders Comment on Eqtedar Military Exercise, Weapons,* February 25, 2007.

55. BBC Monitoring International Reports, "Iran Guards Army Units Test-Fire Short-Range Missiles, Rockets," January 23, 2007.

56. Defense & Foreign Affairs Special Analysis, November 7, 2006, Iranian Military Exercises Continue, Parallel DPRK Exercises, and Highlight Access to Shi'ite Areas of Iraq.

57. Iran Press News, without title, November 23, 2006, http://www.iranpressnews.com/english/source/017875.html.

58. Defense & Foreign Affairs Special Analysis, September 21, 2006: Iranian Claims of Advanced Combat Aircraft Production Seen as Substantial Exaggeration.

59. Ibid.

60. BBC Monitoring International Reports, "Iran's Guard Commander Comments on Tehran's Missile Power," November 13, 2006.

61. Monterey County Herald, "Iran Test-Fires New Anti-Ship Missile," August 28, 2006.

62. BBC Monitoring International Reports, *Paramilitary in Iran's Ardabil Province Begin War Games,* August 28, 2006.

63. Uzi Rubin, *The Global Reach of Iran's Ballistic Missiles* (Tel Aviv: Institute for National Security Studies, November 2006), p. 7.

64. Ibid., p. 16.

65. BBC Monitoring Middle East, *Iran Press: Second Stage of Velayat Exercises Reported,* December 14, 2005; BBC Monitoring Middle East, *Iran to Test Long-Range Shore-to-Sea Missiles in the Sea,* December 12, 2005.

66. BBC Monitoring International Reports, Iran's military exercise has "political impact"—commander, October 3, 2005.

67. BBC Monitoring Middle East, Iranian TV reports "successful" naval exercises in Sea of Oman, May 12, 2005.

68. "Iran," *Jane's World Armies,* October 26, 2006.

69. Ibid.

70. Special Warfare, Iran's republican guard considers new threats; Foreign SOF; Iranian Revolutionary Guard Corps, vol. 17, no. 3, February 1, 2005.

71. "Iran," *Jane's World Armies.*

72. Robin Hughes, "Iran Eyes Long-Range Air Strike Capability," *Jane's Defence Weekly,* February 7, 2007.

73. CIA, *The World Factbook,* 2007, "Iran," http://www.odci.gov/cia/publications/factbook/geos/ir.html.

74. EIA, "OPEC Revenue Fact Sheet, January 2006, http://www.eia.doe.gov/emeu/cabs/OPEC_Revenues/OPEC.html.

75. BP, *Statistical Review of World Energy,* June 2005.

76. Adapted from reporting by the Energy Information Agency of the Department of Energy.

77. International Energy Outlook, 2006, http://www.eia.doe.gov/oiaf/ieo/ieooil.html.

CHAPTER 2

1. CIA, *The World Factbook,* 2007.

2. Energy Information Agency (EIA), "Country Profile Iran," Department of Energy, Washington, August 2006, http://www.eia.doe.gov/emeu/cabs/Iran/Background.html. The CIA has somewhat different estimates. The Central Intelligence Agency (CIA) also estimates Iran's government revenues in 2005 were only $48.82 billion versus expenditures of $60.4 billion, but that total revenues in 2006 were $104.6 billion versus expenditures of $100.6 billion, including capital expenditures of $7.6 billion (2006). Iran's total exports rose to $63.2 billion, versus imports of $45.5 billion.

3. EIA, "Country Profile Iran."

CHAPTER 3

1. Roger Stern, "The Iranian Petroleum Crisis and United States National Security," *Proceedings of the National Academy of Sciences of the United States of America*, vol. 104, no. 1, January 2, 2007, p. 377.

2. Energy Information Agency (EIA), "Country Profile Iran," Department of Energy, Washington, August 2006, http://www.eia.doe.gov/emeu/cabs/Iran/Background.html.

3. Ibid.

4. Gareth Smyth, "Tehran to Ration Petrol and Put up Pump Prices," *Financial Times,* March 9, 2007.

5. EIA, "Country Profile Iran."

6. IISS, *Military Balance,* 2005–2006, 2006, 2007; CIA, *The World Factbook,* 2007, "Iran," http://www.odci.gov/cia/publications/factbook/geos/ir.html.

7. Richard F. Grimmett, *Conventional Arms Transfers To Developing Nations, 1998–2005,* CRS, October 23, 2006.

8. Keri Smith, "Iran Receives Final TOR-M1 Deliveries," *Jane's Defence Weekly,* January 24, 2007.

9. CIA, *The World Factbook,* 2007, "Iran."

10. Based on CIA, *World Factbook,* 2007 edition, https://www.cia.gov/cia/publications/factbook/geos/mu.html.

CHAPTER 4

1. IISS, *Military Balance,* various editions; "Iran," *Jane's Sentinel: The Gulf States,* various editions, p. 24.

2. No reliable data exist on the size and number of Iran's smaller independent formations.

3. There are reports that the lighter and smaller formations in the regular army include an Airmobile Forces group created since the Iran-Iraq War, and which includes the 29th Special Forces Division, which was formed in 1993–1994, and the 55th paratroop division. There are also reports that the regular army and IRGC commando forces are loosely integrated into a corps of up to 30,000 men with integrated helicopter lift and air assault capabilities. The

airborne and special forces are trained at a facility in Shiraz. These reports are not correct. Note that detailed unit identifications for Iranian forces differ sharply from source to source. It is unclear that such identifications are accurate, and now dated wartime titles and numbers are often published, sometimes confusing brigade numbers with division numbers.

4. Global Security, http://www.globalsecurity.org/military/world/iran/zulfiqar.htm.

5. Ibid.

6. Ibid.

7. "Iran," *Jane's World Armies,* October 26, 2006.

8. Ibid.

9. The estimates of Iran's AFV and APC strength are based on interviews with Israeli, British, and U.S. experts, and the IISS, "Iran," *Military Balance;* "Iran," *Jane's Sentinel: The Gulf States.*

10. Federation of American Scientists, http://www.fas.org/man/dod-101/sys/land/row/bmp-1.htm.

11. Federation of American Scientists, http://www.fas.org/man/dod-101/sys/land/row/bmp-2.htm.

12. Wikipedia, http://en.wikipedia.org/wiki/EE-9_Cascavel.

13. Federation of American Scientists, http://www.fas.org/man/dod-101/sys/land/row/btr-60.htm.

14. Christopher Foss, "Iran Reveals Up-Armored Boraq Carrier," *Jane's Defence Weekly,* April 9, 2003, http://jdw.janes.com (accessed January 8, 2004). Labeled 42.

15. Christopher F. Foss, "Iran Reveals Armored Ammunition Carrier," *Jane's Defence Weekly,* August 3, 2005.

16. Lyubov Pronina, "U.S. Sanctions Russian Firm for Alleged Iran Sales," *Defense News,* September 22, 2003, p. 12. Labeled 43.

17. Wikipedia, http://en.wikipedia.org/wiki/Toophan.

18. http://www.nti.org/e_research/profiles/Iran/Missile/1788_1815.html.

19. Wikipedia, http://en.wikipedia.org/wiki/AT-5.

20. http://www.nti.org/e_research/profiles/Iran/Missile/1788_1815.html.

21. http://www.fas.org/nuke/guide/iran/missile/mushak.htm.

22. Wikipedia, http://en.wikipedia.org/wiki/Raad_1.

23. Global Security, http://www.globalsecurity.org/military/world/iran/thunder-2.htm.

24. Ibid.

25. Christopher F. Foss, "Fadjr-5 Artillery Rocket System Gets New Chassis," *Jane's Defence Weekly,* May 10, 2006.

26. Amir Taheir, "The Mullah's Playground," *Wall Street Journal,* December 7, 2004, p. A10.

27. Alon Ben-David, "West doubts Iran missile claims", *Jane's Defence Weekly,* April 12, 2006.

28. Dough Richardson, "Iran's Raad Cruise Missile Enters Production," *Jane's Missiles and Rockets.*

29. *Jane's Defence Weekly,* January 15, 2003, http://jdw.janes.com (accessed January 8, 2004). Labeled 45.

30. *International Defense Review,* 7/1996, pp. 23–26; Anthony H. Cordesman, *Iran's Weapons of Mass Destruction,* CSIS, April 1997.

31. Jane's Armour and Artillery, Aerospace Industries Organization 122 mm (40-round) HADID multiple rocket launcher system, May 14, 2007.

32. NTI, "Iran's Missile Capabilities: Long-Range Artillery Rocket Programs," http://www.nti.org/e_research/profiles/Iran/Missile/3367_3397.html.

33. Ibid.

34. Mark Williams, "The Missiles of August. The Lebanon War and the Democratization of Missile Technology," *Technology Review,* August 16, 2006.

35. NTI, "Iran's Missile Capabilities."

36. Ibid.

37. Ibid.

38. Oliver Schmidt, "Iranische Raketen und Marschflugkörper. Stand und Perspektiven," *SWP-Diskussionspapier,* Dezember 2006, p. 5.

39. NTI, "Iran's Missile Capabilities."

40. Oliver Schmidt, "Iranische Raketen und Marschflugkörper. Stand und Perspektiven," *SWP-Diskussionspapier,* Dezember 2006, p. 6.

41. NTI, "Iran's Missile Capabilities."

42. Ibid.

43. Christopher F. Foss, "Iran Markets Battlefield Radars," *Jane's Defence Weekly,* December 20, 2006.

44. http://www.fas.org/nuke/guide/iran/missile/mushak.htm.

45. "Iran," *Jane's World Armies.*

46. Abbas Bakhtiar, U.S. vs. Iran (II). Hybrid War, http://www.payvand.com/news/06/sep/Scenarios-of-War.pdf, January 27, 2007.

47. Robin Hughes, "Iran Set to Obtain Pantsyr via Syria," *Jane's Missiles and Rockets,* July 1, 2007.

48. "Iran," *Jane's World Armies.*

49. Cnn.com, "Iran, China Exploit U.S. Military Surplus Supermarket," January 16, 2007.

50. World Tribune.com, "Israel Downs Iran UAV over Coast Near Lebanon Border," August 13, 2006.

51. Robin Hughes, "Iran Claims Production and Use of 'stealth' UAV," *Jane's Defence Weekly,* February 21, 2007.

52. Robin Hughes, "Iran and Syria Advance SIGINT Cooperation," *Jane's Defence Weekly,* July 19, 2006, p. 41.

53. "Iran," *Jane's World Armies.*

54. Periscope Daily News Capsules, "Iran—Rapid Deployment Force Launched," January 24, 2005.

CHAPTER 5

1. Michael Slackman, "Seizure of Britons Underlines Iran's Political Split," *New York Times,* April 4, 2007, p. 5; Sarah Lyall, "Iran Sets Free 15 Britons Seized at Sea in March," *New York Times,* April 5, 2007.

2. Robin Wright, "Elite Revolutionary Guard Broadens Its Influence in Iran," *Washington Post,* April 1, 2007, p. A21.

3. UNSCR 1747, United Nations S/RES/1747 (2007), Adopted by the Security Council at its 5647th meeting on 24 March 2007.

4. "Iran," *Jane's World Armies,* October 26, 2006.

5. Michael Connell, "The Influence of the Iraq Crisis on Iranian Warfighting Doctrine and Strategy," CNA Corporation, Alexandria, April 2007; Vision of the Islamic Republic of Iran Network, Network 1. 18:34 GMT, March 9, 2005.

6. Iran has said that experts at its Hossein and Sharif Universities are working on an "impenetrable intranet communications network." Connell indicates that Iran claims such a system was fielded during the Eqtedar exercises in February 2007. *Baztab,* Web edition, February 20, 2007.

7. Connell, "The Influence of the Iraq Crisis on Iranian Warfighting Doctrine and Strategy"; *Keyhan,* February 20, 2007, p. 14.

8. "Iran," Jane's World Armies.

9. "Iran Enhances Existing Weaponry by Optimizing Shahab-3 Ballistic Missile," *Jane's Missiles and Rockets,* January 20, 2004.

10. Reports that the IRGC is operating F-7 fighters do not seem to be correct.

11. Reuters, June 12, 1996, 17:33.

12. See *Time,* March 21, 1994, pp. 50–54; November 11, 1996, pp. 78–82. Also see *Washington Post,* November 21, 1993, p. A-1; August 22, 1994, p. A-17; October 28, 1994, p. A-17; November 27, 1994, p. A-30; April 11, 1997, p. A-1; April 14, 1997, p. A-1; *Los Angeles Times,* November 3, 1994, pp. A-1, A-12; *Deutsche Presse-Agentur,* April 17, 1997, 11:02; Reuters, April 16, 1997; BC cycle, April 17, 1997; *The European,* April 17, 1997, p. 13; *The Guardian,* October 30, 1993, p. 13; August 24, 1996, p. 16; April 16, 1997, p. 10; *New York Times,* April 11, 1997, p. A1; Associated Press, April 14, 1997, 18:37; *Jane's Defence Weekly,* June 5, 1996, p. 15; *Agence France-Presse,* April 15, 1997, 15:13; BBC, April 14, 1997, ME/D2892/MED; Deustcher Depeschen via ADN, April 12, 1997, 0743; *Washington Times,* April 11, 1997, p. A22.

13. Riad Kahwaji and Barbara Opall-Rome, "Hizbollah: Iran's Battle Lab," *Defense News,* December 13, 2004, pp. 1 & 6.

14. Amir Taheir, "The Mullah's Playground," *Wall Street Journal,* December 7, 2004, p. A10.

15. The estimates of such holdings of rockets are now in the thousands, but the numbers are very uncertain. Dollar estimates of what are significant arms shipments are little more than analytic rubbish, based on cost methods that border on the absurd, but significant shipments are known to have taken place.

16. The reader should be aware that much of the information relating to the Al-Quds Force is highly uncertain. Also, however, see the article from the Jordanian publication *Al-Hadath* in FBIS-NES-96-108, May 27, 1996, p. 9, and in *Al-Sharq Al-Awsat,* FBIS-NES-96-110, June 5, 1996, pp. 1, 4; A.J. Venter, "Iran Still Exporting Terrorism," *Jane's Intelligence Review,* November, 1997, pp. 511–516.

17. IntelligenceOnline.com, Tehran targets Mediterranean, March 10, 2006.

18. Michael Gordon and Scott Shane, "Iran Supplied Weapons in Iraq," *New York Times,* March 26, 2007.

19. Michael D. Maples, "Threat Assessment," Statement of Michael D. Maples Director, Defense Intelligence Agency U.S. Army before the Committee on Senate Select Intelligence, January 11, 2007.

20. *New York Times,* May 17, 1998, p. A-15; *Washington Times,* May 17, 1998, p. A-13; *Washington Post,* May 21, 1998, p. A-29.

21. Venter, "Iran Still Exporting Terrorism," *Jane's Intelligence Review,* pp. 511–516.

22. Defense Department Documents and Publications, Coalition Targets Iranian Influence in Northern Iraq, January 14, 2007.

23. Stephen Kaufman, "Bush Says Iranian Group Certainly Providing Weapons in Iraq, February 14, 2007, http://usinfo.state.gov/xarchives/display.html?p=washfile-english&y=2007&m=February&x=20070214171942esnamfuak0.7028467.

24. Bill Gertz, "US General Calls Al Qaeda 'Public Enemy No. 1' in Iraq," *Washington Times,* April 27, 2007, p. 4.

25. "Iran," Jane's World Armies.

26. Connell, "The Influence of the Iraq Crisis on Iranian Warfighting Doctrine and Strategy," p. 4; Vision of the Islamic Republic of Iran Network 1, 18:34 GMT, March 9, 2005.

27. For typical reporting by officers of the IRGC on this issue, see the comments of its acting commander in chief, Brigadier General Seyyed Rahim Safavi, speaking to reporters during IRGC week (December 20–26, 1995). FBIS-NES-95-250, December 25, 1995, IRNA 1406 GMT.

28. UNSCR 1747, United Nations S/RES/1747 (2007), Adopted by the Security Council at its 5647th meeting on March 24, 2007.

CHAPTER 6

1. The range of aircraft numbers shown reflects the broad uncertainties affecting the number of Iran's aircraft that are operational in any realistic sense. Many aircraft counted, however, cannot engage in sustained combat sorties in an extended air campaign. The numbers are drawn largely from interviews; *Jane's Intelligence Review,* Special Report No. 6, May, 1995; *Jane's Sentinel—The Gulf Staffs,* "Iran," various editions; the IISS, *Military Balance,* various editions, "Iran;" Andrew Rathmell, *The Changing Balance in the Gulf,* Whitehall Papers 38 (London, Royal United Services Institute, 1996); Dr. Andrew Rathmell, "Iran's Rearmament: How Great a Threat?" *Jane's Intelligence Review,* July 1994, pp. 317–322; *Jane's World Air Forces* (CD-ROM).

2. Iran Defense Reports, http://www.irandefence.net/archive/index.php/t-744.html.

3. Ibid.

4. Ibid.

5. *Jane's Sentinel Security Assessment: The Gulf States, Armed Forces, Iran,* October 7, 2004.

6. Abbas Bakhtiar, :U.S. vs. Iran (II). Hybrid War," http://www.payvand.com/news/06/sep/Scenarios-of-War.pdf, January 27, 2007.

7. Iran Defense Reports, http://www.irandefence.net/archive/index.php/t-744.html.

8. Cnn.com, "Iran, China Exploit U.S. Military Surplus Supermarket," January 16, 2007.

9. Guy Anderson, "Isonmainer Suspends Sale of F-14 parts," *Jane's Defence Weekly,* February 7, 2007.

10. Iran Defense Reports, http://www.irandefence.net/archive/index.php/t-744.html.

11. Wikipedia, http://en.wikipedia.org/wiki/Chengdu_J-7.

12. "Lockheed C-130H-MP Hercules," *Jane's Fighting Ships,* January 9, 2007.

13. *Wall Street Journal,* February 10, 1995, p. 19; *Washington Times,* February 10, 1995, p. A-19.

14. Periscope, Nations/Alliances/Geographic Regions/Middle East/North Africa, Plans and Programs. Labeled 69.

15. Reports that the IRGC is operating F-7 fighters do not seem to be correct.

16. Reuters, June 12, 1996, 17:33.

17. Robin Hughes, "Iran Eyes Long-Range Air Strike Capability," *Jane's Defence Weekly,* February 7, 2007, p. 11.

18. http://www.missilethreat.com/cruise/id.61/cruise_detail.asp.

19. *Jane's All the World's Aircraft, 2002–2003* (London, Jane's Information Group), pp. 259–263.

20. http://www.irandefence.net/archive/index.php/t-399.html.

21. *Jane's All the World's Aircraft, 2002–2003,* pp. 259–263.

22. "Islamic Republic of Iran Air Force (Ya Hossein Project/Owj Industrial Complex)," *Jane's All The World's Aircraft.* IRIAF (OWJ) Saeghe, December 7, 2006.

23. Robert Hewson, "Iran's New Combat Aircraft Waits in the Wings," *Jane's Defence Weekly,* November 20, 2002, p. 15. Labeled 43; *Jane's All the World's Aircraft, 2002–2003,* pp. 259–263.

24. http://www.irandefence.net/archive/index.php/t-399.html.

25. Federation of American Scientists, http://www.fas.org/man/dod-101/sys/ac/row/azarakhsh.htm.

26. Bakhtiar, "U.S. vs. Iran (II). Hybrid War."

27. BBC Monitoring Middle East, Threat of sanctions prompts Iran to achieve latest technology—defence minister, February 10, 2007.

28. Bakhtiar, "U.S. vs. Iran (II). Hybrid War."

29. Robin Hughes, "Iran and Syria Advance SIGINT Cooperation," *Jane's Defence Weekly,* July 19, 2006, p. 41.

30. *Jane's Defence Weekly,* September 4, 1996, p. 4.

31. Michael Knights, "Iran's Conventional Forces Remain Key to Deterring Potential Threats," *Jane's Intelligence Review,* February 1, 2006.

32. *Jane's Defence Weekly,* "Iran Reveals Shahab Thaqeb SAM Details," September 4, 2002, http://jdw.janes.com (accessed January 9, 2004). Labeled 44.

33. This is based on interviews with British and Israeli experts, and this has given it a rationale for rejecting Russia's offer to provide Iran nuclear fuel without giving Tehran the technology and the expertise needed to use it for weaponization purposes, and the United States agrees with this position.

It has never been clear whether Iran does have a "military" nuclear program that is separate from its "civilian" nuclear research. American and French officials have argued that they believe that Iran's nuclear program would make sense only if it had military purposes. Both governments have yet to provide evidence to prove these claims.

If Iran is a proliferator, it has shown that it is a skilled one that is highly capable of hiding many aspects of its programs, sending confusing and contradictory signals, exploiting both deception and the international inspection process, rapidly changing the character of given facilities, and pausing and retreating when this is expedient. See Michael Eisenstadt, *Iranian Military Power, Capabilities and Intentions* (Washington, DC: Washington Institute, 1996), pp. 9–65; and Anoushiravan Enreshami, "Iran Strives to Regain Military Might," *International Defense Review* 7 (1996) 22–26.

34. Robin Hughes, "Iran Replenishes Hezbollah's Arms Inventory," *Jane's Defence Weekly,* January 3, 2007.

35. Robert Hewson, "Iran Stages Large-Scale Exercises to Underline Defense Capabilities," *Jane's Defense Week,* September 15, 206, p. 5.

36. Alon Ben David, "Iran Launches New Surface to Air Missile Production," *Jane's Defence Weekly,* February 15, 2006.

37. http://www.globalsecurity.org/military/world/russia/sa-15.htm, February 2, 2007.

38. Robin Hughes, "Iran Fires TOR-M1," *Jane's Defence Weekly,* February 14, 2007.

39. http://www.globalsecurity.org/military/world/russia/sa-15.htm; "Russia May Deliver Iranian Tor-M1s Earlier than Expected," *Jane's Missiles and Rockets,* February 1, 2006.

40. Lyubov Provina, "Russian Arms Sale to Iran Draws Scrutiny," DefenseNews.com, December 12, 2005; David, "Iran Launches New Surface to Air Missile Production."

41. For full details, see http://www.globalsecurity.org/military/world/china/qw-1.htm.

42. Reuters, January 5, 1997, 7:00:32 PST; http://www.globalsecurity.org/military/world/russia/s-300pmu2.htm; http://www.globalsecurity.org/military/world/russia/s-300pmu.htm.

43. http://www.globalsecurity.org/military/world/russia/s-300v.htm.

44. Global Security summarizes the capabilities of the two systems as follows:

S-300V / SA-12A GLADIATOR, SA-12B GIANT, HQ-18

The S-300V (SA-12) low-to-high Altitude, tactical surface to air missile system also has anti-ballistic missile capabilities. The HQ-18 is reportedly the designation of a Chinese copy of the Russian S300V, though the details of this program remain rather conjectural. In early 1996 Russia astounded the United States Army by marketing the Russian SA-12 surface-to-air missile system in the UAE in direct competition with the United States Army's Patriot system. Rosvooruzheniye offered the UAE the highest-quality Russian strategic air defense system, the SA-12 Gladiator, as an alternative to the Patriot at half the cost. The offer also included forgiveness of some of Russia's debt to the UAE.

The S-300V consists of:

- 9M82 SA-12b GIANT missile
- 9M83 SA-12a GLADIATOR missile
- 9A82 SA-12b GIANT TELAR
- 9A93 SA-12a GLADIATOR TELAR
- 9A84 GIANT Launcher/Loader Vehicle (LLV)
- 9A85 GLADIATOR Launcher/Loader Vehicle (LLV)
- 9S15 BILL BOARD Surveillance Radar system
- 9S19 HIGH SCREEN Sector Radar system
- 9S32 GRILL PAN Guidance Radar system
- 9S457 Command Station

The 9M83 SA-12a GLADIATOR is a dual-role anti-missile and anti-aircraft missile with a maximum range between 75 and 90 km.

The 9M82 SA-12b GIANT missile, configured primarily for the ATBM role, is a longer range system [maximum range between 100 and 200 km] with a longer fuselage with larger solid-fuel motor.

The 9A82 SA-12b GIANT and 9A93 SA-12a GLADIATOR TELAR vehicles are similar, though the 9A83-1 carries four 9M83 SA-12a GLADIATOR missiles, whereas the 9A82 carries only two 9M82 SA-12b GIANT missiles. The configuration of the vehicles command radar is also different. On the 9A83-1 the radar is mounted on a folding mast providing 360° coverage in azimuth and full hemispheric coverage in elevation.

The radar on the 9M82 TELAR is mounted in a semi-fixed position over the cab, providing 90º coverage on either side in azimuth and 110º in elevation. The TELARs are not capable of autonomous engagements, requiring the support of the GRILL PAN radar.

The 9S457-1 Command Post Vehicle is the command and control vehicle for the SA-12 system, which is supported by the BILL BOARD A surveillance radar and the HIGH SCREEN sector radar. The CPV and its associated radars can detect up to 200 targets, track as many as 70 targets and designate 24 of the targets to the brigade's four GRILL PAN radar systems for engagement by the SA-12a and SA-12b TELARs.

The LLVs (9A85 GLADIATOR and 9A83 GLADIATOR) resemble normal TELARs, but with a loading crane rather than command radars. While the primary role of the LLV is to replenish the TELARs, they can also erecting and launch missiles if needed, though they are dependent on the use of command radars from neighboring TELARs.http://www.globalsecurity.org/military/world/russia/s-300v.htm.

45. http://www.globalsecurity.org/military/world/russia/s-400.htm.

46. "No S-300 Deal with Iran, Says Russian Defense Minister," *Jane's Missiles and Rockets,* March 1, 2006.

CHAPTER 7

1. "Iran," *Jane's,* October 29, 2001.

2. Abbas Bakhtiar, "U.S. vs. Iran (II). Hybrid War," http://www.payvand.com/news/06/sep/Scenarios-of-War.pdf, January 27, 2007.

3. *Jane's Fighting Ships, 2005–2006* (London: Jane's Information Group), pp. 336–343.

4. http://www.globalsecurity.org/military/world/iran/navy.htm.

5. *Jane's Fighting Ships, 2002–2003,* (London: Jane's Information Group), pp. 336–343.

6. Only two torpedo tubes can fire wire guided torpedoes, *Defense News,* January 17, 1994, pp. 1, 29.

7. Ali Akbar Dareini, "Iran Tests Submarine-to-Surface missile," *Washington Post,* August 27, 2006.

8. Agence France-Presse, "Iran Launches Production of First Locally-Built Submarine," May 11, 2005.

9. BBC News, "Iran Launches Its First Submarine," August 29, 2000.

10. *Jane's Fighting Ships, 2002–2003,* pp. 336–343.

11. See David Miller, "Submarines in the Gulf," *Military Technology,* 6/93, pp. 42–45; David Markov, "More Details Surface of Rubin's 'Kilo' Plans," *Jane's Intelligence Review,* May 1997, pp. 209–215.

12. http://www.globalsecurity.org/military/world/iran/navy.htm.

13. Lowell E. Jacoby, Current and Projected National Security Threats to the United States, Statement For the Record, Senate Armed Services Committee, March 17, 2005.

14. Bakhtiar, "U.S. vs. Iran (II). Hybrid War."

15. "Administration, Iran," *Jane's Fighting Ships,* February 19, 2007.

16. Any classification of Iran's missile arsenal evades order and clarity. Most reports about Iran's missiles express uncertainty about parts of Iran's program, and many reports contradict each other, at least partly, either deliberately or not. The following sheds some light into Iranian antiship missile capabilities, but cannot be seen as more than an rough indication:

Iranian designation	Designation in country of origin
Fajr-e-Darya	FL-6 *(Chinese)*
Kosar	FL-8 *(Chinese)*
Nasr	FL-9 *(Chinese)*
Tondar	C-802 *(Chinese)*
Noor	HY-2 *(Chinese)*
Raad	HY-2/C-802

17. Robert Hewson, "Dragon's Teeth—Chinese Missiles Raise Their Game," *Jane's Navy International,* January 1, 2007.

18. Uzi Rubin, *The Global Reach of Iran's Ballistic Missiles* (Tel Aviv: Institute for National Security Studies, November 2006), p. 7.

19. *World Missiles Briefing,* Teal Group Corporation.

20. Global Security, "C-802," http://www.globalsecurity.org/military/world/china/c-802.htm.

21. Hewson, "Dragon's Teeth."

22. *Jane's Defence Weekly,* June 25, 1997, p. 3; Associated Press, June 17, 1997, 1751; United Press, June 17, 1997, 0428; *International Defense Review,* 6/1996, p. 17.

23. Hewson, "Dragon's Teeth."

24. Robert Hewson, "Iran Stages Large-Scale Exercises to Underline Defense Capabilities," *Jane's Defense Week,* September 15, 206, p. 5; Ali Akbar Dareini, "Iran Test-Fires Sub-to-Surface Missile in Persian Gulf," *Philadelphia Inquirer,* August 28, 2006.

25. http://www.fas.org/man/dod-101/sys/missile/row/c-801.htm.

26. Jane's Fighting Ships, Administration, Iran, February 19, 2007.

27. "China Cat (C 14) class (PTGF)," *Jane's Fighting Ships,* February 19, 2007.

28. "Wellington (BH.7) class (HOVERCRAFT) (UCAC)," *Jane's Fighting Ships,* February 19, 2007.

29. "Iran Class (HOVERCRAFT) (UCAC)," *Jane's Fighting Ships,* February 9, 2007.

30. "Introduction," *Jane's Fighting Ships,* February 19, 2007.

31. *Washington Times,* March 27, 1996, p. A-1.

32. *Defense News,* January 17, 1994, pp. 1, 29.

33. "P-3F Orion," *Jane's Fighting Ships,* January 9, 2007.

34. "Sikorsky RH/MH 53D Sea Stallion," *Jane's Fighting Ships,* January 9, 2007; "Agusta AB 204 ASW/212," *Jane's Fighting Ships,* January 9, 2006.

35. In addition to the sources listed at the start of this section, these assessments are based on various interviews, various editions of the IISS *Military Balance;* the *Jaffee Center Middle East Military Balance, Jane's Sentinel: The Gulf States,* "Iran;" and *Jane's Defence Weekly,* July 11, 1987, p. 15.

36. Some sources report they are operated by the Iranian Navy.

37. See Global Security, http://www.globalsecurity.org/military/world/china/c-201.htm.

38. Nadim Hasbani, "The Geopolitics of Weapons Procurement in the Gulf States," *Defense & Security Analysis* 22, no. 1, 84.

39. A. Kozhikov and D. Kaliyeva, "The Military Political Situation in the Caspian Region," Central Asia's Affairs, No. 3.

40. Ibid.

41. "Iran Port Bustles in Shadow of War," *Washington Times,* March 14, 2007, p. 17.

42. *Aftab-e-Yazd,* January 25, 2005 edition.

43. "Iran Port Bustles in Shadow of War," *Washington Times,* March 14, 2007, p. 17.

CHAPTER 8

1. U.S. Department of States, "Iran," *Country Reports on Human Rights Practices,* 2005, http://www.state.gov/g/drl/rls/hrrpt/2005/61688.htm.

2. "The Gulf States: Armed Forces, Iran," *Jane's Sentinel Security Assessment,* October 21, 2005.

3. Alex Vatanka and Fatemeh Aman, "The Making of an Insurgency in Iran's Baluchistan Province," *Jane's Intelligence Review,* June 1, 2006.

4. "The Gulf States: Armed Forces, Iran," *Jane's Sentinel Security Assessment.*

5. Daniel Byman, Shahram Chubin, Anoushiravan Ehteshami, and Jerrold D. Green, *Iran's Security Policy in the Post-Revolutionary Era* (Washington, DC: RAND, 2006), p. 32.

6. Ibid.

7. Globalsecurity.org, *[MOIS] Vezarat-e Ettela'at va Amniat-e Keshvar VEVAK,* http://www.globalsecurity.org/intell/world/iran/vevak.htm.

8. Globalsecurity.org, *Ministry of Intelligence and Security,* http://www.globalsecurity.org/intell/world/iran/vevak.htm.

9. "The Gulf States: Armed Forces, Iran," *Jane's Sentinel Security Assessment.*

10. Globalsecurity.org, *Qods (Jerusalem) Force Iranian Revolutionary Guard Corps (IRGC—Pasdaran-e Inqilab),* http://www.globalsecurity.org/intell/world/iran/qods.htm.

11. "The Gulf States: Armed Forces, Iran," *Jane's Sentinel Security Assessment.*

12. BBC Monitoring Middle East, Iran's Guard commander comments on Tehran's missile power, November 13, 2006.

13. "The Gulf States: Armed Forces, Iran," *Jane's Sentinel Security Assessment.*

14. BBC Monitoring Middle East, Iran's Guard commander comments.

15. Globalsecurity.org, *Niruyeh Moghavemat Basij Mobilisation Resistance Force,* http://www.globalsecurity.org/intell/world/iran/basij.htm.

16. Byman et al., *Iran's Security Policy in the Post-Revolutionary Era,* p. 39.

17. Globalsecurity.org, Qods (Jerusalem) Force.

18. Congressional Research Service, *Country Profile: Iran,* March 2006.

19. Globalsecurity.org, *Ansar-i Hizbullah Followers of the Party of God,* http://www.globalsecurity.org/intell/world/iran/ansar.htm.

CHAPTER 9

1. Stephen Kaufman, "Bush Says Iranian Group Certainly Providing Weapons in Iraq, February 14, 2007, http://usinfo.state.gov/xarchives/display.html?p=washfile-english&y=2007&m=February&x=20070214171942esnamfuak0.7028467.

2. BBC Monitoring Middle East, Iran's Guard commander comments on Tehran's missile power, November 13, 2006.

3. "Iran Enhances Existing Weaponry by Optimizing Shahab-3 Ballistic Missile," *Jane's Missiles and Rockets,* January 20, 2004.

4. "Iran Has Built Underground Missile Factories," *Jane's Missiles and Rockets,* December 8, 2005.

5. Federation of American Scientists, *Iran,* http://www.fas.org/nuke/guide/iran/missile/overview.html, March 5, 2007.

6. Uzi Rubin, *The Global Reach of Iran's Ballistic Missiles* (Tel Aviv: Institute for National Security Studies, November 2006), pp. 21–22.

7. Kenneth Katzman, Congressional Research Service.

8. Rubin, *The Global Reach of Iran's Ballistic Missiles,* p. 7.

9. Rubin, *The Global Reach of Iran's Ballistic Missiles.*

10. "Iran: Missiles" GlobalSecurity.org, http://www.globalsecurity.org/wmd/world/iran/missile.htm; Federation of American Scientists, *Iran.*

11. Robin Hughes, "Long-Range Ambitions," *Jane's Defence Weekly,* September 13, 2006, pp. 22–27.

12. "SCUD-B/Shahab-1," Federation of American Scientists, December 1, 2005, http://www.fas.org/nuke/guide/iran/missile/shahab-1.htm.

13. Kenneth Katzman, *Commission to Assess the Ballistic Missile Threat to the United States,* 1998, http://www.globalsecurity.org/wmd/library/report/1998/rumsfeld/pt2_katz.htm.

14. Robin Hughes, "Iran's Ballistic Missile Developments—Long-Range Ambitions," *Jane's Defence Weekly,* September 13, 2006.

15. Katzman, *Commission to Assess the Ballistic Missile Threat to the United States.*

16. Hughes, "Iran's Ballistic Missile Developments."

17. Katzman, *Commission to Assess the Ballistic Missile Threat to the United States;* Hughes, "Iran's Ballistic Missile Developments."

18. Katzman, *Commission to Assess the Ballistic Missile Threat to the United States.*

19. Ibid.

20. Paul Beaver, "Iran's Shahab-3 IRBM 'Ready for Production,'" *Jane's Missiles and Rockets,* June 1, 1998.

21. Hughes, "Long-Range Ambitions," pp. 22–27.

22. ISS, *The Military Balance 2005–2006.*

23. "Shahab-2," Federation of American Scientists, December 1, 2005, http://www.fas.org/nuke/guide/iran/missile/shahab-2.htm.

24. "Iran: Missiles," GlobalSecurity.org.

25. Katzman, *Commission to Assess the Ballistic Missile Threat to the United States.*

26. Ibid.

27. Rubin, *The Global Reach of Iran's Ballistic Missiles,* p. 37.

28. "Flashpoints: Iran," *Jane's Defence Weekly,* March 4, 1995, p. 18.

29. "Iran Says Shahab-3 Missile Entirely Iranian, Production Ongoing," *Agence France-Presse,* May 5, 2005.

30. Katzman, *Commission to Assess the Ballistic Missile Threat to the United States.*

31. Ibid.

32. "Iran Tests Shahab-3 Ballistic Missile," *Jane's Missiles and Rockets,* August 1, 1998.

33. "Shahab 3/Zelzal 3," Global Security.org, www.globalsecurity.org/wmd/world/iran/shahab-3.htm.

34. David Isby, "Shahab-3 Enters Production," *Jane's Missiles and Rockets,* November 26, 2001.

35. Ed Blanche, "Shahab-3 Ready for Service, Says Iran," *Jane's Missiles and Rockets,* July 23, 2003.

36. Rubin, *The Global Reach of Iran's Ballistic Missiles,* p. 24.

37. Federation of American Scientists, *Iran.*

38. "Shahab-3/Zelzal 3," GlobalSecurity.org.

39. Hughes, "Long-Range Ambitions," *Jane's Defence Weekly,* pp. 22–27.

40. Farhad Pouladi, "Iran Vows to Continue Nuclear Drive at All Costs," *Agence France-Presse,* September 22, 2004.

41. "Iran 'Tests New Missile Engine,'" *BBC News,* May 31, 2005, http://news.bbc.co.uk/2/hi/middle_east/4596295.stm.

42. Hughes, "Long-Range Ambitions," pp. 22–27.

43. BBC Monitoring Middle East, Iran's Guard commander comments on Tehran's missile power; Ed Blanche, "Iran Stages Display of Missile Firepower," *Jane's Missiles and Rockets,* January 1, 2007.

44. Dr. Robert H. Schmucker, "Iran and Its Regional Environment," Schmucker Technologies, Pease Research Institute Frankfurt, March 27, 2006, www.hsfk.de and http://www.hsfk.de/static.php?id=3929&language=de.

45. Hughes, "Iran's Ballistic Missile Developments."

46. Ed Blanche and Doug Richardson, "Iran Gives Details of Latest Shahab 3 Missile," *Jane's Missiles and Rockets,* February 1, 2007.

47. For further details on the history and nature of the Shahab and Iran's programs, see Andrew Feickert, Missile Survey: Ballistic and Cruise Missiles of Selected Foreign Countries, Congressional Research Service, RL30427 (regularly updated); the work of Kenneth Katzman, also of the Congressional Research Service; the "Missile Overview" section of the Iran Profile of the NTI (http://www.nti.org/e_research/profiles/Iran/Missiles/); and the work of Global Security, including http://www.globalsecurity.org/wmd/world/iran/shahab-3.htm.

48. Ed Blanche, "Iran Claims Shahab-3 Range Now 2,000km," *Jane's Missiles and Rockets,* November 1, 2004.

49. "Iran Boasts Shahab-3 is in Mass Production," *Jane's Missiles and Rockets,* November 19, 2004.

50. "Iran Threatens to Abandon the NPT," *Jane's Islamic Affairs Analyst,* September 29, 2004.

51. Douglas Jehl, "Iran Reportedly Hides Work on a Long-Range Missile," *New York Times,* December 2, 2004.

52. "Iran: Missiles Development," GlobalSecurity.org, http://www.globalsecurity.org/wmd/world/iran/missile-development.htm.

53. See the work of Dr. Robert H. Schmucker, "The Shahab Missile and Iran's Delivery System Capabilities," Briefing to the James Shasha Institute conference on a nuclear Iran, May 30–June 2, 2005; and Schmucker, "Iran and Its Regional Environment."

54. IISS, *Iran's Strategic Weapons Programs: A Net Assessment,* IISS Strategic Dossier, 2005, p. 102.

55. Sonni Efron, Tyler Marshall, and Bob Drogin, "Powell's Talk of Arms Has Fallout," *Los Angeles Times,* November 19, 2004.

56. Carla Anne Robbins, "Briefing Iranian Missile to Nuclear Agency," *Wall Street Journal,* July 27, 2005, p. 3.

57. Dafna Linzer, "Strong Leads and Dead Ends In Nuclear Case Against Iran," *Washington Post,* February 8, 2006, p. A01.

58. Hughes, "Iran's Ballistic Missile Developments."

59. Ibid.

60. There is a radical difference in the performance of proven systems, where actual field performance can be measured, and estimates based on engineering theory. With proven

systems, the distribution of the impact of warheads relative to the target tends to be "bivariate normally distributed" relative to the aim point. Most are most reasonably close, and progressively fewer and fewer hit farther away, with only a few missing by long distances.

As an entry in Wikipedia notes, "One component of the bivariate normal will represent range errors and the other azimuth errors. Unless the munition is arriving exactly vertically downwards the standard deviation of range errors is usually larger than the standard deviation of azimuth errors, and the resulting confidence region is elliptical. Generally, the munition will not be exactly on target, i.e. the mean vector will not be (0,0). This is referred to as bias. The mean error squared (MSE) will be the sum of the variance of the range error plus the variance of the azimuth error plus the covariance of the range error with the azimuth error plus the square of the bias. Thus the MSE results from pooling all these sources of error. The square root of the MSE is the circular error probable, commonly abbreviated to CEP. Geometrically, it corresponds to radius of a circle within which 50% of rounds will land."

None of this has proven true, however, of estimates made in the design stage or with very limited tests. The actual hit distribution can be much farther away from the aim point and most or all missiles can fall outside the theoretical CEP.

It should also be noted that the concept of CEP is only strictly meaningful if misses are roughly normally distributed. This is generally not true for precision-guided munitions. As the Wikipedia entry also states, "Generally, if CEP is n meters, 50% of rounds land within n meters of the target, 43% between n and 2n, and 7% between 2n and 3n meters. If misses were exactly normally distributed as in this theory, then the proportion of rounds that land farther than three times the CEP from the target is less than 0.2%. With precision-guided munitions, the number of 'close misses' is higher."

61. "Shahab-3," Federation of American Scientists, December 1, 2005, http://www.fas.org/nuke/guide/iran/missile/shahab-3.htm.

62. See note 33.

63. See the work of Dr. Robert H. Schmucker, "The Shahab Missile and Iran's Delivery System Capabilities"; and Schmucker, "Iran and Its Regional Environment."

64. Blanche and Richardson, "Iran Gives Details of Latest Shahab 3 Missile."

65. "Shahab-3D," Federation of American Scientists, December 1, 2005, http://www.fas.org/nuke/guide/iran/missile/shahab-3d.htm.

66. Doug Richardson, "Iran Is Developing an IRBM, Claims Resistance Group," *Jane's Rockets and Missiles,* January 1, 2005.

67. Hughes, "Long-Range Ambitions," pp. 22–27.

68. Rubin, *The Global Reach of Iran's Ballistic Missiles,* p. 25.

69. "Iran: Missiles" GlobalSecurity.org.

70. "Iran Moves Its Shahab 3 Units," *Jane's Missiles and Rockets,* April 1, 2006.

71. Douglas Jehl, "Iran Is Said to Work on New Missile," *International Herald Tribune,* December 2, 2004, p. 7.

72. "Iran: Missiles Development," GlobalSecurity.org.

73. Stratfor, "Iran: The Potential for a Satellite Launch," January 26, 2007.

74. "Shahab-3D," Federation of American Scientists.

75. "Iran: Missiles Development," GlobalSecurity.org.

76. "Shahab-3D," Federation of American Scientists.

77. Ibid.

78. IISS, *Iran's Strategic Weapons Programs: A Net Assessment,* IISS Strategic Dossier, 2005, p. 102.

79. Hughes, "Long-Range Ambitions," pp. 22–27.

80. Federation of American Scientists, *Iran*.

81. "Shahab-4," Federation of American Scientists, December 1, 2005, http://www.fas.org /nuke/guide/iran/missile/shahab-4.htm.

82. Richardson, "Iran Is Developing an IRBM, Claims Resistance Group."

83. "Shahab-4," Federation of American Scientists.

84. Richardson, "Iran Is Developing an IRBM, Claims Resistance Group."

85. "Western Intelligence Confirms Iranian Missile Developments—German Report," *BBC Monitoring International Report,* February 6, 2006, available through Lexus Nexus.

86. Rubin, *The Global Reach of Iran's Ballistic Missiles,* p. 7.

87. Hughes, "Iran's Ballistic Missile Developments."

88. "Shahab-5," Federation of American Scientists, December 1, 2005, http://www.fas.org /nuke/guide/iran/missile/shahab-5.htm.

89. "Shahab-4," Federation of American Scientists.

90. "Western Intelligence Confirms Iranian Missile Developments—German Report."

91. Rubin, *The Global Reach of Iran's Ballistic Missiles,* p. 39.

92. Federation of American Scientists, *Iran*.

93. Rubin, *The Global Reach of Iran's Ballistic Missiles,* p. 7.

94. Nazila Fathi, "Iran Says It Launched Suborbital Rocket into Space, with Eye toward Lifting Satellites," *New York Times,* February 26, 2007.

95. Stratfor, "Iran: The Potential for a Satellite Launch."

96. Hughes, "Long-Range Ambitions," *Jane's Defence Weekly,* pp. 22–27.

97. Hughes, "Iran's Ballistic Missile Developments."

98. Rubin, *The Global Reach of Iran's Ballistic Missiles,* p. 29.

99. Reportedly, Iran concluded an agreement with North Korea to buy 18 IRBMs (BM-25), which in return are reverse-engineered Russian SS-N-6 SLBMs. Apparently, Iran tested a BM-25 in January 2006; the missile is reported to have flown more than 3,000 km.

100. Richard Fisher, Jr., "China's Alliance with Iran Grows Contrary to U.S. Hopes," http://www.strategycenter.net/research/pubID.109/pub_detail.asp, March 5, 2007.

101. Andrew Koch, "Tehran Altering Ballistic Missile,"*Jane's Defence Weekly,* December 8, 2004.

102. Richardson, "Iran Is Developing an IRBM, Claims Resistance Group."

103. "Iran Tests Shahab-3 Motor," *Jane's Missiles and Rockets,* June 9, 2005.

104. Robin Hughes, "Iranian Resistance Group Alleges Tehran Is Developing New Medium Range Missile," *Jane's Defence Weekly,* March 22, 2006.

105. Schmucker, "Iran and Its Regional Environment"; Hughes, Iran's Ballistic Missile Developments."

106. "KH-55 Granat," Federation of American Scientists, www.fas.org/nuke/guide/russia/ bomber/as-15.htm.

107. Hughes, "Long-Range Ambitions," *Jane's Defence Weekly,* pp. 22–27; http:// www.globalsecurity.org/wmd/world/russia/as-15specs.htm, http://www.globalsecurity.org/ wmd/world/russia/kh-55.htm, and http://www.globalsecurity.org/wmd/world/iran/x-55.htm.

108. "KH-55 Granat," Federation of American Scientists.

109. "Cruise Missile Row Rocks Ukraine," *BBC News,* March 18, 2005, http:// news.bbc.co.uk/2/hi/europe/4361505.stm.

110. Bill Gertz, "Missiles Sold to China and Iran," *Washington Times,* April 6, 2005, http://washingtontimes.com/national/20050405-115803-7960r.htm.

111. Ibid.

112. Paul Kerr, "Ukraine Admits Missile Transfers," Arms Control Association, May 2005, http://www.armscontrol.org/act/2005_05/Ukraine.asp.

113. "Ukraine Investigates Supply of Missiles to China and Iran," *Jane's Missiles and Rockets,* May 1, 2005.

114. "18 Cruise Missiles Were Smuggled to Iran, China" *Associated Press,* March 18, 2005.

115. Hughes, "Iran's Ballistic Missile Developments."

116. Rubin, *The Global Reach of Iran's Ballistic Missiles,* p. 28.

117. Fisher, Jr., "China's Alliance with Iran Grows Contrary to U.S. Hopes."

118. AFX International Focus, *Russian military says Iran 'not capable' of creating intercontinental missiles,* November 2, 2006.

119. NTI, "Iran's Missile Capabilities: Long-Range Artillery Rocket Programs," http://www.nti.org/e_research/profiles/Iran/Missile/3367_3397.html.

120. Aerospace Daily & Defense Report, "Iran Converts Missile into Sat Launch Vehicle," January 29, 2007.

121. Ibid.

CHAPTER 10

1. *Proliferation: Threat and Response,* The Office of Secretary of Defense, 2001, p. 36. http://www.defenselink.mil/pubs/ptr20010110.pdf.

2. CIA, *Unclassified Report: to Congress on the Acquisition of Technology Relating to Weapons of Mass Destruction and Advanced Conventional Munitions,* November 2003, http://www.cia.gov/cia/reports/721_reports/pdfs/721report_july_dec2003.pdf.

3. John R. Bolton, "Iran's Continuing Pursuit of Weapons of Mass Destruction," *Testimony Before the House International Relations Committee Subcommittee on the Middle East and Central Asia,* June 24, 2004, http://www.state.gov/t/us/rm/33909.htm.

4. Quoted in the IISS, *Iran's Strategic Weapons Programs: A Net Assessment,* IISS Strategic Dossier, 2005, p. 67.

5. Merav Zafary, "Iranian Biological and Chemical Weapons Profile Study," *Center for Nonproliferation Studies, Monterey Institute of International Studies,* February 2001.

6. "Iran: Chemical Overview," Nuclear Threat Initiative, Revised in January 2006, http://www.nti.org/e_research/profiles/Iran/Chemical/#fnB15.

7. *Proliferation: Threat and Response,* The Office of Secretary of Defense, 1997, http://www.defenselink.mil/pubs/prolif97/.

8. *Proliferation: Threat and Response,* p. 36.

9. "Iran," *Jane's Sentinel Security Assessment: The Gulf States' Armed Forces,* October 7, 2004.

10. Statement by John A. Lauder, to the Senate Committee on Foreign Relations on Russian Proliferation to Iran's Weapons of Mass Destruction and Missile Programs, October 5, 2000, http://www.cia.gov/cia/public_affairs/speeches/2000/lauder_WMD_100500.html.

11. CIA, "Unclassified Report: to Congress on the Acquisition of Technology Relating to Weapons of Mass Destruction and Advanced Conventional Munitions," July–December 2003, http://www.cia.gov/cia/reports/721_reports/pdfs/721report_july_dec2003.pdf.

12. Bolton, "Iran's Continuing Pursuit of Weapons of Mass Destruction."

13. IISS, *Iran's Strategic Weapons Programs: A Net Assessment,* IISS Strategic Dossier, 2005, pp. 82–83.

CHAPTER 11

1. U.S. Department of State, Statement by Secretary of State Condoleezza Rice, Washington, D.C., May 31, 2006, http://www.state.gov/secretary/rm/2006/67088.htm; U.S. Department of State, Interview on the Doug Wright Radio Show, Salt Lake City, Utah, August 29, 2006, .

2. Department of Public Information, United Nations, "Security Council Demands Iran Suspend Uranium Enrichment by 31 August, or Face Possible Economic, Diplomatic Sanctions," July 31, 2006, http://www.un.org/News/Press/docs/2006/sc8792.doc.htm.

3. Michael Slackman, "Iran Defiant on Nuclear Program as Deadline Approaches," *New York Times,* August 22, 2006.

4. Glenn Kessler and Dafna Linzer, "Brief Nuclear Halt May Lead to Talks with Iran," *Washington Post,* September 12, 2006.

5. Daniel Dombey, "FT-Interview: Mohamed El-Baradei," *Financial Times,* February 19, 2007.

6. Agence France-Presse (AFP), Tehran, April 5, 2007.

7. John Rood, Prepared Statement of the Honorable John C. Rood, Assistant Secretary, Bureau of International Security and Nonproliferation, U.S. Department of State, at the Joint Hearing Before the Subcommittee on Europe and the Subcommittee on Terrorism, Nonproliferation, and Trade of the Committee on Foreign Affairs, House of Representatives, May 3, 2007.

8. David E. Sanger, "Atomic Agency Concludes Iran Is Stepping Up Nuclear Work," *New York Times,* May 14, 2007; [423] David E. Sanger, "Inspectors Cite Big Gain by Iran on Nuclear Fuel," *New York Times,* May 14, 2007.

9. Earlier unclassified CIA reports on problems like the ballistic missile threat often projected alternative levels of current and future capability. The qualifications and possible futures are far less well defined in more recent reports. For example, see CIA, "Unclassified Summary of a National Intelligence Estimate, Foreign Missile Developments and the Ballistic Missile Threat through 2015," National Intelligence Council, December 2001, http://www.cia.gov/nic/pubs/other_products/Unclassifiedballisticmissilefinal.htm.

10. There is no way to determine just how much the Special Plans Office team set up within the office of the Secretary of Defense to analyze the threat in Iraq was designed to produce a given conclusion or politicized intelligence. The Department has denied this and stated that the team created within its policy office was not working Iraqi per se, but on global terrorist interconnections. It also stated that the Special Plans Office was never tied to the Intelligence Collection Program—a program to debrief Iraqi defectors—and relied on CIA inputs for its analysis. It states that it simply conducted a review, presented its findings in August 2002, and its members returned to other duties. See Jim Garamone, "Policy Chief Seeks to Clear Intelligence Record," American Forces Information Service, June 3, 2003; and Briefing on Policy and Intelligence Matters, Douglas J. Feith, Under Secretary of Defense for Policy, and William J. Luti, Deputy Under Secretary of Defense for Special Plans and Near East and South Asian Affairs, June 4, 2003, http://www.defenselink.mil/transcripts/2003/tr20030604-0248.html.

Some intelligence experts dispute this view, however, and claim the team's effort was used to put press on the intelligence community. Such "B teams" also have a mixed history. They did help identify an intelligence community tendency to underestimate Soviet strategic nuclear efforts during the Cold War. The threat analysis of missile threats posed to the United States by the "Rumsfeld Commission," however, was a heavily one-sided assessment designed to justify national missile defense. Also see Greg Miller, "Pentagon Defends Role of Intelligence Unit on Iraq," *Los Angeles Times,* June 5, 2003; and David S. Cloud, "The Case for War Relied on Selective Intelligence," *Wall Street Journal,* June 5, 2003.

11. Some press sources cite what they claim is a deliberate effort to ignore a September 2002 DIA report on Iraqi chemical weapons capabilities called "Iraq—Key WMD Facilities—An Operational Support Study." See James Risen, "Word that n be a weapon; by consistently finding an alternative explanation for all its actions, including concealment and actions that are limited violations of heres. (15 page document in fact, the unclassified excerpts from the DIA report, show that DIA was not stating that Iraq did not have chemical weapons, but rather that it had no reliable information on whether Iraq is producing and stockpiling chemical weapons, or where Iraq has—or will—establish its chemical weapons facilities." The report went on to say that, "although we lack any direct information, Iraq probably possess CW agent in chemical munitions, possibly include artillery rockets, artillery shells, aerial bombs, and ballistic missile warheads. Baghdad also probably possess bulk chemical stockpiles, primarily containing precursors, but that also could consist of some mustard agent of stabilized VX."

If anything, the report is a classic example of what happens when intelligence reports do state uncertainty and of how the user misreads or misuses the result.

12. Alireza Jafarzadeh, "Iranian Regime's Plan and Attempts to Start Uranium Enrichment at Natanz Site," Statement at the National Press Club, Washington, D.C., January 10, 2006.

13. "Iran Says It Will Resume Uranium Conversion Today," *Global Security Newswire,* August 11, 2005, http://www.nti.org/d_newswire/issues/2005/8/1/6860ebe5-d0a1-428e-829d-6005c7b26698.html.

14. Dafna Linzer, "Powell Says Iran Is Pursuing Bomb," *Washington Post,* November 18, 2004, p. A01.

15. "UN Atomic Agency Seeks to Visit Key Iranian Defense Site: Diplomats," *Agence France-Presse,* September 10, 2004.

16. Dafna Linzer, "Nuclear Disclosure on Iran Unverified," *Washington Post,* November 19, 2004, p. A01.

17. Linzer, "Powell Says Iran Is Pursuing Bomb," p. A01.

18. Linzer, "Nuclear Disclosure on Iran Unverified," *Washington Post,* p. A01.

19. Sonni Efron, Tyler Marshall, and Bob Drogin, "Powell's Talk of Arms Has Fallout," *Los Angeles Times,* November 19, 2004.

20. Carla Anne Robbins, "As Evidence Grows of Iran's Program, U.S. Hits Quandary," *Wall Street Journal,* March 18, 2005, p. 1.

21. IAEA, "Implementation of the NPT Safeguards Agreement in the Islamic Republic of Iran: Report by the Director General," November 15, 2004, p. 18, http://www.iaea.org/Publications/Documents/Board/2004/gov2004-83_derestrict.pdf.

22. John R. Bolton, "Preventing Iran from Acquiring Nuclear Weapons," Remarks to the Hudson Institute, Washington, D.C., August 17, 2004.

23. Dafna Linzer, "Strong Leads and Dead Ends in Nuclear Case against Iran," *Washington Post,* February 8, 2006, p. A01.

24. Rowan Scarborough, "U.S. Military Sees Iran's Nuke Bomb 5 Years Away," *Washington Post,* 31 August 2006.

25. Sanger, "Atomic Agency Concludes Iran Is Stepping Up Nuclear Work"; [440] Sanger, "Inspectors Cite Big Gain by Iran on Nuclear Fuel."

26. Donna Abu Nasr, "UN Nuke Chief: Iran's Program Limited," *Washington Post,* April 12, 2007; Dafna Linzer, "Boost In Iran's Capacity to Enrich Uranium Noted," *Washington*

Post, April 19, 2007, p. 23; ISIS, "IAEA Letter to Iran's Representative," April 18, 2007, 5:38:23,
isis@isis-online.org.

27. Frank Barnaby, "World Air Strikes Work?" Oxford Research Group, March 2007, p. 7.

28. Bolton, "Preventing Iran from Acquiring Nuclear Weapons."

29. Paul Kerr, "Russia, Iran Sign Deal to Fuel Bushehr Reactor," *Arms Control Today,* November 2006, http://www.armscontrol.org/act/2006_11/RussiaIran.asp.

30. Bolton, "Preventing Iran from Acquiring Nuclear Weapons."

31. IAEA, "Implementation of the NPT Safeguards Agreement in the Islamic Republic of Iran: Report by the Director General," September 2, 2005, Annex 1, p. 14, http://www.iaea.org/Publications/Documents/Board/2005/gov2005-67.pdf.

32. John R. Bolton, "Nuclear Weapons and Rogue States: Challenge and Response," Remarks to the Conference of the Institute for Foreign Policy Analysis and the Fletcher School's International Security Studies Program Washington, D.C., December 2, 2003.

33. IAEA, "Implementation of the NPT Safeguards Agreement in the Islamic Republic of Iran: Report by the Director General," November 15, 2007, http://www.fas.org/nuke/guide/iran/iaea1104.pdf.

34. IAEA, "Implementation of the NPT Safeguards Agreement in the Islamic Republic of Iran: Report by the Director General," p. 7.

35. Barnaby, "World Air Strikes Work?" p. 7.

36. "Iran Far from Nuclear Bomb-Making Capacity: Ex-UN Weapons Chief Blix," *Agence France-Presse,* June 23, 2005.

37. Barnaby, "World Air Strikes Work?" p. 8.

38. Ali Akbar, "Iran Hits Milestone in Nuclear Technology," *Associated Press,* April 11, 2006.

39. Revati Prasad and Jill Marie Parillo, "Iran's Programs to Produce Plutonium and Enrichment Uranium," *Carnegie Fact Sheet,* February 2006.

40. Ali Akbar Dareini, "Iran to Move to Large Scale Enrichment," *Associated Press,* April 12, 2006.

41. "Iran Says to Go Ahead with Fuel Work," *Reuters,* August 27, 2006.

42. Prasad and Parillo, "Iran's Programs to Produce Plutonium and Enrichment Uranium."

43. Nazila Fathi and Christine Hauser, "Iran Marks Step in Nuclear Development," *New York Times,* April 11, 2006.

44. Prasad and Parillo, "Iran's Programs to Produce Plutonium and Enriched Uranium."

45. IAEA, "Implementation of the NPT Safeguards Agreement in the Islamic Republic of Iran: Report by the Director General," November 15, 2004.

46. Bolton, "Preventing Iran from Acquiring Nuclear Weapons."

47. IAEA, "Implementation of the NPT Safeguards Agreement in the Islamic Republic of Iran: Report by the Director General," September 2, 2005.

48. Ibid.

49. Prasad and Parillo, "Iran's Programs to Produce Plutonium and Enrichment Uranium."

50. IAEA, "Implementation of the NPT Safeguards Agreement in the Islamic Republic of Iran: Report by the Director General," September 2, 2005.

51. David Albright and Corey Hinderstein, "Iran's Next Steps: Final Tests and the Construction of a Uranium Enrichment Plant," Institute for Science and International Security, Issue Brief, January 12, 2006, http://www.isis-online.org/publications/iran/irancascade.pdf.

52. Prasad and Parillo, "Iran's Programs to Produce Plutonium and Enrichment Uranium."

53. IAEA, "Implementation of the NPT Safeguards Agreement and Relevant Provisions of Security Council Resolutions [1696 (2006), 1737 (2006), and 1747 (2007)] in the Islamic, Republic of Iran," Report by the Director General (Gov/2007/8), February 22, 2007.

54. David Albright and Jacqueline Shire, "Latest IAEA Report on Iran: Continued Progress on Cascade Operations, No New Cooperation with IAEA," Institute for Science and International Security, November 14, 2006.

55. David Albright, "Iran's Nuclear Program: Status and Uncertainties," Prepared testimony by David Albright, President, Institute for Science and International Security (ISIS), before the House Committee on Foreign Affairs, Subcommittee on Terrorism, Nonproliferation, and Trade, Subcommittee on the Middle East and Asia, March 15, 2007, p. 4.

56. Jacqueline Shire and David Albright, "Iran's Centrifuges: How Well Are They Working?" Institute for Science and International Security, March 15, 2007.

57. Barbara Slavin, "Iran Claims Nuclear Advance," *USA Today,* April 10, 2007, p. 1; Abu Nasr, "UN Nuke Chief"; Linzer, "Boost In Iran's Capacity to Enrich Uranium Noted," p. 23; ISIS, "IAEA Letter to Iran's Representative"; IAEA, "Communication Dated 18 April 2007 from the Secretariat to the Resident Representative of the Islamic Republic of Iran," IAEA GOV/Inf/2007/10, April 18, 2007.

58. AFP, "Iran Starts Enrichment at Natanz Site: IAEA," April 19, 2007.

59. AFP, "Iran Needs Several Years to Produce Nuclear Fuel: Official," April 20, 2007.

60. AFP, "Iran Installing 3,000 Centrifuges at Natanz—Official," May 17, 2007.

61. Dr. Frank Barnaby, "Iran's Nuclear Activities," Oxford Research Group, February 2006.

62. IAEA, "Implementation of the NPT Safeguards Agreement in the Islamic Republic of Iran: Report by the Director General," September 1, 2004, Annex, p. 7, http://www.iaea.org/Publications/Documents/Board/2004/gov2004-60.pdf.

63. IAEA, "Implementation of the NPT Safeguards Agreement with the Islamic Republic of Iran, Report by the Director General, September 1, 2004, http://www.iaea.org/Publications/Documents/Board/2004/gov2004-60.pdf.

64. IAEA, "Implementation of the NPT Safeguards Agreement in the Islamic Republic of Iran: Report by the Director General," September 1, 2004, Annex, p. 7, http://www.iaea.org/Publications/Documents/Board/2004/gov2004-60.pdf.

65. Ibid.

66. IAEA, "Implementation of the NPT Safeguards Agreement in the Islamic Republic of Iran: Report by the Director General," September 1, 2004, p. 7.

67. Barnaby, "Iran's Nuclear Activities."

68. Ali Akbar, "Iran Confirms Uranium-to-Gas Conversion," *Associated Press,* May 9, 2005.

69. Elaine Sciolino and William J. Broad, "Atomic Agency Sees Possible Link of Military to Iran Nuclear Work," *New York Times,* February 1, 2006, p. 1.

70. Linzer, "Strong Leads and Dead Ends in Nuclear Case Against Iran," p. A01.

71. IAEA, "Implementation of the NPT Safeguards Agreement in the Islamic Republic of Iran: Resolution adopted on 4 February 2006," February 4, 2006, http://www.iaea.org/Publications/Documents/Board/2006/gov2006-14.pdf.

72. IAEA, "Implementation of the NPT Safeguards Agreement in the Islamic Republic of Iran: Report by the Director General," November 18, 2005, p. 11, http://www.iaea.org/Publications/Documents/Board/2005/gov2005-87.pdf.

73. Ian Traynor, "Papers Found in Iran Are Evidence of Plans for Nuclear Weapon Manufacture, Says UK," *The Guardian,* November 25, 2005, http://www.guardian.co.uk/iran/story/0,,1650423,00.html.

74. "Iran Hands over Suspected Atom Bomb Blueprint: IAEA," *Agence France-Presse,* November 18, 2005.

75. David Albright and Corey Hinderstein, "The Clock Is Ticking, But How Fast?" Institute for Science and International Security, Issue Brief, March 27, 2006, http://www.isis-online.org/publications/iran/clockticking.pdf.

76. "Iran Hands over Suspected Atom Bomb Blueprint: IAEA."

77. "Iran Far From Nuclear Bomb-Making Capacity."

78. Kelly Hearn, "Iranian Pact with Venezuela Stokes Fears of Uranium Sales," *Washington Times,* March 13, 2006, p. 1.

79. Drawn from quotes assembled by Y. Mansharof of MEMRI, *Inquiry and Analysis—Iran,* No. 342, www.themeriblog.org.

80. IRNA, Kayhan, April 10, 2007.

81. IRNA, (Iran) April 10, 2007.

82. IRNA (Iran) and Kayhan, April 10, 2007.

83. Sciolino and Broad, "Atomic Agency Sees Possible Link of Military to Iran Nuclear Work," p. 1.

84. Linzer, "Powell Says Iran Is Pursuing Bomb," p. A01.

85. Linzer, "Strong Leads and Dead Ends in Nuclear Case Aagainst Iran," p. A01.

86. Ibid.

87. IAEA, "Implementation of the NPT Safeguards Agreement in the Islamic Republic of Iran: Resolution adopted on 4 February 2006," February 4, 2006.

88. Linzer, "Strong Leads and Dead Ends in Nuclear Case against Iran," p. A01.

CHAPTER 12

1. Rubin, *The Global Reach of Iran's Ballistic Missiles* (Tel Aviv: Institute for National Security Studies, November 2006), p. 1.

2. Gordon Lubold, "DoD Refutes Report of Navy Plans for War with Iran," *ArmyTimes.com,* September 19, 2006.

3. Michael Hirsh and Maziar Bahari, "Hidden Wars with Iran," *Newsweek,* February 19, 2007.

4. Arthur Herman, "How to Fight Iran," *New York Post,* January 26, 2007.

5. Robin Wright and Peter Baker, "Iraq, Jordan See Threat To Election From Iran," *Washington Post,* December 8, 2004, http://www.washingtonpost.com/wp-dyn/articles/A43980-2004Dec7.html.

6. Ibid.

7. *MEHR News,* "Remarks of Jordanian King an Insult on Iraqi Nation: Iran," December 11, 2004, http://www.mehrnews.ir/en/NewsDetail.aspx?NewsID=137699.

8. Ellen Knickmeyer and Omar Fekeiki, "Iraqi Shi'ite Cleric Pledges to Defend Iran," *Washington Post,* January 24, 2006, p. A13.

9. Richard Beeston, "Two Years on, Iran Is the Only Clear Winner of War on Saddam," *London Times,* September 23, 2005.

10. ABCTV News Baghdad Email, September 20, 2005.

11. Robin Hughes, "Rumsfeld Alleges IRGC Al Qods Infiltrating Iraq," *Jane's Defence Weekly,* March 15, 2006.

12. Nawaf Obaid, "Meeting the Challenge of a Fragmented Iraq: A Saudi Perspective," CSIS, April 6, 2006, http://www.csis.org/media/csis/pubs/060406_iraqsaudi.pdf.

13. Matthew Levitt, *Statement before the U.S. House of Representatives, Committee on International Relations, Joint Hearing before the Subcommittee on the Middle East and Central Asia and the Subcommittee on International Terrorism and Nonproliferation of the Committee on International Relations House of Representatives 109th Congress,* 1st Session, February 16, 2005, wwwa.house.gov/international_relations/109/98810.PDF, 15.

14. Mark Mazetti, "Some in G.O.P. Say Iran Is Played Down, *New York Times,* August 24, 2006.

15. Bhushann Bahree and Marc Champion, "In Iran Nuclear Standoff, Scant Leverage for West," *Wall Street Journal,* August 21, 2006.

16. CIA, *The World Fact Book,* "Iran," 2007, https://www.cia.gov/cia/publications/factbook/geos/ir.html.

17. IEA, *World Energy Outlook 2005, Middle East and North Africa Insights,* OECD/IEA, Paris, 2005, p. 361.

18. The EIA reports that Iran has a combined capacity of 1.64 MMBD according to *Oil & Gas Journal.* Major refineries include Abadan (400,000-bbl/d capacity), Isfahan (265,000 bbl/d), Bandar Abbas (232,000 bbl/d), Tehran (225,000 bbl/d), Arak (150,000 bbl/d), and Tabriz (112,000 bbl/d). Gasoline demand is forcast to be growing at around 11.4 percent per year. Iran plans to increase its refining capacity to 2.54 million bbl/d by 2010. One goal of this expansion is to allow Iran's refineries to process a heavier crude slate, while decreasing the fuel oil cut. Currently, Iran's refineries produce around 30 percent heavy fuel oil and just 16 percent gasoline. In addition, diesel sulfur levels are slated for a major reduction from 500 parts per million (ppm) to 50 ppm by 2010, requiring significant additional hydrotreating capacity.

The National Iranian Oil Refining and Distribution Company (NIORDC) plans to begin construction work as early as September 2006 on three units aimed at increasing gasoline production from the Isfahan refinery. Currently, technical proposals are being reviewed for the construction of three units: a 32,000 bbl/d continuous catalytic reformer (CCR) unit, a 27,000 bbl/d isomerization unit, and a 62,000 bbl/d hydrotreater. Construction is expected to cost $300 million. NIORDC is negotiating with bidders to reduce construction time from 36 months to 30 months.

In June 2004, Japan's JGC reached an agreement with Iran to expand Arak to 250,000 bbl/d by 2009. In addition, in 2005 it was announced that a new 180,000-bbl/d-capacity refinery is being planned for Abadan. Bandar Abbas is being expanded in several phases and is on schedule to meet goals of adding around 250,000 bbl/d of capacity by 2010. Two planned grassroots refineries include a 225,000-bbl/d plant at Shah Bahar and a 120,000-bbl/d unit on Qeshm Island. Under Iranian law, foreign companies are permitted to own no more than 49 percent of Iranian oil refining assets.

Iran plans to boost capacity at its northern refineries at Arak, Tebriz, and Tehran in order to process additional Caspian oil. In August 2003, a $500 million tender was issued to upgrade the Tehran and Tabriz refineries in order to handle 370,000 bbl/d of high sulfur Caspian crude. This follows a $330 million project, completed by a Sinopec-led consortium in late 2003, to expand storage at Neka and to upgrade the Tehran and Tabriz refineries. (EIA, "Iran," *Country Analysis Briefs,* January 2006, http://www.eia.doe.gov/emeu/cabs/Iran/pdf.pdf.)

19. Aussenwirtschaft Österreich, Iran—*Newsletter Nr. 15,* November 2005.

20. Kenneth Katzman, "Iran: U.S. Concerns and Policy Responses," *CRS Report for Congress,* November 1, 2006.

21. Bhushann Bahree and Marc Champion, "In Iran Nuclear Standoff, Scant Leverage for West," *Wall Street Journal,* August 21, 2006.

22. EIA, "Iran, A Country Analysis," August 2006, http://www.eia.doe.gov/emeu/cabs/Iran/Background.html.

23. Ibid.

24. Aussenwirtschaft Österreich, Iran—*Newsletter Nr. 15,*.

25. Bahree and Champion, "In Iran Nuclear Standoff, Scant Leverage for West."

26. Jeffrey J. Schott, "Economic Sanctions, Oil, and Iran," Statement by Jeffrey J. Schott before the Joint Economic Committee, United States Congress Hearing on "Energy and the Iranian Economy," July 25, 2006.

27. Bahree and Champion, "In Iran Nuclear Standoff, Scant Leverage for West."

28. EIA, "Iran," *Country Analysis Briefs.*

29. NZZ, Wie resistent ist Irans Wirtschaft gegen Sanktionen? March 1, 2007.

30. EIA, "Iran," *Country Analysis Briefs.*

31. Gareth Smyth, "Expenditure to Rise 20% under Iranian Budget Proposals," *Financial Times,* January 22, 2007.

32. Aussenwirtschaft Österreich, Iran—*Newsletter Nr. 12,* December 2005, p. 3; Daniel Altman, "Quandary over Iran Sanctions," *International Herald Tribune,* January 24, 2006.

33. NZZ, Wie resistent ist Irans Wirtschaft gegen Sanktionen?

34. IEA, *World Energy Outlook 2005, Middle East and North Africa Insights,* OECD/IEA, Paris, 2005, p. 568.

35. Gareth Smyth, "Iranians to Lose Access to Unlimited Cheap Fuel," *Financial Times,* March 9, 2007.

36. Christian Oliver and Alireza Ronaghi, "Iran's Powerful Bazaar Braced for Atomic Storm," *Reuters,* February 7, 2006.

37. Christian Oliver, "Iran Bravado on UN Sanctions May Ring Hallow," *Reuters,* February 1, 2006.

38. CIA, *The World Fact Book,* "Iran."

39. Nazila Fathi and Andrew E. Kramer, "With Threat of Sanctions, Iran Protects Some Assets," *New York Times,* January 21, 2006, p. 5.

40. "Iran Denies Shifting Assets in Europe," *Gulf Daily News,* January 20, 2006, http://www.gulf-daily-news.com/Story.asp?Article=133050&Sn=Be sueID=28306.

41. Aussenwirtscd vereft Österreich, Iran—*Newsletter Nr. 12,* p. 4.

42. World Bank, "Iran," http://web.worldbank.org/WBSITE/EXTERNAL/COUNTRIES/MENAEXT/IRANEXTN/0,,menuPK:312962~pagePK:141159~piPK:141110~theSitePK:312943,00.html.

43. Frank Barnaby, "World Air Strikes Work? " Oxford Research Group, March 2007, pp. 9 and 12; Global Security, Nuclear Threat Initiative, GlobalSecurity.org, http://www.globalsecurity.org/wmd/world/iran/nuke-fac.htm.

44. Barbara Opall-Rome, "Why Israel Won't Strike Iran's Nuclear Facilities Alone," *Defense News,* May 2, 2005.

45. Con Coughlin, "Israel Seeks All Clear for Iran Strike," *Daily Telegraph,* February 24, 2007.

46. http://www.globalsecurity.org/military/world/israel/f-15i-specs.htm.

47. Photos at http://www.fas.org/man/dod-101/sys/smart/gbu-28.htm.

48. Uzi Mahnami and Sarah Baxter, "Revealed: Israel Plans Nuclear Strike on Iran," *Sunday Times,* January 7, 2007.

49. Just how much over time is unclear. See Roger Stern, "The Iranian Petroleum Crisis and United States National Security," PNAS, PNAS 2007; 104,377-382, PNAS.org. Originally published on December 26, 2006 and updated to March 2007.

About the Authors

ANTHONY H. CORDESMAN holds the Arleigh A. Burke Chair in Strategy at the Center for Strategic and International Studies and is an analyst and commentator for ABC News. He has written extensively on energy and Middle Eastern politics, economics, demographics, and security. He has served in a number of senior positions in the U.S. government, including the Department of Energy, and several assignments in the Middle East.

MARTIN KLEIBER is a researcher at the Arleigh A. Burke Chair in Strategy at CSIS. He previously worked on security sector reform and nuclear nonproliferation at the German Foreign Office, in Bosnia, and at the United Nations. He has published on the nuclear nonproliferation regime and Iran as well as U.S. foreign and defense policy and he is the co-author of *Chinese Military Modernization: Force Development and Security Capabilities* together with Anthony H. Cordesman.

Recent Titles by Anthony H. Cordesman

2007
Salvaging American Defense: Ten Challenges of Strategic Overstretch, with Paul S. Frederiksen and William D. Sullivan

2006
Arab-Israeli Military Forces in an Era of Asymmetric Wars
The Changing Dynamics of Energy in the Middle East, with Khalid R. Al-Rodhan
Gulf Military Forces in an Era of Asymmetric Wars, with Khalid R. Al-Rodhan

2005
The Israeli-Palestinian War: Escalating to Nowhere, with Jennifer Moravitz
National Security in Saudi Arabia: Threats, Responses, and Challenges, with Nawaf Obaid
Iraqi Security Forces: A Strategy for Success, with Patrick Baetjer

2004
The Military Balance in the Middle East
Energy and Development in the Middle East

2003
The Iraq War: Strategy, Tactics, and Military Lessons
Saudi Arabia Enters the Twenty-First Century: The Political, Foreign Policy, Economic, and Energy Dimensions
Saudi Arabia Enters the Twenty-First Century: The Military and International Security Dimensions

2001
Peace and War: The Arab-Israeli Military Balance Enters the 21st Century
A Tragedy of Arms: Military and Security Developments in the Maghreb
The Lessons and Non-Lessons of the Air and Missile Campaign in Kosovo
Cyber-threats, Information Warfare, and Critical Infrastructure Protection: Defending the U.S. Homeland, with Justin G. Cordesman
Terrorism, Asymmetric Warfare, and Weapons of Mass Destruction: Defending the U.S. Homeland
Strategic Threats and National Missile Defenses: Defending the U.S. Homeland